*Modern Literature
from
China*

MODERN
LITERATURE
from
CHINA

Edited and introduced by
WALTER J. MESERVE
Indiana University
and RUTH I. MESERVE

1974

NEW YORK: New York University Press
NEW YORK

For
Our Parents

Preface

There are two points we would like to make regarding the selection and form of the material reprinted in this collection. The first refers to translators. Realizing that translation is a highly specialized art—one subject to differing critical opinions and, with particular reference to this collection, political interpretations—we have accepted translations which the People's Republic of China has provided. In all instances, however, the publications which we have used have not indicated the name of the translator involved in a particular work. Book-length translations, for example, frequently omit the name of the translator, but the publication responsibility rests with the Foreign Languages Press in Peking which, of course, prints nothing that does not have the sanction of the Chinese Communist Party.

Transliteration, the second point, also requires a brief note of explanation. It has been our policy to reproduce the transliteration used by the Chinese Communist English language publications. This Chinese system, however, is distinct from both the *pinyin* and Wade-Giles systems of transliteration. For the Chinese, this system is meaningful, and we follow it purposely as the following example may illustrate. Lao Sheh's name was romanized in this fashion throughout his successful writing career under the PRC and until he was purged in 1966. Since then, whenever he has been mentioned (his novel *Cat Country* was criticized in 1970), his name has been romanized as Lau Shaw, the way it appeared when he visited America prior to 1949—thus connecting him subtlely to the "imperialistic" attitudes for which he was purged. For those who wish to know the Wade-Giles transliteration for the names of authors whose selections are represented in this volume they are as follows:

	Wade-Giles
Lu Hsun (Chou Shu-jen)	Lu Hsün
Lao Sheh (Shu Ching-chun)	Lao Shê (Shu Ch'ing-ch'un)
Ai Ching (Chiang Hai-cheng)	Ai Ch'ing (Chiang Hai-ch'eng)
Soong Ching-ling	Sung Ch'ing-ling

Ho Ching-chih	Ho Ch'ing-chih
Yuan Shui-po (Ma Fan-to)	Yüan Shui-p'o (Ma Fan-t'o)
Tsao Yu	Ts'ao Yü

Footnotes with anthologized material have been quoted from original sources unless otherwise noted.

WJM
RIM

Contents

INTRODUCTION 1

SHORT STORIES 25
   Lu Hsun, "The True Story of Ah Q"
   Mao Tun, "Spring Silkworms"
   Chou Li-Po, "The Family on the Other Side
     of the Mountain"
   Lao Sheh, "Brother Yu Takes Office"

TANTZU 111
   Yang Pin-kuei, "Praying for Rain"

POETRY 127
   Mao Tse-tung, "Farewell to the God of Plague"
      "The Long March"
      "Snow"
      "Swimming"
   Ai Ching, "Protect Peace"
   Soong Ching-ling, "The Nameless Nine"
   Yang Yang-tse, "The Mothers' Problem:
   Ho Ching-chih, "Sanmen Gorge"
   Yuan Shui-po, "A Young Sudanese"
      "Artistic Freedom"
      "Museums—London, New York,
        and Points West"

DRAMA 161
   Tsao Yu, *Thunderstorm*

ESSAYS AND SPEECHES 285
   Mao Tse-tung *Talks at the Yenan Forum
     on Literature*
   Kuo Mo-jo, "Romanticism and Realism"

ix

CONTENTS

MISCELLANEOUS FORMS   325
    Anon., "Two Hired Hand Brothers"
    Anon., "Revolutionary Aphorisms"
    Chao Shu-li, "A New Canteen and Old Memories"
    Anon., "Rightful Owners," "On Meals"

*Modern Literature
from
China*

INTRODUCTION

In the eyes of the average American the literature of China—traditional or modern—is non-existent except for the sayings of Confucius. Yet China has its great epic tales, comparable to *The Iliad* and *The Odyssey* or the Norse sagas—tales which challenge the heroic and superhuman feats of Grendel or Robin Hood, Paul Bunyan or Davy Crockett. There are Chinese novels infused with a religious tradition and superstition similar to those Western novels which spread Christianity along with old wives' tales and told of leprechauns and fairies. Like all lyric poets across the world Chinese poets have sung of the bitter tears of loneliness, the smiles of joy, and their awe of nature. Chinese fictional characters have included great lovers no less spectacular than Don Juan, monstrous villainy, and heroic figures epitomized by the adventurous exploits of the fun-loving Monkey who combines qualities of Odysseus, Gargantua, Merlin, and Superman. From among the many stories, poems, and plays of China there are presentations of the hell that men create as well as the gods they worship and the lands of their real and imagined existence. For the Western mind there is tragedy and comedy which, however, for the Chinese may be described better as a gift of laughter and a soul for tears. And all this literary art existed in the traditional China of emperors, courtesans, and Confucian scholars.

With the opening of China by the West during the Ching Dynasty, the Opium War, and the eventual collapse of the Ching in 1911, Chinese literature began to change as China itself entered the modern era. Understandably, Western ideas and Western culture were vitally important in directing this new literature. No doubt it would surprise most Americans to learn that Harriet Beecher Stowe's novel, *Uncle Tom's Cabin*, was translated into Chinese soon after the turn of the twentieth century, while the social problem novels of Upton Sinclair found great popularity among Chinese readers. At the same time, Greek tragedy and the plays of Ibsen, Shaw, and Eugene O'Neill influenced the rise of modern drama which was initiated into China through a 1907 dramatization of *Uncle Tom's Cabin*, while poets such as Walt Whitman and Goethe provided direction for the early poets of modern China. Various Western theories of literature became fascinating to an

1

artistry so recently aware of broadening literary horizons. From the concept of pure "art for art's sake" and the radical idealism of Karl Marx to theories of romanticism, sentimentalism, naturalism, expressionism, and the communist concept of socialist realism—all have played roles in China's developing literature. Visits to China in the early twentieth century by such literary and intellectual notables as George Bernard Shaw, Rabindranath Tagore, Bertrand Russell, and John Dewey also stimulated reflections upon modern thought and writing which was being steadily translated into Chinese. As the world enlarged from China, many Chinese students studied abroad—France, England, Japan, America—and, sometimes anxiously impressionable, returned to China bringing with them strong ideas concerning Western literature. What the Chinese writers then did with the new concepts—either to reject them completely or overwhelmingly accept a new approach—became basic for modern literature in China. However remote and mysterious the Chinese may still seem to Americans, their growing modern literature shows the beauties of their traditional literary artistry combined with Western concepts and, most recently, the revolutionary values they exploit in their art.

LITERATURE AND REVOLUTION

Just as twentieth century China could no longer consider herself as the center of the world but only as a nation among nations, so too could she no longer maintain the literary world of the scholarly elite through which government positions in the old China had been filled to the exclusion of the great mass of people. One consequence of this recognition was the literary revolution or renaissance beginning in 1917, when Chinese students and intellectuals moved to adopt writing in the vernacular language for the masses in place of the classical language which only the minority elite could read and write. Among the leaders of this Literary Renaissance was Hu Shih (1891-1962), a writer educated in America, who had ardently believed in a new literature for the people which would naturally use the spoken vernacular (pai-hua) as its medium. As this modern vernacular literature spread in China, many literary societies were established which accepted the medium but espoused different literary philosophies. Some saw this new literature in terms of "art for art's sake" while others became enamored with politics and incorporated the ideas of Marxism in their writing. But the concept of a vernacular literature persisted, and both the May 4th 1919 Movement and the formation of the Communist Party of China in 1921 lent impetus and purpose to its growth.

During these early years many people played important roles in forming the new literature of China. One of its advocates, for example, was Chen Tu-hsiu (1879-1942), one of the founders of the Communist Party of China who also published the new and significant literary magazine, *New Youth.* "On our banner," he wrote in his 1917 article entitled "On Literary Revolution," "are writ large the aims and tenets of the Revolutionary Army: (1) to establish a simple lyric literature of the people by overthrowing the polite and snobbish literature of the nobility; (2) to establish a new and earnest literature of realism to support the stale and exaggerated literature of classicism; (3) to establish a plain and popular social literature in place of the inept, obscurantist, and cryptic literature of the mountain grove." But perhaps most important among those supporting the new movement, particularly in terms of the Communist Party, was Lu Hsun (1881-1936). Although never a member of the Party, Lu Hsun has been granted the distinction of being the Father of Modern Chinese Literature. For the Western reader he was a writer of short stories, two of which—*The Diary of a Madman* (1918) and *The True Story of Ah Q* (1921)—won him considerable reputation. But it was his essays, particularly those relating literature and revolution, which endeared him to the Party leadership and have, even to the present day, strongly influenced the direction of Chinese Communist literature.

One of his most significant statements for the Chinese Communist movement occurred on April 8, 1927, when he spoke at the Whampoa Military Academy on the subject of "Literature of a Revolutionary Period." "Before a revolution," Lu Hsun told his audience, "nearly all literature expresses dissatisfaction and distress over social conditions, voicing suffering and indignation." But "during a great revolution," he continued, "literature disappears and there is silence, for everyone is swept up in the tide of revolution and turns from shouting to action." For that period following the revolution, his observation suggests the wisdom which the Party admired plus an opinion which it has not always accepted. "When the revolution triumphs, there is less social tension and men are better off; then literature is written again. There are two types of literature in this period. One extols the revolution and sings its praise, because progressive writers are impressed by the changes and advances in society, the destruction of the old and the construction of the new. Rejoicing in the downfall of old institutions, they sing the

3

praise of the new construction. The second type of writing to appear after a revolution—the dirge—laments the destruction of the old. Some consider this 'counter-revolutionary literature,' but I do not think we need take it so seriously." Such was the influence, according to Lu Hsun, which a revolution would have upon literature. In 1927 it was a bold statement, but events—and Party persuasion—also showed it to be true. From the late 1920's the Chinese Communist forces frequently engaged Chiang Kai-shek's Kuomintang forces in battle, although the concentrated revolution occurred from V-J Day 1945 until the People's Republic of China was founded in 1949. For the Party leaders Lu Hsun's comments became both a guide book and a philosophy.

Between the years 1917 and 1945, from the "literary renaissance" to the beginning of the revolution, the literary efforts in China fell into that category of "dissatisfaction and distress over social conditions, voicing suffering and indignation." It was a period of exposé. All aspects of the traditional Chinese society were attacked. From superstitions and clay idols to the century old traditions of family and marriage, all were attacked in novels, short stories, poetry, and drama, along with the wealthy aristocratic society which fostered these conditions. Just as the vernacular was to be considered the language of the new Chinese literature, the poor masses of China and their problems—starvation, landlord usury, sickness, prostitution, and death—became the material for that new literature. Wang Tung-chao (1897-1958), short story writer, novelist, and poet, suggested the prevailing attitude in his story entitled "The Child at the Lakeside" (1922).

> Just think of it. Suffering hunger and discomfort, a child must come to a cove of reeds at dusk and remain half the night. His mother, because the burden of supporting the whole family rests on her, must endure endlessly the worst of all humiliations. Such a life is less than human! The poor of our present society can take only this hopeless, dead-end road.

For this social philosophy and approach to literature the new writers in revolutionary China acknowledged debts to American literary figures. Lu Hsun illustrated that debt in an April 4, 1928, letter to Tung-fen, a student at Peking University, which is generally identified under the title "Literature and Revolution:" "The American writer Upton Sinclair maintains that all literature is propaganda. Our revolutionary writers treasure this saying and have printed it in large type, while the stern critics call him a 'superficial socialist.' But I—being

4

superficial too—agree with Upton Sinclair. All literature becomes propaganda as soon as you show it to anyone. This applies to the individualist works once you write them down. Indeed, the only way to avoid
this is by not writing or opening your mouth. Naturally, then, literature
can be used as a tool for revolution." Given this approach it is not
surprising that a play adaptation of *Uncle Tom's Cabin* was popular.
The Chinese could see their own oppressed plight as a "yellow" race
mirrored in the condition of the American Negro slave, and the propaganda effect of Mrs. Stowe's work is difficult to minimize.

These were years of strong protest—these years before the Communist Party gained a considerable following and a political foothold. The
Chinese writers could expose, and condemn, and demand reform; but
they had no practical solutions. Once again Lu Hsun described the
situation accurately in a lecture on May 22, 1929, entitled "Some
Thoughts on Our New Literature." "All literature is shaped by its
surroundings and, though devotees of art like to claim that literature
can sway the course of world affairs, the truth is that politics comes first,
and art changes accordingly." Accordingly, it would be the task of the
Communist Party of China to find the practical solutions. Literature
would remain an accurate mirror of the times, but in these times people
did not lack hope. The revolutionary poet and later Communist Party
functionary and statesman Kuo Mo-jo (1892-   ) originally published
his poems of *The Goddesses* in 1921. When he prepared a preface for
the English translation of this collection in 1957, he saw his poems as
"recordings of the age in which they were written" yet to be "compared
to a cicada newly emerged from the chrysalis of the old society." There
was hope, the same hope he vizualized in his poetic drama of warlord-
torn China, *The Rebirth of the Goddesses*, in which the Stage Manager
makes a final bow to the audience, saying:

> Ladies and gentlemen, you have become tired of living in the
> foetid gloom of this dark world. You surely thirst for light.
> Your poet, having dramatized so far, writes no more. He has, in
> fact, fled beyond the sea to create new light and heat. Ladies
> and gentlemen, do you await the appearance of a new sun? You
> are bid to create it for yourselves. We will meet again under the
> new sun.

Later, in a 1926 essay entitled "Revolution versus Literature," Kuo
Mo-jo asserted his position with the candor of a true believer: "I wish

5

each of you to be a revolutionary writer, not a deserter of the age, for your sake and for the sake of all our people."

The "literary renaissance" that was born in China during the late years of the second decade of the twentieth century and the ideas of a "revolutionary" literature and art that came out of the numerous literary societies of the 1920's achieved some recognizable results during the 1930's. As antagonism between the Communists and Chiang Kai-shek's wkuomintang grew, the literature of the period reflected and divided the two political positions. For this aspect of the conflict the Communists were well organized. With the formation of the League of Left-Wing Writers in early March of 1930, the goals of a Communist "revolutionary" literature were firmly established. Not only was the League politically significant within the Party, it illustrated, as well, one aspect of the "deepening of the cultural revolution" throughout China.

Formed under Lu Hsun's leadership on March 2, 1930, the League of Left-Wing Writers had its political leadership directly under the auspices of the Communist Party of China, listing among its members some of the most prominent literary figures in the new wave of "revolutionary" literature. Among the nine members of the first Standing Committee were two—Feng Hsueh-feng and Chiang Kwang-tzu—who were also members of the Communist Party plus Feng Nai-chao, Yu Ta-fu (a romantic novelist), Lu Hsun, Ai Ying (pen name of the poet Chien Hsin-chun), Mao Tun (novelist and short story writer, Shen Yen-ping), Tien Han (dramatist) and Hsia Yen (dramatist and scenario writer).

At the initial meeting of the League the members discussed the place of art in a period of social change such as they were now experiencing. Because they saw themselves in opposition to the "feudal" class and the "bourgeoisie" they declared that they must work for a proletarian art and literature. This meant change for art and literature which would, in their opinion, become weapons in the progress toward liberation. With this objective in mind they dedicated their art and literature to a struggle for "victory or death" and determined two essential goals for their literary movement: (1) "to secure the emancipation of the rising class," and (2) to "oppose all kinds of oppression of our movement." With these goals the League bound itself closely to the rising political temper in China and essentially established guiding principles (outlined by Ting Yi, *A Short History of Modern Chinese Literature*, pp. 28-29) which clarified their literary objectives:

a. To assimilate the experience of the new literature in other countries, expand our movement and set up various research organizations;

b. To help new writers gain a literary education and the opportunity to practice and promote worker and peasant writers;

c. To affirm Marxist theories on art and on criticism;

d. To publish magazines, serial books and booklets in the name of the league; and

e. To produce literary works of the rising class.

As the emphasis on workers-peasants-soldiers grew, these principles would continue to develop and eventually determine the literary theories of the People's Republic of China.

In the early 1930's the League of Left-Wing Writers concerned itself with the "popularization" of literature. For the League, however, it was not an interest in providing non-intellectual, simply enjoyable literature but a serious attempt to raise the cultural level of the masses and, more importantly, to make that large heretofore unorganized mass politically aware. With "popularization" the question of form and content arose. Traditional forms of Chinese literature and art, although laden with emotional values alien to Communism, could clearly be useful if the content were "revolutionized." At the same time, however, there was a need to avoid a blind imitation of the past and create new forms of expression. For the newly directed literature, of course, content was of prime importance, although opinions varied. Some felt that content should express an understanding of life; others saw it only as a means to suggest agitation or to actually provoke or incite specific action. In any event, both form and content had to be measured in terms of the socialist-communist world outlook. An understanding of life could not refer to the realistic dramas of Ibsen or Shaw; it was an understanding of life strictly from the "proletarian viewpoint." There could no longer be "art for art's sake" or "art for truth's sake"; it was clearly art or literature for the sake of the revolution.

As undeclared war broke out against Japan after the Mukden Incident (1931), writers added Japanese atrocities to the conditions in China toward which they directed their cries of "suffering and indignation." What followed was one of the most productive periods in modern Chinese literature. Novelists and short story writers such as Mao Tun (1896-   ), Lao Sheh (1898-1966), Pa Chin (1904-   ), Chang Tien-yi (1907-   ), and Ting Ling (c.1902-   ) contributed major

7

works. Some of the best plays were written during this period by Tsao Yu (1910-   ), Tien Han (1898-   ), Hsia Yen (1900-   ), and Chen Pai-chen (1908-   ), while Kuo Mo-jo (1892-   ), Wen I-to (1899-1946), Nieh Erh (1911-1935), and Tien Chien (1914-   ), among others, created some notable poetry. The suffering brought by the war added fuel to writers' indignation and inspiration. They were a voice that had to be heard.

> If we do not go to fight
> the enemy will use his bayonets
> to kill us; and then afterwards
> he will point to our bones and say
> these are the bones of
> slaves.
>
> Tien Chien, "If We Do Not Go to Fight," 1938.

In 1942 Mao Tse-tung presented his now famous *Talks at the Yenan Forum on Literature and Art*. What was then considered an exchange of ideas became the Party dictum and the primary reference point for all future Chinese Communist views on art and literature—the single most important political document on literature for China! Clarifying the nature of revolutionary art and literature, Mao described them as "the products of the reflection of the life of the people" as expressed by revolutionary writers and artists. As such, Mao explained,

> Revolutionary literature and art should create a variety of characters out of actual life and help the masses to propel history onward. There is, for example, suffering from hunger, cold and oppression of man by man. These facts exist every-where and people look upon them as commonplace. Writers and artists concentrate such everyday phenomena, typify the contradictions and struggles within them and produce works which awaken the masses, fire them to enthusiasm and impel them to unite and struggle to transform their environment.

The objective that Mao described was to ensure "that revolutionary literature and art [would] fit well into the whole revolutionary machine as a component part" while at the same time literature and art would become "weapons for uniting and educating the people and for attacking and destroying the enemy."

Such a statement was clear enough, but people had to implement it. For writers and artists to "fit well" into this political objective meant that all must understand such Marxist-Leninist problems as "class stand," "attitude," "audience," and "study" of the Communist point of view and society. In his *Talks at the Yenan Forum*, therefore, Mao clearly defined these problems and answered the basic question of "literature and art for whom?" As more than ninety percent of China's population was divided among the workers, peasants, soldiers, and "urban petty bourgeoisie," he also focused the writers' attention on these —"the broadest masses of the people." Explaining "how to serve" the broad masses, Mao again raised and defined the goals of the "popularization" of literature and the "raising of standards." Most significantly, he defined the relationship between the Communist Party of China and literature and art and paid particular attention to the criteria of literary and art criticism: politics first, then art. What emerged was a well thought out program for revolutionary literature and art—one that would strike those "victory or death" blows that eventually led to bloody struggles for both literary and political figures in modern China.

As World War II ended for China in 1945, once again the two antagonists—Mao's Communist forces and Chiang Kai-shek's Kuomintang—met in full scale revolution. "During a great revolution," Lu Hsun had declared that "literature disappears and there is silence, for everyone is swept up in the tide of revolution and turns from shouting to action." But he was wrong on this point, for during the Civil War there was not silence nor did literature disappear. Indeed, there was still considerable activity, although the quality of the work may have declined in comparison with the previous decade. Changes, however, occurred in form as the Communists continued to build upon the objectives of the League of Left-Wing Writers and the ideas presented by Mao at Yenan. To combat the major problem of illiteracy in China, writers and artists were urged to capitalize upon the oral traditions of China. Consequently, frequent poetry readings were held; story tellers brought the latest news; and dramas were staged to urge all to battle. "Street poetry," "wall poems," declamatory poems, "street plays," "reportage plays," "living newspapers"—all were given significant roles in educating the great masses of people and propagandizing the Communist view. Obviously, the inherent simplicity of these forms of "revolutionary" literature and art made immediate creation possible as the bitterness or joy of any moment was easily captured for an interested population. Undoubtedly, it became, for the most part, a functional literature for immediate political needs, not a treasury of artistic impressions for future generations.

Of literary works written during the revolutionary Civil War, few

9

have received sufficient critical praise to warrant mention here, although the themes were generally limited by the dominant social-political philosophy of the time. Some of the literature, for example, emphasized an exposé of Chinese society; other works set about the task of "exposing the dark, fascist rule of the Kuomintang." Such were the works of Ma Fan-to (pen name, Yuan Shui-po, 1916-   ), Mao Tun, Sha Ting (1905-   ), and Chien Chung-shu (1882-1965). Other writers stressed the heroic struggle of a developing people in what the Western critic might term historical adventure fiction. Just prior to the 1949 "take-over" Liu Pai-yu (1915-   ) wrote a well-received novel, *Flames Ahead* (1947) on the crossing of the Yangtze River by the People's Liberation Army as well as a number of short stories describing the battles and historical events of the war. During the same period Liu Ching published his novel, *Sowing* (1947), on peasants' collective sowing of grain, while life among the workers was described in Tsao Ming's novel *The Moving Force* (1948). Already a world famous novelist, Lao Sheh created his epic-length trilogy *Four Generations Under One Roof* (1946-51). Primarily, however, fiction, poetry, and drama during the revolution were in the same vein as that written from 1917 to 1945. But once the Communist revolution succeeded in uniting China under its banner, changes occurred in the "revolutionary" literature and art of the People's Republic of China.

As Lu Hsun had predicted back in 1927, once the revolution had triumphed, one type of literature that would emerge would sing the praises of the revolution: "Rejoicing in the downfall of old institutions, they sing the praise of the new construction." Shortly after liberation in 1949, Ho Chi-fang's (1910-   ) poem, "Widening Horizons," suggested the optimism of the future.

> The quest for life
> now opens out in front of all
> like a vast expanse of ocean
> for now, wherever people work,
> there is opportunity, rich
> treasure to be found; so much
> that can be done.

The same attitude permeated almost all poetry, drama, story, and novel—praise of the new China under Mao Tse-tung and the new way of life. The artists' mode was generally a comparison of the wretched, evil days gone by with the bright future offered by Communism. Yet not all writers, or Chinese people, for that matter, were quite sure what the new Communism would bring. Some were afraid and fled; most remained and worked—"so much that can be done." Clearly, work would become the key for success in the new China and many who looked back from foreign soil questioned whether or not man could work that hard. True to prophecy and plan, the writers of the People's Republic of China sang the praise of the toilers, the builders of new China. As the time passed, literature in varied forms and styles told of advances made in marriage by choice, of women's rights, bumpercrop seasons, the birth of new industry, the cleaning up of the cities—sewers, prostitution, gambling dens, and so on. As might be expected in a nation building upon a constituency of workers, peasants and soldiers (for this was the emphasis Mao Tse-tung imposed), the new literature and art was popular. People saw the changes in their own lives mirrored by writers, many of whom were workers, peasants and soldiers like themselves rather than professional writers.

But the new China also had problems with its literature and its writers. Many of the established writers felt the pressure of Party censorship and wrote little under the new regime: Tsao Yu, Hsia Yen, Yeh Sheng-tao, Hsieh Ping-hsin, Pa Chin, and Mao Tun among them. The major exception would be Lao Sheh who during the first decade and a half of the People's Republic of China somehow managed to remain ideologically agile and express his true thoughts through effective satire while pleasing the Party with his stories and plays. Essentially, however, even he lost both status and his life in the Cultural Revolution.

For other writers, as Lu Hsun had predicted, there was "the dirge"—the lamenting of "the destruction of the old" literature and art of China. At the urging of many prominent literary figures, the Party tried to contend with these complaints through campaigns advertised by such slogans as "weed through the old to let the new emerge" and "let a hundred flowers bloom and a hundred schools of thought contend." These were attempts to save China's literary heritage from indiscriminate destruction and to use what could be salvaged from the past to serve the Communist future. Consequently, in the early years of the People's Republic many traditional works were reassessed, revised and published for the education and enjoyment of the masses. But as time passed, fewer and fewer of the old works appeared; and new works on historical figures and events were clearly discouraged. As the Party extended its control, most of the older writers lost status, while traditional and historical writing was criticized as "counter-revolutionary."

Originally, Lu Hsun had said of this literary reaction to revolution—the dirge—"I do not think we need take it so seriously." But that
was in the late 1920's. When, in the mid-1960's during the Cultural
Revolution, the Red Guards erupted in fanatical violence, Lu Hsun's
permissive attitude was clearly contradicted. The Party regarded
"counter-revolutionary" literary figures, not as protectors of old Chinese literary traditions but as enemies of the people, attempting to
destroy Communism. These writers, the Party stated, had strayed too
far from the acceptable Party line and, through their literary genius, had
criticized the entire philosophy of a Communist state. The purges that
resulted were indeed part of the struggles for "victory or death" that the
League of the early 1930's had dedicated itself to pursue. Many artists
and literary figures were ostracized; some lost their lives, either by their
own hands in consequence of their own artistic integrity and sense of
human responsibility or by the Party forces. The literature that followed this cultural upheaval, while still singing praise to "the destruction of the old and the construction of the new," began to emphasize
the new Communist utopian goals and the superhuman Communist
hero. "The age of Mao Tse-tung breeds heroes" reads one line of a
collective poem entitled "Song of Chin Hsun-hua" by three Shanghai
workers. And it is this "age" and such utopian styled "heroes" that seem
to mark the direction that Chinese literature will now follow.

LITERARY GENRES IN MODERN CHINA

Revolutionary literature and art in China includes all of the major
literary genres, and each had its place in the well integrated schematic of
the revolutionary mechanism. Back in 1931, the League of Left-Wing
Writers urged that writers "must study and adopt, with discrimination,
the methods of China's traditional popular literature, the reportage
literature of Western Europe, propaganda technique, popular stories
published as wall newspapers, and poems for recitation." [1] Consequently, branches of the League were formed for the drama (the League
of Left-Wing Dramatists and Stage Workers), and for poetry (China
Poetry Society). After Mao's *Talks at the Yenan Forum on Literature
and Art* (1942) there was a concrete effort to broaden the base of the
literature being created as well as the creators of that literature. Attempts were made to get the professional writers to go out among the
people in order to learn their way of life and refresh themselves with the

struggle experienced and the knowledge gained. Similarly, workers, peasants, and soldiers were encouraged to become "spare-time" writers, sharing their experiences and impressions. It also became clear as time went on that in the revolutionary scheme for literature writing in Communist China was no longer an individual matter to be resolved within the author's mind and heart. The creation of literature became the concern of all and, therefore, frequently a cooperative venture. Teams or groups might write a single poem or a story or a play, and when the work was completed, mass criticism followed for improvement of both the work and the writers. Not all literature in modern China is created in this fashion, but the method is encouraged in a country with the "utopian" goals of the People's Republic of China.

That first decade of the PRC, from 1949 to 1959, brought rapid growth in all literary endeavors, encouraged by the newly created All-China Federation of Literary and Art Circles. Literary books published in 1950, for example, number 156; in 1958 there were 2,600 new books published. In 1949 there were eighteen literary journals; by 1959 there were eighty-six. The one literary research institute in 1950 was increased to nine such institutes by 1959. The number of recognized writers also increased dramatically during this ten year period. In 1950 the Union of Chinese Writers had 401 members with one central and six local branches; by 1959 membership totalled 3,136 within the twenty-three structured branches. Undoubtedly, there were good reasons for this advance, and one critic explained the Party position after ten years.

> The richness and diversity of actual life, the aspiring revolutionary spirit of the age, the close links between literature and the masses and improved craftsmanship have helped our literature develop in a healthier direction, become more varied in style, more truly Chinese and more popular.[2]

Whatever the reasons and in whatever genre it appeared, Chinese literature had become, quite assuredly, a literature of the masses, by the masses, and for the masses.

The Novel. In December, 1962, the Union of Chinese Writers sent a team of investigators to three rural counties in Hopei Province to discover whether China's peasants enjoyed reading novels, what kind of novels they read, and why. Their stated objective was as typical of the People's Republic of China—to serve the peasants better through literature and art—as was the underlying motivation to determine more effective means of propaganda. For East and West, however, the study

13

proved interesting for what it revealed about literate people in general and their reading habits. It should also be noted here that the Communists have undertaken elaborate campaigns to teach the peasants and workers the Chinese characters necessary to read newspapers and simple fiction. Mainly, the team investigated reactions toward new novels such as Chao Shu-li's *Sanliwan Village*, Chou Li-po's *Hurricane* and *Great Changes in a Mountain Village*, Tu Peng-cheng's *Defend Yenan!*, Wu Chiang's *Red Sun*, Liang Pin's *Keep the Red Flag Flying*, Malchinhu's *On the Boundless Steppe* (a national minority writer from Inner Mongolia), Chu Po's *Tracks in the Snowy Forest*, Yang Mo's *Song of Youth*, and Feng Teh-ying's *Bitter Herbs*. As might be expected, the older people rejected the list of current suggested reading for the traditional Chinese novels such as *Water Margin;* while the young people preferred modern stories such as the heroic deeds of the People's Liberation Army in *Tracks in the Snowy Forest*—a tale so popular with the Chinese that it was adapted to the stage as a model Peking opera with the title *Taking Tiger Mountain by Strategy*. Pursuing their investigation, the team found that the peasants enjoyed the novels best which were (1) "militant and inspiring, packed with fascinating incidents," (2) "written in popular language, racy and easy to understand," and (3) had "characters [that] are well-conceived and are full of vitality, the breath of real life." [3] Certainly, man's taste in fiction does not vary a great deal from one part of the world to another. In China, however, the investigators took particular satisfaction in their findings. They attributed the popularity in fiction to the literary campaigns of the PRC, the spread of primary and middle school education in the villages, and the campaign to "return the intellectuals to the farm" to learn from the people in the countryside.

Whether retelling the struggles of the people during the "feudal" past or recounting the heroic deeds of the present fighters for Communism, the novel has been an expressive force among China's people. To do this it has involved the great masses of people both as characters in fiction and as amateur writers. Minority groups have also participated in this force by writing of their life styles and experiences in the border regions. This activity has been considered a political necessity, and as a part of the effort to solve "the contradiction among the different nationalities" in China, the novel has done its share in erasing misunderstandings and prejudices. The only significant drawback to the novel, in terms of Party attitude, is the amount of time it takes the individual to read a novel, for time is work and work is progress.

The Short Story. As Lu Hsun explained in his Preface to *Modern Short Stories of the World*, the short story has a very definite place in modern fiction.

> In addition to magnificent, huge and monumental works, short stories also have every right to exist. This is not simply because the small is needed to compliment the great. It is also like going into a large monastery where, in addition to the whole splendid, dazzling and inspiring scene, by looking closely you can see carved balustrades and frescoes. Though these are small, the impression made on you is particularly sharp, so that you receive a more intimate idea of the whole.

It is this "more intimate idea of the whole" in modern Chinese life that appeals to the Communist literary world. Because it is brief the short story answers one problem posed by the novel. Another concept of time is also satisfied by the short story which can quickly reflect social, political, or economic changes within China or abroad. When, for example, socialist villages were established, short stories such as Chou Li-po's "A Visitor from Peking" and "The Family on the Other Side of the Mountain" celebrated the new concept of community life. Other stories described other events or problems the Party considered important. Li Chun's "The Letter" and Liu Pai-yu's collection of stories, *Joy of Battle*, tell of Chinese volunteers in the Korean War; Li Chun's "Not That Road" and Chao Shu-li's "Steeling" deal with discussions among peasants in the early days of the PRC as they considered "the socialist road." Ma Feng's "I Knew All Along" and Wang Wen-shih's "The Shrewd Vegetable Vendor" and "By the Well" present "middle" peasants and "rich middle" peasants in the process of joining a cooperative.

Like the novelists, the short story writers in modern China distinguish themselves from past generations of writers by producing stories of "revolutionary realism" in the "spirit" of the new age under Mao Tse-tung. Since most of these writers are workers, peasants, and soldiers, the literary quality of their work varies considerably. In modern China, however, literary quality is not the foremost consideration for the reader or the critic: politics always comes first, artistry second. Wherever the story takes place—in field or factory or in battle—and whether it concerns old or young, men or women, proletariat or bourgeoisie, the hero or heroine must be presented in the spirit of the "socialist age" and in the style of "revolutionary realism" where the best of man lives in the best of all possible worlds. Chinese short story writers have been effective in describing such heroes and conditions.

Story-telling. Closely allied to the novel and short story is the oral form of story-telling. Dating back many centuries, story-telling traditions began among Buddhist teachers and developed to a popular entertainment art. An art of the common man, heard in any tea house that he might pass, rather than an art stylized by the literati of old China, it was an ideal form for Communist purposes. Hence, the Communist revival of this traditional art, like the established poetry readings and theatre, was responsive to the needs of the uneducated masses of China. It was also an educational tool concerned not only with a people's daily needs but with information that kept them aware of technical advances in a modern world. Story-telling, therefore, transmitted necessary propaganda to the people and explained to them what their individual positions would be in the newly formed Communist state.

Although not used to best advantage during the early years of the People's Republic of China, story-telling as an art form has been actively stressed since 1962. Clearly, its practicality speaks for its usefulness in a Communist society: simple, mobile, immediate, personal, as effective as the narrator can make it, and requiring no costumes or properties. As soon as an event occurred, story-tellers were dispersed with the news. This art form is a true expression of the Party policy: "weed through the old to let the new emerge."

Poetry. In a peasant song, the poets are asked to take on new tasks in China:

> Where can good poems be found?
> We suggest poets should come to the villages;
> Hills, streams, and fields are changing every day;
> Each change is a moving story.
>
> Their hearts as one, the people break old conventions,
> Everywhere heroes are working miracles;
> There are songs and epic legends everywhere—
> Why don't you poets make haste to pick them up? [4]

China's new poets, like other literary workers, come from the masses. Using the simple language of their fellow workers, they sing praises to Mao, to Communism, to factory production, commune yield, or their soldiers' heroics. If a distinction may be made between poetry and verse, most of that written in modern China is verse—straightforward thoughts generally unencumbered by imagery or profundity, effective mainly in terms of the propaganda impulse. Yet in this simplicity there is occasionally the strength and vigor of the convert who though limited by the common quality of his thoughts and a pre-determined conclusion is inspired by the vision itself. Mainly, however, the modern Chinese poet writes verse—to be read, recited, or to be sung, for song writing in a mass culture oriented to popular slogans is a logical extension of traditional poetry.

The reading of poems before large groups had been used during World War II when it became necessary to inspire the people to fight the Japanese. Successful then, the PRC continued its use "for military revolutionary calls to action" such as the Korean War, the Sino-Indian Border War, the Quemoy-Matsu Incident, and various other wars of "liberation" in Asia, Africa, and Latin America. Poems written for this purpose would include Liang Nan's "Guatemalan Brothers," Wei Yang's "Three Eulogies on Korea," Ai Ching's "Visit to South America," Kuo Mo-jo's "Fearless Heroic Nation," Tsung Kch-chai's "Viet Nam, Oh, Heroic Viet Nam," and Yuan Shui-po's "Life in Hungary Begins Again," or "Hail, Latin America." Since 1949 poetry has also been used to inspire the Chinese people to reach for higher and higher goals in work. The Big Leap Forward represented the Party's campaign for higher goals, while such poems as Liu Su-ying's "Committee Members," Liu Yi-ting's "The Lathe Worker," Hsiao Yu's "Now I Have Land," and Chang Ming-chuan's "On the Wish for Grain Stacked High" show the poet writing within particular Party objectives.

The writing of poetry in China was once regarded as a supreme literary accomplishment, a means for judging a person's worth for social or governmental activities. With the art of calligraphy it designated the talent or genius of the literary elite. Now, for the most part, that concept has changed, and poetry has become the province of the people. It can be written on a hoe as well as on rice paper; yet what was traditionally controlled by the demands of examiners or the intellect and imagination of the poet himself is now determined by Party policies. Within these limitations the momentous change in Chinese poetry is that, like all literature in modern China, it is now largely written by and for the masses.

The Drama. For more than 2000 years theatre has been a popular art in China, and like theatre throughout the world it has served different purposes and appeared in a variety of forms. When China stepped into the modern world early in the twentieth century, she brought her

17

traditional highly stylized opera form. Then in 1907 with a production in Shanghai of an adaptation of *Uncle Tom's Cabin* China was first introduced to Western style spoken drama. Interest in this form, particularly in the plays of Ibsen, grew with the liberal movement in China. By the 1930's, however, distinctive changes were being made both in politics and art, and during the war years (1931-1949) drama became a powerful weapon to help propagandize the new political ideas. There were some exceptions, of course, and Tsao Yu's work during the 1930's was noteworthy as art distinctive in itself yet showing the influence of the plays of Aeschylus, Shakespeare, Ibsen, and O'Neill. Traditional theatre during this time was thoroughly enjoyed, but much of the playwriting was being done in the Western form. By the early years of the PRC there was still strong emphasis on the creation and re-creation of both traditional opera-drama as well as the spoken drama. While many of the traditional operas were being revised to meet Party goals or discarded if revisions proved impossible, numerous forms of theatre were encouraged: one-act plays, variety theatre skits, children's plays, historical plays, agit-prop plays, and new revolutionary Chinese operas on contemporary themes. All, of course, had to conform to the strictures of Party ideology, sometimes necessitating many revisions before acceptance by the board of censors. Yet regardless of such problems, there has been considerable theatre and drama activity in contemporary China.

Since 1949, however, playwriting and theatrical productions in China have acquired distinctive characteristics. Of the major writers before the "take-over" only Lao Sheh continued as a reasonably prolific playwright with *Dragon Beard Ditch*, *Magic Boxing*, *The Magic Boat*, *Paper-Tiger Fortress*, *Tea House*, *Saleswomen*, *Red Compound*, and *Family Re-united*, among others. Tsao Yu wrote a blatant propaganda play on germ warfare in 1954, *Bright Skies*, and then turned to historical plays as did Kuo Mo-jo and Tien Han. Hsia Yen produced a play on workers entitled *The Test* and then turned most of his efforts to film work. Chen Pai-chen wrote some propaganda pieces on American "atrocities." In playwriting as in other art forms the dictum of demanding the subserviance of art to politics became more carefully adhered to, although with certain Party concessions such as the Hundred Flowers movement ("Let a hundred flowers bloom; let a hundred schools of thought contend."). As China celebrated her first decade under the PRC and approached the Cultural Revolution, more and more plays were written by workers, peasants, and soldiers, either individually or in groups.

Partially as a consequence of this innovation, the drama was more aggressively used in the area of problem solving. If a problem arose in a factory or commune or mine, a play would be written and produced in an effort to solve that particular problem. In such instances the audience was limited to those involved in the factory, or commune, and the play was seldom produced more than once or published. This was another function of the drama which was encouraged by the Party, but the practice had an effect upon the art of the theatre. Once professional playwrights and all writers had been urged to live and work among the common people of China in order to increase their understanding. Now they were being by-passed for "spare-time" writers from among these workers, peasants, and soldiers. Lacking in both artistic and intellectual sophistication, these writers created at best weak melodramas with disappointing third acts. Westerners enjoy exciting action and spectacular conclusions in their melodramas. Chinese playwrights have a distinct disadvantage in the censorship imposed because whereas the conflicts leading to Communist goals are dramatically exciting, the Communist utopia represented in the third act is invariably dull and wearisome. Hell has always been far more interesting than heaven.

The use of the spoken drama for problem solving and propaganda purposes has reached a degree of efficiency in modern China never before attained on the stage. But this does not mean that traditional forms, such as the Chinese opera, have been completely abandoned. Rather they have been changed to suit Party demands. During the early years of the Cultural Revolution in the mid-1960's (the concept of cultural revolution, its four periods of attainment prior to 1970, and a detailed analysis of it was presented by Mao Tse-tung in January, 1940, in an essay entitled "On New Democracy"), Madam Chiang Ching, Mao's wife, selected five model revolutionary Peking operas which combined some traditional acting practices with stories on contemporary themes: *The Red Lantern, Taking Tiger Mountain By Strategy, Raid on the White Tiger Regiment, On the Docks* and *Shachiapang*. Since then each has been revised by groups of writers and the list has been multiplied by works such as *Song of Dragon River* which are called revolutionary Peking operas.

The Essay. The essay in contemporary China has changed greatly from the times of Lu Hsun and those more traditionally oriented to explore their philosophical views. Theoretically, there is now only one philosophy: Communism. Consequently, the essay has become, essentially, an exercise in Party politics. Emphasizing, explaining, threatening—the essay is limited to interpreting the single, if changing, Party line. The elements of wit and humor and satire have given way to political jargon, while the essayist has the unenviable task of demonstrating his semantic agility as well as his ability to remain abreast of current dogma. If he falls behind, he may well meet a fate similar to that accorded other men of arts and letters—criticism that can lead to purging if the essayist does not admit his errors and open himself to public confession of guilt. Like other art forms in China, the essay has become a tool and weapon for the Communist, to be used with careful but persuasive effect by excellent writers such as Mao Tse-tung, Chou Yang, Kuo Mo-jo and innumerable Party critics and leaders. Supplementary to the essay is a form called reportage.

Reportage. Of all the genres, reportage literature, is the newest and most rapidly developing in China. Called "the light cavalry on our literary front," reportage is "a sharp weapon to transform reality and build a new world." [5] This literary form came to prominence in China in the early 1960's as a part of the current movement to discover new writers. Describing events in the lives of real persons as well as recording particular changes taking place in factories, mines, grasslands, villages, the army, schools, shops, or offices, reportage literature was essentially given the task of inspiring the people to move toward the goals of Communism and eliminating certain backward elements from society. And in this task the new art form has had some success. Progress was recorded not only toward Communist goals in agriculture and industry but also in science, sports, city life, and commune life. It was regarded by Party policy as a constant reflection of "socialist construction" and the people who were bringing about the changes in the Chinese life style. Written by the workers, peasants, and soldiers, and only occasionally by well-known writers, reportage literature is also a recording of history (albeit from the Communist point of view)—not of wars, and elections, and leaders, but of the common, everyday man. It may describe the life of a pedicurist in a public bath *(Master Cheng's Fate)*, the Taching oil fields *(Taching Spirit, Taching Men)*, a peasant commune *(Spring Over Nanliu, Heroes of Tachai)*, or even Ox Street, the center of the Muslim community of Peking. As such, the reportage literature, by workers, peasants, and soldiers, is a major recording tool of China's successes in the past and its expectations for the future.

RECURRING THEMES AND HEROES

"The Chinese literary scene has changed fundamentally. Most significant is the change in the content of our literary works. The old decadent or reactionary works of feudalism, imperialism and the bourgeoisie are completely out of the picture which now consists of socialist, revolutionary works with incomparably rich and varied themes and subject matter closely linked with the people." This was the opinion of Chung Ho as he discussed "A Decade of Chinese Literature." [6] There is certainly truth in what he wrote, but one would have to take issue with his conclusion that revolutionary works have "incomparably rich and varied themes." Considering the writers involved and the great variety of people making up the population of modern China, there is a clear eclecticism in the subject matter of revolutionary works, but there is a predictability of theme in these works that leads to boredom simply because there can be no point of view or idea presented that is not consistent with the thought of Chairman Mao. For some there may be richness in these ideas; this is not the place to discuss the efficacy or value, in any terms, of Chinese Communism. But there is little room for variety of theme in literature which places politics before art. In fact, the consistency of repetition in good propaganda is part of its effectiveness. Unfortunately, however, the control of plot, character development, and even choice of characters places severe control on writing which might otherwise be limited only by the artistry, imagination, inspiration, and genius of the writer. Where the literature of the past was filled with beautiful courtesans, wise judges and ministers, virtuous scholars and proud all-powerful emperors, the characters that people the literature of modern China are common men— workers, peasants, and soldiers. There are some villains, of course, but they are only stereotypes of a different nature. That incomparable richness of plot, character, and idea that distinguished traditional Chinese literature is gone.

In the early years of the People's Republic of China youth provided all of the answers. Generally, the old person (whether in story, poem, or play) was stereotyped as "old-fashioned" with "feudal" ideas and superstitions. Young people carried just the opposite stereotype; they had the correct Communist view of life which the old should learn from them. As the years passed, however, the Party realized the error of this over-simplified interpretation of youth and age and gradually began to show impatient youths needing the wisdom and guidance of experience.

21

Nevertheless, with the direction of literature carefully determined, there is always the aura of stereotyped characteristics.

For the young and old in China there is little opportunity for escape into the world of fantasy or the days of long ago. For the past dozen years the emphasis in literature and the arts has been on the all-important present. Myth, legend, and superstition, which went through periods of Party acceptance and rejection during the first decade of the PRC have now been discarded along with the evils of the past. In play, comic book, and story Chinese children learn Mao's views on war: *Heroes Blow Up the Tiger's Den, Join the Guerrillas, Capturing the Enemy's Guns*. (Yet this is a reflection of our violent world which American children easily discover in TV cartoons and comic books.) The Chinese children also learn many other Mao-taught lessons, but they never feel the light touch of the fairy godmother. Their heroes are all in the present which they are not at all anxious to escape. Instead, all Chinese must learn to contend with the exigencies of the present and discover the world through "revolutionary realism" in literature. The old learn to be vital members of the community while the time-honored oriental tradition of filial piety has become the obligation of the State. In modern China everyone must do his share—a fact and a recurrent theme in China's inescapable politico-socio-economic literature.

Another popular theme in Chinese literature relates to the position of women. In traditional China women had no rights in society although they did exercise a considerable control within the family compound. In Mao's China the woman is a dominant force, free to choose her husband, to get a divorce, to speak her mind in public, and to assume the position of a leader. More frequently than not the virtuous Communist character in any piece of modern literature is a woman—hard working, self-confident, well-versed in her job, determined, extremely efficient, and sensitive to the needs of man while exercising a forceful leadership. However she may be opposed—by husband, mother-in-law, employer, foreign villain, or enemy of the people—and whatever problem may occur, she invariably turns out to be correct in her opinions and competent to complete the correct actions. In every way that relates to the progress of the State toward a Communist "utopia" the woman of modern China is frequently cast as an heroic figure.

On a broader base the heroes of Maoist China are the "workers, peasants, and soldiers"—a phrase that appears with such frequency in all modern Chinese writing that its representative significance in the creation of Communist China cannot be mistaken. Upon the workers, peasants, and soldiers Mao has built his dream of a utopian state.

22

Consequently, in order to establish a true "proletarian literature" it has been absolutely necessary that writers and artists come from the ranks of the common man. China has wanted the "free literature" that Lenin spoke of—"free" because it was sympathetic to the working people, "free" because it would not be greed that attracted those who would create this literature. "It will be a free literature," Lenin wrote in 1905 ("Party Organization and Party Literature"), "because it will serve, not some satiated heroine, not the bored 'upper ten thousand' suffering from petty degeneration, but the millions and tens of millions of working people—the flower of its country, its strength and its future." This concern for the toiling masses as those for whom literature is created has been extended by the Chinese to inspire those "millions of working people" to help create their own literature. Consequently, the worker-peasant-soldier as spare-time writer has become an essential part of the plan for reaching the goals of Communism. This approach clearly helps to abolish the differences between mental and physical labor, and it illustrates the Communist dictum that professional writers and artists must go out and help the people with their common labors in order to write that "free" literature which Lenin described.

A most natural result of these objectives, in theme and genre in modern Chinese literature as well as in its creation, has been the development of a proletarian hero. Interestingly enough, there is a kind of cyclical pattern involved. As the Foundation for Chinese Communism rests squarely upon the workers, peasants, and soldiers, their acts become the logical subject matter for the literature and art, perhaps most accurately portrayed by the people themselves. Once their lives are re-created in novel, short story, poem, or play there is a transformation which takes place. Propaganda merges with literature, and the result is a portrayal of life as it must be in the future "utopian" state of Chinese Communism —a "revolutionary realism" combined with "revolutionary romanticism." In this "realistic" literature there emerges the Utopian hero or heroine, a natural culmination of the cult of Mao: from worker, peasant, soldier model through proletarian writer to revolutionary hero. The activities of Lei Feng illustrate this pattern very clearly. Lei Feng, an ordinary soldier, was quite unheroically killed when a pole fell on him during a military maneuver. But writers capitalized on the act and emphasized Lei Feng in story and play until the government recognized a campaign for Lei Feng and Mao himself watched a play commemorating Lei Feng, the common man hero in the Communist state.

Modern China is not interested in returning to the China of the past; rather it looks eagerly to the China of the future where modernity

23

precludes an "art for art's sake" approach and, instead, determines a functioning body of literature, versatile in politics, economics, and social problems as well as future dreams. A mirror of the present it also attempts to be the crystal ball of the future.

NOTES

1. Ting Yi, *A Short History of Modern Chinese Literature* (Peking: Foreign Languages Press, 1959), p. 211.

2. Chung Ho, "A Decade of Chinese Literature," *Peking Review* (December 8, 1959), pp. 13-15.

3. "Do China's Farmers Like Novels," *Peking Review* (March 29, 1963), pp. 25-26.

4. Chao Chuan-lin, "Chinese Literature in 1958," *Chinese Literature* (1959, No. 1), p. 6.

5. Mo Kan, "Reportage in Contemporary Chinese Writing," *Chinese Literature* (1965, No. 2), pp. 79-85.

6. Chung Ho, p. 13.

SHORT STORIES

Representing the distinctive artistry of four writers, the short stories in this volume suggest the variety of style and attitude which has made this literary genre increasingly popular reading over the past fifty years. For the Western readers the two best known writers are Lu Hsun and Lao Sheh. Lu Hsun (pen name of Chou Shu-jen, 1881-1936), has been called the greatest writer of modern China. As the earliest practitioner of Western style fiction in China, Lu Hsun began his writing career, though without success, during the first decade of this century. With the later Literary Revolution and particularly the publication of "The Diary of a Mad Man" in 1918 he gained a sympathetic audience and also a teaching position in the National Peking University. His best stories may be found in two collections—*Outcry* (1923) and *Hesitation* (1926)—which show both his sensitivity to the position of man in traditional China and the penetrating yet unassuming force of his style. A significant writer before Communism was a strong factor in Chinese politics and never a member of the Party, his despondency and intellectual development aligned him with the League of Left-Wing Writers in a way that has since made him a hero of the Communist struggle. Even Mao Tse-tung paid him the highest compliment in *On New Democracy* (1940) by stating that "the direction of Lu Hsun is the direction of the new Chinese culture."

On the other hand, Lao Sheh (pseudonym of Shu Ching-chun, 1898-1966) slipped from Party favor and was purged during the Cultural Revolution. Prior to the 1949 "take-over" Lao Sheh had won considerable praise for his novels which showed the influence of Western writers as well as his own Western travels and illustrated his particular insight into social problems relating to traditional China. A wit and a keen understanding of satire and irony underlined his writing style. In America he was best known for a novel entitled *Rickshaw Boy*. After 1949 he wrote a number of plays, seemingly in praise of the new Communist government, which were later criticized during his purging. In 1950 his play, *Dragon Beard Ditch*, won him the citation of "People's Artist" and throughout the 1950's he continued writing plays such as *Tea House* and *Red Compound*. His purging and death came as Party

25

officials recognized the satire in his plays and earlier novels, and he has since been judged "an enemy of the people."

Mao Tun (pseudonym of Shen Yen-ping, 1896-   ) is another writer who was influenced by Western writers but distinct from Lu Hsun and Lao Sheh through his active association with the Communist Party in China. A novelist, short story writer, essayist, editor, he wrote in a highly literary style but very early advocated a realism that would serve the people. An early member of the League of Left-Wing Writers, his list of activities with the People's Republic of China takes three full columns in *Who's Who in Communist China,* while his most significant post was as Minister of Culture, 1949-1965. Yet like many writers he was criticized during the Cultural Revolution. His novels include *Rainbow* (1930) and *Midnight* (1933) while the story in this volume is part of a trilogy—*Spring Silkworms, Autumn Harvest, Winter Ruin.* He has also written essays such as "On Lu Hsun," "What Is Literature?" and "Talks on Western Literature." Although the Communist view is clear in most of his writings, there is also a psychological penetration which distinguishes his work.

Chou Li-po (1908-   ) showed his radicalism early by being imprisoned by the Kuomintang in 1932 and joining both the League of Left-Wing Writers and the Communist Party in 1934. Prior to 1949 he worked as an editor, a war correspondent, and a teacher. Then in 1951 his novel, *The Hurricane,* on land reform in northeast China, won the Stalin Prize. In the preceeding year he had shared the Stalin Prize as one of the authors of a film scenario entitled *Liberated China.* During the next dozen years he worked as a professional writer producing novels (*Great Changes in a Mountain Village,* 1957) and reportage (*March into the South*). During the Cultural Revolution, however, he was criticized as a "revisionist" whose novels distorted the nature of land reform.

The True Story of Ah Q*

by Lu Hsun

CHAPTER 1

INTRODUCTION

I have been meaning to write the true story of Ah Q for several years now. But while wanting to write I had some trepidations, too, which goes to show that I am not one of those who achieve glory by writing; for an immortal pen has always been required to record the deeds of an immortal man, the man becoming known to posterity through the writing and the writing known to posterity through the man—until finally it is not clear who is making whom known. But in the end, as though possessed by some fiend, I always came back to the idea of writing the story of Ah Q.

And yet no sooner had I taken up my pen than I became conscious of huge difficulties in writing this far-from-immortal work. The first was the question of what to call it. Confucius said, "If the name is not correct, the words will not ring true"; and this axiom should be most scrupulously observed. There are many types of biographies: official biographies, autobiographies, unauthorized biographies, legends, supplementary biographies, family histories, sketches . . . but unfortunately none of these suited my purpose. "Official biography?" This account will obviously not be included with those of many eminent people in some authentic history. "Autobiography?" But I am obviously not Ah Q. If I were to call this an "unauthorized biography," then where is his "authenticated biography"? The use of "legend" is

*Reprinted from *Selected Works of Lu Hsun*, Vol. 1 (Peking: Foreign Languages Press, 1956), pp. 76-135.

impossible, because Ah Q was no legendary figure. "Supplementary biography?" But no president has ever ordered the National Historical Institute to write a "standard life" of Ah Q. It is true that although there are no "lives of gamblers" in authentic English history, the famous author Conan Doyle nevertheless wrote *Rodney Stone;** but while this is permissible for a famous author it is not permissible for such as I. Then there is "family history"; but I do not know whether I belong to the same family as Ah Q or not, nor have I ever been entrusted with such a task by his children or grandchildren. If I were to use "sketch," it might be objected that Ah Q has no "complete account." In short, this is really a "life," but since I write in vulgar vein using the language of hucksters and pedlars, I dare not presume to give it so high-sounding a title; so from the stock phrase of the novelists, who are not reckoned among the Three Cults and Nine Schools:** "Enough of this digression, and back to the *true story*," I will take the last two words as my title; and if this is reminiscent of the *True Story of Calligraphy**** of the ancients, it cannot be helped.

The second difficulty confronting me was that a biography of this type should start off something like this: "So-and-so, whose other name was so-and-so, was a native of such-and-such a place"; but I don't really know what Ah Q's surname was. Once, he seemed to be named Chao, but the next day there was some confusion about the matter again. This was after Mr. Chao's son had passed the county examination, and his success was being announced in the village, to the sounding of gongs. Ah Q, who had just drunk two bowls of yellow wine, began to prance about declaring that this reflected credit on him too, since he belonged to the same clan as Mr. Chao, and by an exact reckoning was three generations senior to the successful candidate. At the time several of the bystanders even began to stand slightly in awe of him. But the next day the bailiff summoned Ah Q to Mr. Chao's house. When the old gentleman set eyes on him, his face turned crimson with fury and he roared:

"Ah Q, you miserable wretch! Did you say I belonged to the same clan as you?"

Ah Q made no reply.

---

*In Chinese this novel was called *Supplementary Biographies of the Gamblers.*
**The Three Cults were Confucianism, Buddhism and Taoism. The Nine Schools included the Confucian, Taoist, Legalist and Moist schools, as well as others. Novelists, who did not belong to any of these, were considered not quite respectable.
***A book by Feng Wu of the Ching Dynasty (1644-1911).

The more he looked at him the angrier Mr. Chao became, and advancing menacingly a few steps he said, "How dare you talk such nonsense! How could I have such a relative as you? Is your surname Chao?"

Ah Q made no reply, and was planning a retreat; but Mr. Chao darted forward and gave him a slap on the face.

"How could *you* be named Chao!—Do you think you are worthy of the name Chao?"

Ah Q made no attempt to defend his right to the name Chao, but rubbing his left check went out with the bailiff. Once outside, he had to listen to another torrent of abuse from the bailiff, and thank him to the tune of two hundred cash. All who heard of this said Ah Q was a great fool to ask for a beating like that. Even if his surname *were* Chao—which wasn't likely—he should have known better than to boast like that when there was a Mr. Chao living in the village. After this, no further mention was made of Ah Q's ancestry, so that I still don't know what his surname really was.

The third difficulty I encountered in writing this work was that I don't know how Ah Q's personal name should be written either. During his lifetime everybody called him Ah Quei, but after his death not a soul mentioned Ah Quei again; for he was obviously not one of those whose name is "preserved on bamboo tablets and silk." * If there is any question of preserving his name, this essay must be the first attempt at doing so. Hence I am confronted with this difficulty at the outset. I have given the question careful thought: Ah Quei—would that be the "Quei" meaning cassia or the "Quei" meaning nobility? If his other name had been Moon Pavilion, or if he had celebrated his birthday in the month of the Moon Festival, then it would certainly be the "Quei" for cassia.** But since he had no other name—or if he had, no one knew it—and since he never sent out invitations on his birthday to secure complimentary verses, it would be arbitrary to write Ah Quei (cassia). Again, if he had had an elder or younger brother called Ah Fu (prosperity), then he would certainly be called Ah Quei (nobility). But he was all on his own: thus there is no evidence for writing Ah Quei (nobility). All the other, unusual characters with the sound Quei are even less suitable. I once put this question to Mr. Chao's son, the successful county candidate, but even such a learned man as he was

---

*A phrase first used in the third century B.C. Bamboo and silk were writing materials in ancient China.

**The cassia blooms in the month of the Moon Festival. Also, according to Chinese folklore, it is believed that the shadow on the moon is a cassia tree.

baffled by it. According to him, however, the reason that this name could not be traced was that Chen Tu-hsiu* had brought out the magazine *New Youth*, advocating the use of the Western alphabet, so that the national culture was going to the dogs. As a last resort, I asked someone from my district to go and look up the legal documents recording Ah Q's case, but after eight months he sent me a letter saying that there was no name anything like Ah Quei in those records. Although uncertain whether this was the truth or whether my friend had simply done nothing, after failing to trace the name this way I could think of no other means of finding it. Since I am afraid the new system of phonetics has not yet come into common use, there is nothing for it but to use the Western alphabet, writing the name according to English spelling as Ah Quei and abbreviating it to Ah Q. This approximates to blindly following the *New Youth* magazine, and I am thoroughly ashamed of myself; but since even such a learned man as Mr. Chao's son could not solve my problem, what else can I do?

My fourth difficulty was with Ah Q's place of origin. If his surname were Chao, then according to the old custom which still prevails of classifying people by their districts, one might look up the commentary in *The Hundred Surnames** and find "A native of Tienshui in Kansu Province." But unfortunately this surname is open to question, with the result that Ah Q's place of origin must also remain uncertain. Although he lived for the most part in Weichuang, he often stayed in other places, so that it would be wrong to call him a native of Weichuang. It would, in fact, amount to a distortion of history.

The only thing that consoles me is the fact that the character "Ah" is absolutely correct. This is definitely not the result of false analogy, and is well able to stand the test of scholarly criticism. As for the other problems, it is not for such unlearned people as myself to solve them, and I can only hope that disciples of Dr. Hu Shih, who has such "a passion for history and antiquities," ** may be able in the future to throw new light on them. I am afraid, however, that by that time my *True Story of Ah Q* will have long since passed into oblivion.

The foregoing may be considered as an introduction.

---

*1880-1942. A professor of Peking University at this time, he edited *New Youth*, the monthly which led the new cultural movement.

*A school primer, in which the surnames were written into verse.

**This phrase was often used in self-praise by Hu Shih, the well-known reactionary politician and writer.

CHAPTER 2

A BRIEF ACCOUNT OF AH Q'S VICTORIES

In addition to the uncertainty regarding Ah Q's surname, personal name, and place of origin, there is even some uncertainty regarding his "background." This is because the people of Weichuang only made use of his services or treated him as a laughing-stock, without ever paying the slightest attention to his "background." Ah Q himself remained silent on this subject, except that when quarrelling with someone he might glance at him and say, "We used to be much better off than you! Who do you think you are anyway?"

Ah Q had no family but lived in the Tutelary God's Temple at Weichuang. He had no regular work either, simply doing odd jobs for others: if there was wheat to be cut he would cut it, if there was rice to be ground he would grind it, if there was a boat to be punted he would punt it. If the work lasted for a considerable period he might stay in the house of his temporary employer, but as soon as it was finished he would leave. Thus whenever people had work to be done they would remember Ah Q, but what they remembered was his service and not his "background"; and by the time the job was done even Ah Q himself would be forgotten, to say nothing of his "background." Once indeed an old man remarked, "What a good worker Ah Q is!" At that time Ah Q, stripped to the waist, listless and lean, was standing before him, and other people did not know whether the remark was meant seriously or derisively, but Ah Q was overjoyed.

Ah Q, again, had a very high opinion of himself. He looked down on all the inhabitants of Weichuang, thinking even the two young "scholars" not worth a smile, though most young scholars were likely to pass the official examinations. Mr. Chao and Mr. Chien were held in great respect by the villagers, for in addition to being rich they were both the fathers of young scholars. Ah Q alone showed them no exceptional deference, thinking to himself, "My sons may be much greater!"

Moreover, after Ah Q had been to town several times, he naturally became even more conceited, although at the same time he had the greatest contempt for townspeople. For instance, a bench made of a wooden plank three feet by three inches the Weichuang villagers called a "long bench." Ah Q called it a "long bench" too; but the townspeople called it a "straight bench," and he thought, "This is wrong. How

31

ridiculous!" Again, when they fried large-headed fish in oil the Wei-chuang villagers all added shallot leaves sliced half an inch long, whereas the townspeople added finely shredded shallots, and he thought, "This is wrong too. How ridiculous!" But the Weichuang villagers were really ignorant rustics who had never seen the fried fish of the town!

Ah Q who "used to be much better off," who was a man of the world and "a good worker," would have been almost the perfect man had it not been for a few unfortunate physical blemishes. The most annoying consisted of some places on his scalp where in the past, at some uncer-tain date, shiny ringworm scars had appeared. Although these were on his own head, apparently Ah Q did not consider them as altogether honorable, for he refrained from using the word "ringworm" or any words that sounded anything like it. Later he improved on this, making "bright" and "light" forbidden words, while later still even "lamp" and "candle" were taboo. Whenever this taboo was disregarded, whether intentionally or not, Ah Q would fly into a rage, his ringworm scars turning scarlet. He would look over the offender, and if it were someone weak in repartee he would curse him, while if it were a poor fighter he would hit him. And yet, curiously enough, it was usually Ah Q who was worsted in these encounters, until finally he adopted new tactics, con-tenting himself in general with a furious glare.

It so happened, however, that after Ah Q had taken to using this furious glare, the idlers in Weichuang grew even more fond of making jokes at his expense. As soon as they saw him they would pretend to give a start, and say:

"Look! It's lighting up."

Ah Q would rise to the bait as usual, and glare furiously.

"So there is a kerosene lamp here," they would continue, not in the least intimidated.

Ah Q could do nothing, but rack his brains for some retort: "You don't even deserve. . . ." At this juncture it seemed as if the scars on his scalp were noble and honorable, not just ordinary ringworm scars. However, as we said above, Ah Q was a man of the world: he knew at once that he had nearly broken the "taboo" and refrained from saying any more.

If the idlers were still not satisfied, but continued to bait him, they would in the end come to blows. Then only after Ah Q had, to all appearances, been defeated, had his brownish pigtail pulled and his head bumped against the wall four or five times, would the idlers walk away, satisfied at having won. Ah Q would stand there for a second, thinking to himself, "It is as if I were beaten by my son. What is the world coming to nowadays. . . ." Thereupon he too would walk away, satisfied at having won.

Whatever Ah Q thought he was sure to tell people later; thus almost all who made fun of Ah Q knew that he had this means of winning a psychological victory. So after this anyone who pulled or twisted his brown pigtail would forestall him by saying: "Ah Q, this is not a son beating his father, it is a man beating a beast. Let's hear you say it: A man beating a beast!"

Then Ah Q, clutching at the root of his pigtail, his head on one side, would say: "Beating an insect—how about that? I am an insect—now will you let me go?"

But although he was an insect the idlers would not let him go until they had knocked his head five or six times against something nearby, according to their custom, after which they would walk away satisfied that they had won, confident that this time Ah Q was done for. In less than ten seconds, however, Ah Q would walk away also satisfied that he had won, thinking that he was the "foremost self-belittler," and that after subtracting "self-belittler" what remained was "foremost." Was not the highest successful candidate in the official examination also the "foremost"? "And who do you think you are anyway?"

After employing such cunning devices to get even with his enemies, Ah Q would make his way cheerfully to the wineshop to drink a few bowls of wine, joke with the others again, quarrel with them again, come off victorious again, and return cheerfully to the Tutelary God's Temple, there to fall asleep as soon as his head touched the pillow. If he had money he would go to gamble. There would be a group of men squatting on the ground, Ah Q sandwiched in the midst, his face streaming with perspiration; and his voice would be the loudest to shout: "Four hundred on the Green Dragon!"

"Hey—open there!" the stakeholder, his face streaming with perspiration too, would open the box and chant: "Heavenly Gate! . . . Nothing for the Corner! . . . No stakes on the Popularity Passage! Pass over Ah Q's coppers!"

"The Passage—one hundred—one hundred and fifty."

To the tune of this chanting, Ah Q's money would gradually vanish into the pockets of other perspiring people. Finally, he would be forced to squeeze his way out of the crowd and watch from the back, taking a vicarious interest in the game until it broke up, when he would return reluctantly to the Tutelary God's Temple. And the next day he would go to work with swollen eyes.

However, the truth of the proverb "Misfortune may be a blessing in

33

disguise" was shown when Ah Q was unfortunate enough to win and almost suffered defeat in the end.

This was the evening of the Festival of the Gods in Weichuang. According to custom there was a play; and close to the stage, also according to custom, were numerous gambling tables. The drums and gongs of the play sounded about three miles away to Ah Q who had ears only for the stakeholder's chant. He staked successfully again and again, his coppers turning into silver coins, his silver coins into dollars, and his dollars mounting up. In his excitement he cried out, "Two dollars on Heavenly Gate!"

He never knew who started the fighting, nor for what reason. Curses, blows and footsteps formed a confused medley of sound in his head, and by the time he clambered to his feet the gambling tables had vanished and so had the gamblers. Several parts of his body seemed to be aching as if he had been kicked and knocked about, while a number of people were looking at him in astonishment. Feeling as if there were something amiss, he walked back to the Tutelary God's Temple, and by the time he regained his composure he realized that his pile of dollars had disappeared. Since most of the people who ran gambling tables at the Festival were not natives of Weichuang, where could he look for the culprits?

So white and glittering a pile of silver! It had all been his . . . but now it had disappeared. Even to consider it tantamount to being robbed by his son could not comfort him. To consider himself as an insect could not comfort him either. This time he really tasted something of the bitterness of defeat.

But presently he changed defeat into victory. Raising his right hand he slapped his own face hard twice, so that it tingled with pain. After this slapping his heart felt lighter, for it seemed as if the one who had given the slap was himself, the one slapped some other self, and soon it was just as if he had beaten someone else—in spite of the fact that his face was still tingling. He lay down satisfied that he had gained the victory.

Soon he was asleep.

CHAPTER 3

A FURTHER ACCOUNT OF AH Q'S VICTORIES

Although Ah Q was always gaining victories, it was only after he was favored with a slap on the face by Mr. Chao that he became famous.

After paying the bailiff two hundred cash he lay down angrily. Later he said to himself, "What is the world coming to nowadays, with sons beating their parents...." Then the thought of the prestige of Mr. Chao, who was now his son, gradually raised his spirits, and he got up and went to the wineshop singing *The Young Widow at Her Husband's Grave*. At that time he did feel that Mr. Chao was a cut above most people.

After this incident, strange to relate, it was true that everybody seemed to pay him unusual respect. He probably attributed this to the fact that he was Mr. Chao's father, but actually such was not the case. In Weichuang, as a rule, if the seventh child hit the eighth child or Li So-and-so hit Chang So-and-so, it was not taken seriously. A beating had to be connected with some important personage like Mr. Chao before the villagers thought it worth talking about. But once they thought it worth talking about, since the beater was famous, the one beaten enjoyed some of his reflected fame. As for the fault being Ah Q's, that was naturally taken for granted, the reason being that Mr. Chao could not possibly be wrong. But if Ah Q were wrong, why did everybody seem to treat him with unusual respect? This is difficult to explain. We may put forward the hypothesis that it was because Ah Q had said he belonged to the same family as Mr. Chao; thus, although he had been beaten, people were still afraid there might be some truth in what he said and therefore thought it safer to treat him more respectfully. Or, alternatively, it may have been like the case of the sacrificial beef in the Confucian temple: although the beef was in the same category as the sacrificial pork and mutton, being of animal origin just as they were, later Confucians did not dare touch it since the sage had enjoyed it.

After this Ah Q prospered for several years.

One spring, when he was walking along in a state of happy intoxication, he saw Whiskers Wang sitting stripped to the waist in the sunlight at the foot of a wall, catching lice; and at this sight his own body began to itch. Since Whiskers Wang was scabby and bewhiskered, everybody called him "Ringworm Whiskers Wang." Although Ah Q omitted the

35

word "Ringworm," he had the greatest contempt for him. Ah Q felt that while scabs were nothing to take exception to, such hairy cheeks were really too outlandish, and could excite nothing but scorn. So Ah Q sat down by his side. If it had been any other idler, Ah Q would never have dared sit down so casually; but what had he to fear by the side of Whiskers Wang? To tell the truth, the fact that he was willing to sit down was an honor for Wang.

Ah Q took off his tattered lined jacket, and turned it inside out; but either because he had washed it recently or because he was too clumsy, a long search yielded only three or four lice. He saw that Whiskers Wang, on the other hand, was catching first one and then another in swift succession, cracking them in his mouth with a popping sound.

Ah Q felt first disappointed and then resentful: the despicable Whiskers Wang could catch so many while he himself had caught so few—what a great loss of face! He longed to catch one or two big ones, but there were none, and it was only with considerable difficulty that he managed to catch a middle-sized one, which he thrust fiercely into his mouth and bit savagely; but it only gave a small sputtering sound, again inferior to the noise Whiskers Wang was making.

All Ah Q's scars turned scarlet. Flinging his jacket on the ground, he spat and said, "Hairy worm!"

"Mangy dog, who are you calling names?" Whiskers Wang looked up contemptuously.

Although the relative respect accorded him in recent years had increased Ah Q's pride, when confronted by loafers who were accustomed to fighting he remained rather timid. On this occasion, however, he was feeling exceptionally pugnacious. How dare a hairy-cheeked creature like this insult him?

"Anyone who the name fits," said Ah Q standing up, his hands on his hips.

"Are your bones itching?" demanded Whiskers Wang, standing up too and putting on his coat.

Thinking that Wang meant to run away, Ah Q stepped forward raising his fist to punch him. But before his fist came down, Whiskers Wang had already seized him and given him a tug which sent him staggering. Then Whiskers Wang seized Ah Q's pigtail and started dragging him towards the wall to knock his head in the time-honored manner.

" 'A gentleman uses his tongue but not his hands!' " protested Ah Q, his head on one side.

Apparently Whiskers Wang was no gentleman, for without paying the slightest attention to what Ah Q said he knocked his head against the wall five times in succession, and gave him a great shove which sent him staggering two yards away. Only then did Whiskers Wang walk away satisfied.

As far as Ah Q could remember, this was the first humiliation of his life, because he had always scoffed at Whiskers Wang on account of his ugly whiskered cheeks, but had never been scoffed at, much less beaten by him. And now, contrary to all expectations, Whiskers Wang had beaten him. Perhaps what they said in the market-place was really true: "The Emperor has abolished the official examinations, so that scholars who have passed them are no longer in demand." As a result of this the Chao family must have lost prestige. Was it a result of this, too, that people were treating him contemptuously?

Ah Q stood there irresolutely.

From the distance approached another of Ah Q's enemies. This was Mr. Chien's eldest son whom Ah Q also despised. After studying in a foreign school in the city, it seemed he had gone to Japan. When he came home half a year later, his legs were straight* and his pigtail had disappeared. His mother cried bitterly a dozen times, and his wife tried three times to jump into the well. Later his mother told everyone, "His pigtail was cut off by some scoundrel when he was drunk. He would have been able to be an official, but now he will have to wait until it has grown again before he thinks of that." Ah Q did not, however, believe this, and insisted on calling him "Imitation Foreign Devil" and "Traitor in Foreign Pay." As soon as he saw him he would start cursing under his breath.

What Ah Q despised and detested most in him was his false pigtail. When it came to having a false pigtail, a man could scarcely be considered as human; and the fact that his wife had not attempted to jump into the well a fourth time showed that she was not a good woman either.

Now this "Imitation Foreign Devil" was approaching.

"Baldhead—Ass—" In the past Ah Q had cursed under his breath only, inaudibly; but today, because he was in a bad temper and wanted to work off his feelings, the words slipped out involuntarily.

Unfortunately this "baldhead" was carrying a shiny, brown stick which Ah Q called a "staff carried by the mourner." With great strides

---

* When the Chinese of those days saw foreigners walking with big strides —unlike the usual Chinese gait—they imagined that foreigners had no joints at the knees.

he bore down on Ah Q who, guessing at once that a beating was impending, hastily braced himself to wait with a stiffened back. Sure enough, there was a resounding thwack which seemed to have alighted on his head.

"I meant him!" explained Ah Q, pointing to a nearby child.

Thwack! Thwack! Thwack!

As far as Ah Q could remember, this was the second humiliation of his life. Fortunately, after the thwacking stopped, it seemed to him that the matter was closed, and he even felt somewhat relieved. Moreover, the precious "ability to forget" handed down by his ancestors stood him in good stead. He walked slowly away and by the time he was approaching the wineshop door he felt quite happy again.

Just then, however, a small nun from the Convent of Quiet Self-improvement came walking towards him. The sight of a nun always made Ah Q swear; how much more so, then, after his humiliations? When he recalled what had happened, all his anger revived.

"So all my bad luck today was because I had to see you!" he thought to himself.

He went up to her and spat noisily. "Ugh! . . . Pah!"

The small nun paid not the least attention, but walked on with lowered head. Ah Q went up to her and shot out a hand to rub her newly shaved scalp, then laughing stupidly said, "Baldhead! Go back quickly, your monk is waiting for you. . . ."

"Who are you pawing? . . ." demanded the nun, blushing crimson as she began to hurry away.

The men in the wineshop roared with laughter. Seeing that his feat was admired, Ah Q began to feel elated.

"If the monk paws you, why can't I?" said he, pinching her cheek.

Again the men in the wineshop roared with laughter. Ah Q felt even more pleased, and in order to satisfy those who were expressing approval, he pinched her hard again before letting her go.

During this encounter he had already forgotten Whiskers Wang and the Imitation Foreign Devil, as if all the day's bad luck had been avenged. And, strange to relate, even more relaxed than after the beating, he felt light and buoyant as if ready to float into the air.

"Ah Q, may you die sonless!" sounded the little nun's voice tearfully in the distance.

Ah Q roared with delighted laughter.

The men in the wineshop roared too, with only slightly less satisfaction.

CHAPTER 4

THE TRAGEDY OF LOVE

There are said to be some victors who take no pleasure in a victory unless their opponents are as fierce as tigers or eagles: if their adversaries are as timid as sheep or chickens they find their triumph empty. There are other victors who, having carried all before them, with the enemy slain or surrendering and cowering in utter subjection, realize that now they are left with no foe, rival, or friend—they have only themselves, supreme, solitary, desolate, and forlorn. And then they find their triumph a tragedy. But our hero was not so spineless. He was always exultant. This may be a proof of the moral supremacy of China over the rest of the world.

Look at Ah Q, light and elated, as if about to fly!

This victory was not without strange consequences, though. For quite a time he seemed to be flying, and he flew into the Tutelary God's Temple, where he would normally have snored as soon as he lay down. This evening, however, he found it very difficult to close his eyes, for he felt as if there were something the matter with his thumb and first finger, which seemed to be smoother than usual. It is impossible to say whether something soft and smooth on the little nun's face had stuck to his fingers, or whether his fingers had been rubbed smooth against her cheek.

"Ah Q, may you die sonless!"

These words sounded again in Ah Q's ears, and he thought, "Quite right, I should take a wife; for if a man dies sonless he has no one to sacrifice a bowl of rice to his spirit . . . I ought to have a wife." As the saying goes, "There are three forms of unfilial conduct, of which the worst is to have no descendants," * and it is one of the tragedies of life that "spirits without descendants go hungry." ** Thus his view was absolutely in accordance with the teachings of the saints and sages, and it is indeed a pity that later he should have run amok.

"Woman, woman! . . ." he thought.

". . . The monk paws. . . . Woman, woman! . . . Woman!" he thought again.

*A quotation from Mencius (372-289 B.C.).
**A quotation from the old classic *Tso Chuan*.

We shall never know when Ah Q finally fell asleep that evening. After this, however, he probably always found his fingers rather soft and smooth, and always remained a little light-headed. "Woman . . ." he kept thinking.

From this we can see that woman is a menace to mankind.

The majority of Chinese men could become saints and sages were it not for the unfortunate fact that they are ruined by women. The Shang Dynasty was destroyed by Ta Chi, the Chou Dynasty was undermined by Pao Szu; as for the Chin Dynasty, although there is no historical evidence to that effect, yet if we assume that it fell on account of some woman we shall probably not be far wrong. And it is a fact that Tung Cho's death was caused by Tiao Chan.*

Ah Q, too, had been a man of strict morals to begin with. Although we do not know whether he was guided by some good teacher, he had always shown himself most scrupulous in observing "strict segregation of the sexes," and was righteous enough to denounce such heretics as the little nun and the Imitation Foreign Devil. His view was, "All nuns must carry on in secret with monks. When a woman walks alone on the street, she must be wanting to seduce bad men. When a man and a woman talk together, they must be arranging to meet." In order to correct such people, he would glare furiously, pass loud, cutting remarks, or, if the place were deserted, throw a small stone from behind.

Who could tell that close on thirty, when a man should "stand firm," ** he would lolse his head like this over a little nun? Such light-headedness, according to the classical canons, is most reprehensible; thus women certainly are hateful creatures. For if the little nun's face had not been soft and smooth, Ah Q would not have been bewitched by her; nor would this have happened if the little nun's face had been covered by a cloth. Five or six years before, when watching an open-air opera, he had pinched the leg of a woman in the audience; but because it was separated from him by the cloth of her trousers he had not had this light-headed feeling afterwards. The little nun had not covered her face, however, and this is another proof of the odiousness of the heretic.

"Woman . . ." thought Ah Q.

*Ta Chi, of the twelfth century B.C., was the concubine of the last king of the Shang Dynasty. Pao Szu, of the eighth century B.C., was the concubine of the last king of the Western Chou Dynasty. Tiao Chan was the concubine of Tung Cho, a powerful minister of the third century B.C.

**Confucius said that at thirty he "stood firm." The phrase was later used to indicate that a man was thirty years old.

He kept a close watch on those women who he believed must be "wanting to seduce bad men," but they did not smile at him. He listened very carefully to those women who talked to him, but not one of them mentioned anything relevant to a secret rendezvous. Ah! this was simply another example of the odiousness of women: they all assumed a false modesty.

One day when Ah Q was grinding rice in Mr. Chao's house, he sat down in the kitchen after supper to smoke a pipe. If it had been anyone else's house, he could have gone home after supper, but they dined early in the Chao family. Although it was the rule that you must not light a lamp, but go to bed after eating, there were occasional exceptions to the rule: before Mr. Chao's son passed the county examination he was allowed to light a lamp to study the examination essays; and when Ah Q came to do odd jobs he was allowed to light a lamp to grind rice. Because of this latter exception to the rule, Ah Q was still sitting in the kitchen smoking before going on with his work.

When Amah Wu, the only maidservant in the Chao household, had finished washing the dishes, she sat down too on the long bench and started chatting to Ah Q:

"Our mistress hasn't eaten anything for two days, because the master wants to get a concubine. . . ."

"Woman . . . Amah Wu . . . this little widow," thought Ah Q.

"Our young mistress is going to have a baby in the eighth moon. . . ."

"Woman . . ." thought Ah Q.

He put down his pipe and stood up.

"Our young mistress—" Amah Wu chattered on.

"Sleep with me!" Ah Q suddenly rushed forward and threw himself at her feet.

There was a moment of absolute silence.

"Ai ya!" Dumbfounded for an instant, Amah Wu suddenly began to tremble, then rushed out shrieking and could soon be heard sobbing.

Ah Q kneeling opposite the wall was dumbfounded too. He grasped the empty bench with both hands and stood up slowly, dimly aware that something was wrong. In fact, by this time he was in rather a nervous state himself. In a flurry, he stuck his pipe into his belt and decided to go back to the rice. But—bang!—a heavy blow landed on his head, and he spun round to see the successful county candidate standing before him brandishing a big bamboo pole.

"How dare you . . . you. . . ."

The big bamboo pole came down across Ah Q's shoulders. And when

41

he put up both hands to protect his head, the blow landed on his knuckles, causing him considerable pain. As he was escaping through the kitchen door, it seemed as if his back also received a blow.

"Turtle's egg!" shouted the successful candidate, cursing him in mandarin from behind.

Ah Q fled to the hulling-floor where he stood alone, still feeling a pain in his knuckles and still remembering that "turtle's egg" because it was an expression never used by the Weichuang villagers, but only by the rich who had seen something of official life. This had made him more frightened, and left an exceptionally deep impression on his mind. By now, however, all thought of "Woman . . ." had flown. After this cursing and beating it seemed as if something was done with, and he began quite light-heartedly to grind rice again. After grinding for a time he grew hot, and stopped to take off his shirt.

While he was taking off his shirt he heard an uproar outside, and since Ah Q always liked to join in any excitement that was going, he went out in search of the sound. He traced it gradually right into Mr. Chao's inner courtyard. Although it was dusk he could see many people there: all the Chao family including the mistress who had not eaten for two days. In addition, there was their neighbor Mrs. Tsou, as well as their relatives Chao Pai-yen and Chao Szu-chen.

The young mistress was leading Amah Wu out of the servants' quarters, saying as she did so:

"Come outside . . . don't stay brooding in your own room."

"Everybody knows you are a good woman," put in Mrs. Tsou from the side. "You mustn't think of committing suicide."

Amah Wu merely wailed, muttering something inaudible.

"This is interesting," thought Ah Q. "What mischief can this little widow be up to?" Wanting to find out, he was approaching Chao Szu-chen when suddenly he caught sight of Mr. Chao's eldest son rushing towards him with, what was more, the big bamboo pole in his hand. The sight of this big bamboo pole reminded him that he had been beaten by it, and he realized that apparently he was connected in some way with this scene of excitement. He turned and ran, hoping to escape to the hulling-floor, not foreseeing that the bamboo pole would cut off his retreat; thereupon he turned and ran in the other direction, leaving without further ado by the back door. In a short time he was back in the Tutelary God's Temple.

After Ah Q had sat down for a time, his skin began to form goose pimples and he felt cold, because although it was spring the nights were still quite frosty and not suited to bare backs. He remembered that he had left his shirt in the Chao house, but he was afraid if he went to fetch it he might get another taste of the successful candidate's bamboo pole.

Then the bailiff came in.

"Curse you, Ah Q!" said the bailiff. "So you can't even keep your hands off the Chao family servants, you rebel! You've made me lose my sleep, curse you! . . ."

Under this torrent of abuse Ah Q naturally had nothing to say. Finally, since it was night-time, Ah Q had to pay double and give the bailiff four hundred cash. But because he happened to have no ready money by him, he gave his felt hat as security, and agreed to the following five terms:

1. The next morning Ah Q must take a pair of red candles, weighing one pound, and a bundle of incense sticks to the Chao family to atone for his misdeeds.
2. Ah Q must pay for the Taoist priests whom the Chao family had called to exorcize evil spirits.
3. Ah Q must never again set foot in the Chao household.
4. If anything unfortunate should happen to Amah Wu, Ah Q must be held responsible.
5. Ah Q must not go back for his wages or shirt.

Ah Q naturally agreed to everything, but unfortunately he had no ready money. Luckily it was already spring, so it was possible to do without his padded quilt which he pawned for two thousand cash to comply with the terms stipulated. After kowtowing with bare back he still had a few cash left, but instead of using these to redeem his felt hat from the bailiff, he spent them all on drink.

Actually, the Chao family burnt neither the incense nor the candles, because these could be used when the mistress worshipped Buddha and were put aside for that purpose. Most of the ragged shirt was made into diapers for the baby which was born to the young mistress in the eighth moon, while the tattered remainder was used by Amah Wu to make shoe soles.

CHAPTER 5

THE PROBLEM OF LIVELIHOOD

After Ah Q had kowtowed and complied with the Chao family terms, he went back as usual to the Tutelary God's Temple. The sun had gone

43

down, and he began to feel that something was wrong. Careful thought led him to the conclusion that this was probably because his back was bare. Remembering that he still had a ragged lined jacket, he put it on and lay down, and when he opened his eyes again the sun was already shining on the top of the west wall. He sat up, saying, "Curse it. . . ."

After getting up he loafed about the streets as usual, until he began to feel that something else was wrong, though this was not to be compared to the physical discomfort of a bare back. Apparently, from that day onwards all the women in Weichuang became shy of Ah Q: whenever they saw him coming they would take refuge indoors. In fact, even Mrs. Tsou who was nearly fifty years old retreated in confusion with the rest, calling her eleven-year-old daughter to go inside. This struck Ah Q as very strange. "The bitches!" he thought. "They have suddenly become as coy as young ladies. . . ."

A good many days later, however, he felt even more strongly that something was wrong. First, the wineshop refused him credit; secondly, the old man in charge of the Tutelary God's Temple made some uncalled-for remarks, as if he wanted Ah Q to leave; and thirdly, for many days—how many exactly he could not remember—not a soul had come to hire him. To be refused credit in the wineshop he could put up with; if the old man kept urging him to leave, Ah Q could just ignore his complaints; but when no one came to hire him he had to go hungry; and this was really a "cursed" state to be in.

When Ah Q could stand it no longer, he went to his regular employers' houses to find out what was the matter—it was only Mr. Chao's threshold that he was not allowed to cross. But he met with a very strange reception. The one to appear was always a man, who looked thoroughly annoyed and waved Ah Q away as if he were a beggar, saying:

"There is nothing, nothing at all! Go away!"

Ah Q found it more and more extraordinary. "These people always needed help in the past," he thought. "They can't suddenly have nothing to be done. This looks fishy." And after making careful enquiries he found out that when they had any odd jobs they all called in Young D. Now this Young D was a lean and weakly pauper, even lower in Ah Q's eyes than Whiskers Wang. Who could have thought that this low fellow would steal his living from him? So this time Ah Q's indignation was greater than usual, and going on his way, fuming, he suddenly raised his arm and sang: "*I'll thrash you with a steel mace. . . .*" *

* A line from *The Battle of Dragon and Tiger*, an opera popular in Shaohsing. It told how Chao Kuang-yin, the first emperor of the Sung Dynasty, fought with another general.

A few days later he did indeed meet Young D in front of Mr. Chien's house. "When two foes meet, their eyes flash fire." As Ah Q went up to him, Young D stood still.

"Stupid ass!" hissed Ah Q, glaring furiously and foaming at the mouth.

"I'm an insect—will that do? . . ." asked Young D.

Such modesty only made Ah Q angrier than ever, but since he had no steel mace in his hand all he could do was to rush forward with out-stretched hand to seize Young D's pigtail. Young D, protecting his pigtail with one hand, with the other tried to seize Ah Q's, whereupon Ah Q also used one free hand to protect his own pigtail. In the past Ah Q had never considered Young D worth taking seriously, but since he had recently suffered from hunger himself he was now as thin and weakly as his opponent, so that they presented a spectacle of evenly matched antagonists. Four hands clutched at two heads, both men bending at the waist, casting a blue, rainbow-shaped shadow on the Chien family's white wall for over half an hour.

"All right! All right!" exclaimed some of the onlookers, probably trying to make peace.

"Good, good!" exclaimed others, but whether to make peace, ap-plaud the fighters or incite them on to further efforts, is not certain.

The two combatants turned deaf ears to them all, however. If Ah Q advanced three paces, Young D would recoil three paces, and so they would stand. If Young D advanced three paces, Ah Q would recoil three paces, and so they would stand again. After about half an hour—Wei-chuang had few striking clocks, so it is difficult to tell the time; it may have been twenty minutes—when steam was rising from both their heads and perspiration pouring down their cheeks, Ah Q let fall his hands, and in the same second Young D's hands fell too. They straightened up simultaneously and stepped back simultaneously, pushing their way out through the crowd.

"You'll be hearing from me again, curse you! . . ." said Ah Q over his shoulder.

"Curse you! You'll be hearing from me again . . ." echoed Young D, also over his shoulder.

This epic struggle had apparently ended neither in victory nor defeat, and it is not known whether the spectators were satisfied or not, for none of them expressed any opinion. But still not a soul came to hire Ah Q.

One warm day, when a balmy breeze seemed to give some foretaste of summer, Ah Q actually began to feel cold; but he could put up with

45

this—his greatest worry was an empty stomach. His cotton quilt, felt hat and shirt had disappeared long ago, and after that he had sold his padded jacket. Now nothing was left but his trousers, and these of course he could not take off. He had a ragged lined jacket, it is true; but this was certainly worthless, unless he gave it away to be made into shoe soles. He had long been hoping to pick up a sum of money on the road, but hitherto he had not been successful; he had also hoped he might suddenly discover a sum of money in his tumbledown room, and had looked wildly all around it, but the room was quite, quite empty. Thereupon he made up his mind to go out in search of food.

As he was walking along the road "in search of food" he saw the familiar wineshop and the familiar steamed bread, but he passed them by without pausing for a second, without even hankering after them. It was not these he was looking for, although what exactly he was looking for he did not know himself.

Weichuang was not a big place, and soon he had left it behind. Most of the country outside the village consisted of paddy fields, green as far as the eye could see with the tender shoots of young rice, dotted here and there with round, black, moving objects, which were peasants cultivating the fields. But blind to the delights of country life, Ah Q simply went on his way, for he knew instinctively that this was far removed from his "search for food." Finally, however, he came to the walls of the Convent of Quiet Self-improvement.

The convent too was surrounded by paddy fields, its white walls standing out sharply in the fresh green, and inside the low earthen wall at the back was a vegetable garden. Ah Q hesitated for a time, looking around him. Since there was no one in sight he scrambled on to the low wall, holding on to some milkwort. The mud wall started crumbling, and Ah Q shook with fear; however, by clutching at the branch of a mulberry tree he managed to jump inside. Within was a wild profusion of vegetation, but no sign of yellow wine, steamed bread, or anything edible. By the west wall was a clump of bamboos, with many bamboo shoots, but unfortunately these were not cooked. There was also rape which had long since gone to seed; the mustard was already about to flower, and the small cabbages looked very tough.

Ah Q felt as resentful as a scholar who has failed in the examinations, and was walking slowly towards the gate of the garden when he gave a start for joy, for there before him what should he see but a patch of turnips! As he knelt down and began picking, a round head suddenly appeared from behind the gate, only to be withdrawn again at once, and this was no other than the little nun. Now though Ah Q had always had the greatest contempt for such people as little nuns, there are times when "Discretion is the better part of valor." He hastily pulled up four turnips, tore off the leaves and folded them in his jacket. By this time an old nun had already come out.

"May Buddha preserve us, Ah Q! What made you climb into our garden to steal turnips! . . . Oh dear, what a wicked thing to do! Oh dear, Buddha preserve us! . . ."

"When did I ever climb into your garden and steal turnips?" retorted Ah Q, looking at her as he started off.

"Now—aren't you?" said the old nun, pointing at the folds of his jacket.

"Are these yours? Can you make them answer you? You. . . ."

Leaving his sentence unfinished, Ah Q took to his heels as fast as he could, followed by an enormously fat, black dog. This dog had originally been at the front gate, and it was a mystery how it had reached the back garden. The black dog gave chase, snarling, and was just about to bite Ah Q's leg when a turnip fell most opportunely from the latter's jacket, and the dog, taken by surprise, stopped for a second. During this time Ah Q scrambled up the mulberry tree, scaled the mud wall and fell, turnips and all, outside the convent. He left the black dog still barking by the mulberry tree, and the old nun saying her prayers.

Fearing that the nun would let the black dog out again, Ah Q gathered together his turnips and ran, picking up a few small stones as he went. But the black dog did not reappear. Ah Q threw away the stones and walked on, eating as he went, thinking to himself: "There is nothing to be had here; I had better go to town. . . ."

By the time he had finished the third turnip, he had made up his mind to go to town.

CHAPTER 6

FROM RESTORATION TO DECLINE

Weichuang did not see Ah Q again till just after the Moon Festival that year. Everybody was surprised to hear of his return, and this made them think back and wonder where he had been all this time. The few previous occasions on which Ah Q had been to town, he had usually informed people in advance with great gusto; but since he had not done so this time, no one had noticed his going. He might have told the old man in charge of the Tutelary God's Temple, but according to the custom of Weichuang it was only when Mr. Chao, Mr. Chien, or the successful county candidate went to town that it was considered important. Even the Imitation Foreign Devil's going was not talked about, much less Ah Q's. This would explain why the old man had not spread the news for him, with the result that the villagers had had no means of knowing it.

But Ah Q's return this time was very different from before, and in fact quite enough to occasion astonishment. The day was growing dark when he appeared blinking sleepily before the door of the wineshop, walked up to the counter, pulled a handful of silver and coppers from his belt and tossed them on the counter. "Cash!" he said. "Bring the wine!" He was wearing a new, lined jacket, and evidently a large purse hung at his waist, the great weight of which caused his belt to sag in a sharp curve. It was the custom in Weichuang that when there seemed to be something unusual about anyone, he should be treated with respect rather than insolence, and now, although they knew quite well that this was Ah Q, still he was very different from the Ah Q of the ragged coat. The ancients say, "A scholar who has been away three days must be looked at with new eyes," and so the waiter, innkeeper, customers and passers-by, all quite naturally expressed a kind of suspicion mingled with respect. The innkeeper started by nodding, then said:

"Hullo, Ah Q, so you're back!"

"Yes, I'm back."

"You've made money . . . er . . . where . . . ?"

"I went to town."

By the next day this piece of news had spread through Weichuang. And since everybody wanted to hear the success story of this Ah Q of the ready money and the new lined jacket, in the wineshop, teahouse, and under the temple eaves, the villagers gradually ferreted out the news. The result was that they began to treat Ah Q with a new deference.

According to Ah Q, he had been a servant in the house of a successful provincial candidate. This part of the story filled all who heard it with awe. This successful provincial candidate was named Pai, but because he was the only successful provincial candidate in the whole town there was no need to use his surname: whenever anyone spoke of the successful provincial candidate, it meant him. And this was so not only in Weichuang but everywhere within a radius of thirty miles, as if everybody imagined his name to be Mr. Successful Provincial Candidate. To have worked in the household of such a man naturally called for respect; but according to Ah Q's further statements, he was unwilling to go on working there because this successful candidate was really too much of a "turtle's egg." This part of the story made all who heard it sigh, but with a sense of pleasure, because it showed that Ah Q was actually not fit to work in such a man's household, yet not to work was a pity.

According to Ah Q, his return was also due to the fact that he was not satisfied with the townspeople because they called a long bench a straight bench, used shredded shallots to fry fish, and—a defect he had recently discovered—the women did not sway in a very satisfactory manner as they walked. However, the town had its good points too; for instance, in Weichuang everyone played with thirty-two bamboo counters, and only the Imitation Foreign Devil could play mah-jong, but in town even the street urchins excelled at mah-jong. You had only to place the Imitation Foreign Devil in the hands of these young rascals in their teens, for him straightaway to become like "a small devil before the King of Hell." This part of the story made all who heard it blush.

"Have you seen an execution?" asked Ah Q. "Ah, that's a fine sight. . . . When they execute the revolutionaries. . . . Ah, that's a fine sight, a fine sight. . . ." As he shook his head, his spittle flew on to the face of Chao Szu-chen directly opposite. This part of the story made all who heard it tremble. Then with a glance around, he suddenly raised his right hand and dropped it on the neck of Whiskers Wang, who was listening raptly with his head thrust forward.

"Kill!" shouted Ah Q.

Whiskers Wang gave a start, and drew in his head as fast as lightning or a spark struck from a flint, while the bystanders shivered with pleasurable apprehension. After this, Whiskers Wang went about in a daze for many days, and dared not go near Ah Q, nor did the others.

Although we cannot say Ah Q's status in the eyes of the inhabitants of Weichuang at this time was superior to that of Mr. Chao, we can at least affirm without any danger of inaccuracy that it was about the same.

Not long after, Ah Q's fame suddenly spread into the women's apartments of Weichuang too. Although the only two families of any pretensions in Weichuang were those of Chien and Chao, and nine-tenths of the rest were poor, still women's apartments are women's apartments, and this spreading of Ah Q's fame into them was something of a miracle. When the womenfolk met they would say to each other, "Mrs. Tsou bought a blue silk skirt from Ah Q. Although it was old, still it only cost ninety cents. And Chao Pai-yen's mother (this has yet to be verified, because some say it was Chao Szu-chen's mother) bought a child's costume of crimson foreign calico, which was nearly new, only spending three hundred cash, less eight per cent discount."

Then those who had no silk skirt or needed foreign calico were most anxious to see Ah Q in order to buy from him. Far from avoiding him now, they would sometimes follow him when he passed, calling to him to stop.

"Ah Q, have you any more silk skirts?" they would ask. "No? We want foreign calico too. Do you have any?"

This news later spread from the poor households to the rich ones, because Mrs. Tsou was so pleased with her silk skirt that she took it to Mrs. Chao for her approval, and Mrs. Chao told Mr. Chao, speaking very highly of it.

Mr. Chao discussed the matter that evening at dinner with his son, the successful county candidate, suggesting that there must be something queer about Ah Q, and that they should be more careful about their doors and windows. They did not know, though, whether Ah Q had any things left or not, and thought he might still have something good. And Mrs. Chao happened to be wanting a good, cheap, fur vest. So after a family council it was decided to ask Mrs. Tsou to find Ah Q for them at once, and for this a third exception was made to the rule, special permission being given for a lamp to be lit that evening.

A considerable amount of oil had been burnt, but still there was no sign of Ah Q. The whole Chao household was yawning with impatience, some of them resenting Ah Q's undisciplined ways, some of them angrily blaming Mrs. Tsou for not trying harder to get him there. Mrs. Chao was afraid that Ah Q dared not come because of the terms agreed upon that spring, but Mr. Chao did not think this anything to worry about, because, as he said, "This time *I* sent for him." And sure enough, Mr. Chao proved himself a man of insight, for Ah Q finally arrived with Mrs. Tsou.

"He keeps saying he has nothing left," panted Mrs. Tsou as she came in. "When I told him to come and tell you so himself, he would go on talking. I told him. . . ."

"Sir!" said Ah Q with an attempt at a smile, coming to a halt under the eaves.

"I hear you got rich out there, Ah Q," said Mr. Chao, going up to him and looking him carefully over. "Very good. Now . . . they say you have some old things. . . . Bring them all here for us to have a look at. . . . This is simply because I happen to want. . . ."

"I told Mrs. Tsou—there is nothing left."

"Nothing left?" Mr. Chao could not help sounding disappointed. "How could they go so quickly?"

"They belonged to a friend, and there was not much to begin with. People bought some. . . ."

"There must be something left."

"Now there is only a door curtain left."

"Then bring the door curtain for us to see," said Mrs. Chao hurriedly.

"Well, it will be all right if you bring it tomorrow," said Mr. Chao without much enthusiasm. "When you have anything in future, Ah Q, you must bring it to us first. . . ."

"We certainly will not pay less than other people!" said the successful county candidate. His wife shot a hasty glance at Ah Q to see his reaction.

"I need a fur vest," said Mrs. Chao.

Although Ah Q agreed, he slouched out so carelessly that they did not know whether he had taken their instructions to heart or not. This made Mr. Chao so disappointed, annoyed and worried that he even stopped yawning. The successful candidate was also far from satisfied with Ah Q's attitude, and said, "People should be on their guard against such a turtle's egg. It might be best to order the bailiff not to allow him to live in Weichuang."

But Mr. Chao did not agree, saying that he might bear a grudge, and that in a business like his it was probably a case of "the eagle does not prey on its own nest": his own village need not worry, and they need only be a little more watchful at night. The successful candidate was much impressed by this parental instruction, and immediately withdrew his proposal for driving Ah Q away, cautioning Mrs. Tsou on no account to repeat what he had said.

The next day, however, when Mrs. Tsou took her blue skirt to be dyed black she repeated these insinuations about Ah Q, although not actually mentioning what the successful candidate had said about driving him away. But even so, it was most damaging to Ah Q. In the first place, the bailiff appeared at his door and took away the door curtain. Although Ah Q protested that Mrs. Chao wanted to see it, the bailiff would not give it back, and even demanded a monthly payment of hush-money. In the second place, the villagers' respect for him suddenly changed. Although they still dared not take liberties, they avoided him as much as possible. And while this differed from their previous fear of his "Kill!", it closely resembled the attitude of the ancients to spirits: keeping a respectful distance.

But there were some idlers who wanted to get to the bottom of the business, who went to question Ah Q carefully. And with no attempt at concealment, Ah Q told them proudly of his experiences. They learned that he had merely been a petty thief, not only unable to climb walls, but even unable to go through openings: he simply stood outside an opening to receive the stolen goods.

One night he had just received a package and his chief had gone in again, when he heard a great uproar inside, and took to his heels as fast as he could. He fled from the town that same night, back to Weichuang; and after this he dared not return to that business. This story, however, was even more damaging to Ah Q, since the villagers had been keeping a respectful distance because they did not want to incur his enmity; for who could have guessed that he was only a thief who dared not steal again? But now they knew he was really too low to inspire fear.

CHAPTER 7

THE REVOLUTION

On the fourteenth day of the ninth moon of the third year in the reign of Emperor Hsuan Tung*—the day on which Ah Q sold his purse to Chao Pai-yen—at midnight, after the fourth stroke of the third watch, a large boat with a big black awning came to the Chao family's landing place. This boat floated up in the darkness while the villagers were sound asleep, so that they knew nothing about it; but it left again about dawn, when quite a number of people saw it. Investigation revealed that this boat actually belonged to the successful provincial candidate!

This boat caused great uneasiness in Weichuang, and before midday the hearts of all the villagers were beating faster. The Chao family kept very quiet about the errand of the boat, but according to the gossip in the tea-house and wineshop, the revolutionaries were going to enter the town and the successful provincial candidate had come to the country to take refuge. Mrs. Tsou alone thought otherwise, maintaining that the successful provincial candidate had merely wanted to deposit a few battered cases in Weichuang, but Mr. Chao had sent them back. Actually the successful provincial candidate and the successful county candidate in the Chao family were not on good terms, so that it was scarcely logical to expect them to prove friends in adversity; moreover, since Mrs. Tsou was a neighbor of the Chao family and had a better idea of what was going on, she ought to have known.

Then a rumor spread to the effect that although the scholar had not arrived himself, he had sent a long letter tracing some distant relationship with the Chao family; and Mr. Chao after thinking it over had decided it could, after all, do him no harm to keep the cases, so they

* The day on which Shaohsing was freed in the 1911 Revolution.

were now stowed under his wife's bed. As for the revolutionaries, some people said they had entered the town that night in white helmets and white armor—the mourning dress for Emperor Tsung Cheng.*

Ah Q had long since heard of the revolutionaries, and this year had with his own eyes seen revolutionaries being decapitated. But since it had occurred to him that the revolutionaries were rebels and that a rebellion would make things difficult for him, he had always detested and kept away from them. Who could have guessed they could so frighten a successful provincial candidate renowned for thirty miles around? In consequence, Ah Q could not help feeling rather "entranced," the terror of all the villagers only adding to his delight.

"Revolution is not a bad thing," thought Ah Q. "Finish off the whole lot of them . . . curse them! . . . I would like to go over to the revolutionaries myself."

Ah Q had been hard up recently, and was probably rather dissatisfied; added to this was the fact that he had drunk two bowls of wine at noon on an empty stomach. Consequently, he got drunk more quickly than ever; and as he walked along thinking to himself, he felt again as if he were treading on air. Suddenly, in some curious way, he felt as if the revolutionaries were himself, and all the people in Weichuang were his captives. Unable to contain himself for joy, he could not help shouting loudly:

"Rebellion! Rebellion!"

All the villagers looked at him in consternation. Ah Q had never seen such pitiful looks before, and found them as refreshing as a drink of iced water in midsummer. So he walked on even more happily, shouting:

"All right . . . I shall take what I want! I shall like whom I please!

> "*Tra la, tra la!*
> "*I regret to have killed by mistake my sworn*
>   *brother Cheng, in my cups.*
> "*I regret to have killed. . . . Yah, yah, yah!*
> "*Tra la, tra la, tum ti tum tum!*
> "*I'll thrash you with a steel mace.*"

Mr. Chao and his son were standing at their gate with two relatives discussing the revolution. But Ah Q did not see them as he went past singing with his head thrown back: "*Tra la la, tum ti tum!*"

---

* Tsung Cheng, the last emperor of the Ming Dynasty, reigned from 1628 to 1644. He hanged himself before the Manchus entered Peking.

"Q, old chap!" called Mr. Chao timidly in a low voice.

"*Tra la!*" sang Ah Q, unable to imagine that his name could be linked with those words "old chap." Sure that he had heard wrongly and was in no way concerned, he simply went on singing, "*Tra la la, tum ti tum!*"

"Q, old chap!"

"*I regret to have killed. . . .*"

"Ah Q!" The successful candidate had to call his name.

Only then did Ah Q come to a stop. "Well?" he asked with his head on one side.

"Q, old chap . . . now. . . ." But Mr. Chao was at a loss for words again. "Are you getting rich now?"

"Getting rich? Of course. I take what I like. . . ."

"Ah—Q, old man, poor friends of yours like us can't possibly matter . . ." said Chao Pai-yen apprehensively, as if sounding out the revolutionaries' attitude.

"Poor friends? Surely you are richer than I am," said Ah Q, and walked away.

They stood there despondent and speechless; then Mr. Chao and his son went back to the house, and that evening discussed the question until it was time to light the lamps. When Chao Pai-yen went home, he took the purse from his waist and gave it to his wife to hide for him at the bottom of a chest.

For some time Ah Q seemed to be walking on air, but by the time he reached the Tutelary God's Temple he was sober again. That evening the old man in charge of the temple was also unexpectedly friendly and offered him tea. Then Ah Q asked him for two flat cakes, and after eating these demanded a four-ounce candle that had been used, and a candlestick. He lit the candle and lay down alone in his little room. He felt inexpressibly refreshed and happy, while the candlelight leapt and flickered as on the Lantern Festival and his imagination too seemed to soar.

"Revolt? It would be fun. . . . A group of revolutionaries would come, all wearing white helmets and white armor, carrying swords, steel maces, bombs, foreign guns, double-edged knives with sharp points and spears with hooks. They would come to the Tutelary God's Temple and call out, 'Ah Q! Come with us, come with us!' And then I would go with them. . . .

"Then all those villagers would be in a laughable plight, kneeling down and pleading, 'Ah Q, spare our lives.' But who would listen to them! The first to die would be Young D and Mr. Chao, then the successful county candidate and the Imitation Foreign Devil . . . but

54

perhaps I would spare a few. I would once have spared Whiskers Wang, but now I don't even want him either. . . .

"Things . . . I would go straight in and open the cases: silver ingots, foreign coins, foreign calico jackets. . . . First I would move the successful county candidate's wife's Ningpo bed to the temple, and also move in the Chien family tables and chairs—or else just use the Chao family's. I would not lift a finger myself, but order Young D to move the things for me, and to look smart about it, unless he wanted a slap in the face. . . .

"Chao Szu-chen's younger sister is very ugly. In a few years Mrs. Tsou's daughter might be worth considering. The Imitation Foreign Devil's wife is willing to sleep with a man without a pigtail, hah! She can't be a good woman! The successful county candidate's wife has scars on her eyelids. . . . I have not seen Amah Wu for a long time, and don't know where she is—what a pity her feet are so big."

Before Ah Q had reached a satisfactory conclusion, there was a sound of snoring. The four-ounce candle had burnt down only half an inch, and its flickering red light lit up his open mouth.

"Ho, ho!" shouted Ah Q suddenly, raising his head and looking wildly around. But when he saw the four-ounce candle, he lay back and went to sleep again.

The next morning he got up very late, and when he went out to the street everything was the same as usual. He was still hungry, but though he racked his brains he did not seem able to think of anything. Then suddenly an idea came to him, and he walked slowly off, until either by design or accident he reached the Convent of Quiet Self-improvement.

The convent was as peaceful as it had been that spring, with its white wall and shining black gate. After a moment's reflection, he knocked at the gate, whereupon a dog started barking within. He hastily picked up several pieces of broken brick, then went up again to knock more heavily, knocking until a number of small dents appeared on the black gate. And at last he heard someone coming to open the door.

Ah Q hastily got ready his broken bricks, and stood with his legs wide apart, prepared to do battle with the black dog. But the convent door only opened a crack, and no black dog rushed out. When he looked in all he could see was the old nun.

"What are you here for again?" she asked, giving a start.

"There is a revolution . . . did you know?" said Ah Q vaguely.

"Revolution, revolution . . . there has already been one," said the old nun, her eyes red from crying. "What do you think will become of us with all your revolutions?"

"What?" asked Ah Q in astonishment.

"Didn't you know? The revolutionaries have already been here!"

"Who?" asked Ah Q in even greater astonishment.

"The successful county candidate and the Imitation Foreign Devil."

This came as a complete surprise to Ah Q, who could not help being taken aback. When the old nun saw that he had lost his aggressiveness, she quickly shut the gate, so that when Ah Q pushed it again he could not budge it, and when he knocked again there was no answer.

It had happened that morning. The successful county candidate in the Chao family got news quickly, and as soon as he heard that the revolutionaries had entered the town that night, he had immediately wound his pigtail up on his head and gone out first thing to call on the Imitation Foreign Devil in the Chien family, with whom he had never been on good terms. This was a time for all to work for reforms, so they had had a very pleasant talk and became on the spot comrades who saw eye to eye and pledged themselves to become revolutionaries.

After racking their brains for some time, they remembered that in the Convent of Quiet Self-improvement was an imperial tablet inscribed "Long Live the Emperor" which ought to be done away with at once. Thereupon they lost no time in going to the convent to carry out their revolutionary activities. Because the old nun tried to stop them, and put in a few words, they considered her as the Manchu government and knocked her many times on the head with a stick and with their knuckles. The nun, pulling herself together after they had gone, made an inspection. Naturally the imperial tablet had been smashed into fragments on the ground, but the valuable Hsuan Te censer* before the shrine of Kuan-yin, the goddess of mercy, had also disappeared.

Ah Q only learned this later. He deeply regretted having been asleep at the time, and resented the fact that they had not come to call him. But then he said to himself, "Maybe they still don't know I have joined the revolutionaries."

* Highly decorative bronze censers were made during the Hsuan Te period (1426-1435) of the Ming Dynasty.

CHAPTER 8

BARRED FROM THE REVOLUTION

The people of Weichuang became more reassured every day. From the news that was brought they knew that, although the revolutionaries had entered the town, their coming had not made a great deal of difference. The magistrate was still the highest official, it was only his title that had changed; and the successful provincial candidate also had some post—the Weichuang villagers could not remember these names clearly—some kind of official post; while the head of the military was still the same old captain. The only cause for alarm was that there were also some bad revolutionaries making trouble, who had started cutting off people's pigtails the day after their arrival. It was said that the boatman "Seven Pounds" from the next village had fallen into their clutches, and that he no longer looked presentable. Still, the danger of this was not great, because the Weichuang villagers seldom went to town to begin with, and those who had been considering a trip to town at once changed their plans in order to avoid this risk. Ah Q had been thinking of going to town to look up his old friends, but as soon as he heard the news he gave up the idea in resignation.

It would be wrong, however, to say that there were no reforms in Weichuang. During the next few days the number of people who coiled their pigtails on their heads gradually increased, and, as has already been said, the first to do so was naturally the successful county candidate; the next were Chao Szu-chen and Chao Pai-yen, and after them Ah Q. If it had been summer it would not have been considered strange if everybody had coiled their pigtails on their heads or tied them in knots; but this was late autumn, so that this autumn observance of a summer practice on the part of those who coiled their pigtails could be considered nothing short of a heroic decision, and as far as Weichuang was concerned it could not be said to have had no connection with the reforms.

When Chao Szu-chen approached with the nape of his neck bared, people who saw him would say, "Ah! here comes a revolutionary!"

When Ah Q heard this, he was greatly impressed. Although he had long since heard how the successful county candidate had coiled his pigtail on his head, it had never occurred to him to do the same. Only now when he saw that Chao Szu-chen had followed suit was he struck with the idea of doing the same himself, and made up his mind to copy them. He used a bamboo chopstick to twist his pigtail up on his head, and after hesitating for some time eventually summoned up the courage to go out.

As he walked along the street people looked at him, but nobody said anything. Ah Q was very displeased at first, and then he became very resentful. Recently he had been losing his temper very easily. As a matter of fact his life was no harder than before the revolution, people treated him politely, and the shops no longer demanded payment in cash, yet Ah Q still felt dissatisfied. He thought since a revolution had taken place, it should involve more than this. And then he saw Young D, and the sight made his anger boil over.

Young D had also coiled his pigtail on his head and, what was more, he had actually used a bamboo chopstick to do so too. Ah Q had never imagined that Young D would also have the courage to do this; he certainly could not tolerate such a thing! Who was Young D anyway? He was greatly tempted to seize him then and then, break his bamboo chopstick, let down his pigtail and slap his face several times in the bargain to punish him for forgetting his place and for his presumption in becoming a revolutionary. But in the end he let him off, simply fixing him with a furious glare, spitting, and exclaiming, "Pah!"

These last few days the only one to go to town was the Imitation Foreign Devil. The successful county candidate in the Chao family had thought of using the deposited cases as a pretext to call on the successful provincial candidate, but the danger that he might have his pigtail cut off had made him defer his visit. He had written an extremely formal letter, and asked the Imitation Foreign Devil to take it to town; he had also asked the latter to introduce him to the Liberty Party. When the Imitation Foreign Devil came back, he asked the successful county candidate for four dollars, after which the successful county candidate wore a silver peach on his chest. All the Weichuang villagers were overawed, and said that this was the badge of the Persimmon Oil Party,* equivalent to the rank of a Han Lin.** As a result, Mr. Chao's prestige suddenly increased, far more so in fact than when his son first passed the official examination; consequently, he started looking down on everyone else, and, when he saw Ah Q, tended to ignore him a little.

* The Liberty Party was called *Tzu Yu Tang.* The villagers, not understanding the word Liberty, turned *Tzu Yu* into *Shih Yu,* which means persimmon oil.

** The highest literary degree in the Ching Dynasty (1644-1911).

Ah Q was thoroughly discontented at finding himself always ignored, but as soon as he heard of this silver peach he realized at once why he was left out in the cold. Simply to say that you had gone over was not enough to make anyone a revolutionary; nor was it enough merely to wind your pigtail up on your head; the most important thing was to get into touch with the revolutionary party. In all his life he had known only two revolutionaries, one of whom had already lost his head in town, leaving only the Imitation Foreign Devil. Unless he went at once to talk things over with the Imitation Foreign Devil there was no way left open to him.

The front gate of the Chien house happened to be open, and Ah Q crept timidly in. Once inside he gave a start, for there he saw the Imitation Foreign Devil standing in the middle of the courtyard dressed entirely in black, no doubt in foreign dress, and also wearing a silver peach. In his hand he held the stick with which Ah Q was already acquainted to his cost, and the foot or so of hair which he had grown again fell over his shoulders, hanging dishevelled like Saint Liu's.* Standing erect before him were Chao Pai-yen and three others, all of them listening with the utmost deference to what he was saying.

Ah Q tiptoed inside and stood behind Chao Pai-yen, wanting to utter a greeting, but not knowing what to say. Obviously, he could not call the man "Imitation Foreign Devil," and neither "Foreigner" nor "Revolutionary" seemed suitable. Perhaps the best form of address would be "Mr. Foreigner."

But Mr. Foreigner had not seen him, because with eyes raised he was talking most animatedly:

"I am so impulsive that when we met I kept saying, 'Old Hung, we should get on with it!' But he always answered 'Nein!'—that's a foreign word which you wouldn't understand. Otherwise, we should have succeeded long ago. This is an instance of how cautious he is. He asked me again and again to go to Hupeh, but I wouldn't agree. Who wants to work in a small district town? . . ."

"Er—er—" Ah Q waited for him to pause, and then screwed up his courage to speak. But for some reason or other he still did not call him Mr. Foreigner.

The four men who had been listening gave a start and turned to stare at Ah Q. Mr. Foreigner, too, caught sight of him for the first time.

"What?"

"I. . . ."

* An immortal in Chinese folk legend, always portrayed with flowing hair.

"Clear out!"

"I want to join. . . ."

"Get out!" said Mr. Foreigner, lifting the "mourner's stick."

Then Chao Pai-yen and the others shouted, "Mr. Chien tells you to get out, don't you hear!"

Ah Q put up his hands to protect his head, and without knowing what he was doing fled through the gate; but this time Mr. Foreigner did not give chase. After running more than sixty steps Ah Q began to slow down, and now he began to feel most upset, because if Mr. Foreigner would not allow him to be a revolutionary, there was no other way open to him. In future he could never hope to have men in white helmets and white armor coming to call him. All his ambition, aims, hope and future had been blasted at one stroke. The fact that people might spread the news and make him a laughing-stock for the likes of Young D and Whiskers Wang was only a secondary consideration.

Never before had he felt so flat. Even coiling his pigtail on his head now struck him as pointless and ridiculous. As a form of revenge he was very tempted to let his pigtail down at once, but he did not do so. He wandered about till evening, when after drinking two bowls of wine on credit he began to feel in better spirits, and saw again in his mind's eye fragmentary visions of white helmets and white armor.

One day he loafed about until late at night. Only when the wineshop was about to close did he start to stroll back to the Tutelary God's Temple.

"Bang—bump!"

He suddenly heard an unusual sound, which could not have been firecrackers. Ah Q always liked excitement and enjoyed poking his nose into other people's business, so he went looking for the noise in the darkness. He seemed to hear footsteps ahead, and was listening carefully when a man suddenly rushed out in front of him. As soon as Ah Q saw him, he turned and followed him as fast as he could. When that man turned, Ah Q turned too, and when after turning a corner that man stopped, Ah Q stopped too. He saw there was no one behind, and that the man was Young D.

"What is the matter?" asked Ah Q resentfully.

"Chao . . . the Chao family have been robbed," panted Young D.

Ah Q's heart went pit-a-pat. After telling him this, Young D left. Ah Q ran on and then stopped two or three times. However, since he had once been in the business himself, he felt exceptionally courageous. Emerging from the street corner, he listened carefully and thought he could hear shouting; he also looked carefully and thought he could see a lot of men in white helmets and white armor, carrying off cases, carrying off furniture, even carrying off the Ningpo bed of the successful county candidate's wife; he could not, however, see them very clearly. He wanted to go nearer, but his feet were rooted to the ground.

There was no moon that night, and Weichuang was very still in the pitch darkness, as quiet as in the peaceful days of the ancient Emperor Fu Hsi.* Ah Q stood there until he lost interest, yet everything still seemed the same as before; in the distance were people moving to and fro, carrying things, carrying off cases, carrying off furniture, carrying off the Ningpo bed of the successful county candidate's wife . . . carrying until he could hardly believe his own eyes. But he decided not to go nearer, and went back to the temple.

It was even darker in the Tutelary God's Temple. When he had closed the big gate, he groped his way into his room, and only after he had been lying down for some time did he feel calm enough to begin to think how this affected him. The men in white helmets and white armor had evidently arrived, but they had not come to call him; they had moved out a lot of things, but there was no share for him—this was all the fault of the Imitation Foreign Devil, who had barred him from the rebellion. Otherwise, how could he have failed to have a share this time?

The more Ah Q thought of it the angrier he grew, until he was in a towering rage. "So no rebellion for me, only for you, eh?" he exclaimed, nodding maliciously. "Curse you, you Imitation Foreign Devil—all right, be a rebel! A rebel is punished by having his head chopped off. I shall have to turn informer, to see you carried into town to have your head cut off—you and all your family. . . . Kill, kill!"

CHAPTER 9

THE GRAND FINALE

After the Chao family was robbed, most of the people in Weichuang felt pleased yet fearful, and Ah Q was no exception. But four days later Ah Q was suddenly dragged into town in the middle of the night. It happened to be a dark night when a squad of soldiers, a squad of militia, a squad of police and five secret servicemen made their way quietly to Weichuang, and under cover of darkness surrounded the Tutelary God's Temple, posting a machine gun opposite the entrance. Yet Ah Q

* One of the earliest legendary monarchs in China.

did not rush out. For a long time nothing stirred in the temple. The captain grew impatient and offered a reward of twenty thousand cash. Only then did two militiamen summon up courage to jump over the wall and enter. Then with co-operation from within, the others rushed in and dragged Ah Q out. But not until he had been carried out of the temple to somewhere near the machine gun did he begin to sober up.

It was already midday by the time they reached town, and Ah Q found himself carried to a dilapidated yamen where, after taking five or six turnings, he was pushed into a small room. No sooner had he stumbled inside than the door, made of wooden bars forming a grating, closed upon his heels. The rest of the room consisted of three blank walls, and when he looked round carefully he saw two other men in a corner of the room.

Although Ah Q was feeling rather uneasy, he was by no means too depressed, because the room where he slept in the Tutelary God's Temple was in no way superior to this. The two other men also seemed to be villagers. They gradually fell into conversation with him, and one of them told him that the successful provincial candidate wanted to dun him for the rent owed by his grandfather; the other did not know why he was there. When they questioned Ah Q, he answered quite frankly, "Because I wanted to revolt."

That afternoon he was dragged out through the barred door and taken to a big hall, at the far end of which was sitting an old man with his head shaved clean. Ah Q first took him for a monk, but when he saw soldiers standing beneath and a dozen men in long coats on both sides, some with their heads clean-shaved like this old man and some with a foot or so of hair hanging over their shoulders like the Imitation Foreign Devil, but all glaring at him furiously from grim faces, then he knew this man must be someone important. At once the joints of his knees relaxed of their own accord, and he sank down.

"Stand up to speak! Don't kneel!" shouted all the men in the long coats.

Although Ah Q understood, he felt incapable of standing up: his body had involuntarily dropped to a squatting position, and improving on it he finally knelt down.

"Slave! . . ." exclaimed the long-coated men contemptuously. They did not insist on his getting up, however.

"Tell the truth and you will receive a lighter sentence," said the old man with the shaved head, in a low but clear voice, fixing his eyes on Ah Q. "I know everything already. When you have confessed, I will let you go."

62

"Confess!" repeated the long-coated men loudly.

"The fact is I wanted . . . to come . . ." muttered Ah Q disjointedly, after a moment's confused thinking.

"In that case, why didn't you come?" asked the old man gently.

"The Imitation Foreign Devil wouldn't let me!"

"Nonsense! It is too late to talk now. Where are your accomplices?"

"What? . . ."

"The people who robbed the Chao family that night."

"They didn't come to call me. They moved the things away themselves." Mention of this made Ah Q indignant.

"Where did they go? When you have told me, I will let you go," said the old man even more gently.

"I don't know . . . they didn't come to call me. . . ."

Then, at a sign from the old man, Ah Q was dragged again through the barred door. The next time that he was dragged out was the following morning.

Everything was unchanged in the big hall. The old man with the clean-shaved head was still sitting there, and Ah Q knelt down again as before.

"Have you anything else to say?" asked the old man gently.

Ah Q thought, and decided there was nothing to say, so he answered, "Nothing."

Then a man in a long coat brought a sheet of paper and held a brush in front of Ah Q, which he wanted to thrust into his hand. Ah Q was now nearly frightened out of his wits, because this was the first time in his life that his hand had ever come into contact with a writing brush. He was just wondering how to hold it when the man pointed out a place on the paper, and told him to sign his name.

"I—I—can't write," said Ah Q, nervous and shamefaced, holding the brush.

"In that case, to make it easy for you, draw a circle!"

Ah Q tried to draw a circle, but the hand with which he grasped the brush trembled, so the man spread the paper on the ground for him. Ah Q bent down and, as painstakingly as if his life depended on it, drew a circle. Afraid people would laugh at him, he determined to make the circle round; however, not only was that wretched brush very heavy, but it would not do his bidding, wobbling instead from side to side; and just as the line was about to close it swerved out again, making a shape like a melon seed.

While Ah Q was ashamed because he had not been able to draw a round circle, that man had already taken back the paper and brush without any comment; and then a number of people dragged him back for the third time through the barred door.

This time he did not feel particularly irritated. He supposed that in this world it was the fate of everybody at some time to be dragged in and out of prison, and to have to draw circles on paper; it was only because his circle had not been round that he felt there was a blot on his escutcheon. Presently, however, he regained composure by thinking, "Only idiots can make perfect circles." And with this thought he fell asleep.

That night, however, the successful provincial candidate was unable to go to sleep, because he had quarrelled with the captain. The successful provincial candidate had insisted that the most important thing was to recover the stolen goods, while the captain said the most important thing was to make a public example. Recently the captain had come to treat the successful provincial candidate quite disdainfully. So, banging his fist on the table, he said, "Punish one to awe one hundred! See now, I have been a member of the revolutionary party for less than twenty days, but there have been a dozen cases of robbery, none of them solved yet; and think how badly that reflects on me. And now that one case has been solved, you come to argue like a pedant. It won't do! This is my affair."

The successful provincial candidate had been very upset, but had still persisted, saying that if the stolen goods were not recovered, he would resign immediately from his post as assistant civil administrator. "As you please!" said the captain.

In consequence the successful provincial candidate did not sleep that night, but happily he did not hand in his resignation after all the next day.

The third time that Ah Q was dragged out of the barred door, was the morning following the night on which the successful provincial candidate had been unable to sleep. When he reached the big hall, the old man with the clean-shaved head was still sitting there as usual, and Ah Q also knelt down as usual.

Very gently the old man questioned him: "Have you anything more to say?"

Ah Q thought, and decided there was nothing to say, so he answered, "Nothing."

A number of men in long coats and short jackets put on him a white vest of foreign cloth, with some black characters on it. Ah Q felt considerably disconcerted, because this was very like mourning dress, and to wear mourning was unlucky. At the same time his hands were bound behind his back, and he was dragged out of the yamen.

Ah Q was lifted on to an uncovered cart, and several men in short jackets sat down with him. The cart started off at once. In front were a number of soldiers and militiamen shouldering foreign rifles, and on both sides were crowds of gaping spectators, while what was behind Ah Q could not see. But suddenly it occurred to him—"Can I be going to have my head cut off?" Panic seized him and everything turned dark before his eyes, while there was a humming in his ears as if he had fainted. But he did not really faint. Although he felt frightened some of the time, the rest of the time he was quite calm. It seemed to him that in this world probably it was the fate of everybody at some time to have his head cut off.

He still recognized the road and felt rather surprised: why were they not going to the execution ground? He did not know that he was being paraded round the streets as a public example. But if he had known, it would have been the same; he would only have thought that in this world probably it was the fate of everybody at some time to be made a public example of.

Then he realized that they were making a detour to the execution ground, so he must be going to have his head cut off, after all. He looked round him regretfully at the people swarming after him like ants, and unexpectedly in the crowd of people by the road he caught sight of Amah Wu. So that was why he had not seen her for so long: she had been working in town.

Ah Q suddenly became ashamed of his lack of spirit, because he had not sung any lines from an opera. His thoughts revolved like a whirlwind: *The Young Widow at Her Husband's Grave* was not heroic enough. The words of "I regret to have killed" in *The Battle of Dragon and Tiger* were too poor. *I'll thrash you with a steel mace* was still the best. But when he wanted to raise his hands, he remembered that they were bound together; so he did not sing *I'll thrash you* either.

"In twenty years I shall be another...." * In his agitation Ah Q uttered half a saying which he had picked up himself but never used before. The crowd's roar "Good!!!" sounded like the growl of a wolf.

---

* "In twenty years I shall be another stout young fellow" was a phrase often used by criminals before execution, to show their scorn of death. Believing in the transmigration of the soul, they thought that after death their souls would enter other living bodies.

The cart moved steadily forward. During the shouting Ah Q's eyes turned in search of Amah Wu, but she did not seem to have seen him for she was looking raptly at the foreign rifles carried by the soldiers.

So Ah Q took another look at the shouting crowd.

At that instant his thoughts revolved again like a whirlwind. Four years before, at the foot of the mountain, he had met a hungry wolf which had followed him at a set distance, wanting to eat him. He had nearly died of fright, but luckily he happened to have an axe in his hand, which gave him the courage to get back to Weichuang. But he had never forgotten that wolf's eyes, fierce yet cowardly, gleaming like two will-o'-the-wisps, as if boring into him from a distance. And now he saw eyes more terrible even than the wolf's: dull yet penetrating eyes that seemed to have devoured his words and to be still eager to devour something beyond his flesh and blood. And these eyes kept following him at a set distance.

These eyes seemed to have merged in one, biting into his soul.

"Help, help!"

But Ah Q never uttered these words. All had turned black before his eyes, there was a buzzing in his ears, and he felt as if his whole body were being scattered like so much light dust.

As for the after-effects of the robbery, the most affected was the successful provincial candidate, because the stolen goods were never recovered. All his family lamented bitterly. Next came the Chao household; for when the successful county candidate went into town to report the robbery, not only did he have his pigtail cut off by bad revolutionaries, but he had to pay a reward of twenty thousand cash into the bargain; so all the Chao family too lamented bitterly. From that day forward they gradually assumed the air of survivors of a fallen dynasty.

As for any discussion of the event, no question was raised in Weichuang. Naturally all agreed that Ah Q had been a bad man, the proof being that he had been shot; for if he had not been bad, how could he have been shot? But the census of opinion in town was unfavorable. Most people were dissatisfied, because a shooting was not such a fine spectacle as a decapitation; and what a ridiculous culprit that had been too, to have passed through so many streets without singing a single line from an opera. They had followed him for nothing.

Spring Silkworms*

by Mao Tun

Old Tung Pao sat on a rock beside the road that skirted the canal, his long-stemmed pipe lying on the ground next to him. Though it was only a few days after "Clear and Bright Festival" the April sun was already very strong. It scorched Old Tung Pao's spine like a basin of fire. Straining down the road, the men towing the fast junk wore only thin tunics, open in front. They were bent far forward, pulling, pulling, pulling, great beads of sweat dripping from their brows.

The sight of others toiling strenuously made Old Tung Pao feel even warmer; he began to itch. He was still wearing the tattered padded jacket in which he had passed the winter. His unlined jacket had not yet been redeemed from the pawn shop. Who would have believed it could get so hot right after "Clear and Bright"?

Even the weather's not what it used to be, Old Tung Pao said to himself, and spat emphatically.

Before him, the water of the canal was green and shiny. Occasional passing boats broke the mirror-smooth surface into ripples and eddies, turning the reflection of the earthen bank and the long line of mulberry trees flanking it into a dancing grey blur. But not for long! Gradually the trees reappeared, twisting and weaving drunkenly. Another few minutes, and they were again standing still, reflected as clearly as before. On the gnarled fists of the mulberry branches, little fingers of tender green buds were already bursting forth. Crowded close together, the trees along the canal seemed to march endlessly into the distance. The unplanted fields as yet were only cracked clods of dry earth; the mulberry trees reigned supreme here this time of the year! Behind Old Tung

---

* Reprinted from *Spring Silkworms and Other Stories* (Peking: Foreign Languages Press, 1956).

Pao's back was another great stretch of mulberry trees, squat, silent. The little buds seemed to be growing bigger every second in the hot sunlight.

Not far from where Old Tung Pao was sitting, a grey two-story building crouched beside the road. That was the silk filature, where the delicate fibres were removed from the cocoons. Two weeks ago it was occupied by troops; a few short trenches still scarred the fields around it. Everyone had said that the Japanese soldiers were attacking in this direction. The rich people in the market town had all run away. Now the troops were gone and the silk filature stood empty and locked as before. There would be no noise and excitement in it again until cocoon selling time.

Old Tung Pao had heard Young Master Chen—son of the Master Chen who lived in town—say that Shanghai was seething with unrest, that all the silk weaving factories had closed their doors, that the silk filatures here probably wouldn't open either. But he couldn't believe it. He had been through many periods of turmoil and strife in his sixty years, yet he had never seen a time when the shiny green mulberry leaves had been allowed to wither on the branches and become fodder for the sheep. Of course if the silkworm eggs shouldn't ripen, that would be different. Such matters were all in the hands of the Old Lord of the Sky. Who could foretell His will?

"Only just after Clear and Bright and so hot already!" marvelled Old Tung Pao, gazing at the small green mulberry leaves. He was happy as well as surprised. He could remember only one year when it was too hot for padded clothes at Clear and Bright. He was in his twenties then, and the silkworm eggs had hatched "two hundred per cent": that was the year to get married. His family was flourishing in those days. His father was like an experienced plough ox—there was nothing he didn't understand, nothing he wasn't willing to try. Even his old grandfather—the one who had first started the family on the road to prosperity—seemed to be growing more hearty with age, in spite of the hard time he was said to have had during the years he was a prisoner of the "Long Hairs." *

Old Master Chen was still alive then. His son, the present Master Chen, hadn't begun smoking opium yet, and the "House of Chen" hadn't become the bad lot it was today. Moreover, even though the House of Chen was of the rich gentry and his own family only ordinary tillers of the land, Old Tung Pao had felt that the destinies of the two

---

* The reference is to the Taiping Army men, those Chinese peasants who rebelled against the Manchu rulers in what is known as the Taiping Revolution (1851-1864).

families were linked together. Years ago, "Long Hairs" campaigning through the countryside had captured Tung Pao's grandfather and Old Master Chen and kept them working as prisoners for nearly seven years in the same camp. They had escaped together, taking a lot of the "Long Hairs' " gold with them—people still talk about it to this day. What's more, at the same time Old Master Chen's silk trade began to prosper, the cocoon raising of Tung Pao's family grew successful too. Within ten years grandfather had earned enough to buy three acres of rice paddy, two acres of mulberry grove, and build a modest house. Tung Pao's family was the envy of the people of East Village, just as the House of Chen ranked among the first families in the market town.

But afterwards, both families had declined. Today, Old Tung Pao had no land of his own; in fact, he was over three hundred silver dollars in debt. The House of Chen was finished, too. People said the spirit of the dead "Long Hair" had sued the Chens in the underworld, and because the King of Hell had decreed that the Chens repay the fortune they had amassed on the stolen gold, the family had gone down financially very quickly. Old Tung Pao was rather inclined to believe this. If it hadn't been for the influence of devils, why would a decent fellow like Master Chen have taken to smoking opium?

What Old Tung Pao could never understand was why the fall of the House of Chen should affect his own family? They certainly hadn't kept any of the "Long Hairs' " gold. True, his father had related that when grandfather was escaping from the "Long Hairs' " camp he had run into a young "Long Hair" on patrol and had to kill him. What else could he have done? It was "fate"! Still from Tung Pao's earliest recollections, his family had prayed and offered sacrifices to appease the soul of the departed young "Long Hair" time and time again. That little wronged spirit should have left the nether world and been reborn long ago by now! Although Old Tung Pao couldn't recall what sort of man his grandfather was, he knew his father had been hard-working and honest—he had seen that with his own eyes. Old Tung Pao himself was a respectable person; both Ah Sze, his elder son, and his daughter-in-law were industrious and frugal. Only his younger son, Ah To, was inclined to be a little flighty. But youngsters were all like that. There was nothing really bad about the boy. . . .

Old Tung Pao raised his wrinkled face, scorched by years of hot sun to the color of dark parchment. He gazed bitterly at the canal before him, at the boats on its waters, at the mulberry trees along its banks. All were approximately the same as they had been when he was twenty. But the world had changed. His family now often had to make their meals of

69

pumpkin instead of rice. He was over three hundred silver dollars in debt. . . .

Toot! Toot-toot-toot. . . .

Far up the bend in the canal a boat whistle broke the silence. There was a silk filature over there, too. He could see vaguely the neat lines of stones embedded as reinforcement in the canal bank. A small oil-burning river boat came puffing up pompously from beyond the silk filature, tugging three larger craft in its wake. Immediately the peaceful water was agitated with waves rolling toward the banks on both sides of the canal. A peasant, poling a tiny boat, hastened to shore and clutched a clump of reeds growing in the shallows. The waves tossed him and his little craft up and down like a see-saw. The peaceful green countryside was filled with the chugging of the boat engine and the stink of its exhaust.

Hatred burned in Old Tung Pao's eyes. He watched the river boat approach; he watched it sail past and glared after it until it went tooting around another bend and disappeared from sight. He had always abominated the foreign devils' contraptions. He himself had never met a foreign devil, but his father had given him a description of one Old Master Chen had seen—red eyebrows, green eyes and a stiff-legged walk! Old Master Chen had hated the foreign devils, too. "The foreign devils have swindled our money away," he used to say. Old Tung Pao was only eight or nine the last time he saw Old Master Chen. All he remembered about him now were things he had heard from others. But whenever Old Tung Pao thought of that remark—"The foreign devils have swindled our money away."—he could almost picture Old Master Chen, stroking his beard and wagging his head.

How the foreign devils had accomplished this, Old Tung Pao wasn't too clear. He was sure, however, that Old Master Chen was right. Some things he himself had seen quite plainly. From the time foreign goods—cambric, cloth, oil—appeared in the market town, from the time the foreign river boats increased on the canal, what he produced brought a lower price in the market every day, while what he had to buy became more and more expensive. That was why the property his father left him had shrunk until it finally vanished completely; and now he was in debt. It was not without reason that Old Tung Pao hated the foreign devils!

In the village, his attitude toward foreigners was well-known. Five years before, in 1927, someone had told him: The new Kuomintang government says it wants to "throw out" the foreign devils. Old Tung

Pao didn't believe it. He heard those young propaganda speech makers the Kuomintang sent when he went into the market town. Though they cried "Throw out the foreign devils," they were dressed in Western style clothing. His guess was that they were secretly in league with the foreign devils, that they had been purposely sent to delude the countryfolk! Sure enough, the Kuomintang dropped the slogan not long after, and prices and taxes rose steadily. Old Tung Pao was firmly convinced that all this occurred as part of a government conspiracy with the foreign devils.

Last year something had happened that made him almost sick with fury: Only the cocoons spun by the foreign strain silkworms could be sold at a decent price. Buyers paid ten dollars more per load for them than they did for the local variety. Usually on good terms with his daughter-in-law, Old Tung Pao had quarrelled with her because of this. She had wanted to raise only foreign silkworms, and Old Tung Pao's younger son Ah To had agreed with her. Though the boy didn't say much, in his heart he certainly had also favored this course. Events had proved they were right, and they wouldn't let Old Tung Pao forget it. This year, he had to compromise. Of the five trays they would raise, only four would be silkworms of the local variety; one tray would contain foreign silkworms.

"The world's going from bad to worse! In another couple of years they'll even be wanting foreign mulberry trees! It's enough to take all the joy out of life!"

Old Tung Pao picked up his long pipe and rapped it angrily against a clod of dry earth. The sun was directly overhead now, foreshortening his shadow till it looked like a piece of charcoal. Still in his padded jacket, he was bathed in heat. He unfastened the jacket and swung its opened edges back and forth a few times to fan himself. Then he stood up and started for home.

Behind the row of mulberry trees were paddy fields. Most of them were as yet only neatly ploughed furrows of upturned earth clods, dried and cracked by the hot sun. Here and there, the early crops were coming up. In one field, the golden blossoms of rape-seed plants emitted a heady fragrance. And that group of houses way over there, that was the village where three generations of Old Tung Pao's family were living. Above the houses, white smoke from many kitchen stoves was curling lazily upwards into the sky.

After crossing through the mulberry grove, Old Tung Pao walked along the raised path between the paddy fields, then turned and looked

71

again at that row of trees bursting with tender green buds. A twelve-year-old boy came bounding along from the other end of the fields, calling as he ran:

"Grandpa! Ma's waiting for you to come home and eat!"

It was Little Pao, Old Tung Pao's grandson.

"Coming!" the old man responded, still gazing at the mulberries. Only twice in his life had he seen these finger-like buds appear on the branches so soon after Clear and Bright. His family would probably have a fine crop of silkworms this year. Five trays of eggs would hatch out a huge number of silkworms. If only they didn't have another bad market like last year, perhaps they could pay off part of their debt.

Little Pao stood beside his grandfather. The child too looked at the soft green on the gnarled fist branches. Jumping happily, he clapped his hands and chanted:

> Green, tender leaves at Clear and Bright,
> The girls who tend silkworms,
> Clap hands at the sight!

The old man's wrinkled face broke into a smile. He thought it was a good omen for the little boy to respond like this on seeing the first buds of the year. He rubbed his hand affectionately over the child's shaven pate. In Old Tung Pao's heart, numbed wooden by a lifetime of poverty and hardship, suddenly hope began to stir again.

II

The weather remained warm. The rays of the sun forced open the tender, finger-like, little buds. They had already grown to the size of a small hand. Around Old Tung Pao's village, the mulberry trees seemed to respond especially well. From a distance they gave the appearance of a low grey picket fence on top of which a long swath of green brocade had been spread. Bit by bit, day by day, hope grew in the hearts of the villagers. The unspoken mobilization order for the silkworm campaign reached everywhere and everyone. Silkworm rearing equipment that had been laid away for a year was again brought out to be scrubbed and mended. Beside the little stream which ran through the village, women and children, with much laughter and calling back and forth, washed the implements.

None of these women or children looked really healthy. Since the coming of spring, they had been eating only half their fill; their clothes were old and torn. As a matter of fact, they weren't much better off than beggars. Yet all were in quite good spirits, sustained by enormous patience and grand illusions. Burdened though they were by daily mounting debts, they had only one thought in their heads—If we get a good crop of silkworms, everything will be all right! . . . They could already visualize how, in a month, the shiny green leaves would be converted into snow-white cocoons, the cocoons exchanged for clinking silver dollars. Although their stomachs were growling with hunger, they couldn't refrain from smiling at this happy prospect.

Old Tung Pao's daughter-in-law was among the women by the stream. With the help of her twelve-year-old son, Little Pao, she had already finished washing the family's large trays of woven bamboo strips. Seated on a stone beside the stream, she wiped her perspiring face with the edge of her tunic. A twenty-year-old girl, working with other women on the opposite side of the stream, hailed her.

"Are you raising foreign silkworms this year too?"

It was Sixth Treasure, sister of young Fu-ching, the neighbor who lived across the stream.

The thick eyebrows of Old Tung Pao's daughter-in-law at once contracted. Her voice sounded as if she had just been waiting for a chance to let off steam.

"Don't ask me; what the old man says, goes!" she shouted. "He's dead set against it, won't let us raise more than one batch of foreign breed! The old fool only has to hear the word 'foreign' to send him up in the air! He'll take dollars made of foreign silver, though; those are the only 'forcign' things he likes!"

The women on the other side of the stream laughed. From the threshing ground behind them a strapping young man approached. He reached the stream and crossed over on the four logs that served as a bridge. Seeing him, his sister-in-law dropped her tirade and called in a high voice:

"Ah To, will you help me carry these trays? They're as heavy as dead dogs when they're wet!"

Without a word, Ah To lifted the six big trays and set them, dripping, on his head. Balancing them in place, he walked off, swinging his hands in a swimming motion. When in a good mood, Ah To refused nobody. If any of the village women asked him to carry something heavy or fish something out of the stream, he was usually quite willing. But today he probably was a little grumpy, and so he walked empty-handed with only six trays on his head. The sight of him, looking as if he were wearing six layers of the wide straw hats, his waist twisting at each step in imitation of the ladies of the town, sent the women into peals of laughter. Lotus, wife of Old Tung Pao's nearest neighbor, called with a giggle:

"Hey, Ah To, come back here. Carry a few trays for me too!"

Ah To grinned. "Not unless you call me a sweet name!" He continued walking. An instant later he had reached the porch of his house and set down the trays out of the sun.

"Will 'kid brother' do?" demanded Lotus, laughing boisterously. She had a remarkably clean white complexion, but her face was very flat. When she laughed, all that could be seen was a big open mouth and two tiny slits of eyes. Originally a slave in a house in town, she had been married off to Old Tung Pao's neighbor—a prematurely aged man who walked around with a sour expression and never said a word all day. That was less than six months ago, but her love affairs and escapades already were the talk of the village.

"Shameless hussy!" came a contemptuous female voice from across the stream.

Lotus's piggy eyes immediately widened. "Who said that?" she demanded angrily. "If you've got the brass to call me names, let's see you try it to my face! Come out into the open!"

"Think you can handle me? I'm talking about a shameless, man-crazy baggage! If the shoe fits, wear it!" retorted Sixth Treasure, for it was she who had spoken. She too was famous in the village, but as a mischievous, lively young woman.

The two began splashing water at each other from opposite banks of the stream. Girls who enjoyed a row took sides and joined the battle, while the children whooped with laughter. Old Tung Pao's daughter-in-law was more decorous. She picked up her remaining trays, called to Little Pao and returned home. Ah To watched from the porch, grinning. He knew why Sixth Treasure and Lotus were quarrelling. It did his heart good to hear that sharp-tongued Sixth Treasure get told off in public.

Old Tung Pao came out of the house with a wooden tray-stand on his shoulder. Some of the legs of the uprights had been eaten by termites, and he wanted to repair them. At the sight of Ah To standing there laughing at the women, Old Tung Pao's face lengthened. The boy hadn't much sense of propriety, he well knew. What disturbed him particularly was the way Ah To and Lotus were always talking and laughing together. "That bitch is an evil spirit. Fooling with her will bring ruin on our house," he had often warned his younger son.

"Ah To!" he now barked angrily. "Enjoying the scenery? Your

brother's in the back mending equipment. Go and give him a hand!" His inflamed eyes bored into Ah To, never leaving the boy until he disappeared into the house.

Only then did Old Tung Pao start work on the tray-stand. After examining it carefully, he slowly began his repairs. Years ago, Old Tung Pao had worked for a time as a carpenter. But he was old now; his fingers had lost their strength. A few minutes' work and he was breathing hard. He raised his head and looked into the house. Five squares of cloth to which sticky silkworm eggs were adhered, hung from a horizontal bamboo pole.

His daughter-in-law, Ah Sze's wife, was at the other end of the porch, pasting paper on big trays of woven bamboo strips. Last year, to economize a bit, they had bought and used old newspaper. Old Tung Pao still maintained that was why the eggs had hatched poorly—it was unlucky to use paper with writing on it for such a prosaic purpose. Writing meant scholarship, and scholarship had to be respected. This year the whole family had skipped a meal and with the money saved, purchased special "tray pasting paper." Ah Sze's wife pasted the tough, gosling-yellow sheets smooth and flat; on every tray she also affixed three little colored paper pictures, bought at the same time. One was the "Platter of Plenty"; the other two showed a militant figure on horseback, pennant in hand. He, according to local belief, was the "Guardian of Silkworm Hatching."

"I was only able to buy twenty loads of mulberry leaves with that thirty silver dollars I borrowed on your father's guarantee," Old Tung Pao said to his daughter-in-law. He was still panting from his exertions with the tray-stand. "Our rice will be finished by the day after tomorrow. What are we going to do?"

Thanks to her father's influence with his boss and his willingness to guarantee repayment of the loan, Old Tung Pao was able to borrow the money at a low rate of interest—only twenty-five per cent a month! Both the principal and interest had to be repaid by the end of the silkworm season.

Ah Sze's wife finished pasting a tray and placed it in the sun. "You've spent it all on leaves," she said angrily. "We'll have a lot of leaves left over, just like last year!"

"Full of lucky words, aren't you?" demanded the old man, sarcastically. "I suppose every year'll be like last year? We can't get more than a dozen or so loads of leaves from our own trees. With five sets of grubs to feed, that won't be nearly enough."

"Oh, of course, you're never wrong!" she replied hotly. "All I know is

75

with rice we can eat, without it we'll go hungry!" His stubborn refusal to raise any foreign silkworms last year had left them with only the un-salable local breed. As a result, she was often contrary with him.

The old man's face turned purple with rage. After this, neither would speak to the other.

But hatching time was drawing closer every day. The little village's two dozen families were thrown into a state of great tension, great determination, great struggle. With it all, they were possessed of a great hope, a hope that could almost make them forget their hungry bellies.

Old Tung Pao's family, borrowing a little here, getting a little credit there, somehow managed to get by. Nor did the other families eat any better; there wasn't one with a spare bag of rice! Although they had harvested a good crop the previous year, landlords, creditors, taxes, levies, one after another, had cleaned the peasants out long ago. Now all their hopes were pinned on the spring silkworms. The repayment date of every loan they made was set for the "end of the silkworm season."

With high hopes and considerable fear, like soldiers going into a hand-to-hand battle to the death, they prepared for their spring silk-worm campaign!

"Grain Rain" day—bringing gentle drizzles—was not far off. Almost imperceptibly, the silkworm eggs of the two dozen village families began to show faint tinges of green. Women, when they met on the public threshing ground, would speak to one another agitatedly in tones that were anxious yet joyful.

"Over at Sixth Treasure's place, they're almost ready to incubate their eggs!"

"Lotus says her family is going to start incubating tomorrow. So soon!"

"Huang 'the Priest' has made a divination. He predicts that this spring mulberry leaves will go to four dollars a load!"

Old Tung Pao's daughter-in-law examined their five sets of eggs. They looked bad. The tiny seed-like eggs were still pitch black, without even a hint of green. Her husband, Ah Sze, took them into the light to peer at them carefully. Even so, he could find hardly any ripening eggs. She was very worried.

"You incubate them anyhow. Maybe this variety is a little slow," her husband forced himself to say consolingly.

Her lips pressed tight, she made no reply.

Old Tung Pao's wrinkled face sagged with dejection. Though he said nothing, he thought their prospects were dim.

The next day, Ah Sze's wife again examined the eggs. Ha! Quite a few were turning green, and a very shiny green at that! Immediately, she told her husband, told Old Tung Pao, Ah To . . . she even told her son Little Pao. Now the incubating process could begin! She held the five pieces of cloth to which the eggs were adhered against her bare bosom. As if cuddling a nursing infant, she sat absolutely quiet, not daring to stir. At night, she took the five sets to bed with her. Her husband was routed out, and had to share Ah To's bed. The tiny silkworm eggs were very scratchy against her flesh. She felt happy and a little frightened, like the first time she was pregnant and the baby moved inside her. Exactly the same sensation!

Uneasy but eager, the whole family waited for the eggs to hatch. Ah To was the only exception. We're sure to hatch a good crop, he said, but anyone who thinks we're going to get rich in this life, is out of his head. Though the old man swore Ah To's big mouth would ruin their luck, the boy stuck to his guns.

A clean dry shed for the growing grubs was all prepared. The second day of incubation, Old Tung Pao smeared a garlic with earth and placed it at the foot of the wall inside the shed. If, in a few days, the garlic put out many sprouts, it meant the eggs would hatch well. He did this every year, but this year he was more reverential than usual, and his hands trembled. Last year's divination had proved all too accurate. He didn't dare to think about that now.

Every family in the village was busy "incubating." For the time being there were few women's footprints on the threshing ground or the banks of the little stream. An unofficial "martial law" had been imposed. Even peasants normally on very good terms stopped visiting one another. For a guest to come and frighten away the spirits of the ripening eggs—that would be no laughing matter! At most, people exchanged a few words in low tones when they met, then quickly separated. This was the "sacred" season!

Old Tung Pao's family was on pins and needles. In the five sets of eggs a few grubs had begun wriggling. It was exactly one day before Grain Rain. Ah Sze's wife had calculated that most of the eggs wouldn't hatch until after that day. Before or after Grain Rain was all right, but for eggs to hatch on the day itself was considered highly unlucky. Incubation was no longer necessary, and the eggs were carefully placed in the special shed. Old Tung Pao stole a glance at his garlic at the foot of the wall. His heart dropped. There were still only the same two small green shoots the garlic had originally! He didn't dare to look any closer. He prayed silently that by noon the day after tomorrow the garlic would have many, many more shoots.

At last hatching day arrived. Ah Sze's wife set a pot of rice on to boil and nervously watched for the time when the steam from it would rise straight up. Old Tung Pao lit the incense and candles he had bought in anticipation of this event. Devoutly, he placed them before the idol of the Kitchen God. His two sons went into the fields to pick wild flowers. Little Pao chopped a lamp-wick into fine pieces and crushed the wild flowers the men brought back. Everything was ready. The sun was entering its zenith; steam from the rice pot puffed straight upwards. Ah Sze's wife immediately leaped to her feet, stuck a "sacred" paper flower and a pair of goose feathers into the knot of hair at the back of her head and went to the shed. Old Tung Pao carried a wooden scale-pole; Ah Sze followed with the chopped lamp-wick and the crushed wild flowers. Daughter-in-law uncovered the cloth pieces to which the grubs were adhered, and sprinkled them with the bits of wick and flowers Ah Sze was holding. Then she took the wooden scale-pole from Old Tung Pao and hung the cloth pieces over it. She next removed the pair of goose feathers from her hair. Moving them lightly across the cloth, she brushed the grubs, together with the crushed lamp-wick and wild flowers, on to a large tray. One set, two sets . . . the last set contained the foreign breed. The grubs from this cloth were brushed on to a separate tray. Finally, she removed the "sacred" paper flower from her hair and pinned it, with the goose feathers, against the side of the tray.

A solemn ceremony! One that had been handed down through the ages! Like warriors taking an oath before going into battle! Old Tung Pao and family now had ahead of them a month of fierce combat, with no rest day or night, against bad weather, bad luck and anything else that might come along!

The grubs, wriggling in the trays, looked very healthy. They were all the proper black color. Old Tung Pao and his daughter-in-law were able to relax a little. But when the old man secretly took another look at his garlic, he turned pale! It had grown only four measly shoots! Ah! Would this year be like last year all over again?

III

But the "fateful" garlic proved to be not so psychic after all. The silkworms of Old Tung Pao's family grew and thrived! Though it rained continuously during the grubs' First Sleep and Second Sleep, and the weather was a bit colder than at Clear and Bright, the "little darlings" were extremely robust.

The silkworms of the other families in the village were not doing badly either. A tense kind of joy pervaded the countryside. Even the small stream seemed to be gurgling with bright laughter. Lotus's family was the sole exception. They were only raising one set of grubs, but by the Third Sleep their silkworms weighed less than twenty catties. Just before the Big Sleep, people saw Lotus's husband walk to the stream and dump out his trays. That dour, old-looking man had bad luck written all over him.

Because of this dreadful event, the village women put Lotus's family strictly "off limits." They made wide detours so as not to pass her door. If they saw her or her taciturn husband, no matter how far away, they made haste to go in the opposite direction. They feared that even one look at Lotus or her spouse, the briefest conversation, would contaminate them with the unfortunate couple's bad luck!

Old Tung Pao strictly forbade Ah To to talk to Lotus. "If I catch you gabbing with that baggage again, I'll disown you!" He threatened in a loud, angry voice, standing outside on the porch to make sure Lotus could hear him.

Little Pao was also warned not to play in front of Lotus's door, and not to speak to anyone in her family....

The old man harped at Ah To morning, noon and night, but the boy turned a deaf ear to his father's grumbling. In his heart, he laughed at it. Of the whole family, Ah To alone didn't place much stock in taboos and superstitions. He didn't talk with Lotus, however. He was much too busy for that.

By the Big Sleep, their silkworms weighed three hundred catties. Every member of Old Tung Pao's family, including twelve-year-old Little Pao, worked for two days and two nights without sleeping a wink. The silkworms were unusually sturdy. Only twice in his sixty years had Old Tung Pao ever seen the like. Once was the year he married; once when his first son was born.

The first day after the Big Sleep, the "little darlings" ate seven loads of leaves. They were now a bright green, thick and healthy. Old Tung Pao and his family, on the contrary, were much thinner, their eyes bloodshot from lack of sleep.

No one could guess how much the "little darlings" would eat before they spun their cocoons. Old Tung Pao discussed the question of buying more leaves with Ah Sze.

"Master Chen won't lend us any more. Shall we try your father-in-law's boss again?"

"We've still got ten loads coming. That's enough for one more day,"

79

replied Ah Sze. He could barely hold himself erect. His eyelids weighed a thousand catties. They kept wanting to close.

"One more day? You're dreaming!" snapped the old man impatiently. Not counting tomorrow, they still have to eat three more days. We'll need another thirty loads! Thirty loads, I say!"

Loud voices were heard outside on the threshing ground. Ah To had arrived with men delivering five loads of mulberry branches. Everyone went out to strip the leaves. Ah Sze's wife hurried from the shed. Across the stream, Sixth Treasure and her family were raising only a small crop of silkworms; having spare time, she came over to help. Bright stars filled the sky. There was a slight wind. All up and down the village, gay shouts and laughter rang in the night.

"The price of leaves is rising fast!" a coarse voice cried. "This afternoon, they were getting four dollars a load in the market town!"

Old Tung Pao was very upset. At four dollars a load, thirty loads would come to a hundred and twenty dollars. Where could he raise so much money! But then he figured—he was sure to gather over five hundred catties of cocoons. Even at fifty dollars a hundred, they'd sell for two hundred and fifty dollars. Feeling a bit consoled, he heard a small voice from among the leaf-strippers.

"They say the folks east of here aren't doing so well with their silkworms. There won't be any reason for the price of leaves to go much higher."

Old Tung Pao recognized the speaker as Sixth Treasure, and he relaxed still further.

The girl and Ah To were standing beside a large basket, stripping leaves. In the dim starlight, they worked quite close to each other, partly hidden by the pile of mulberry branches before them. Suddenly, Sixth Treasure felt someone pinch her thigh. She knew well enough who it was, and she suppressed a giggle. But when, a moment later, a hand brushed against her breasts, she jumped; a little shriek escaped her.

"Aiya!"

"What's wrong?" demanded Ah Sze's wife, working on the other side of the basket.

Sixth Treasure's face flamed scarlet. She shot a glance at Ah To, then quickly lowered her head and resumed stripping leaves. "Nothing," she replied. "I think a caterpillar bit me!"

Ah To bit his lips to keep from laughing aloud. He had been half starved the past two weeks and had slept little. But in spite of having lost a lot of weight, he was in high spirits. While he never suffered from any of Old Tung Pao's gloom, neither did he believe that one good crop,

80

whether of silkworms or of rice, would enable them to wipe off their debt and own their own land again. He knew they would never "get out from under" merely by relying on hard work, even if they broke their backs trying. Nevertheless, he worked with a will. He enjoyed work, just as he enjoyed fooling around with Sixth Treasure.

The next morning, Old Tung Pao went into town to borrow money for more leaves. Before leaving home, he had talked the matter over with daughter-in-law. They had decided to mortgage their grove of mulberries that produced fifteen loads of leaves a year as security for the loan. The grove was the last piece of property the family owned.

By the time the old man ordered another thirty loads, and the first ten were delivered, the sturdy "little darlings" had gone hungry for half an hour. Putting forth their pointed little mouths, they swayed from side to side, searching for food. Daughter-in-law's heart had ached to see them. When the leaves were finally spread in the trays, the silkworm shed at once resounded with a sibilant crunching, so noisy it drowned out conversation. In a very short while, the trays were again empty of leaves. Another thick layer was piled on. Just keeping the silkworms supplied with leaves, Old Tung Pao and his family were so busy they could barely catch their breath. But this was the final crisis. In two more days the "little darlings" would spin their cocoons. People were putting every bit of their remaining strength into this last desperate struggle.

Though he had gone without sleep for three whole days, Ah To didn't appear particularly tired. He agreed to watch the shed alone that night until dawn to permit the others to get some rest. There was a bright moon and the weather was a trifle cold. Ah To crouched beside a small fire he had built in the shed. At about eleven, he gave the silkworms their second feeding, then returned to squat by the fire. He could hear the loud rustle of the "little darlings" crunching through the leaves. His eyes closed. Suddenly, he heard the door squeak, and his eyelids flew open. He peered into the darkness for a moment, then shut his eyes again. His ears were still hissing with the rustle of the leaves. The next thing he knew, his head had struck against his knees. Waking with a start, he heard the door screen bang and thought he saw a moving shadow. Ah To leaped up and rushed outside. In the moonlight, he saw someone crossing the threshing ground toward the stream. He caught up in a flash, seized and flung the intruder to the ground. Ah To was sure he had nabbed a thief.

"Ah To, kill me if you want to, but don't give me away!"

The voice made Ah To's hair stand on end. He could see in the moonlight that queer flat white face and those round little piggy eyes fixed upon him. But of menace, the piggy eyes had none. Ah To snorted.

"What were you after?"

"A few of your family's 'little darlings'!"

"What did you do with them?"

"Threw them in the stream!"

Ah To's face darkened. He knew that in this way she was trying to put a curse on the lot. "You're pure poison! We never did anything to hurt you."

"Never did anything? Oh, yes you did! Yes, you did! Our silkworm eggs didn't hatch well, but we didn't harm anybody. You were all so smart! You shunned me like a leper. No matter how far away I was, if you saw me, you turned your heads. You acted as if I wasn't even human!"

She got to her feet, the agonized expression on her face terrible to see. Ah To stared at her. "I'm not going to beat you," he said finally. "Go on your way!"

Without giving her another glance, he trotted back to the shed. He was wide awake now. Lotus had only taken a handful and the remaining "little darlings" were all in good condition. It didn't occur to him either to hate or pity Lotus, but the last thing she had said remained in his mind. It seemed to him there was something eternally wrong in the scheme of human relations; but he couldn't put his finger on what it was exactly, nor did he know why it should be. In a little while, he forgot about this, too. The lusty silkworms were eating and eating, yet, as if by some magic, never full!

Nothing more happened that night. Just before the sky began to brighten in the east, Old Tung Pao and his daughter-in-law came to relieve Ah To. They took the trays of "little darlings" and looked at them in the light. The silkworms were turning a whiter color, their bodies gradually becoming shorter and thicker. They were delighted with the excellent way the silkworms were developing.

But when, at sunrise, Ah Sze's wife went to draw water at the stream, she met Sixth Treasure. The girl's expression was serious.

"I saw that slut leaving your place shortly before midnight," she whispered. "Ah To was right behind her. They stood here and talked for a long time! Your family ought to look after things better than that!"

The color drained from the face of Ah Sze's wife. Without a word, she carried her water bucket back to the house. First, she told her husband about it; then she told Old Tung Pao. It was a fine state of affairs when a baggage like that could sneak into people's silkworm sheds! Old Tung Pao stamped with rage. He immediately summoned Ah To. But the boy denied the whole story; he said Sixth Treasure was dreaming. The old man then went to question Sixth Treasure. She insisted she had seen everything with her own eyes. The old man didn't know what to believe. He returned home and looked at the "little darlings." They were as sturdy as ever, not a sickly one in the lot.

But the joy that Old Tung Pao and his family had been feeling was dampened. They knew Sixth Treasure's words couldn't be entirely without foundation. Their only hope was that Ah To and that hussy had played their little games on the porch rather than in the shed!

Old Tung Pao recalled gloomily that the garlic had only put forth three or four shoots. He thought the future looked dark. Hadn't there been times before when the silkworms ate great quantities of leaves and seemed to be growing well, yet dried up and died just when they were ready to spin their cocoons? Yes, often! But Old Tung Pao didn't dare let himself think of such a possibility. To entertain a thought like that, even in the most secret recesses of the mind, would only be inviting bad luck!

IV

The "little darlings" began spinning their cocoons, but Old Tung Pao's family was still in a sweat. Both their money and their energy were completely spent. They still had nothing to show for it; there was no guarantee of their earning any return. Nevertheless, they continued working at top speed. Beneath the racks on which the cocoons were being spun fires had to be kept going to supply warmth. Old Tung Pao and Ah Sze, his elder son, their backs bent, slowly squatted first on this side then on that. Hearing the small rustlings of the spinning silkworms, they wanted to smile, and if the sounds stopped for a moment their hearts stopped, too. Yet, worried as they were, they didn't dare to disturb the silkworms by looking inside. When the silkworms squirted fluid in their faces as they peered up from beneath the racks, they were happy in spite of the momentary discomfort. The bigger the shower, the better they liked it.*

Ah To had already peeked several times. Little Pao had caught him at it and demanded to know what was going on. Ah To made an ugly face at the child, but did not reply.

* The emission of the fluid means the silkworm is about to spin its cocoon.

After three days of "spinning," the fires were extinguished. Ah Sze's wife could restrain herself no longer. She stole a look, her heart beating fast. Inside, all was white as snow. The brush that had been put in for the silkworms to spin on was completely covered with cocoons. Ah Sze's wife had never seen so successful a "flowering"!

The whole family was wreathed in smiles. They were on solid ground at last! The "little darlings" had proved they had a conscience; they hadn't consumed those mulberry leaves, at four dollars a load, in vain. The family could reap its reward for a month of hunger and sleepless nights. The Old Lord of the Sky had eyes!

Throughout the village, there were many similar scenes of rejoicing. The Silkworm Goddess had been beneficent to the tiny village this year. Most of the two dozen families garnered good crops of cocoons from their silkworms. The harvest of Old Tung Pao's family was well above average.

Again women and children crowded the threshing ground and the banks of the little stream. All were much thinner than the previous month, with eyes sunk in their sockets, throats rasping and hoarse. But everyone was excited, happy. As they chattered about the struggle of the past month, visions of piles of bright silver dollars shimmered before their eyes. Cheerful thoughts filled their minds—they would get their summer clothes out of the pawnshop; at Spring Festival perhaps they could eat a fat golden fish. . . .

They talked, too, of the farce enacted by Lotus and Ah To a few nights before. Sixth Treasure announced to everyone she met, "That Lotus has no shame at all. She delivered herself right to his door!" Men who heard her laughed coarsely. Women muttered a prayer and called Lotus bad names. They said Old Tung Pao's family could consider itself lucky that a curse hadn't fallen on them. The gods were merciful!

Family after family was able to report a good harvest of cocoons. People visited one another to view the shining white gossamer. The father of Old Tung Pao's daughter-in-law came from town with his little son. They brought gifts of sweets and fruits and a salted fish. Little Pao was happy as a puppy frolicking in the snow.

The elderly visitor sat with Old Tung Pao beneath a willow beside the stream. He had the reputation in town of a "man who knew how to enjoy life." From hours of listening to the professional story-tellers in front of the temple, he had learned by heart many of the classic tales of ancient times. He was a great one for idle chatter, and often would say anything that came into his head. Old Tung Pao therefore didn't take him very seriously when he leaned close and queried softly:

"Are you selling your cocoons, or will you spin the silk yourself at home?"

"Selling them, of course," Old Tung Pao replied casually.

The elderly visitor slapped his thigh and sighed, then rose abruptly and pointed at the silk filature rearing up behind the row of mulberries, now quite bald of leaves.

"Tung Pao," he said, "the cocoons are being gathered, but the doors of the silk filatures are shut as tight as ever! They're not buying this year! Ah, all the world is in turmoil! The silk houses are not going to open, I tell you!"

Old Tung Pao couldn't help smiling. He wouldn't believe it. How could he possibly believe it? There were dozens of silk filatures in this part of the country. Surely they couldn't all shut down? What's more, he had heard that they had made a deal with the Japanese; the Chinese soldiers who had been billeted in the silk houses had long since departed.

Changing the subject, the visitor related the latest town gossip, salting it freely with classical aphorisms and quotations from the ancient stories. Finally he got around to the thirty silver dollars borrowed through him as middleman. He said his boss was anxious to be repaid.

Old Tung Pao became uneasy after all. When his visitor had departed, he hurried from the village down the highway to look at the two nearest silk filatures. Their doors were indeed shut; not a soul was in sight. Business was in full swing this time last year, with whole rows of dark gleaming scales in operation.

He felt a little panicky as he returned home. But when he saw those snowy cocoons, thick and hard, pleasure made him smile. What beauties! No one wants them?—Impossible. He still had to hurry and finish gathering the cocoons; he hadn't thanked the gods properly yet. Gradually, he forgot about the silk houses.

But in the village, the atmosphere was changing day by day. People who had just begun to laugh were now all frowns. News was reaching them from town that none of the neighboring silk filatures was opening its doors. It was the same with the houses along the highway. Last year at this time buyers of cocoons were streaming in and out of the village. This year there wasn't a sign of even half a one. In their place came dunning creditors and government tax collectors who promptly froze up if you asked them to take cocoons in payment.

Swearing, curses, disappointed sighs! With such a fine crop of cocoons the villagers had never dreamed that their lot would be even worse than usual! It was as if hailstones dropped out of a clear sky. People like Old

Tung Pao, whose crop was especially good, took it hardest of all.

"What is the world coming to!" He beat his breast and stamped his feet in helpless frustration.

But the villagers had to think of something. The cocoons would spoil if kept too long. They either had to sell them or remove the silk themselves. Several families had already brought out and repaired silk reels they hadn't used for years. They would first remove the silk from the cocoons and then see about the next step. Old Tung Pao wanted to do the same.

"We won't sell our cocoons; we'll spin the silk ourselves!" said the old man. "Nobody ever heard of selling cocoons until the foreign devils' companies started the thing!"

Ah Sze's wife was the first to object. "We've got over five hundred catties of cocoons here," she retorted. "Where are you going to get enough reels?"

She was right. Five hundred catties was no small amount. They'd never get finished spinning the silk themselves. Hire outside help? That meant spending money. Ah Sze agreed with his wife. Ah To blamed his father for planning incorrectly.

"If you listened to me, we'd have raised only one tray of foreign breed and no locals. Then the fifteen loads of leaves from our own mulberry trees would have been enough, and we wouldn't have had to borrow!"

Old Tung Pao was so angry he couldn't speak.

At last a ray of hope appeared. Huang the Priest had heard somewhere that a silk house below the city of Wusih was doing business as usual. Actually an ordinary peasant, Huang was nicknamed "The Priest" because of the learned airs he affected and his interests in Taoist "magic." Old Tung Pao always got along with him fine. After learning the details from him, Old Tung Pao conferred with his elder son Ah Sze about going to Wusih.

"It's about 270 *li* by water, six days for the round trip," ranted the old man. "Son of a bitch! It's a goddamn expedition! But what else can we do? We can't eat the cocoons, and our creditors are pressing hard!"

Ah Sze agreed. They borrowed a small boat and bought a few yards of matting to cover the cargo. It was decided that Ah To should go along. Taking advantage of the good weather, the cocoon selling "expeditionary force" set out.

Five days later, the men returned—but not with an empty hold. They still had one basket of cocoons. The silk filature, which they reached after a 270-*li* journey by water, offered extremely harsh terms—Only thirty-five dollars a load for foreign breed, twenty for local; thin cocoons not wanted at any price. Although their cocoons were all first class, the people at the silk house picked and chose only enough to fill one basket; the rest were rejected. Old Tung Pao and his sons received a hundred and ten dollars for the sale, ten of which had to be spent as travel expenses. The hundred dollars remaining was not even enough to pay back what they had borrowed for that last thirty loads of mulberry leaves! On the return trip, Old Tung Pao became ill with rage. His sons carried him into the house.

Ah Sze's wife had no choice but to take the ninety odd catties they had brought back and reel the silk from the cocoons herself. She borrowed a few reels from Sixth Treasure's family and worked for six days. All their rice was gone now. Ah Sze took the silk into town, but no one would buy it. Even the pawnshop didn't want it. Only after much pleading was he able to persuade the pawnbroker to take it in exchange for a load of rice they had pawned before Clear and Bright.

That's the way it happened. Because they raised a crop of spring silkworms, the people in Old Tung Pao's village got deeper into debt. Old Tung Pao's family raised five trays and gathered a splendid harvest of cocoons. Yet they ended up owing another thirty silver dollars and losing their mortgaged mulberry trees—to say nothing of suffering a month of hunger and sleepless nights in vain!

The Family on the Other Side
of the Mountain*

by Chou Li-po

Treading on the shadows of the trees cast on the slope by the moon, we were on our way to a wedding on the other side of the mountain.

Why should we go to a wedding? If anyone should ask, this is our

* Reprinted from Sowing the Clouds (Peking: Foreign Languages Press, 1961), pp. 26-33.

answer: Sometimes people like to go to weddings to watch the happiness of others and to increase one's own joy.

A group of girls were walking in front of us. Once girls gather in groups, they laugh all the time. These now laughed without cease. One of them even had to halt by the roadside to rub her aching sides. She scolded the one who provoked such laughter while she kept on laughing. Why were they laughing? I had no idea. Generally, I do not understand much about girls. But I have consulted an expert who has a profound understanding of girls. What he said was "they laugh because they want to laugh." I thought that was very clever. But someone else told me that "although you can't tell exactly what makes them laugh, generally speaking, youth, health, the carefree life in the co-op, the fertile green fields where they labor, being paid on the same basis as the men, the misty moonlight, the light fragrance of flowers, a vague or real feeling of love . . . all these are sources of their joy."

I thought there was a lot of sense in what he said, too.

When we had climbed over the mountain we could see the home of the bridegroom—two little rooms in a big brick house. A little ancient red lantern was hung at the door. The girls rushed inside like a swarm of bees. According to local tradition, they have this privilege when families celebrate this happy event. In the past, unmarried girls used to eavesdrop the first night of a friend's marriage under the window or outside the bridal chamber. When they heard such questions as "Uh . . . are you sleepy?" they would run away and laugh heartily. They would laugh again and again the next day, too. But there were times when they could hear nothing. Experienced eavesdroppers would keep entirely silent on their own first night of bliss and make the girls outside the window walk away in disappointment.

The group of girls ahead of us had crowded into the door. Had they come to eavesdrop, too?

I had picked several camellias to present to the bride and groom. When I reached the door, I saw it was flanked with a pair of couplets written on red paper. By the light of a red lantern one could make out the squarely written words:

> Songs wing through the streets,
> Joy fills the room.

As we entered, a young man who was all smiles walked up to welcome us. He was the bridegroom, Tsou Mai-chiu, the storekeeper of the co-op. He was short and sturdy with nice features. Some said he was a simple, honest man, but others insisted he wasn't so simple, because he found himself a beautiful bride. It is said that beautiful girls do not love simple men. Who knows? Let's take a look at the bride first.

After presenting the camellias to the bridegroom, we walked towards the bridal chamber. The wooden lattice of the window was pasted with fresh paper and decorated in the center with the character "happiness," cut out of red paper. In the four corners were charming paper-cuts of carps, orchids and two beautiful vases with two fat pigs at the side.

We walked into the room. The girls were there already, giggling softly and whispering. When we were seated, they left the room in a flock. Laughter rang outside the door.

Then we scrutinized the room. Many people were seated there. The bride and her matron, who was her sister-in-law, sat on the edge of the bed. The sister-in-law had brought her three-year-old boy along and was teaching him to sing:

> In his red baby shoes a child of three,
> Toddles off to school just like his big brother.
> Don't spank me, teacher, right back I shall be
> After going home for a swig of milk from mother.

I stole a glance at the bride, Po Tsui-lien. She was not strikingly beautiful, but she wasn't bad looking either. Her features and figure were quite all right. So we reached the conclusion that the bridegroom was a simple and yet not too simple man. Though everyone in the room had his eyes on the bride, she remained composed and was not a bit shy. She took her nephew over from her sister-in-law, tickled him to make him laugh and then took him out to play for a while in the courtyard. As she walked past, she trailed behind a light fragrance.

A kerosene lamp was lit. Its yellowish flame lit up the things in the room. The bed was an old one, the mosquito-net was not new either and its embroidered red brocade fringes were only half new. The only thing new were the two pillows.

On the red lacquer desk by the window were two pewter candlestands and two small rectangular mirrors. Then there were china bowls and a teapot decorated with "happiness" cut out of red paper. Most outstanding of all the bric-a-brac presents were two half-naked porcelain monks, with enormous pot bellies, laughing heartily. Why did they laugh? Since they were monks they should have considered such merry-making as frivolous and empty. Why had they come to the wedding then? And they looked so happy too. They must have learned to take a more enlightened view of life, I suppose.

Among the people chatting and laughing were the township head, the chairman of the co-op, the veterinarian and his wife. The township head was a serious man. He never laughed at the jokes others cracked. Even when he joked himself, he kept a straight face. He was a busy man. He hadn't intended to come to the wedding. But since Tsou was on the co-op's administrative staff and also his neighbor, he had to show up. As soon as he stepped into the door, the bridegroom's mother came up to him and said:

"You have come just at the right moment. We need a responsible person to see to things." She meant that she wanted him to officiate.

So he had to stay. He smoked and chatted, waiting for the ceremony to begin.

The head of the co-op was a busy person, too. He usually had to attend at least two meetings a day and give not less than three serious talks. He also had to work in the fields. He was often scolded by his wife for coming home too late at night. He was hard working and never complained. Indeed, he was a busy man, but he had to come to congratulate the union of these two young people however busy he was. Tsou Mai-chiu was one of his best assistants. He had come to express his goodwill and to offer his help.

Of all the guests, the veterinarian talked the most. Talking on all subjects, he finally came to the marriage system.

"There are some merits to arranged marriages, too. You don't have to take all the trouble of looking for a wife yourself," said he, for he had obtained his beautiful wife through an old-fashioned arbitrarily arranged marriage, and he was extremely satisfied. With his drink-mottled pock-marked face, he would never have been able to get such a beautiful wife by himself.

"I advocate free choice in marriage," said the chairman. His wife, who married him also in the old-fashioned way, often scolded him, and this made him detest the arbitrary marriage system.

"I agree with you." The township head sided with the co-op chairman. "There is a folk song about the sorrows caused by the old marriage system."

"Recite it to us," urged the co-op chairman.

"The old marriage system promises no freedom.

"The woman cries and the man grieves.

"She cries till the Yangtse River overflows,

90

"And he grieves till the green mountain is crested with white."

"Is it as bad as that?" laughed the co-op chairman.

"We neither cry nor grieve," said the veterinarian proudly, looking at his wife.

"You are just a blind dog who happened on a good meal by accident," said the township head. "Talking about crying reminds me of the custom in Tsinshih." He paused to light his pipe.

"What kind of custom?" asked the chairman.

"The family who is marrying off a daughter must hire many people to cry. Rich families sometimes hire several dozen."

"What if the people they hire don't know how to cry?" asked the veterinarian.

"The purpose is to hire those who do. There are people in Tsinshih who are professional criers and specialists in this trade. Their crying is as rhythmic as singing, very pleasing to the ear."

Peals of laughter burst forth outside the window. The girls, who had been away for some time, evidently were practicing eavesdropping already. All the people in the bridal chamber, including the bride, laughed with them. The only persons who did not laugh were the township head and the veterinarian's beautiful wife who knitted her brows.

"Anything wrong with you?" the veterinarian asked softly.

"I feel a little dizzy and there's a sick feeling in my stomach."

"Perhaps you're pregnant?" suggested the township head.

"Have you seen a doctor?" the bride's sister-in-law asked.

"She's in bed with a doctor every night! She doesn't have to look for one," laughed the chairman.

"How can you say such things at your age!" said the veterinarian's beautiful wife. "And you a chairman of the co-op!"

"Everything is ready," someone called. "Come to the hall, please." All crowded into the hall. With her little boy in her arms the bride's sister-in-law followed behind the bride. The girls also came in. They leaned against the wall, shoulder to shoulder and holding hands. They looked at the bride, whispered into each other's ears and giggled again.

On one side of the hall were barrows, baskets and bamboo mats which belonged to the co-op. On the table in the center, two red candles were lit, shining on two vases of camellias.

The ceremony began. The township head took his place. He read the marriage lines, talked a little and withdrew to sit beside the co-op chairman. The girl who acted as the conductor of ceremonies announced that the next speaker was to be one of the guests. Whoever arranged the program had put the most interesting item, the bride's turn to speak, at the very end. So everyone waited eagerly for the guests to finish their chatter.

The first one called upon was the co-op chairman. But he said:

"Let the bride speak. I have been married for more than twenty years and have quite forgotten what it is like to be a newly-wed. What can I say?"

All laughed and clapped. However the person who walked up to speak was not the bride but the veterinarian with his drink-mottled pock-marked face. He spoke slowly, like an actor. Starting from the situation in our country before and after liberation and using a lot of special terms, he went on to the international situation.

"I have an appointment. I must leave early," said the township head softly to the co-op chairman. "You stay to officiate."

"I should be leaving, too."

"No, you can't. We shouldn't both leave," said the township head. He nodded to the bridegroom's mother apologetically and left. The co-op chairman had to stay. Bored by the talk, he said to the person sitting beside him:

"What on earth is the relation between the wedding and the situation at home and abroad?"

"This is his usual routine. He has only touched on two points, so far. There are still a lot yet."

"We should invent some kind of device that makes empty talkers itch all over so that they have to scratch and cannot go on speaking," said the chairman.

After half an hour or so, the guests clapped hands again. The veterinarian had ended his speech at last. This time the bride took the floor. Her plaits tied up with red wool, she was blushing crimson in spite of her poise. She said:

"Comrades and fellow villagers, I am very happy this evening, very, very happy."

The girls giggled. But the bride who was saying that she was very, very happy didn't even smile. On the contrary, she was very nervous. She continued:

"We were married a year ago."

The guests were shocked, and then they laughed. After a while it came home to them that she had said married instead of engaged because she was too nervous.

"We are being married today. I'm very happy." She paused and glanced at the guests before continuing. "Please don't misunderstand me when I say I'm happy. That doesn't mean I shall enjoy my happiness by sitting idly at home. I do not intend to be a mere dependent on my husband. I shall do my share of work. I'll do my work well in the co-op and compete with him."

"Hurrah! And beat Tsou down, too." A young man applauded.

"That's all I have to say." The bride, blushing scarlet, escaped from the floor.

"Is that all?" Someone wanted to hear more.

"She has spoken too little." Another was not satisfied.

"The bride's relative's turn now," said the girl conductor of ceremony.

Holding her boy of three the bride's sister-in-law stood up.

"I have not studied and I don't know how to talk." She sat down blushing scarlet, too.

"Let the bridegroom say whether he accepts the bride's challenge," someone suggested.

"Where is the bridegroom?"

"He's not here," someone discovered.

"He's run away!" another decided.

"Run away? Why?"

"Where has he run to?"

"This is terrible. What kind of a bridegroom is he!"

"He must be frightened by the bride's challenge to compete."

"Look for him immediately. It's unbelievable! The bride's relative is still here," said the co-op chairman.

With torches and flashlights people hurried out. They looked for him in the mountains, by the brooks and pools and everywhere. The co-op chairman and several men, about to join in the hunt, noticed a light in the sweet potato cellar.

"So you are here. You are the limit, you. . . ." A young man felt like cursing him.

"Why have you run away? Are you afraid of the challenge?" asked the chairman.

Tsou Mai-chiu climbed out of the cellar with a lantern. Brushing the dust from his clothes he raised his eyebrows and said calmly in a low voice:

"Rather than sit there listening to the veterinarian's empty talk, I thought I might as well come to see whether our sweet potatoes are in good condition."

93

"You are a good storekeeper, but certainly a poor bridegroom. Aren't you afraid your bride'll be offended?" said the chairman half reproachfully and half encouragingly.

After escorting the bridegroom back, we took our leave. Again treading on the tree shadows cast by the moonlight, which by now was slanting in the west, we went home. The group of girls who had come with us remained behind.

In the early winter night the breeze, fragrant with the scent of camellia, brought to our ears the peals of happy open laughter of the girls. They must have begun their eavesdropping. Had they heard something interesting already?

Brother Yu Takes Office*

by Lao Sheh

Brother Yu set out to take office.

When he came in sight of the building where he would be working, he slowed down. It wasn't very large. He knew the place. He had visited nearly all the offices, gambling houses and opium dens in the city. He remembered this place—when the door was open you could see the Mountain of the Thousand Buddhas. Naturally at the moment he had no interest in the Mountain of the Thousand Buddhas; his duties would be heavy! But he showed no agitation. He'd knocked about for years, he knew how to mask his feelings. Yu walked slower still.

Fat, fortyish, heavy brows, a sallow clean-shaven face. A grey serge gown, wide sleeves, black satin shoes. He moved sedately, with never a glance at the Mountain of the Thousand Buddhas. Maybe I should have come in a car, he thought. No, what for? His men were all his own kind. Everyone knew each other. Why put on a show? Besides, his was

* Reprinted from *Chinese Literature*, No. 6 (1962), pp. 58-76. (Translated by Sidney Shapiro.)

an important job. Why throw his weight around? It wasn't as if he had anything to worry about. Black satin shoes, grey serge gown—just right for a man of his position. Yu strolled slowly, calm and composed. No need to wear a military uniform. A "hard guy" was stuck in his belt beneath his gown. Yu smiled to himself.

No signboard hung outside the two-room office but, like Yu's clothing, there were hard guys inside. The door was open. His four men were seated on stools, smoking, their heads down. No one was looking at the Mountain of the Thousand Buddhas. On a large table by the wall were several teacups. On the floor, a new iron kettle was surrounded by cigarette butts. One was still burning. As the men rose to greet him, Yu again thought about the car. Assuming office this way really was a little cheap. But his old friends stood very ceremoniously. Although everyone was smiling warmly, there was respect in their manner. They didn't look down on him because he hadn't arrived in a car. When you came to think of it, the inspector and his office operated secretly. The less attention they attracted, the better. Of course, his men knew this. Yu felt somewhat easier.

After pausing before the large table and smiling at the men, he went into the inner room. Its furnishings consisted of a desk and two chairs. On the wall was a calendar, decorated with the blood of a departed bed-bug. The office is a bit too bare, Yu mused. But he couldn't think of what to add.

Chao brought in a cup of tea with a piece of twig floating in it. Yu didn't speak to him. Rubbing his forehead, Yu got an idea. Ah, that's right, he needed a wash basin. But he didn't tell Chao to buy one. He had to think this over carefully. The money for the office expenses was in his hands. Should he use it, or keep it all for himself? His salary was a hundred and twenty dollars. The expense account gave him eighty more. On a job where you risked your life, another eighty wasn't too much. But weren't his men also risking their lives? And they were old friends. Yu had eaten and drunk with them for years. When they lived in the earthen cave dwelling, hadn't they all slept on the same platform bed? No, he couldn't keep the whole expense account for himself.

Chao went out. When Chao was leader of his own band, had he ever privately pocketed money? Yu blushed. From the next room, Liu glanced at him through the open door. Although over fifty, Liu had come to work as one of his men. But three years ago, Liu had fifty rapid fire rifles under his command. No, he couldn't keep all the expense money. But in that case, what was the use of being boss? Share the eighty with the others? Of course they too had been leaders, but only of

95

bandit gangs in the mountains. Although Yu kept in constant touch with them, he had never formally become a bandit. There was a difference. They, to put it bluntly, were crooks who had given up crime to join the forces of law and order. He was an official. An official had his own way of doing things. Very well, then, he'd run his office in an official manner—the eighty dollars would be reserved for his personal use. But he still needed that wash basin, and a couple of towels, too.

There were also certain things he ought to do. For instance, an inspector ought to read the newspaper, or lecture his men. The newspaper he had to have. Whether he read it or not didn't matter. Just spreading it on his desk would make an impression. As for lecturing people, he was no novice at that. He had been a corporal in the army, and a member of the tax commission. Yes, he'd have to lecture his men; otherwise, it wouldn't seem like a real office-taking. Anyhow, these fellows had all been up in the hills, and at various times they'd been in the army. If he didn't give them a couple of stingers, they wouldn't respect him.

Chao had left the room. Liu kept coughing. He definitely had to lecture them. He'd teach them how to behave. Yu cleared his throat and stood up. He wanted to wash his face. But he still had no basin and towel. He sat down again. He'd lecture them. What should he say? Hadn't he made everything clear when he asked them to help? Hadn't he said exactly the same thing to Chao and Liu and Wang and Chu? "Give me a hand, old friend. When there's food on Yu's table, nobody goes hungry. We're brothers!" And he'd said it more than once. Why repeat it?

As for their duties, they were all quite clear. It was simply a case of set a thief to catch a thief. Every one of them knew it, though it wasn't a good idea to put it into words.

The main thing was to look out for himself, to protect his own neck. If he really tried to make good on this job and arrested a few of his underworld friends, Liu and the others might let their pistols off in his direction. It was best for him to keep one eye closed. He couldn't start off with a big flourish. They'd all be meeting again some day. But could Yu say this? How could he lecture them? Get a load of the eyes of that Liu—those lids wouldn't close even when he was dead. The help the men were giving Yu was a form of bandit loyalty. He couldn't get rid of the code of the hills in one sweep. True, the police commissioner had put him on this job to nab bandits. But they were all his friends. Intimate friends. A tough problem!

Yu took off his grey serge gown, then went out and smiled at his men.

"Inspector," Liu hailed him. Contempt was plain in his eyes. "How about assigning us some work?" he said.

Yu nodded. He'd show them. "I'm going to write a list. I have to make a report to Commissioner Li. As I told you brothers the other day, our job is to help Commissioner Li nab bandits. The commissioner called me in and said: Yu, you've got to help me, I don't know the layout here. How could I refuse? He's an old friend, too. I can do it, I thought. Why? Because I thought of you fellows. I know the set up pretty well, and you know it right down to the ground. Working together, we can put it over. Commissioner, I said, leave it to me. Since he did me the honor of offering me the job, I couldn't be ungrateful enough to refuse. Brothers, whatever Commissioner Li gets, there's a share for me. Whatever I get, you're in it, too. I've got it all figured out. Now I'm going to write this list—who does what. After we've talked it over, I'll hand it in; then we'll get started. We'll do it all official and proper. Right?" Yu asked with a laugh.

No one replied. Chu blinked. Although there wasn't any awkward silence, Yu couldn't very well say any more. He'd have to prepare his list, write it out with a pomp that would crush Liu and his pals. After all, Yu recalled, wasn't he the one who wrote the ransom note the year Chu kidnapped that rich young Wang? Yes, he'd certainly wriggle that writing brush. But where was his brush and ink slab? These men couldn't get anything done!

"Say, Chao. . . ." Yu thought he'd send Chao to buy the writing brush. But then he checked himself. Why Chao? You had to be discriminating where money was involved. This wasn't up in the hills where they did things any old way. This was official business. Who should do the buying, who should deliver letters—these jobs had to be assigned right. It wasn't easy. The man who bought things got a rake-off from the store. You didn't earn anything delivering letters. Who should be stuck with the messenger job?

"Ah . . . nothing . . . nothing," he told Chao. He wouldn't buy the writing brush just yet. He'd have to give the matter more thought. Yu was rather disturbed. He never imagined being an inspector was so troublesome. It wasn't such a wonderful job. Yet it might not be too bad, particularly if he could keep the eighty dollars expense money. But he couldn't do that. His men had all been bandits. If he held on to the money too tightly, their pistols might pump him full of "black dates." That wouldn't be so funny.

It was a tricky situation. An official with bandits for his assistants. What kind of an official was that? Yet he couldn't operate without

them. Could he nab crooks by himself? A fat chance! He patted the
pistol in his belt.

"Brothers, have you got your hardware?"

Everyone nodded.

Are the bastards mute! What was the idea? Was it scorn, or fear? Just
nodding, that was no way for a friend to behave. If they had anything to
say, they ought to say it. Look at that Liu, his face all grim and solemn.
Yu laughed again. He wasn't being quite officious enough. But he
couldn't be too officious with this crowd. Maybe they'd like it better if
he swore at them. But he didn't dare. He wasn't a real bandit. Yu felt as
if he were standing with his feet in two different boats. He hated himself
for not being a genuine bandit. At the same time, he felt he was
high-class. If he weren't, would he have been made an official? Lighting
a cigarette, he pondered. He'd have to feed this bunch. He could hang
on to the office expense money, but he'd have to spend a bit on food.

"Let's go, brothers, to the Wufu Restaurant!" Yu went to put on his
grey serge gown.

Chou's face cracked into wrinkles, like an overripe pumpkin. Two
smile lines appeared in Liu's fifty-year-old stony cheeks. Wang and Chu
also revived. Moisture had evidently returned to everyone's throat.
Those who couldn't find anything to say, licked their lips.

At the restaurant, they were all great friends again. They didn't stand
on ceremony. For their joint feast this one proposed a jellied fresh ham,
that one wanted a mixed roast with sea-slugs. Liu suggested grilled whole
chicken—two of them. When they were half full, they started to talk
business. Liu, of course, spoke first, since he was by far the eldest. His
stony cheeks were red with feasting. He took another drink of liquor,
another bite of the ham, another drag on his cigarette.

"Inspector," he began. His eyes swept the others. "Opium pedlars,
pimps—we can take them easy. But with bandits, we've got to be
careful. Are we going to sell our brothers for a small heap of silver
dollars?"

Drink had given Yu courage. "That's no way to talk, Brother Liu.
Commissioner Li appointed us to catch bandits. There are too many of
them around. If we don't nab some fast, Commissioner Li may lose his
job. If he goes, where will that leave us?"

"Suppose we do nab some, knock a couple off?" A strong liquor
breath accompanied the smoke Chao exhaled. "Sure, we've got guns,
but so have they. Anyhow we're not going to keep these jobs for ever.
It's not that I'm scared."

"Whoever's scared is a son of a bitch," was the analysis Chu drew.

"A stinking son of a bitch," Chao confirmed. And he added: "Nobody's scared, and everybody's willing to give Commissioner Li a hand. Fraternity—that's the problem. It's true you've helped us, Brother Yu, and you've been around more than we, but you've never been up in the hills."

"Don't I know what the code is?" Yu gazed off into space and laughed coldly.

"Who says you don't?" countered gourd-mouthed Wang.

"It's this way, brothers." Yu decided to needle them. "If we're friends, you'll stick with me. If you don't want to stick with me," again he laughed off into space, "that's all right, too."

"Inspector." Once more it was Liu. His eyes were piercing. "If you really want us to go at it, we will. But don't forget this. We're just your assistants; you're the head man. Any comebacks will go direct to you. You're a friend, so I'm talking straight. If you want us to nab guys, that's a cinch. Nothing to it."

The lovely sea-slugs Yu had consumed turned to ice in his stomach. This was just what he was afraid of. His men would do the work and he would report the victories. But when the bandits started dishing out black dates, he would be first on the list!

He mustn't worry in advance. He'd take things as they came. Eating black dates was uncomfortable, but reporting success and being rewarded was very sweet. He had been around for years. He knew no matter what you did, you had to strike first. When you played, you played for keeps! Yu was over forty. If he didn't get much out of this himself, at least he could leave a little something for his son. He wasn't going to be like Liu and the others. Always guarding their heads but leaving their backsides sticking out. Doing dirty work all their lives but ending up without even a burial plot to lie in when they died. He was shrewd, he could plan. He wouldn't listen to Liu. Yu decided to go ahead. He'd play along with Commissioner Li. If he cracked a couple of cases, he might even be transferred to headquarters. Who could tell? With a car to ride around in wherever he went. He couldn't always walk to take office!

The concluding soup expanded spirits and stomachs together. Everyone grew much more cordial. Although Yu was still quite firm, his tone mellowed:

"You've got to help me, brothers. Pick someone with no connections and bring him in. It'll serve him right. We've got to put on some kind of a show. We're all carrying hardware. How will it look if we just nab a few pimps? All right, then. This is how we'll do it. First find some small fry.

99

Nab the kind that can't cause any trouble; then, we'll see. When we finish that, we'll come back here for another feed, what do you say? That cold ham wasn't bad."

"It's autumn, it's getting cool. We ought to have hot roast pork from now on." Wang didn't talk much, but when he said something it was to the point.

Yu decided to keep Wang with him in the office and send the other three out to investigate. No need to write a list. When they came back, he'd make a report. Yes, he'd have to buy a writing brush and an ink slab, and also a wash basin. He'd buy it himself so there'd be no question of favoritism. What he needed was a secretary, but he had forgotten to mention this to Commissioner Li. For the time being, he'd do his own writing. He'd ask for a secretary after they'd cracked their first case. There was no rush. Yu was a man who kept both feet on the ground. People said Erh-tieh's son could write. Yu would give him a start in the world. He'd make Erh-tieh's son his secretary. Good. For his first day in office he wasn't doing badly.

Chatting with Wang on the way back, he forgot all about the brush and the ink slab. The office wasn't a bit like a real office. Still, it was just as well. All that business about writing with a great flourish was only something in his mind. When it came to actually writing, he didn't know many words. They always seemed to escape him whenever he wanted to put them down on paper. It was just as well that he had no brush and ink slab.

But what should he do with his time? He ought to have a newspaper, even if it was only to look at the pictures. He couldn't just keep gabbing with Wang. Although they were old friends, he was an official and Wang was an underling. Yu had to think of his dignity. He had already stood in the doorway. He couldn't drink any more tea. He had looked twice through the pages of the calendar. There was nothing else for him to do. Yu thought over his family finances. Their condition was hopeful. Salary a hundred and twenty, plus eighty dollars expense money—even if he didn't take it all. He could count on at least a hundred and fifty a month. Gradually, he could save up for a little house.

Mother's—! Dog Shang did just one job with warlord Chang Tsung-chang and they raked in a hundred thousand! There was never anything like it. Never. They were the kind of bandits Li was after. Who could be as careful with his money as Dog Shang? With money in your hands, you went dizzy. Take himself, for instance. Yu had picked up twenty or thirty thousand when he was working in the tax office. And now where was it? No wonder men went crooked. He was used to eating and drinking and playing around. Live on bran muffins again? He couldn't stand it. Nobody could stand it.

Yes, to tell the truth, they all—including Yu—were waiting for Marshal Chang's return. Naturally. Mother's—! Ting the Third alone was storing two trunks full of military notes* which Chang had printed. If Chang came back, Ting would be a rich man with those trunks!

How could Yu talk about arresting bandits? They were all old friends. But on a salary of a hundred and twenty, plus eighty in expense money, what else could he do? He had to! Mother's—! Get on with it. Who could worry about so much? Every man for himself. Whose fault was it that Marshal Chang couldn't come back? Nab them! Shoot a couple! Yu had never been up in the hills. He wouldn't be betraying any of his own gang.

It was after four, and still no sign of Liu and the other two. Had they really gone to pry into nests, or were they just fooling around? He'd have to set office hours. Everyone must be back by four-thirty to report. What kind of an office would it be like, if they never showed up? Without them he couldn't operate. With them, they were a headache. Mother's—!

He wouldn't wait for them any longer than five. He started work at eight; at five he quit. His men could go out whenever they liked. It wasn't unusual for arrests to be made in the middle of the night. But the inspector couldn't always be waiting around for his assistants. He ought to tell them, but it was rather hard to say. What was so hard about it? Wasn't he the boss? He immediately notified Wang. Wang grunted. What did that mean?

"It's five o'clock!" Yu glanced at the Mountain of the Thousand Buddhas. The sun was gilding its summit. In the sunlight the autumn grass still had a bit of green. "Look after things, Wang. See you tomorrow at eight."

Wang's gourd-shaped mouth was closed in a tight line.

The next morning Yu deliberately came a half hour late. He had to hold back. Suppose he arrived before his men? How embarrassing.

But the men were all there, seated on stools, smoking, their heads down. Yu felt like punching them. What clods! When he entered, they rose as they had the day before, but very slowly, as if they all had athlete's foot. Yu smiled at them, though he felt more like swearing. It would be awkward if he did. He had to act big. Who told him to

---

* At that time China was ruled by various big warlords, who issued notes which they used as money in the areas under their control.

become a leader of men? He had to act shrewd. Yu gave a grandiose laugh. Casual, unconcerned.

"Ah, Liu, do any business?" Natural, pleasant, humorous. Yu mentally praised himself.

"There was business," Liu, grim-visaged, bored into Yu with his eyes. "But we didn't do any."

"Why not?" Yu laughed.

"We didn't have to. They'll be coming in themselves soon."

"Oh!" Yu tried to laugh again, but no sound emerged. "What about you?" he asked Chao and Chu.

The two just shook their heads.

"Shall we go out again today?" queried Liu.

"Ah, wait a while," Yu walked towards his room. "Let me think." He turned his head back and looked. The men were again seated, their eyes on the cigarette butts. They weren't saying a word. Clods.

Yu sat down in his office. He was puzzled. They'll be coming in themselves? He couldn't ask Liu what that meant. He couldn't admit they had him stumped. They'd lose respect. But what did it mean—they'll be coming in themselves? He'd just have to wait and see.

Should he send Liu and the others out on their rounds today? That had to be decided immediately. "Hey, Chu, get going. Keep your eyes open, do you hear?" Yu waited for them all to laugh. That would show they appreciated his carefree humor. No one laughed.

"Liu, you'd better wait. Didn't you say they were coming to see me? You and I will keep them company. We're all old friends." He didn't send Wang and Chao out either. The more men he had around the more secure he'd feel. But suppose they wanted to go out themselves? He couldn't stop them. You had to act reserved on a job like this. If they asked him, then he'd speak. But Wang and Chao didn't say anything, so that was all right.

It was on the tip of his tongue to ask, "How many of them are coming?" but he swallowed back the words. Didn't he have three assistants with him, all packing guns? If they came in a big gang, well, he'd just have to close his eyes. He'd act according to the situation. Mother's—!

He still had no newspaper. What kind of an office was this anyhow! The official had to sit around waiting for bandits. It was really too much. Why not telephone Commissioner Li to send down a company of soldiers, nab the bandits as they came in, then shoot the whole lot! No, better not be too hasty. Better wait and see. Nine-thirty.

"Hey, Liu, when are they coming?"

"Soon, inspector." Was there a mocking note in Liu's voice?

"Go out and get me a paper." Yu simply had to have his newspaper. When it was brought, he turned to the local news section. He pretended to chuckle at something he saw. He'd read it learnedly aloud. But there were too many words he didn't recognize. Like the name of that cafe hostess there. What the devil was it?

"They're here, inspector." Liu was quite formal.

Yu was calm. Setting aside the irritating cafe hostess, he said softly, "Come in." He felt for the pistol in his belt.

A whole crowd entered, headed by Big Yang. Following him was Fancy Brow, another hulking brute. Walking between them, Monkey Four looked particularly small. Sixth Horse, Big Mouth Tsao and White Chang Fei also walked into the room.

"Brother Yu," they hailed him cordially.

He had to admit he knew them. Yu stood up and smiled.

Everybody talked at the same time. There was such a clamor no one could hear himself think.

"Big Yang, you tell him." Gradually everyone's interest focussed on one point. They urged one another: "Listen to Big Yang!"

Frowning, Big Yang leaned forward and rested his hands on the desk. His mouth virtually against Yu's nose, he said: "We've come to congratulate you, Brother Yu."

"Listen!" White Chang Fei gave Monkey Four a poke in the back.

"Congratulations are congratulations, but you ought to give us a treat. Actually, we should be treating you, but the last few days we're a little short of this." Big Yang's index finger and thumb pinched together in a circle like a silver dollar. "So you'll have to treat us."

"Anything I can do, brothers—" Yu began.

Big Yang rolled right on. "You don't have to invite us to a restaurant. That's not necessary. We want this." Again his thumb and index finger formed a circle. "We want money for train tickets."

"Train tickets?" said Yu.

"That's right." Big Yang nodded thoughtfully. "You see, brother, you're now in charge of this district. How can we keep on operating here? We're all friends. You come, we go. There can't be any squabbles between us. You do your official job. We'll go back to the hills. You pay the fare. No hard words. We part friends. We'll be meeting again some day." Big Yang turned to his cronies. "Isn't that the idea?"

"Right. It's just that," cried Monkey Four. "Now let's hear from Brother Yu."

This was something Yu had never expected. He hadn't thought that it would be so easy. But he certainly hadn't expected it would be so hard either. These six wanted train fares. Suppose another sixty, or another six hundred, came in, all wanting him to pay their fares? Besides, Commissioner Li had appointed him to arrest them. If Yu gave them all fares, spoke to them gently, and sent them off one by one, how would it look? And where would the money come from? He could hardly ask Li for it. Should he spend his hundred and twenty dollars salary, plus eighty dollars expense money?

The trouble was these birds were giving him a lot of face. Not a hard word out of them. "You come, we go." Short and sweet. Spoken like a real friend. It was easy enough, if a man was willing to lay out the money. With a smiling face, Yu invited them to have some tea. He couldn't make up his mind. He didn't dare offend them. They might talk nicely, but they also could be very rough. If they said they'd go, they'd definitely go. But they wouldn't leave unless Yu gave them the fares. It would make an awful dent in his expense money. And he'd have to pretend to be happy about it, too. They wouldn't stand for any tough talk.

"How much, friends?" he asked casually.

"Ten dollars apiece," said Big Yang, speaking for all.

"It's just the train fare. Once we're up in the hills, we'll manage fine," Monkey Four added.

"We'll leave this afternoon, friend. When we say a thing, we mean it," said Big-mouth Tsao.

Yu couldn't be so decisive. Ten dollars apiece meant sixty dollars! Three-fourths of his eighty dollars expense money!

White Chang Fei got a bit impatient. "Fork over the sixty dollars and we'll be moving along. It's either you or us. With you here, we've got to leave. Isn't that the answer? If you give us the money, we'll go. If you don't—but why talk about that? We understand each other. Real men don't beat about the bush. Brother Yu, I'm holding out my hand for that train fare."

"Right, we're all holding out our hands. We'll pay it back later. Our friendship hasn't been just for a day," said Big Yang. The others also chimed in. Although their words were different, the meaning was the same.

Yu could no longer delay. He took out the wallet next to the pistol in his belt and counted out sixty dollars. "Here you are, brothers." He didn't smile.

"Thanks, brother," chorused Big Yang and his gang. Monkey Four rolled up the bills and stuffed them into his waist-band. "We'll be seeing you, brother," he said. The bandits left. In the outer room they nodded at Liu and the others. "Come up and see us in the hills." Yu's men smiled and escorted them to the door.

Yu was miserable. If he had known this was going to happen he would have sent for soldiers and had those six birds arrested. But maybe this way of handling it was better. He'd be running into them in the future. Sixty dollars gone. A few more visits like this and his hundred and twenty dollars of salary would also vanish. What kind of an inspector was he? An inspector who gets squeezed by bandits. He was like a mute who's eaten wormwood—it was more bitter than he could say. Had Liu been trying to be helpful, or was he just kidding around? He ought to ask him! Not only hadn't Liu captured any bandits—he had invited them to the office. Was that any way to do things?

Still, maybe he shouldn't be too strict with Liu. He might go back to the hills. Yu had to have him. He couldn't afford to offend anyone. What a life. If he had brought a couple of green hands along when he took office, when those bandits came he'd have had to eat black dates. Those sixty dollars bought him his life. If you looked at it that way, it was worth it.

Yu had no choice. What's done was done. He was only afraid that another gang might show up tomorrow asking for railway fares. He couldn't tell this to his men. He had to smile, show that Yu was big-hearted to his friends, as if sixty dollars or a hundred were nothing at all. But if he kept handing money out at this rate, what would the inspector have to eat? The northwest wind? A fine thing!

Again he picked up the newspaper, but he'd lost interest. He had no interest in anything. Like a fool he'd given away sixty dollars. It was really sickening. He ought to be ashamed—being afraid for his life. It was as if his life didn't belong to him—he had to buy it. Mother's—! He had to admire Monkey Four and the others. They dared come to the inspector's office and demand train fares. Weren't they afraid of being nabbed? No, the devils. But he, Yu, had lost face. Not only hadn't he arrested them, he hadn't even dared to speak a harsh word. What a disgrace. Next time would be different. He wouldn't act so soft again. It wasn't worth going soft just to remain an inspector. An inspector had to arrest people. There were no two ways about it. Blast that cafe hostess. What *was* her name?

Chu had returned. At least he ought to come in and report. The inspector couldn't very well run out and question him. In the next room Chu and Liu talked and talked. He would wait. He'd see whether Chu came in or not. Who could reason with bandits?

Finally Chu entered. "Brother . . . er . . . inspector. There's a gang holed up north of the city. Want to go see them?"

"Where are they?" Yu couldn't be afraid again. Sixty dollars gone already. If he had to die, then he'd die. He'd go even if they were gods.

"On the lake shore."

"Take your gun. Let's go." Yu didn't hesitate. He'd clean out that nest. No one would get any more railway fare out of him.

"Just us two?" Chu certainly could be infuriating.

"What kind of talk is that? Tell me the address and I'll go myself." If he didn't act bold, his assistants wouldn't know what sort of man the inspector was. Just handing out train fares, not cracking a single case. How could he face the commissioner? What was he being paid a salary of a hundred and twenty a month for?

Silently, Chu poured himself a bowl of tea. He seemed to be getting ready to go along. Ignoring him, Yu stalked out. Chu followed. That was more like it. Yu felt a little braver. Of course two on this job were much better than one. If they ran into trouble, they could talk it over.

By the lakeside was a lane about the size of a nostril. In it was a small inn. Yu was very familiar with this area. Of course, he recognized the inn. You needed only one look to see that it was a nest of thieves. He should have brought more men along. Yu, he said to himself, you've wasted your years of experience. When you lost your temper, your brains went with it. Why didn't you bring more men? Who told you to get mad at them?

Since he'd come, he'd have to see it through. He'd show his men —although he'd never been up in the hills, he had plenty of guts. If he could haul a couple of crooks out of this place, the next time he spoke his words would carry a lot more weight. He'd try his luck. Maybe he was a goner. Who could tell?

"Chu, will you guard the door or shall I?"

"There they are," said Chu, pointing inside. "No need to guard the door. None of them want to run."

Another farce. Yes, they would talk about fraternity. Mother's—! Yu looked in. Several toughs were sitting in a small hallway: Colored Butterfly, Nose Six, Burly Sung, Young Teh-sheng, and two others he hadn't seen before. Finished. Again old friends.

"Come in, Brother Yu. We haven't even dared go to congratulate you. Come in and meet the gang. Dog Chang, Jewels Hsu, this is Brother Yu. Old friends. Our own brother." Greetings exchanged, the gangsters chatted animatedly.

"Have a seat, brother." Young Teh-sheng—his pa, Old Teh-sheng,

106

had just been executed in Honan Province—was particularly courteous.

Yu hated himself. Why couldn't he think of what to say? In the end it was Chu who found just the right words.

"Brothers, the inspector has come personally. Speak up if you have anything on your mind."

The inspector smiled and nodded.

"Then we'll talk frankly," said Nose Six. "Brother Sung, take Brother Yu and show him."

"This way, Brother Yu." Burly Sung jerked his thumb towards the rear and went into a small room.

Yu followed. There was no danger. He was sure of that. He couldn't risk his life even if he wanted to. How irritating. The little room was pitch dark. Its earthen floor stank of mildew. Against the wall was a small wooden bed strewn with straw. Burly Sung pulled the bed away from the wall and squatted in the corner. Removing two or three moist bricks, he extracted several pistols and threw them on the bed.

"That's the lot." Burly Sung smiled and wiped his hands on his tunic. "Things are too hot around here. If we carry those, we can't even get on a train. That's our problem. We didn't know you were in charge till Brother Chu dropped in. Now we have a way out. We'll turn this pile over to you. You give us a little railway fare and have Chu put us on the train. That's how it's got to be. We're asking you this favor."

Yu wanted to vomit. The stench of the mildew was seeping into his brain. Holding his nose, he said: "Why give them to me?" As they went back to the hallway, he added: "I can't keep that stuff for you."

"But if we take them with us, we can't leave. The heat's on," Burly Sung explained earnestly.

"If I take them, I can hand them over to the authorities. I'm not turning in any men. At least if I've got some weapons to show, that will be something. You've got to think of it from my angle. Right?" Yu was enraged to hear himself speak like this. Much too soft.

"That's up to you, Brother Yu."

He had been hoping they would refuse.

"Whatever you say, brother. Of course, you know we need guns in our line of work. Would we give them up if we had any other way out? Do whatever you like with them. All we want is to hit the road right now. Without your help we can't get away. Have Brother Chu put us on the train."

The bandits were giving orders to the inspector. Their own brother. Yu had nothing to say. He had no ideas, no energy. He had ideas, but they didn't work. He had a position, but he couldn't use it. The truth was out. He scratched his head. He couldn't turn in those weapons. But could he refuse to take them? He'd have to give the gang railway fares and look after their guns to boot. What kind of official business was that? The only alternative was to refuse the weapons and not give them any money either. Let them do as they pleased. But did he dare? Arresting them was even more unthinkable. A dead body could be pushed off the lake bank at any time. Yu didn't want to end up in a watery grave.

"Brother Yu," Burly Sung was extremely sincere, "it's hard for you. Anyone who says different is a son of a bitch. But we can't help it. Take the hardware, give us a couple of dollars, and we'll say no more. The words are in our hearts."

"How much?" Yu gave a sickly smile.

"Six sixes are thirty-six. The man's a bastard who asks for a dollar more. Thirty-six dollars."

"But I don't want those guns."

"That's up to you. Anyhow, we can't take them along. If we're nabbed, at most we'll get six months. But if they catch us with that hardware on us, it's black dates or something very much like it. That's the truth. We're not scared—we brothers don't have to boast—but when you ought to be careful, you'd better be careful. Well then, brother, thirty-six dollars, and we'll be seeing you again." Burly Sung turned up his palm.

Thirty-six dollars changed hands. The inspector had no choice. "What are we going to do with these guns, Chu?"

"Take them back first, then we'll see." Chu seemed very self-assured.

"Brother Chu," called the gangsters, "take us to the train."

"Brother Yu," they were very polite, "thanks a lot."

"Thanks" was all Yu got. So many guns in one bundle would be too heavy to carry. He divided them with Chu, and each tucked several in his belt. How awesome. A belt full of pistols. But Yu couldn't fire a single one. These fellows all trusted him. That's why they gave him their guns. It never occurred to them that he might turn them down. How could he even think of arresting them. They had guts. He had to admire them. By now, he had spent sixteen dollars more than his eighty dollars office expense money. What else could he do? He'd probably lose his hundred and twenty dollars salary, too.

Yu's lunch was tasteless to him that day, though he drank two big tumblers of liquor. What was the use of talking? He was a dud. He had let Commissioner Li down. Yu was not without a sense of dignity. He thought it over. One more fiasco and the only course left would be to resign. But what a disgrace—to resign. And where else could he find a job paying a hundred and twenty a month these days? Commissioner Li certainly wouldn't give him another appointment. Not only hadn't he captured any bandits—on the contrary, the bandits had taken him in. What a joke. When they got back to the hills, they'd surely laugh at him. He was just one big joke. The more he thought about it, the worse Yu felt.

The best thing to do was capture some opium. Could opium be considered illegal? Yes. But what a dull pastime for an inspector of a special bureau. Anyhow, he couldn't resign. First he'd collect some opium; it wasn't a bad idea. Yu determined his policy. He'd confiscate opium for a while, then he'd see. At least here he knew his ground.

A week passed. Several stores of opium were brought in. Commissioner Li wanted bandits, but Yu couldn't push his men. His expense money was already sixteen dollars overdrawn.

It was a Monday, and his men were all out looking for opium, (opium!) when a big swarthy fellow staggered into Yu's office.

"Brother Yu," he called smilingly.

"You, Money Five? You've got your nerve."

"With Brother Yu in office, what have I to fear?" Money Five sat down. "Give me a smoke."

"What have you come for?" Yu reached for his money pouch. More railway fare.

"First to congratulate you, second to thank you. When the brothers got back to the hills, they all praised you. That's the truth."

Oh? They didn't laugh at me? Yu thought to himself.

"Brother," Money Five pulled out a roll of bills. "We can't let you lose anything. The brothers in the hills will never forget your kindness."

"Really—" Yu tried to make a show of courteous refusal.

"Not a word, brother. Take it. Now where is Brother Sung's hardware?"

Am I a weapons keeper, or something? Yu didn't dare say it aloud. "Chu's got them," he replied.

"Good, I'll ask him for them."

"Just down from the hills?" Yu felt he ought to make conversation.

"Just down from the hills. I've come to advise you to chuck this job." Money Five was very sincere.

"You want me to resign?"

"That's right. Maybe you're one of us, maybe you're not. Anyhow, with you in office, we stay out of the way. You couldn't operate if we were here. You're good to us, and we're good to you. Leave this job.

109

That's all I've got to say. I have over three hundred men up in the hills, but I've come down to say this to you personally. We're friends. When I tell you to quit, you'd better quit. A smart fellow catches on fast. I'm going, brother. Tell Chu I'll be waiting for him in the inn by the lakeshore."

"Tell me one thing, brother." Yu stood up. "If I quit, what will our friends think?"

"No one will laugh. Don't worry about that, brother. Well, goodbye."

Two or three days later, there was a new man in the post of inspector. Yu, fat and stately, often strolled down the street. At times, he glanced serenely at the Mountain of the Thousand Buddhas.

TANTZU

Praying for Rain is a traditional *tantzu* story, one of a great number which have been popular for generations. Yang Pin-kuei, an old and talented *tantzu* artist, provided the version of the story on which this translation is based. Like other such story-tellers and singing artists, Yang was a one-man show. Sitting at a table with a clapper or fan in his hands, he also played a three-string guitar while acting all of the character parts, providing a running commentary on the background, status, appearance, and reactions of each character and even adding sound effects—a barking dog, a bird singing in the woods, a storm overtaking his hero, or the sounds of a horse racing across a battlefield. It was a simple but extremely popular entertainment, and many towns or cities had special places where the *tantzu* would be performed. Occasionally, there would be a two-man show, the second man playing the lute, and other stringed instruments were used as performers were added.

Praying for Rain *

a tantzu story

by Yang Pin-Kuei

CHIEN: I am Chien Chih-chieh, a Soochow citizen. I make my living by telling fortunes, and I manage pretty well. Today, I'm taking a leisurely stroll to the Hsuantu Temple to watch the praying for rain.

The Narrator: This Chien is a fortune-teller who practices divination by various gadgets. Though he tells nothing but lies, his business is better than most. This is because Chien has a pair of sharp eyes and a slick tongue. His business is thriving and he has become quite popular. People call him Chien the Demi-god. He has put that name on his signboard.

Today, he is dressed like a Taoist priest. He is wearing a priest's cap, a robe of blue gauze, white linen trousers, white stockings and sandals of fine straw. Chien carries a feather fan with a bone handle. He is tall and big-boned and sports a fine beard.

For more than six months there has been no rain in Soochow. Due to the drought, the price of rice and firewood has soared. Life is very hard for the people. The officials are helpless. But since they have to make some pretence of earning their salaries, they have had a high platform erected at the Hsuantu Temple to be used for praying for rain—leave everything to Heaven! An imperial decree has even been posted on the front wall of the temple.

Chien is now fifty-three years of age. Although he has heard of praying for rain, he has never actually seen it. That's why he is going to

* Reprinted from *Chinese Literature*, No. 8 (August, 1959), pp. 120-38. [Translated by Chang Su.]

the temple today. Usually crowded and bustling, the mainstreet is now quiet and deserted. The shops have few customers. People passing by look weary and ill-nourished. When acquaintances meet they just sigh and complain of their plight.

Quite a big crowd has gathered before the temple to see the praying for rain. On the wall beside the closed front gate is posted an imperial decree. Chien waits patiently for the crowd to thin out a bit so that he can read it. But more and more people keep coming. How long will he have to wait? Chien decides to squeeze through the crowd.

CHIEN (*reading aloud the imperial decree*): "On the thirtieth day of the fifth month of Wan Li Era of the great Ming dynasty, the Heaven-appointed emperor issues the following decree: According to the memorandum submitted by Fang Po-nien, governor of Kiangsu, there is a serious drought. The officials should be responsible to relieve the people's suffering. In the city of Soochow, there has been no moisture since the snowfall in the middle of the eleventh month last year. The fields are parched. Unless wheat and rice can be planted, there will be no autumn harvest. Now is the time for sowing, and rain is badly needed. The governor and his subordinates have submitted themselves to the emperor for punishment on the grounds that their lack of virtue and ability has enraged Heaven and caused it to impose this disaster upon the people.

"The emperor states that ever since ancient times there have been droughts and floods. The drought is not the governor's fault. Let this imperial decree be dispatched to Soochow and put up immediately. Let it be known to all civilians, officers and people that whoever has the power to summon rain can take down the decree, mount the platform and drive away the evil spirit of drought. If he succeeds in bringing rain and is an official he will be promoted; if he is not, he shall be made one; if he does not want to be an official he shall be rewarded by other means. If he prays to no avail. . . ."

The Narrator: Chien cannot see the remaining words. For the day is hot, the paste has dried and a corner of the paper has rolled up. What it says is: ". . . he shall be punished for the crime of defrauding the emperor." Chien reaches for the corner of the paper, intending to flatten it out. The crowd thinks this priest is ready to undertake praying for rain. Someone says, "Look, he's taking down the imperial decree!" A commotion is created. Everyone crowds forward to have a look at the

113

man who dares to take down the imperial decree. Chien is nearly jostled off his feet.

CHIEN: Hey! don't push!

The Narrator: Chien's hand, which is holding the paper, is also jostled and half the decree comes away in his fingers. He has taken down the decree! Official messengers, across the street, hearing the people shout and seeing a priest with a piece of the imperial decree in his hand, also think he has torn it down. They dash forward, pushing aside the on-lookers.

MESSENGER A: Make way, make way. . . . Aha! I wondered who would have the courage to take down the imperial decree. So it is Chien the Demi-god.

CHIEN: No, no. . . .

MESSENGER A: Of course. Who in Soochow is better qualified? It is very good of you to pray for rain for the sake of the people of your native place.

CHIEN: I didn't take down the imperial decree. I was just trying to read the words in the rolled-up corner and somebody pushed my hand. Only a small piece was torn. . . .

MESSENGER A: A small piece is quite enough. Even a tiny corner will do!

CHIEN: Please paste this bit back on. . . .

MESSENGER A: Mr. Chien, imperial decrees can't be torn down and pasted up again at will!

CHIEN: What shall I do, then?

MESSENGER A: Pray for rain!

CHIEN: Please don't make fun of me. What do I know about praying for rain?

MESSENGER A: You don't know how to pray for rain; yet you tore down the imperial decree! Come on, come to the perfect!

CHIEN: I have something to say. . . .

MESSENGER A: You can tell it to the city prefect in person.

CHIEN (*aside*): What bad luck! These messengers know me well. They even borrow money from me. But now they are so official. There's no use talking to them. For one thing, they wouldn't believe me; for another, they can't make decisions anyway. All right, let's go to the prefect. If I pray and it doesn't rain, at most I'll get thirty strokes on my palm.

The Narrator: Chien hands the piece of the imperial decree to the messenger, deciding to trust to his own wit. There is a shout.

MESSENGER B: The prefect of Soochow and the magistrates of Chang-chow and Wuhsien Counties are waiting for the diviner at the East Corner Gate.

MESSENGER A: Please come this way.

CHIEN (aside): Ah, this looks as if I won't get away with a mere thirty strokes on the palm. Perhaps, I shall have to stay in for thirty days.

The Narrator: Chien strolls to the East Corner Gate. More than a hundred servants and messengers are standing there in two rows. The prefect and two magistrates come forward.

Prefect: Ah, venerable sir, it is indeed the good fortune of the people of Soochow that you have taken down the imperial decree. I and my colleagues have been sent by the governor to meet you. We humbly beg your pardon for not having come earlier. We humbly beg your pardon.

CHIEN (*aside*): It looks like even thirty days in jail won't do. I shall serve three years, at least. But never mind. With officials, money talks. I'm ready to pay. Business has been good for me the past six months. I've plenty of money.

The Narrator: The prefect and the two magistrates accompany Chien into the temple compound. As they walk up to a temporary shelter, a guard announces loudly.

GUARD: The governor and the local gentry have come to welcome the diviner.

CHIEN (aside): Well! Even the governor has come! This is serious. If I fail to bring rain, they won't let me off with only three years—I'll be exiled three thousand *li* away! It's no joke. I'd better confess to the governor that I know nothing about praying for rain and that the imperial decree was torn down because I was pushed by the crowd. I must keep cool.

The Narrator: Governor Fang, having heard that someone has torn down the imperial decree and volunteered to pray for rain, arrives with the local gentry. He sees a priest holding a feather fan, his beard long

115

and fine, looking quite ethereal. The governor comes forward from the shelter.

GOVERNOR: Ah, venerable sir, your disciple heard that you had arrived, but he has not had time to bathe and perfume himself in order to welcome you and has been late in coming. I hope you will pardon me. Please accept my greetings.

THE GENTRY: Venerable sir, your disciples are late in coming to welcome you. Respectfully, we bow. . . .

CHIEN: What virtue and ability have I that I should cause you such trouble? I bow respectfully.

GOVERNOR: Please come this way.

CHIEN: Please, you first.

GOVERNOR: Let's go together hand in hand then. (*Grasps Chien's hand.*)

CHIEN (*shivering*): Please.

GOVERNOR: Remarkable! (*Aside.*) It's so hot and yet his hand is icy cold. He must be an immortal. They never eat cooked food.

CHIEN (*aside*): I eat everything. But I'm worried frigid!

GOVERNOR: A real immortal!

The Narrator: They enter the shelter. Chien is offered the seat of honor. The officials and gentry also sit down in accordance with their rank. Cooling drinks are served. All take them except Chien who shakes his head indicating that he does not want any. Chien is already shivering; he couldn't bear being any cooler.

GOVERNOR: Venerable sir, may I have the honor to know your name?

CHIEN: My name is Chien Chih-chieh.

GOVERNOR: Where is your celestial abode? Who is your divine teacher?

CHIEN (aside): He treats me like a genuine immortal. If the thing were of small consequence, I could afford to fool with him. But it's deadly serious. I must reply in a dignified manner. (*Aloud.*) My humble hut is located in the Purple Cloud Cave of the Purple Gold Mount. My teacher is Li Tai-po. As he was sitting on his straw mattress in deep meditation, suddenly it occurred to him that for six months there has been no rain in Soochow. He ordered me to descend from the clouds, and I came here. Originally, I intended to pray for rain, but the officials of Soochow have committed so much sin that I—

GOVERNOR: What great mercy! You have come here specially. How fortunate for the people of Soochow! Please enlighten me, immortal sir, what method will you use to command the rain?

CHIEN (*aside*): I was going to say that I could do nothing. But he has interrupted me and twisted my sentence. I'd better tell him the truth. ... (*Aloud.*) First, I cannot remove mountains or empty oceans; second, I cannot scatter beans and turn them into soldiers; third, I have no power to call forth the wind or summon the rain. . . .

GOVERNOR: Ah, so you are the great diviner! (*Aside.*) He's just an ordinary Taoist priest who tells fortune with pieces of wood. Well, since he's torn down the decree, we mustn't let him go. If he succeeds in summoning the rain, I can report it to the emperor as my own accomplishment. If he fails, I'll condemn him for defrauding the emperor and have him executed. That will show that we officials are concerned with the people's suffering. No one will be able to say that we have done nothing about the drought. By killing this priest, we shall free ourselves of responsibility. (*Smiling aloud.*) Ah, venerable sir, please apply your magic.

CHIEN: All right. I'll do my best. First, let a table laid with incense be set up in the hall. Your Honor must kowtow in piety. Then I shall practice divination.

GOVERNOR: Servant! Set up a table with incense in the hall.

SERVANT: Yes, Your Honor.

GOVERNOR: Venerable sir, shall we have a look at the praying platform?

CHIEN (*aside*): When I left home today, I intended to see how people pray for rain. But now I myself must do the praying! I'll have a look at the platform anyway. (*Aloud.*) All right.

GOVERNOR: Gentlemen, this way please

All: After you, Your Honor.

The Narrator: They follow the governor to the platform in the front courtyard. Chien, the governor and the gentry mount the platform. Chien walks around on it, then all come down.

GOVERNOR: Venerable sir, is there anything lacking or improper about the platform? We don't want to offend Heaven. Please correct it if anything's amiss.

CHIEN (*aside*): How do I know whether there's anything lacking or amiss? The ones who built the platform must be experts. I'd better not complain. (*Aloud.*) Your Honor, so far as I can see, the platform is fine. Everything is complete. If it does not rain, it will be because the officials

117

have offended Heaven by their wickedness; it has nothing to do with the platform.

GOVERNOR: Oh!

The Narrator: Just then a servant comes to say that the table with incense is laid in the front hall. The governor nods and beckons to the diviner. They walk together into the big hall. An attendant hands long sticks of burning incense to the governor. The governor puts the sticks in the tripod on the table and prays to Heaven. The prefect, two magistrates and all the officials and gentry stand by on both sides. Silence reigns in the hall.

GOVERNOR (*sings*)):
Long sticks of incense burn in the tripod,
The governor kneels in communion with the gods.
Ever since I took office there's been no rain,
So the people inevitably complain.
I'm not bothered by the drought a bit,
All I fear is the emperor's anger.
Pray Heaven be merciful,
Let it rain in Soochow city,
Let there be a bumper harvest,
So that the emperor will not blame me,
And the people will be grateful.
Then I shall be promoted for certain.
(*Speaks.*) Now let the diviner practice his art, please.
CHIEN: Yes, Your Honor.

The Narrator: From his bag Chien takes two divining sticks and a "divination book"—actually a few blank sheets bound together. Of course, no one can read them except Chien. Each of the two pieces of wood has a face and a back. When thrown, if they fall both face upward it's called yang, *or brightness; if both are backs, it's called* yin, *or darkness. If they fall one face and another back, it is considered a good omen.*

Chien places the divination book on the table, waves the sticks over the tripod while murmuring an incantation, then throws them. Three times in succession the sticks fall face upward. Chien is worried, for yang *also means sun. If there's plenty of sunshine it will not rain. Chien turns the leaves of the divination book. Of course it makes no difference*

whether he looks into the book or not. If I predict rain, thinks Chien, I
may be able to get away. He assumes a smiling face.

CHIEN: Congratulations, Your Honor. All's well, all's well.

GOVERNOR: Congratulations for what?

CHIEN: It is written clearly in the book here, "Within three days there
will be rain. No cause for doubt or worry." Isn't that good news?

GOVERNOR: Within three days? What is the exact date?

CHIEN (*aside*)): Today is the first of the sixth month; let me pick the
third day. That will give me the maximum of time. (*Aloud.*) Ah, yes
. . . the third day of the sixth month.

GOVERNOR: What hour?

CHIEN: Three quarters past noon.

GOVERNOR: How much rain?

CHIEN: Three point three inches.

GOVERNOR: Then I shall trouble you to stay at the temple for two days
more and mount the platform to pray for rain on the third. That will
save you the trouble of leaving and coming back again. Servant, call
the abbot.

ABBOT: I'm here. What is Your Honor's order?

GOVERNOR: Abbot, the diviner Chien has come to pray for rain. He will
stay for two days in your temple. Have a comfortable and clean room
ready for him. You must look after him well.

ABBOT: Yes, Your Honor. The back hall is clean and quiet. Sir, this way
please.

CHIEN (*aside*): Too bad! It looks as if I'll really have to produce some
rain! But I'll think of something. I'll make so much trouble for them
that they'll be glad to get rid of me!

The Narrator: Chien follows the old abbot into the back hall. The
room is quiet and clean. Two novices are there to wait upon him. The
vegetarian food is of first quality and prepared by famous cooks. But
Chien is bent on creating trouble.

CHIEN: Come here, novices. (*The two novices come forward. One is*
nine and the other ten years old.)

NOVICE: Sir, what do you want?

CHIEN: Go and tell the abbot that I am a disciple of the poet Li Tai-po
and like to drink. Bring me some wine.

NOVICES: Yes.

119

CHIEN: Wait a minute. Say also that I want meat. I cannot dine without it. If you want me to pray for rain, you must let me eat my fill. If I'm hungry, I cannot succeed. Understand?

NOVICES: Yes.

The Narrator: The novices report to the old abbot. The abbot can get wine easily enough, but meat is not so simple. Because of the serious drought the yamen has ordered that no living thing should be slaughtered in order not to infuriate the Creator who is merciful. The meat shops are closed; fishing boats have been forbidden to cast and haul nets. Where can the abbot get meat? He reports his problem to the yamen. The officials have already decided that if Chien fails to call forth rain, he shall be burned, platform and all. They grant his request for meat without the slightest hesitation. An emergency order is issued to slaughter a pig. Chefs are sent from the yamen to cook for him. Although the dinner is rather late that night, it is truly a feast.

CHIEN (*aside*): Since they have managed it, I might as well eat.

The Narrator: For two days Chien keeps the cooks extremely busy. And he drinks heavily. The novices wait on him every minute. On the second night, he is still drinking. The ten-year-old novice, eager to learn some magic, questions Chien while fanning him.

NOVICE: Sir, how do you pray for rain?

CHIEN: Pray for rain? It's very easy. The main thing is to have a pair of eyes which can analyze the clouds and the wind. For instance, if the sun is shining brightly and the sky is without clouds, the day will be rainless. If the sun is hidden by thick clouds, and drops of water fall from the sky, then it is—

NOVICE: Raining.

CHIEN: Right. You're beginning to get the idea. Let me test you: Suppose the sun is shining and it's raining at the same time. What do you call that weather?

NOVICE: Fickle.

CHIEN: I'll test you again. Suppose there is no sun and the clouds are thick but no drops fall. What is it?

NOVICE: Cloudy.

CHIEN: Right! You already know all that's necessary.

NOVICE (*aside*): He's light-hearted. Doesn't he know that if he fails to bring rain he will be burned to death? I'll tell him and see how merry he remains! (*Aloud.*) Sir, you are joking. Don't you know if you succeed in summoning the rain you will be made an official, but you will be burnt to death if you fail?

The Narrator: Chien is alarmed. A spell of cold sweat makes him sober. How awful, he thinks.

CHIEN (*sings*):
The words shock me so
My soul nearly flies off to heaven
You've only yourself to blame for taking things so easily.
You thought tearing down the imperial decree was nothing but a trifle,
Who knew that you'd be burnt if you couldn't bring the rain!
It's painful and unbearable when
You even slightly scorch a finger.
And now my whole body is to be burnt.
I roll my eyes and clench my teeth—But what's the use of worrying?
The die is cast, better to laugh than to cry.
(*Having made up his mind, Chien assumes a lighthearted air. Aloud.*)
Ha, ha, ha. . . .
NOVICE: What's the matter with you?
CHIEN: The officials are only foolish mortals. They've eyes, but they don't see me in my true self. How ridiculous. Ha, ha, ha. . . .
NOVICE: Sir, If you are laughing, why are there tears in your eyes?
CHIEN (*aside*): My laugh is forced. My grief is genuine. But I mustn't let the novice see through me. (*Aloud.*) You are young; you don't understand. I'm offended that these officials should be disrespectful to me. My tears are tears of anger.
NOVICE: You said you were offended. Anyone who's offended doesn't feel like laughing.
CHIEN: There's an old saying that one can feel offended and amused at the same time. Haven't you heard of it?
ABBOT: Sir, the third day is drawing near. The governor has sent me to see if you want anything else. Please give me your orders.
CHIEN (*aside*): All I want is to live. But it's too late for that now. Well, since I'm going to die, I might as well do it in style. (*Aloud.*) Abbot, I want forty-nine monks and forty-nine priests. Let there be plenty of music while I pray for rain.
ABBOT: Your order will be carried out.

121

CHIEN: And one thing more. I want to borrow your robe and a hat to wear when I mount the platform. After the ceremony I'll return them to you.

ABBOT (*unwillingly*): Yes, yes, of course. (*Aside.*) The robe and hat are sure to be burnt together with you into ashes. But I dare not refuse; otherwise, he will put the blame on me when he fails to call forth the rain.

The Narrator: The old abbot with brows tightly knit goes out and sends his robe and hat to Chien by a novice. Ready to die, Chien drinks profusely. As the proverb has it, time is as precious as gold, but gold cannot buy time. Soon it is the first hour of the third day. A servant comes and tells Chien it is time to mount the platform.

CHIEN: I know. (*Stands up, drunkenly.*) Ah, the house is whirling.
NOVICE: Be careful, sir, walk carefully.

The Narrator: Outside, servants hold the torches high. They help the drunken Chien to the platform. The monks and priests are playing music feverishly. Sounds of drums, big and small wood clappers, gongs, horns, trumpets and cymbals.

CHIEN (*aside*): Lovely. The rich always hire monks and priests to play music at their funerals, but the dead can never hear it. Now I can see and hear my funeral ceremony perfectly. I can consider these officers and officials as my grieving sons and grandsons. It's a fine sight.
GOVERNOR: Sir, your disciples are waiting for you. You are truly merciful to release the people of Soochow from misfortune. We are very grateful.
CHIEN (*aside*): So it's the governor. Detestable creature! He's the one who decreed that I should be burned; yet he speaks as if he were the soul of virtue. I'll deal with him properly if I get the chance.
GOVERNOR: Ah, you have drunk too much. Come, help the diviner to the platform.

The Narrator: Two servants, one on each side, help Chien walk to the north side of the platform. Chien catches sight of the pile of firewood at the base. Heaven, let it rain! he prays. He wonders whether there is still hope. With one servant pulling from above and another pushing him from below, Chien crawls up the ladder. After they have helped Chien reach the platform, which is three stories high, the servants descend.

Chien looks around. On the left are the monks, on the right the priests. Some of his old acquaintances among them nod to him. Chien pulls himself together and walks to the front of the platform. He strikes the table and waves the magic banner. Then he takes up a wooden sword in one hand and makes a magic sign with the other. He faces the northeast and murmurs incantations. Puttering about, he appears to be very busy. Finally he takes up the divining rod. That was a mistake! For when the monks and priests see that Chien means to try his magic power, they all cease playing. Chien is dismayed. He wants them to be absorbed in their music so that no one will see what he is doing. But now all is silent. Everyone is watching him attentively. How awkward! Fortunately, Chien has been in the profession ever since childhood and is an experienced trickster. He begins to chant incantations. He chants and stops, stops and chants again. Not bad. But the summer night is short. In a wink it is dawn. In no time at all, the sun is high. The people who have gathered at the foot of the platform are worried for him. The hum of their voices is heard.

CHIEN (*looking at the east, aside*): What a big sun! Oh, Sun, usually you don't rise so early. You look as if you didn't have a wink of sleep last night either. But what's the use of complaining? While there's still time, let me bid farewell to my family and country. (*He kneels down facing northwest, thinking of his wife and children.*)

The Narrator: Chien has been drinking ever since he came to the temple, and has not had a single moment's sleep. Now that the sun is high, he feels there is no hope of rain. Chien's bravado crumbles; he becomes dispirited. The heat makes him dizzy and the wine makes him sleepy. Chien yawns and kneels on the platform. The next moment he is fast asleep. The monks and priests think the diviner is kneeling there to receive the angels, but wonder why he kneels so long. Next they hear him snoring. Clearly, he is asleep.

PRIEST A: Brother, the master is asleep.
PRIEST B: Brother, I don't think he is asleep. It must be that the angels have failed to come, and his spirit has gone out to invite them. That's why he's snoring.
PRIEST A: I doubt it.
PRIEST B: It's certain. Otherwise, how can he fall asleep with the flames virtually licking his backside?
PRIEST A: True. If he's really asleep, it is something quite remarkable.

123

Anyone who can fall asleep under such circumstances is certainly an immortal.

The Narrator: Time passes. It is already a quarter past noon. The governor, the officials and the gentry, convinced that it is not going to rain, order everyone except Chien to come down from the platform. After this is done, the ladder is removed. Twelve-thirty. The servants wait with torches in hand. At three quarters past noon, if there is still no rain, they are to set fire to the platform. The people do not have the heart to watch Chien be burned to death, and they turn to go. But exactly at three quarters past noon, clouds gather at the northeast and rush forward like ten thousand galloping horses. The wind blows and drives away the heat. All of a sudden, the sun is hidden. It becomes very dark and cool. Seeing that the rain is coming, the people shout, "Don't start the fire!" The governor hastily orders the servants to put out the torches. All rush forward to the platform. The wind blows hard. Chien, fast asleep on the platform, is awakened by the wind.

CHIEN: Ah, it's cold, why don't you cover me with a quilt? Where am I? (*Thinks for a moment and suddenly becomes sober.*) I was praying for rain on the platform. If there was no rain at three quarters past noon, I was to be burned. But I saw with my own eyes that the sun was up and there was no hope at all. Does that mean I'm already dead? Where am I? (*Stands up.*)

The Narrator: As he rises, the people and the officials, the monks and the priests, all cheer. The master's magic power is indeed wonderful. They are sure he was not asleep but that his soul had left his body to consult the gods in Heaven. And now it will rain.

All: Wonderful magic, bravo. . . .

CHIEN (*hears the cheers and looks downward*): Ah, I haven't been burned to death. I see the governor; he certainly wouldn't accompany me to the next world. But why are the people still there? (*Looks up at the sky.*) How dark! Is it really going to rain? This rain-praying trick is actually quite simple. All you have to do is eat your fill, get drunk and go to sleep; then the rain comes. It certainly looks like rain. Now I can hold my head high. Even if it only thunders, I can say that I've succeeded in summoning the wind and the clouds. Let me think. I've got it! I'll shift the whole responsibility to the officials. (*Chien takes up the divining rod from the table. Aloud.*) Let the governor, the prefect, the magistrates, the officers, officials and the gentry put on straw hats and straw capes and kneel before the platform and welcome the rain. If anybody disobeys or offends Heaven, the rain will be taken back and will not come. It will be your own fault; don't let anyone say the diviner is no good!

GOVERNOR: Yes, master.

The Narrator: The governor gives the order. All the officers and officials and gentry put on straw hats and straw capes and kneel before the platform. Chien looks down. All is quiet and orderly. Serves you right, you rotten officials, Chien thinks to himself. He continues to chant and gesticulate. The wind blows harder and harder. It begins to rain heavily. The people rush for shelter. But the officials dare not move. They have to wait for the diviner's order. Their clothes are not warm enough and their knees are beginning to ache from kneeling. The cold rain falls on their backs, and they grow chilled. The wind makes them shiver with cold. They are all drenched like chickens in the soup. The governor is soaked to the bone. Since the rain has already come, he thinks, must we remain kneeling like this? He raises his head to look hopefully at the diviner for permission to stand. Acha! He sneezes. As if in response to his lead, everybody begins to sneeze.

CHIEN (*looks down*): Well, you've had enough for today. This thick robe felt too hot before the rain, but now it's nice and warm. Let me issue my command. (*Aloud.*) The officials and gentry may retire to the shelter.

The Narrator: The officials and gentry hurry to the shelter. The governor sends servants up the platform to help the diviner down and lead him to the shelter. The officials and gentry are full of praise for Chien. Chien changes into dry garments brought from the temple. The officials are still in their wet clothes. An attendant comes in to report.

Attendant: Your Honor, the rain amounts to three point three inches.

GOVERNOR: Good. (*Aside.*) The diviner is truly marvelous. He said three point three inches and it turns out exactly so.

The Narrator: Chien himself cannot believe it. It's too much of a coincidence. Obviously, the weather officer has sent this report just to

125

please them. But the rain is not likely to stop at once. If it continues, it will surpass three point three inches. Chien decides to use another trick to make these scurvy officials believe in him even more.

CHIEN: Ah, Your Honor, originally I intended to summon three point three inches of rain. But since the drought is very serious, I am adding some more.
GOVERNOR: How much?
CHIEN: Thirty-three feet!
GOVERNOR: Oh, no!

The Narrator: The governor exclaims in alarm. Although three point three inches of rain is a bit too little, thirty-three feet would certainly cause a flood.

CHIEN: Your Honor need not worry. The thirty-three feet of rain will not fall all at once. It will rain several times to reach that amount.
GOVERNOR: Good, good.

The Narrator: Chien has covered himself neatly. If the rain does not come up to quota this time, he can always claim that it will the following time, or the next.

GOVERNOR: Master, you have been working hard for several days; you must take a rest. Won't you please come to my humble residence so that I may show my respect?
CHIEN: It's not necessary. My family lives near by. I want to go home to see them.
GOVERNOR: All right. Bring the sedan-chair. See the master home.
SERVANT: Yes, Your Honor.

The Narrator: Chien the Diviner rides in the governor's sedan-chair carried by eight bearers and goes home in triumph. The governor rides in the prefect's chair and the prefect rides in the chair of one of the magistrates. The magistrate is compelled to walk home with the officials and gentry. As there has been no rain for six months, the ditches have become blocked with debris. Water overflows into the streets. The officials and gentry are in a bedraggled state. Some take off their shoes and walk barefoot, some roll up their trousers and wade through the puddles. They look like refugees from a flood.
   This ends our story of praying for rain.

126

POETRY

To most scholars the quiet beauty which epitomized the best of Chinese poetry exists mainly in those poems written during the Tang dynasty (618-906). It would also be generally agreed that the modern period in China has not produced poets of the first rank. The reasons for this lack of distinction in modern poetry may be found in the uncertainty which accompanied China's emergence into the twentieth century, in her "literary revolution" beginning in 1917 when Hu Shih suggested a modern vernacular to replace the classical language in the growing rebellion against feudal traditions in society and classical poetic conventions, and, most recently, in the government's encouragement of writers among its workers, peasants, and soldiers. Certainly, there have been changes in the poetry of modern China as there have been changes in its people and their approach to life. Where once beauty was the only persuasion, argument has been declared a necessary force. Where man once blended with nature to find whatever meaning he needed, there is now an individual energy which may be exemplified by a few to show the flow of a single thought which unites all men.

The poems collected here are intended to suggest the great variety in poetry which has been written in China during the past fifty-odd years. Some of it has a place in the poetry of the modern world; much of it is undistinguished. With reference to the most recent Chinese poetry, however, one must remember two things: politics comes before art; the people who write the poems are as significant as the calibre of the poetry being written. This volume, therefore, includes the work of poets such as Mao Tse-tung and Kuo Mo-jo, who have admired classical styles, as well as the poems of common men such as Yang Yang-tse. Together it becomes the poetry of modern China.

Interesting to Western readers who tend to divorce world leaders from literary circles, Mao Tse-tung (1893-   ) is one of the most significant poets in modern China. As a leader of his country, he has always placed a high priority upon art and literature, and in his own poetry he shows an extensive knowledge of the classics which he uses to celebrate the value of individual man against a background of nature's inescapable grandeur. Ai Ching, the pen name of Chiang Hai-cheng

(1910-   ), came from a wealthy family and studied in France before travelling to North China where he became a teacher at the Lu Hsun Academy of Arts. He felt the revolutionary force in the poetry of Whitman, Rimbaud, and Mayakovsky. Like Whitman he learned from the common man and in his poems shows the intensity of his feelings. He was at the height of his career when he attended the Yenan Forum in 1942. Continuing to write, edit, and promote young poets, he was criticized by the Party as a "rightist" during the late 1950's but was cleared in 1961.

Soong Ching-ling (1890-   ), the wife of Sun Yat-sen and sister of Madame Chiang Kai-shek has been extremely active in political, cultural, and humane affairs since the late 1920's. In 1951 she was awarded the Stalin Prize. Yuan Shui-po (1916-   ) also wrote under the name of Ma Fan-to and has gained considerable reputation as a satirical poet who combines humor and simple, ordinary expressions to burlesque the follies of man. Little known before World War II, he has since used his bitter comedy to discuss world affairs. Ho Ching-chih (1924-   ) also has a recognized reputation in literature. As one of the authors of the celebrated opera, *The White-haired Girl,* he shared a Stalin Prize for literature. He has also served on the editorical board of *The Drama Monthly.* Yang Yang-tse represents those workers, peasants, and soldiers whom Mao encourages to express their feelings in both poetry and prose.

Four Poems by Mao Tse-tung

Farewell to the God of Plague*

After reading in the Remin Ribao of June 30, 1958, of how schisto-somiasis was wiped out in Yukiang County, so many fancies crossed my mind that I could not sleep. In the warm morning breeze, as sunlight fell on my window, I looked towards the distant southern sky and in my happiness wrote the following lines.

—the author

Green streams, blue hills—but all to what avail?
This tiny germ left even Hua To[1] powerless;
Weeds choked hundreds of villages, men wasted away;
Thousands of households dwindled, phantoms sang with glee.
On earth I travel eighty thousand *li* a day,[2]
Ranging the sky I see a myriad rivers.
Should the Cowherd[3] ask tidings of the God of Plague,
Say: past joys and woe have vanished with the waves.

* Reprinted from *Chinese Literature*, No. 1 (1960), p. 4. (Translated by Gladys Yang.) ,
1. A great physician of the Three Kingdoms Period.
2. Referring to the rotation of the earth.
3. According to Chinese mythology the Milky Way is a celestial river where a cowherd lives. By association, the Cowherd here also refers to the Chinese peasants.

The spring wind blows amid ten thousand willow branches,
Six hundred million in this Sacred Land all equal Yao and Shun.[4]
Flowers falling like crimson rain swirl in waves at will.
Green mountains turn to bridges at our wish;
Gleaming mattocks fall on heaven-high peaks;
Mighty arms move rivers, rock the earth.
We ask the God of Plague: "Where are you bound?"
Paper barges aflame and candle-light illuminate the sky.[5]

4. Two ancient sage kings.
5. Burning paper barges and candles was a traditional rite for sending off spirits.

The Long March[1]*

—a lu shih[2]

The Red Army fears not the trials of a distant march;
To them a thousand mountains, ten thousand rivers are nothing;
To them the Five Ridges[3] ripple like little waves,
And the mountain peaks of Wumeng[4] roll by like mud balls.
Warm are the cloud-topped cliffs washed by the River of Golden Sand,[5]
Cold are the iron chains that span the Tatu River.[6]
The myriad snows of Minshan[7] only make them happier,
And when the Army has crossed, each face is smiling.

---

* Reprinted from *Nineteen Poems* (Peking: Foreign Languages Press, 1958), p. 18.

1. In October, 1934, the Red Army set out from the Kiangsi base and marched for 25,000 *li* or about 8,000 miles, through the provinces of Fukien, Kiangsi, Kwangtung, Hunan, Kwangsi, Kweichow, Yunnan, Sikang, Szechuan and Kansu. In October, 1935, it reached the anti-Japanese base in north Shensi.

2. A *lu shih* has eight lines with seven characters in each.

3. The Five Ridges stretch across the provinces of Hunan, Kwangtung, Kwangsi and Kweichow.

4. A mountain range between Yunnan and Kweichow.

5. A river in the upper reaches of the Yangtse in Yunnan.

6. A river in Szechuan. Luting Bridge over this river was made of thirteen iron chains supporting loose wooden planks.

7. A mountain range in Chinghai, Kansu, Shensi and Szechuan.

Snow[1]*

—to the melody Shen Yuan Chun

This is the scene in that northern land;
A hundred leagues are sealed with ice,
A thousand leagues of whirling snow.
On either side of the Great Wall
One vastness is all you see.
From end to end of the great river
The rushing torrent is frozen and lost.
The mountains dance like silver snakes,
The highlands roll like waxen elephants,
As if they sought to vie with heaven in their height;
    And on a sunny day
You will see a red dress thrown over the white,
    Enchantingly lovely!

Such great beauty like this in all our landscape
Has caused unnumbered heroes to bow in homage.
But alas these heroes! —Chin Shih Huang and Han Wu Ti[2]

* Reprinted from *Nineteen Poems* (Peking: Foreign Languages Press, 1958), pp. 22-23.

1. In August, 1945, the author went to Chungking for peace negotiations with the Kuomintang. There he met Mr. Liu Ya-tse, who asked him for a poem. Mr. Liu wrote another in return, in the same metre. (The name of this melody, which literally means Shen Garden Spring, is taken from the garden of the Princess of Shenshui who lived in the late Han dynasty. When a poem in the *tzu* form is said to be set to a certain melody, that means that it follows a specified traditional pattern. The name of the melody has no other bearing on the poem.)

2. Chin Shih Huang, first emperor of Chin, reigned from 246 to 210 B.C.; Han Wu Ti, or Emperor Wu of the Han dynasty, reigned from 140 to 87 B.C.

Were rather lacking in culture;
Rather lacking in literary talent
Were the emperors Tang Tai Sung and Sung Tai Tsu;[3]
   And Genghis Khan,[4]
Beloved Son of Heaven for a day,
Only knew how to bend his bow at the golden eagle.
   Now they are all past and gone:
To find men truly great and noble-hearted
We must look here in the present.

Mao's note: The highlands are those of Shensi and Shansi.

3. Tang Tai Tsung, or Emperor Tai Tsung of Tang, reigned from 627 to 649; Sung Tai Tsu, first emperor of Sung, reigned from 960 to 976.

4. The famous Mongol conqueror who reigned from 1206 to 1227.

133

Swimming[1]*

—to the melody *Shui Tiao Keh Tou*[2]

I have just drunk the waters of Changsha,
And eaten the fish of Wuchang;[3]
Now I am crossing the thousand-mile long river,
Looking afar to the open sky of Chu.[4]
I care not that the wind blows and the waves beat;
It is better than idly strolling in a courtyard.
Today I am free!
It was on a river that the Master said:
"Thus is the whole of Nature flowing! "[5]

* Reprinted from *Nineteen Poems* (Peking: Foreign Languages Press, 1958), pp. 28-29.
1. In May, 1956, the author swam the Yangtse River from Wuchang to Hankow. That summer he swam it a second and third time from Hanyang to Wuchang. This poem refers to his first crossing.
2. *Shui Tiao* was an ancient tune; *Keh Tou* means the first section.
3. A folk song of the Three Kingdoms period ran:
   We would rather drink the waters of Chienyeh
   Than eat the fish of Wuchang.
The people of Wu were opposed to the removal of the capital from Chienyeh, present-day Nanking, to Wuchang.
4. Wuchang was a part of the ancient land of Chu.
5. *The Analects of Confucius* record that when the page came to the bank of a river he exclaimed: "Thus is the whole of Nature flowing ceaselessly day and night!"

134

Masts move in the swell;
Tortoise and Snake are still.[6]
Great plans are being made;
A bridge will fly to join the north and south,
A deep chasm become a thoroughfare;
Walls of stone will stand upstream to the west[7]
To hold back Wushan's clouds and rain,[8]
And the narrow gorges will rise to a level lake.
The mountain goddess, if she is still there,
Will be startled to find her world so changed.

6. The Tortoise Hill at Hanyang and the Snake Hill at Wuchang face each other across the Yangtse. The Yangtse Bridge is constructed between these two hills.

7. Referring to a dam to be built further upstream.

8. A famous mountain in the Yangtse Gorges. Legend has it that the goddess of this mountain controls the clouds and the rain.

Protect Peace*

by Ai Ching

I

In the morning when I awakened
I heard the sound of birds a-singing;
getting up, I pushed open the window
yet did not catch a glimpse of the singers;
only between the branches of a tree
seeing the dawn breaking, dew-drops between
the leaves glinting with the light of morning;
through the evergreen creepers on the wall
came a little breeze, gently moving the leaves;

and on the other side of the wall
lies a maternity hospital; listen!
on this clear morning, comes
the sound of faint but touching cries
of some new-born babe; another new life
has come into the world;

and quietly in the lane outside
road sweepers are cleaning the road
so well; passing them, flocks of
school children, wearing every kind
of colored clothing, hand in hand and

* Reprinted from Rewi Alley, translator and editor, *Peace Through the Ages* (Peking, 1954), pp. 151-158.

with laughing voices, go to this local
primary school; farmers come with two
handcarts, filled with the fruits
of their labors, carrying something
of the dew of the suburbs, into the
vegetable market!

factory whistles blow
sending out their happy summons;
from this side and then that,
come many such sounds, echoing each other and
among the high poplars, stand factory
chimneys; from them comes smoke
like long tails of horses racing;
numberless workmen, with voices
raised, and with swift strides, go
along the roads leading to the chimneys
and enter the factory gates;
on the power lines, insulators
gleam white; like so many flowers
threaded together;
hung in the blue of the heavens
throwing the reflections of the sun
down on the streets;

a bunch of little girls
riding bicycles, facing
the sun,
with happy shouts, speed
over the ground;

on the main street, busy
people and vehicles
flow along like the waters of a river
sending out all the sounds
of a great city, blended together
like those of some great symphony
orchestra; songs of labor,
a choir of production;

II

this is a city that has come back
to life; a city liberated from the
grasp of the enemy; one that has
been stamped over by the aggressors,
suffering so much disgrace; this city
is like the body of a man, torn by
the claws of wild beasts, with wounds
that have just been healed;

this city
through the long night of tyranny
became paralyzed; now
it has begun to awaken, and be itself
through the efforts of the great
working class and its enthusiasm
for construction; now
has this city begun to lift its head;

daily, workers
dig deeply down into the earth
and descend to repair sewers,
clearing out the refuse of ages,
connecting all drainage;
daily, workers
with their welding sets, sit
through the night without rest
in the middle of flashing sparks
welding the tram tracks;
daily, workers
on the ruins of houses
demolished by war
start to build up homes again;
if you go to the suburbs of the city
to the wide fields or country places
nearby, or else to further localities
all over the liberated areas, in liberated
cities, villages, there you will see
all the strength of the people's hands
healing the wounds of war;

this the people's will for peace, with
all they have done, directed
towards this end;
our wars, over all the past hundred
years, all directed towards the victory
of peace; yet not the kind of peace
that comes from kneeling and begging,
not that which comes from weeping;
peace
not just some blessing showered from heaven,
peace
not just something that comes
out of its own free will like doves;
for us peace is something won
putting forth all the stubborn strength
of a great people; this peace
cost us much blood; for this peace
have we sacrificed tens of millions
of lives; so that our country has come
to understand the value of peace; for
those who have been through the long
and evil dreams of the dark night
know how to love
the beauty of a quiet morning;

III

but
one thinks of a great building
supported by shining columns; yet
with these columns inwardly eaten
by white ants; then looks towards
the war-makers of the world, stealthily
sharpening their weapons, waiting
for that moment when people are unprepared
then swooping down for murder;

in Washington
in London
leaders of the old gang
sit; like slave-traders
or opium-runners, discussing
all their secret plans; how
to evolve more dreadful weapons
that will murder more men, how
to occupy more military bases;
how to get their munitions taken
by reactionary groups in foreign
countries; how to suppress
the people, send out secret agents,
buy up the traitors of the people,
smash the construction of New
Democracies; using as their tools
gold dollars, slander, murder,
atoms, gas and germs; together
with those scamps Tito, Rajk, Trotskyites
who are their most useful weapons,
for all the shameful business
of starting new wars, to throw
all the people of the world into
the fiery pit, so that they, the gangsters,
may expand their colonial empire,
all the world becoming their slaves,
and so let more profit come
to the merchants of death; none
could be more brutal
and greedy than these, worse scoundrels
than Hitler even; that they should remain
alive, a disaster for all men;

IV

resist
these loafers and bandits,
oppose their intrigue for new wars,
oppose pacts against the people
in the Atlantic and in the Pacific;

all peace fighters must combine; all
oppressed peoples join together; so shall
all these people of the five continents
seeking the welfare of mankind
be united
round the Soviet Union and her allies
round the figure of the Great Stalin
and the everlastingly victorious people
of the USSR; with the people of China
who have stood up and those of
the New Democracies;
together
we will put forth all our strength
to halt war;

all the workers of the world, unite
to use together the strength of our
arms; to change the fate of humanity;
not allowing the enemy to push us
into the abyss; soldiers of the imperialist
countries, American soldiers
British soldiers
French soldiers
this is the moment for you to awake;
the wounds on your body have only just
healed; do you still wish to die?
you have been
to the Philippine Islands,
you have been to Greece,
you have been to Iran,
you have been to China,
and also Japan; except for
gaining the hatred of millions of people
what exactly have you gained?
Nothing else!
Nothing at all!
While the medals on MacArthur's breast
were glittering
tens of thousands of you were wiped out;

and we—
we are numberless;
and we are all as one body
the peoples of the whole world
who do not want war;

but should there be a day
when war does come, then there
will be no question of fear; we are
ready for any struggle needed; and we have
complete confidence in victory;

our hungry guns,
our ammunition so full of hatred
our angry though now silent-lying
explosives; all of these
are waiting for the aggressor
who would dare to invade
our homeland.

"The Nameless Nine"*

by Soong Ching-Ling

Here in the heart of our land,[1]
   in times gone by, were
   nine women of China whose names
   are lost with the years, who would
   not kneel, nor bow their heads,
   but who fought for the people,
   giving their all;
      and here too,
      in later times did I see
      the host of those who came
      after them, aflame with the fire
      of revolution; binding up their wounds,
      marching, struggling on
      to the new song of mankind;
      and there were those whose names too
      have not survived, but who for their fellows
      gave all they had;
so in this place,
with the rulers now the people,
we build this monument to the unknown nine,
giving them honor, and not only them
but all Chinese women who today
unforgetful of the past look into the future,
build for it
and for all people.

* Rewi Alley, ed., *The People Sing* (Peking, 1958), pp. 359-360.
1. Refers to the city of Wuhan, Hupeh Province, where the nameless nine were buried.

"The Mothers' Problem"*

by Yang Yang-tse

Almost everyone
  has a pretty good mother,
  so it is quite natural
  that I have one too;
  so did I finally decide
  to ask for leave to return home
  and see her, after
  our ten years' separation;
    recently

    many letters had come to me
    from relatives, saying
    reproachfully:
    a man like you was stupid,
    casting off the family
    relationship; completely
    unconcerned with parental
    affairs. . . .

The Szeming Hills first
came into view, then those
of Tientai; a drizzling rain
covered the blue mountains
in a haze all around me, it all

* Reprinted from Rewi Alley, ed., *The People Sing* (Peking, 1958), pp. 361-371.

144

looking like some foolish
landscape scroll; and while
I tramped along, I pondered
on what I should say to her
first; the rain wetted
my cotton uniform, and with my hand
I kept my pocket as dry as I could,
for in it was a diary
and in the diary a picture of Lao Liang,
a picture that had been stained
with blood; I fearing it would
become yellow if the rain wet it;
at length I came to the top
of the pass over the hills, staying
awhile in the rest house there
where tea was sold, taking out my diary
to dry it a bit in the wind
and involuntarily taking out
the picture; looking at the round eyes,
pointed chin; it was stubborn, gay
Lao Liang, Liang Ah-hsiang;
the picture looked ten years younger
than he actually was; he seemed
the same carefree lad as he was
when we were kids together,
both running over this path
on this selfsame mountain; sleeping
at noon on the stone benches
of this rest house; who would have thought
after these ten years he would be
a fallen hero, his name inscribed
on the Huai-Hai battle memorial
and that were it not for him, I would not
be able to return to this rest house today,
unable to come
to find my mother again . . .

it was that last stage
of the Huai-Hai battle
when Lao Liang was supporting us
as we went into the attack;

then the enemy was reinforced
with a new regiment, so that
counter-attack developed on both
flanks; Lao Liang led
the third company; three platoons
became three sections, and three sections
reduced to nine fighters only;
Lao Liang telephoned me
asking us to do our job, and he
would go on trying to cover us;
just then, a bullet made in U.S.A.
pierced this picture and tore
into the chest of Lao Liang.

and somehow I let my finger
go through the hole in the picture,
thinking of his straightness,
trueness, his strength of character
like that of men born amongst
the mountains; of his steadfastness
like that of other sons
of the poor; he pressed one hand
against the wound, laid on the ground
still fighting, directing
his eight men for over an hour,
even threatening with his pistol
the bearers who came to carry him off
to the rear; using a barrier of dead enemy
bodies to halt the attack;

then when all was over and before
we had combed the prisoners even,
I went to look for him,
finding him stretched out
on a bamboo bed, blood
staining his clothes; his face
showing a greenish white,
medical workers washing
and bandaging him as he lay
eyes closed; "Lao Liang!
Lao Liang!" I said, and when

he heard my voice he opened
his eyes and said, "From here
to Szeming Hills, the road now
becomes easy; even south
of the Yangtse, there will be
no very great battle to fight;
I am sad that I cannot work
for more years; my task
must be handed over to you all . . .

in the future when you go
back to our home village,
I hope you will have the chance
to see my mother for me, telling her
that I am well—that I
have done my best . . ."
then from
his pocket he took out
this blood-stained picture,
asking me to pass it over
to his mother; and he held
my hand with his cold fingers
for the last time . . .

it was in the valley
of the blue mountains, that I found her—
her hair as white as snow; it was not
my mother, for first I came to the home
of Lao Liang;
his mother lifted her head
blankly, standing under
the low eaves of their home,
her sunken eyes staring,
thin lips, and powerful chin,
so much thinner than when
I had known her, but yet
she looked like Lao Liang;
I called her "Ma"—and after
some time, she suddenly realized
and said, "So . . . it is you
who have come back," and starting

147

to weep, her tears bigger than beans,
saying, "Before my eyes
you two played together,
grew up together, went away
together to fight the Japanese
and make a revolution; day
and night always fearing the worst
for you; remembering that when
he went away from home, he said
to me, he wanted to be like
that hero who saved his mother,
asking me not to worry about him;
now I see you come back, but I'll
never see him!"

I sat with her, face to face,
trying to console her with
a long story; calling her "Ma"
many times, both for myself
and the dead Lao Liang;
several times I thought
of pulling out the picture of Lao Liang,
but when my fingers touched the hole
I dared not . . .

at last I invited her
to come to supper at my home,
and then drying my own eyes
went to look for my mother,
finding her also under the low eaves
and she too looking at me, a passing soldier,
without recognition; but for me
there could be no mistake,
and I shouted out, "Ma!"
and then she said, "So . . . it is you,
it is you who have come back!"
and the man she had dreamed to see
for the last ten years was there
with her; and then she filled
with laughter, smiles turning up
the corners of her mouth;

it had been so long that I had not
seen her! Indeed she was much older,
her eyes not so good, but however dim
they could well recognize me,
for they were the eyes that had
followed me to manhood; her face
was so full of gladness; but like
the mother of Lao Liang, her mouth
was a little shrunken and she seemed
more silent; looking at me more,
speaking less; she did say though
that I was much taller, my face
longer; something that had not
occurred to me, for over the years
no one had told me this.
Now the whole village was excited to hear
I had come back, and I was like
a grain rolling into an ant hill;
neighbors from all sides, from
the furthest ends of the village,
surrounded me,
as if they were coming to see
some bit of drama; the old relations
said I still talked my native dialect
very well; all the lads in blue jackets
were especially interested
in my khaki uniform; my mother
killed a chicken, and was busy
cooking it; my brother-in-law
brought two catties of Shaohsing wine;
relatives and friends made me sit
as guest of honor; when he heard
that Lao Liang's mother would also
come, we all waited; and my brother-in-law
asked me, saying, "We have heard
that you have married; when was it?"
And I answered, "No—never!"
my sister interrupted, stove tongs
in hand, "Some said you have already
got sons!" And I replied,
"Who says this is boasting for me!"

149

Then the family head said,
"Some say that men like you
become like monks, or as if
you had joined a secret society;
think of nothing,
desire nothing,
even giving up your own mother
and your father; is this
true or not?" And I replied,
"If so, we are surely a
funny sort of people!" Then
taking out the picture of Lao Liang
and pointing to the hole in it
with my finger, I said, "Many comrades
have given up their lives
for the parents, the wives and children
of the hundreds of millions of China,
so that they could stand up
on their own feet; live better;
no one of us has ever said
we do not want our families";
then the faces showed a little tension
as they crowded around the picture
under the lamp, asking me to tell
about it; so that I told them
in detail the story of Lao Liang
from the very beginning; all
the good things he did
for the people, and while all were
absorbed in the story, suddenly
at the back of the crowd someone
discovered the mother
of Lao Liang; and involuntarily
all stood up, really because
of a true spontaneous respect
for her; so we invited her
to sit and take supper;
she said politely
she had already eaten, but now
she had heard the story of her son
and all my trying to hide it from her

was useless; I forced myself
to put the picture in
her withered hand, and she came
near to the lamp, peering at it,
she touched his hair,
his eyes, and then the hole
of the bullet with her finger
and his field glasses in the picture;
and I said, my voice hoarse with emotion,
trying to comfort her,
"If it were not for your son
I would never be able to see
my mother again; your son
has helped me, but I have done
nothing for you";

she said, as she dried her eyes,
"What did Ah-hsiang say to you
when he was dying?
Tell me everything!"
And I told her how he had asked me
to come back home and see his mother
for him; how he had asked me
to tell her not to grieve and said
he had done his best; and I said
to her
"It is surely your glory
to have had such a son; you
have suffered so much
all your life, and now
you can live better; he wanted
to save you and a thousand of others,
poor mothers of China,
from the bitterness of hell"; she
lifted her head and looked at me
solemnly, and nodded saying,
"Yes, when I see you it seems
that I see the daybreak; it is true
it is just like that old story of him
who gave his life to save his mother;
the poor have begun to stand up

and to change; land is being
given to them; the government
grants me a pension; I hope that
in the future, no one will have to eat
grass and bran; you have done
what you have set out to do;
I shall not feel sad again";

two mothers
with two pairs of eyes
and the same loving hearts
looking at me,
holding their bowls in their hands
and eating slowly,
and I was filled with happiness,
the more so now because
no longer did anyone ask me:
did you Communists
love your parents or not?

Sanmen Gorge*

by Ho Ching-chih

See Sanmen Gorge,[1] its three gates open wide—
"The Yellow River rushes down drom heaven"[2]—
Dire Gate of Gods, gaunt Gate of Ghosts,
And the sheer precipice of the Gate of Men.
The Yellow River thunders at these gates,
Gales sweep a thousand leagues to the Eastern Sea.

See Sanmen Gorge, its three gates open wide;
East flows the Yellow River, ever east;
Kunlun is high, Mount Mang is low,
Where Great Yu's horse trod, green moss grows;[3]
The horse has gone, no house remains,
Only a dressing-table by the open gates.[4]

* Reprinted from *Chinese Literature*, No. 8 (1960), pp. 3-5. (Translated by Gladys Yang.)

1. Sanmen (Three Gates) is a most perilous gorge of the Yellow River, the turbulent stream widely known as "China's Sorrow" which has caused so much death and destruction down the centuries. Since liberation, many steps have been taken to tame the river. In April, 1957, work started on the first key project—the vast water conservancy scheme at the Sanmen Gorge in Honan. The huge dam built to regulate the flow of the river detains enormous amounts of water in the reservoir above it. The Sanmen Gorge project has ended the threat of serious floods on the lower Yellow River, and ensures the needs of irrigation and navigation.
2. A line from a poem by Li Po, a famous Tang Dynasty poet.
3. At the Gate of Ghosts there is a hollow in the rock shaped like a hoof print. Legend has it that this was made when Great Yu, the pacifier of floods in Chinese mythology, rode this way.
4. Not far from the gorges stands a platform of rock known as the "dressing-table."

For centuries the dressing-table has stood,
But where is she who should use it?
Darkling clouds dim the bright mirror,
Muddy waters swallow up her golden head-dress;
Whole generations of boatmen die in despair,
The Yellow River's daughter neglects her toilet.

Come to your dressing-table, lady, come!
White is the hair of the Yellow River's daughter;
Leagues long, her white hair streams out in despair
Over the perennial floods of the Yellow River.
She climbs the gorge, she asks the Eastern Sea:
    Will youth come back to me?

Will youth come back?
Pan Ku's[5] new heirs are here!
Red flags are flying, a new world is born.
We trample on the tomes of all past history,
With a huge brush we write a brave new page—
    Socialism—here we come!

We come, we come!
Kunlun takes fright and Mount Mang is aghast.
We unfold the mighty plan to tame this torrent,
First grasp the Yellow River by the waist,
Raze the Gate of Gods, sweep off the Gate of Ghosts,
Three crashes and the Gate of Men is dust!

See Sanmen Gorge now that its gates are gone
Tomorrow a great dam will loom up there.
We must ask Li Po to revise that line,
"The Yellow River rushes from our hands."
A galaxy of stars will fall from heaven,
Clear water will follow the breeze to the Eastern Sea.

It will flow to the Eastern Sea and back again,
The river's age-old crimes must be redeemed;
The Yellow River's daughter grows young again,

5. Man's earliest ancestor, the mythical figure who separated heaven and earth.

Her dressing-table is set in order for her,
In blue sky a bright mirror hangs,
The water of the lake throws back its brightness,
Come, Yellow River's daughter, dress your hair!

Come, lady, dress your hair
And take your choice
Of all the hundred flowers of spring,
Of this far-flung countryside lovely as brocade.
The workers on the Sanmen Dam are young,
For them the Gate of Happiness is open;
Shoulder to shoulder, hand in hand they sing
Of youth that will endure for ever more!

Three Poems by Yuan Shui-po

A Young Sudanese*

At the Peace Conference in Vienna
I met a handsome young Negro;
Often we sat together,
Asia and Africa, shoulder to shoulder.

His face was black as night,
His eyes shone like the stars
—Bright and friendly, yet at times
Burning with a furious anger.

He was from the Sudan, he said,
East of the Sahara Desert;
He drew me a map of Africa,
Sketching in deftly his country's borders.

Not one of these distant lands
Had escaped the white man's lash;
Marking place after place with his red pencil,
He said: "Much blood flowed here.

"We have English hangmen, French butchers,
And Truman's 'Point Four Program';
They plunder and murder openly,
Or conceal their violence behind elaborate words.

* Reprinted from *Soy Sauce and Prawns* (Peking: Foreign Languages Press, 1963), pp. 16-17. (Translated by Sidney Shapiro.)

"Tanks have levelled hundreds of homes,
Charged barbed wire surrounds our villages;
In the night women listen fearfully
To the yelps of patriot-hunting police dogs.

"Bomber runways cut through our fields,
Deadly warships clog our bays;
The warmongers want to turn our Africa
Into one huge military base."

"But," said the young Negro decisively,
"Force cannot make us change our aims;
Africans will never be Wall Street's cannon fodder;
We shall strike off colonialism's chains."

He showed me a golden commemorative badge,
Stamped with the image of Mao Tse-tung;
"We agree completely with your Chairman Mao,"
He announced, gazing at it smilingly.

At the Peace Conference in Vienna
I met a young Negro with eyes like stars;
Whenever courage and pride are mentioned,
I think of this patriot from the Sudan.

February 1953

"Artistic Freedom" *

A middle-aged man kneels on the curb
In London's Trafalgar Square,
Drawing pictures with colored chalks,
The dirty pavement his art gallery.

Cold wind ruffles his sparse hair,
Fog seeps through his muffler;
Passers-by toss him glances of contempt, or pity,
But not a penny falls in his upturned old hat.

A beggar who's learned to paint?
Or a painter who's learned to beg?
"Artistic freedom," a tenet of the "Free World,"
Includes the freedom to decorate its gutters.

Of course, fortune blesses other favorites, too,
Even more creative freedom is found in the city zoo;
There, "paintings" by black apes form an exhibition grand,
Hairy simian paws have replaced Gainsborough's hand.

June 1957

* Reprinted from *Soy Sauce and Prawns* (Peking: Foreign Languages Press, 1963), p. 26.

Museums—London, New York, and Points West*

Rooms full of loot
From the east, from the west,
Carved Buddhist hands
By stone horse-heads rest;
Jewels and porcelain
—Yuan Ming Yuan,[1]
Ancient skull fragments
—The Peking Man,
Great art from Paris,
Mummies Egyptian,
Embroidery, murals,
That beggar description;
What if your own country
Is culturally drab?
Just reach into others
And what you like—grab.

February 1960

---

* Reprinted from *Soy Sauce and Prawns* (Peking: Foreign Languages Press, 1963), p. 33.
1. Magnificent Ching dynasty palace in the Peking suburbs pillaged by British and French troops in 1860.

DRAMA

With the growing influence of the West upon the art and literature of China, no changes were more distinctive than those in drama and theatre. The production of *Uncle Tom's Cabin* in 1907 introduced both Western staging and the concept of a spoken drama. Ten years later the initiators of the "literary revolution" found great satisfaction in the realistic plays of Ibsen. As more Chinese intellectuals either studied abroad or read widely among Western writers, the spoken drama (as distinct from the traditional Chinese opera) became an accepted part of Chinese theatre.

Generally acknowledged as the most significant playwright in modern China, Tsao Yu (pseudonym of Wan Chai-pao, 1910-　) wrote six major plays during the 1930's and early 1940's. *Thunderstorm* (1934) is his first play and, like the others, suggests his admiration of Western literature from the Greeks through Shakespeare to Ibsen and O'Neill. *Sunrise* (1936), his second play, is a story of prostitution and of a young girl who lived the life of a prostitute, facing its horrors and finally accepting death. *Wilderness* (1937), which forms a vague trilogy with the earlier plays, deals with a peasant's violent revenge upon an evil landlord. Although *Thunderstorm* had been tremendously successful and the others had received a popular success, the Communist critics had not been satisfied. With *Transformation* (1940), which dealt with a corrupt military hospital that was transformed into a well-organized unit, these critics could feel that Tsao Yu's political ideas were progressing properly. *Peking Man* (1940) was a much better play, treating as it did the emergence of a new order and the decay of the old way of life in China, but less acceptable to the Communist critics. They felt the same way about Tsao Yu's dramatization of Pa Chin's novel, *The Family* (1941), in which he showed the evils of the feudalistic family system in China but did not suggest Communism as the solution. His next important play, *Bright Skies* (1954) showed a distinct change in Tsao Yu's work. A thoroughly anti-American play concerned with germ warfare in Korea, this play lacked any suggestion of the dramatist's former talents. By the early 1960's he was reported writing historical dramas, perhaps as a means to escape the strict Party censorship. With

161

the emphasis on contemporary man demanded during the Cultural Revolution Tsao Yu seemingly stopped writing for the stage.

As originally written, *Thunderstorm* included a prologue and an epilogue which take place in a Catholic Hospital two years after the action of the play and dramatize the pathetic existence of Chou Pu-yuan and Ma Shih-ping, those who first sinned. Of the two Greek themes present in the play—the Phaedra-Hippolytus love and the House of Atreus concept of sins of the past visited upon the present—the epilogue shows the furries still at work. Greek concern for Unity of Time and Unity of Action is also followed. The version of the play included here, however, has undergone some changes by Communist censors. Western music (the epilogue ended with Bach's Mass in B Minor) and Western philosophy were eliminated as were all references to religion. Chou Pu-yuan no longer reads Buddhist scriptures. Lu Ta-hai is demoted from foreman to worker to glorify the Communist worker. Fate, however, which the Communists have regarded as feudalistic, remains strong in the play. In a review of *Thunderstorm* in the *Drama Gazette* (*Hsi Chü Pao*), August 20, 1954, the actors were urged to give prominence to the "positive social meaning," the "truth in history," in the play. By emphasizing Lu Ta-hai, who "opposes the corruption of the bourgeois family," and playing Fan Yi as a victim of "the oppressors" rather than as a mentally disturbed person, the director eliminated some of the "unhealthy elements of the script." For Western readers, however, the play is reasonably free from the Communist interpretation of the "evil dregs of the feudalistic past." It is, rather, a frequently moving and powerful illustration of a concept which unifies all men.

Thunderstorm*

by Tsao Yu
Translated By Wang Tso-liang
and A. C. Barnes

THE CHARACTERS

CHOU PU-YUAN, 55, *chairman of the board of directors of a coal-mining company*
CHOU FAN-YI, 35, *his wife*
CHOU PING, 28, *his son by a former marriage*
CHOU CHUNG, 17, *his younger son by his present wife*
LU KUEI, 48, *his servant*
LU SHIH-PING *or* LU MA, 47, *Lu Kuei's wife, employed as a servant in a school*
LU TA-HAI, 27, *her son by a former marriage, a miner*
LU SSU-FENG, 18, *her daughter by her present husband, a maid at the Chous'*
Various other servants in the house

*   *   *

ACT I—*In the Chous' drawing-room.* TIME—*a sultry summer morning.*
ACT II—*The same.* TIME—*the afternoon of the same day.*
ACT III—*In a little inner room at the Lus'.* TIME—*ten o'clock that evening.*
ACT IV—*The same as Act I.* TIME—*after midnight that night.*

* Reprinted from *Thunderstorm* (Peking: Foreign Languages Press, 1958).

163

ACT ONE

It is a summer morning in the drawing-room at the Chous'. A door on the left leads to the dining-room and one on the right to the study. A third door stands open in the middle, and through the wire-gauze screen in front of it the shady green of the trees in the garden can be seen and the shrilling of cicadas can be heard. An old-fashioned bureau stands against the wall to the right of the door, covered with a yellow runner. A number of objets d'art are arranged on it and also, conspicuously out of place, an old photograph. On the right-hand wall is the fireplace, with a clock on the mantelpiece, and on the wall above hangs an oil painting. In front of the fireplace are two armchairs. To the left of the center door is a glass case full of curios, with a stool in front of it. The left-hand corner is occupied by a sofa with several plump, satin-covered cushions on it. In front of this stands as a low table with a cigarette-box and ash-trays on it. In the center of the stage and slightly to the right are two small sofas with a round table between them, and on this table are a cigar-box and a fan.

The curtains are new, the furniture is spotless, and all the metal fittings are gleaming.

It is close and oppressive, and the room is stuffy. Outside is a grey, overcast sky. A thunderstorm seems imminent.

When the curtain rises, Lu Ssu-feng is standing at a table against the center wall with her back to the audience, filtering medicine and wiping her perspiring face every now and then. Her father, Lu Kuei, is polishing the silver cigarette-box on the low table in front of the sofa.

Ssu-feng is a healthy, rosy-cheeked girl of eighteen with a well-developed figure and large white hands. When she walks, the movement of her over-developed breasts is plainly visible under her clothes. Her silk slacks and cloth slippers are old and slightly worn, yet she is neatly dressed and brisk in her movements. Her two years' service with the Chous has taught her poise and ease of manner, but this does not mean that she does not know her place. Her big, limpid eyes with their long lashes will dance with animation or, when she frowns, stare gravely. Her mouth is large, with full lips that are naturally and deliciously red. When she smiles, we see that her teeth are good, and a dimple appears at each corner of her mouth; yet her face as a whole retains its expression of dignity and sincerity. Her complexion is not particularly fair. The heat has brought a faint perspiration to her nose, and she dabs it from time to time with a handkerchief. She is aware of her good looks and usually enhances them with a smile—though just at the moment she is frowning.

Her father, Lu Kuei, is a mean-faced man in his forties, whose most conspicuous features are his thick, bushy eyebrows and his swollen eyelids. His loose, pendulous lips and the dark hollows under his eyes tell a tale of unbridled sensual indulgence. He is rather fat, and his flabby face remains expressionless most of the time, though he will put on a cringing, obsequious smile when occasion demands. Like most servants in big houses, he is shrewd and has faultless manners. He has a slight stoop, which gives him the appearance of being for ever on the point of saying "Very good, sir," but the look of greed and slyness never leaves his sharp, wolfish eyes. He is astute and calculating. His clothes are showy but untidy. At the moment he is rubbing the silver cigarette-box over with a duster. On the floor at his feet is a pair of brown shoes which he has just polished. Every now and then he wipes his perspiring face with the loose skirts of his long gown.

Lu Kuei: Ssu-feng!

(*She pretends not to hear, but goes on filtering the medicine.*)

Lu: Ssu-feng!

Ssu-feng (*with a glance at her father*): Whew, isn't it hot! (*She walks over to the bureau, picks up a palm-leaf fan, and begins to fan herself with it.*)

Lu (*stopping what he is doing and looking across at her*): Did you hear what I said, Ssu-feng?

Feng (*unconcernedly*): Why, what is it now, Dad?

Lu: I mean did you hear what I was telling you a moment ago?

Feng: Yes, every word of it.

Lu (*who is used to being treated like this by his daughter and so can do nothing more than make a feeble protest*): Oh, what's the use of talking to you?

Feng (*looking round at him*): You talk too much! (*Fanning herself vigorously.*) Whew! With the weather as close as this, ten to one it'll rain presently. (*Suddenly.*) Have you cleaned the master's shoes that he'll be wearing to go out? (*She goes across, picks up one of the shoes and glances contemptuously at it.*) You call this cleaned? Just a couple of wipes with a duster! You just wait till the master sees them, and then you'll be for it!

Lu (*snatching the shoe from her*): I'll thank you to mind your own business!—Now listen, Ssu-feng, while I tell you again: when you see

165

your mother presently, don't forget to get all your new clothes out and show them to her.

FENG *(impatiently):* I heard you the first time.

LU: Let her see who knows what's best for you, she or your dad!

FENG *(contemptuously):* Why, you, of course!

LU: And don't forget to tell her how well you're treated here—good food, light work, just waiting on the mistress and the young gentlemen in the daytime and going straight home in the evening just as she told you to do.

FENG: There's no need for me to tell her that, because she's sure to ask anyway.

LU *(gloatingly):* And then, the money! *(Laughing avariciously.)* You must have quite a bit put by!

FENG: Money?

LU: Yes, two years' pay, and tips, and—*(meaningfully)* and the odd little sums every now and then, which they—

FENG *(cutting him short):* Yes, and you've relieved me of every penny of it, a dollar or two at a time! And it's all gone on drinking and gambling!

LU: There you go again! Getting worked up over nothing! Don't worry, I'm not after your money. No, what I mean is—*(lowering his voice)* he—er—hasn't he been giving you money?

FENG *(taken aback):* He? Who?

LU *(bluntly):* Master Ping.

FENG *(crimsoning):* What on earth do you mean? Master Ping giving me money, indeed! You must be off your head, Dad, talking such nonsense!

LU: All right, all right, so he hasn't, then. But in any case you must have saved quite a bit these last two years.—Don't worry, I'm not after your money. All I meant was you can show it to your mother when she comes. That'll be an eye-opener for her!

FENG: Humph! Mother isn't like you—show you a handful of coppers and you'll break your neck to get at it! *(She goes back to the table to attend to the medicine.)*

LU *(sitting down on the sofa with a smirk):* Money or no money, where do you think you'd be without your old dad? If you'd taken your mother's advice over the last two years instead of coming to work in a big house like this, you surely don't imagine you'd be living as comfortably as you are now? And you wouldn't be wearing nice, cool silk clothes in the middle of summer, either!

FENG: Yes, but mother has her principles. She's educated, and she can't bear to see her own daughter at someone else's beck and call. She's got her pride, you know.

Lu: Pride be damned! If that isn't just like her! What do you think you are, an heiress? Pooh! A servant's daughter, and it's beneath her dignity to go into service!

Feng (*disgustedly*): Look at your face, Dad. You might at least wipe it!—And you'd better have another go at those shoes, too.

Lu: Pride indeed! If you insist on giving yourself airs you'll end up a poor, miserable creature like her. Pride? Just look at her! She travels three hundred miles to be a skivvy in this girls' school of hers, and all for the sake of eight dollars a month and the privilege of coming home once every two years! That's where her "principles" have got her! So much for her "education"! A lot of good *that's* done her!

Feng (*restraining herself*): You'd better keep that until we get home. Remember you're at the Chous' now, not in your own house.

Lu: Why should that stop me discussing my family affairs with my own daughter? Now, listen here: your mother—

Feng (*suddenly*): Just a minute! I've got something to tell *you* first. It isn't every day that mother can get home, and when she does it's only to see Ta-hai and me. If you so much as say a word to upset her, I'll tell Ta-hai just what you've been up to these last two years.

Lu: Me? And what have I done, pray? (*Feeling that his paternal dignity is at stake.*) If you mean I've had a little drink and a flutter now and then, and a bit of fun with the girls, well, what of it? After all, I'm nearly fifty. What's it to him, anyway?

Feng: Oh, he couldn't care less about that sort of thing! But what's happened to the money he sends home from the mine every month for mother? You've spent every penny of it on the sly, and if he found out about it he wouldn't let you get away with it!

Lu: What could he do about it? (*Raising his voice.*) His mother's married to me, so I'm his father!

Feng: Ssh! No need to shout.

Lu: Humph! (*With sudden eloquence.*) Now just you listen to me. I've never stopped blaming myself for marrying your mother. To think that a smart chap like me should go and do a thing like that! Now is there a single person in all this big house who doesn't think I'm one of the best? I hadn't been here two months when I got my own daughter a nice job in the house, and even your brother—he'd never have got that job in the Chous' mine if I hadn't put in a word for him. Could your mother ever have done as much for the two of you? And what thanks do I get for it? Your mother and your brother are still ganged up against me as much as ever! If she still tries to put on airs and come the great lady over me this time, I'll disown her, and in front of your brother, too! I may even divorce her, even if she has given me a daughter—and brought along that come-by-chance of hers into the bargain!

FENG: Dad! How can—

LU: God knows what bastard fathered him!

FENG: What right have you to say such things about Ta-hai? What's he ever done to upset you?

LU: What's he ever done to make me feel proud of him, I'd like to know? He's tried his hand at being a soldier, a rickshaw boy, a mechanic, a student—he's been a Jack of all trades, but hasn't stuck to any of them for long. After all the trouble I had getting him this job in the mine, he has to go and spoil everything by picking a quarrel with his foreman and beating him up!

FENG (cautiously): But from what I heard, the men didn't do anything until the master told the police at the mine to open fire on them.

LU: Whatever happened, the boy's a bloody fool. He should have had enough sense to realize that if somebody's paying your wages you've got to take orders from them. But no: he has to throw down his tools, and then come and try and get round his poor old dad to smooth things out with the master for him.

FENG: You've got it all wrong, I'm afraid. He's not asking you to do anything of the sort. He said he's coming to see the master himself.

LU (smugly): Well, after all, I am his father, and I can't very well just stand aside and let him get on with it on his own, now, can I?

FENG (eyeing him contemptuously and heaving a sigh): Well, if you'll excuse me I'll take this medicine up to the mistress. (She picks up the little bowl and goes towards the dining-room door.)

LU: Just a minute. I've got something else to tell you—

FENG (in an effort to change the subject): It's nearly lunch-time. Have you made the Yunnan tea yet?

LU: That's no concern of mine. The girls will have seen to that.

FENG: Mm, well, I'd better be off.

LU (standing in her way): What's the hurry, Ssu-feng? There's something I'd like to talk over with you.

FENG: What?

LU: You know yesterday was the master's birthday? Well, Master Ping gave me a tip—four dollars.

FENG: Very nice, too. (Letting her tongue run away with her.)—Though I wouldn't give you a penny if I were him!

LU (*laughing coarsely*): There's something in that, too! What can you do with four dollars, anyway? I paid off a debt or two and now I'm broke again.

FENG (*adroitly*): You'd better touch Ta-hai for a few dollars, then, when he comes.

.LU: Don't be like that, Ssu-feng. When did I ever borrow money and not pay it back? Now, what about a little loan of seven or eight dollars, now that you're in the money?

FENG: I haven't got any money. (*She pauses a moment.*) Did you really use that money to pay off your debts?

LU: Of course! (*With an air of injured innocence.*) You don't think I'd sink so low as to tell lies to my own daughter!—Though it isn't really my fault that I'm in debt now. The measly little tip I got yesterday wasn't enough to pay off the big debts, though there was some left over after I'd paid off the small ones, so I had a couple of games of cards with the rest—you see, I hoped I'd win enough to get out of debt once and for all. How was I to know I was going to have a run of bad luck? Anyway, what with the losses and a few drinks, I'm now in debt to the tune of ten dollars. (*Ssu-feng stares hard at her father.*) And that's the truth, every word of it.

FENG: Then let me tell you something that's just as true: I haven't got any money, either! (*She goes to pick up the bowl of medicine again.*)

LU (*becoming agitated*): Now, Ssu-feng. What's the matter? You're my own daughter, aren't you?

FENG: Yes, but even your own daughter can't be expected to pay your gambling debts for ever!

LU (*solemnly*): Now, my dear girl, be reasonable. Your mother only talks about loving you, whereas I take a real interest in everything that concerns you.

FENG (*realizing that he is hinting at something*): What else is worrying you?

LU (*after a swift glance all round he moves closer to her*): Listen. Master Ping often talks to me about you. Well, he says—

FENG (*unable to contain herself*): Master Ping, Master Ping all the time! You're off your head!—Well, I'm going. The mistress will be asking for me in a minute.

LU: No, don't go. Just let me ask you one thing. The other day I saw Master Ping buying material for a dress—

FENG (*darkly*): Well, what of it?

LU (*looking her up and down*): Well—(*his eyes now rest on her hand*) this ring—(*laughing*) didn't he give you this, too?

169

FENG (*with disgust*): The nasty-minded way you talk about everything!

LU: You don't have to put on an act with me. After all, you are my daughter. (*With a sudden avaricious laugh.*) Don't worry, there's nothing wrong in a servant's daughter accepting gifts or money from people. Nothing wrong at all. I quite understand.

FENG: Don't beat about the bush. Exactly how much do you want?

LU: Not much. Thirty dollars would do.

FENG: I see. Well, you'd better try and touch your Master Ping for it.

LU (*mortified and angered*): Now look here, my girl, you don't really think I'm such a fool that I don't know what's going on between you and that young scoundrel?

FENG (*suppressing her anger*): Call yourself a father? That's a fine way to talk to your own daughter, I must say!

LU: It's just because I am your father that I have to keep an eye on you. Now, tell me, the night before last—

FENG: The night before last?

LU: Yes, the night when I wasn't at home. You didn't turn up till midnight. What had you been doing all that time?

FENG (*inventing an excuse*): I had to hunt out some things for the mistress.

LU: And what kept you out so late?

FENG (*contemptuously*): A father like you has no right to ask such questions.

LU: Ho, getting superior, aren't we! You still can't tell me where you were, though.

FENG: Who says I can't?

LU: Come on, then, let's hear it.

FENG: Well, as a matter of fact, the mistress heard that the master had just got back, and she wanted me to get his clothes out ready for him.

LU: I see. (*In a menacing undertone.*) And who was the gentleman who brought you home in a car at midnight that night?—The one who'd had a drop too much and kept talking a lot of nonsense to you? (*He smiles triumphantly.*)

FENG: Well—er—

LU (*with a roar of laughter*): No, you needn't tell me: it was our rich son-in-law, of course! To think that our rickety little hovel should be honored by a visit from a gentleman in a car, running round after a servant's daughter! (*Suddenly stern.*) Now, tell me, who was it? (*Ssu-feng is speechless.*)

(*At this moment. Lu Ta-hai—Ssu-feng's half-brother and Lu Kuei's stepson—comes in. He is tall and powerfully built, with bushy black eyebrows and slightly hollow cheeks. His stubborn character shows in his square jaw and his piercing eyes. His lips are thin, in striking contrast to his sister's, which are the full, red lips of a passionate southerner. He speaks with a slight stutter, but when he gets excited his tongue can have a sharp edge to it. At the moment he has just arrived from the coal-mine two hundred miles away where he has helped to organize a strike. The strain of the past few months has told on him and aged him. Weary and unshaven, he looks old enough to be Lu Kuei's brother, and only the closest observation reveals that his eyes and his voice are just as youthful and ardent as his sister's. Like her, he is inwardly consumed by the white-hot passions of youth and has the latent energy of a simmering volcano. He wears a miner's short jacket of coarse blue cotton and in his hand is a greasy straw hat. One of his shoes has lost its lace. As he comes in, he seems rather ill at ease. His speech is terse, which makes him appear cold and aloof.)*

TA-HAI: Ssu-feng!

FENG: Ta-hai!

LU (*to Ssu-feng*): Now, come on! Don't pretend you're dumb.

FENG (*appealing to her brother*): Ta-hai!

LU (*ignoring this*): It makes no difference with your brother here. I still want to know.

HAI: What's the matter?

LU: None of your business.

FENG: It's nothing important, Ta-hai. (*To her father.*) It's all right, Dad, we can talk it over later on.

LU: Later on? (*He gives her a significant glance.*) All right, then, we'll leave it. (*To Ta-hai, haughtily.*) Now then, what do you mean by just barging in like this! Where's your manners?

HAI (*simply*): I got fed up with waiting in the porter's lodge.

LU: That's just like you, Ta-hai, a ham-fisted miner without the least idea how to behave in a big house.

FENG: He's not a servant here, you know.

LU: His wages still come out of the Chous' pocket, though.

HAI (*coldly*): Where is he?

LU (*pretending not to understand*): "He"? Who's "he"?

HAI: The company chairman.

LU: If you mean the master, then say so. Whatever he's called at the mine, he's "the master" to you while you're in this house.

HAI: Tell him the miners' representative has come to see him.

LU: I think you'd better go home first. (*Confidently.*) You needn't worry about your job at the mine; leave it to your old dad to straighten everything out for you. Have a couple of days at home with your mother and your sister, and when your mother's gone you can go back to the mine, and you'll find your job still waiting for you there.

HAI: You don't understand what it's all about. You needn't bother.

FENG (*anxious that her father should go and leave them alone together*): Why don't you go and see if the visitors have gone, Dad? If they have, you could take Ta-hai in to see the master.

LU (*shaking his head*): I doubt very much if he'll see you.

HAI (*with the confidence of a man convinced of the rightness of his cause*): Tell him that Lu Ta-hai, the miners' representative, wants to see him. He asked us to come, and we saw him in the office only the day before yesterday.

LU (*hesitantly*): Well, in that case I'd better find out if you can see him.

FENG: Yes, go on, Dad.

LU (*turning round as he reaches the door of the study*): If he does agree to see you, you'd better watch your tongue, see? (*He disappears into the study with the confident tread of a senior servant with years of lucrative service behind him.*)

HAI (*watching Lu Kuei out of sight and shaking his head*): Ugh! He forgets he's a man!

FENG (*rather reproachfully*): Ta-hai! (*Looking timidly at him.*) I shouldn't speak so loud if I were you. Remember the master's through there.

HAI (*looking at her*): All right. Mother will be back soon. I think you'd best pack up this job here and go back home.

FENG (*surprised*): But why?

HAI: This is no place for you.

FENG: Why not?

HAI (*bitterly*): The Chous are rotten through and through. I've seen enough of their doings at the mine these last two years. (*Deliberately.*) I hate them.

FENG: And what are these things you've seen?

HAI: Take this house, Ssu-feng. A "stately home," you might say. Tcha! Built with the blood of miners crushed at the coal-face!

FENG: Don't *you* start: they say this room's haunted as it is.

HAI (*with sudden scorn*): Just now as I was coming in I saw a young man in the garden. He was lying there with his eyes closed and his face so pale that I shouldn't think he'd last much longer. And they tell me this is our chairman's eldest son. Ah, it's a punishment, it's what he deserves!

172

FENG (*indignant*): How dare you—(*checking herself*) He treats people very decently, you know.

HAI: He can't be any good with a father who'll stoop to any dirty trick to make money!

FENG (*looking at him*): It's two years since I saw you last. You've changed a lot.

HAI: These past two years—(*he walks a few steps, then turns and looks her full in the face*) I think it's you that's changed.

(*Lu Kuei reappears from the study.*)

LU: Well, the visitors went at last, but just as I was going to tell him you were here another one came in. (*Turning to Ta-hai.*) I think we'd better go out the back way and wait.

HAI: In that case I'll go in and see him myself. (*He goes towards the door of the study.*)

LU (*blocking the way*): Where do you think you're going?

FENG: Stop, Ta-hai, don't go in. You'd better—

HAI: All right—(*after a moment's thought*) perhaps you're right: we don't want him thinking that miners have got no manners.

LU: Come down off your high horse! If the old man says he won't see you, then he won't. Now, why not go down and wait a bit longer in the servants' quarters? Come on, I'll take you along; otherwise, in a big house like this you'll be losing your way and blundering into places where you shouldn't be. (*As he goes towards the center door he calls over his shoulder to his daughter.*) You stay here, Ssu-feng. I won't be a minute. Got it?

FENG: Yes, all right.

(*Lu Kuei and Lu Ta-hai go out.*)

(*Ssu-feng sits down wearily on a sofa.*)

(*A young man's cheerful voice is heard outside in the garden calling her name. It comes nearer and nearer until it is just outside the center door.*)

FENG (*slightly alarmed*): Oh dear, it's Master Chung!

CHOU CHUNG'S VOICE: Ssu-feng! Ssu-feng!

(*Ssu-feng jumps hurriedly to her feet and hides behind the sofa.*)

(*Chou Chung, Chou Pu-yuan's seventeen-year-old younger son, comes briskly into the room. He is dressed for tennis and carries a racket under his left arm. He is mopping his perspiring face with a towel. Like all youngsters of his age, he is something of an idealist. Just now his face is flushed and his eyes are dancing merrily.*)

CHOU CHUNG: Ssu-feng! Ssu-feng! (*Looking all round the room.*) Oh, she's not here. (*Tiptoes across to the door of the dining-room, opens*

it, and speaks in a low voice.) Come on out, Ssu-feng. I've got
something to tell you. *(He now goes quietly across to the door of the
study and speaks in a lower voice still.)* Ssu-feng.

CHOU PU-YUAN'S VOICE *(from inside the study)*: Is that you, Chung?

CHUNG *(timidly)*: Yes, Father.

THE VOICE: What do you want?

CHUNG: I'm looking for Ssu-feng.

THE VOICE: Well, she's not in here.

CHUNG *(turning away from the door with a puzzled frown)*: Well, that's
odd. *(Disappointed, he walks across the room and disappears into the
dining-room.)*
*(Now that he has gone, Ssu-feng comes out of her hiding-place and
heaves a sigh of relief.)*
(Lu Kuei comes in through the center door.)

LU *(to Ssu-feng)*: Who was that calling you just now?

FENG: Master Chung.

LU: What did he want you for?

FENG: God knows.

LU *(reproachfully)*: Why did you dodge him like that?

FENG: You told me to stay here, didn't you? Now, let's hear what you've
got to say.

LU: Well, it's like this. When I went down to the servants' quarters just
now, I found all these bloody people I owe money to crowded round
the door waiting for me. They stopped me in front of everybody and
demanded their money back on the spot. Unless I can raise twenty
dollars I won't be able to get rid of them.

FENG *(producing some money)*: That's every penny I've got. I'd been
keeping it to buy mother a new dress, but you'd better have it.

LU *(hypocritically)*: But won't that leave you broke?

FENG: Forget it. You're getting very considerate all of a sudden, aren't
you?

LU *(taking the money with a smile and counting it)*: Only twelve
dollars?

FENG *(flatly)*: It's all I've got.

LU *(trying to look as if the loan is more trouble than it is worth)*: How
am I going to get rid of these people, then?

FENG *(controlling herself with difficulty)*: Tell them to come round to
our place tonight. I'll see what I can do after mother's arrived. You'd
better keep this money for your own use.

LU *(delighted)*: For me, eh? Then I'll accept it as a token of your affection for your father. I always knew you loved your old dad, my dear.

FENG (*helplessly*): Perhaps now you'll let me go upstairs after all that? (*She picks up the bowl of medicine.*)

LU: Why, who's stopping you? Go on, and tell the mistress that Lu Kuei is anxious to know how she's getting on.

FENG: All right, I won't forget.

LU (*rather pleased with himself*): Oh yes, Ssu-feng, there's something else I want to tell you.

FENG: Couldn't you save it for later on?

LU (*mysteriously*): Ah, but this is something that concerns you. (*He smiles hypocritically.*)

FENG (*scowling*): Me again? Now what? (*Putting down the bowl.*) All right. Let's get everything cleared up once and for all before we go any farther.

LU: There you go again. Flying off the handle at the slightest excuse! Quite the young lady, aren't you, with your airs and your tantrums!

FENG: Come on, out with it.

LU: Now don't be like that, my dear. (*Seriously.*) I just want to warn you to be on your guard.

FENG (*sarcastically*): What have I got to be on my guard for, now that you've cleaned me out?

LU: Listen. I don't think the mistress has been in a very good mood these last few days.

FENG: What's that got to do with me?

LU: It seems to upset her to have you around.

FENG: Why?

LU: Why? Let me remind you of one thing or two. The master is years older than the mistress, and they don't get on very well with one another. Master Ping is only her stepson, and there's not much difference in their ages.

FENG: I know all that.

LU: But do you know why no one ever comes into this room after dark, and why it's not even used in the daytime all the time the master's away at the mine?

FENG: Well, it's because the room's haunted, isn't it?

LU: Haunted? Oh yes, it certainly is. And I've seen the ghosts, too.

FENG: You have?

LU (*complacently*): Yes, and lucky for me that I did.

FENG: How's that?

175

Lu: It was before you came. The master was away at the mine, and the mistress and the two young gentlemen were left alone in this big, gloomy house. This room was already haunted then, and Master Chung, who was still only a child, was afraid and insisted I should sleep at his door to keep him company. I remember it was in the autumn. Well, one night, about midnight, he suddenly woke me up and said he'd heard ghosts in the drawing-room. He insisted that I should go and have a look. I was shaking in my shoes at the thought of it, but I was new here then, and I didn't dare disobey the young master.

Feng: So you went, then?

Lu: I had a little drink to steady my nerves, then I went round past the lotus-pond and crept up to the verandah outside this room. As soon as I got near the door, I heard a faint noise. It sounded like a woman sobbing her heart out. I was scared out of my wits, but the noise made me all the more determined to have a look. Finally, I plucked up courage and peeped in through this window here.

Feng (*gazing tensely at him*): What did you see?

Lu: There was a candle on this table here. It had burned right down and it was just flickering as if it was going out. There was just enough light to make out two ghosts all in black sitting side by side with their backs towards me. They looked like a man and a woman. The woman seemed to be leaning on the man's shoulder and crying, and the man sat with his head bent, sighing to himself.

Feng: You're not making it all up?

Lu: Of course not! Well, with the drink inside me, I managed to pluck up enough courage to put my face close to the window and give a little cough. The two ghosts sprang apart with a jerk and looked round towards me. Just for a moment I got a clear view of both their faces.—And then I really did think I was seeing things!

Feng: Why?

(*Lu Kuei pauses and looks quickly all round.*)

Feng: Who were they?

Lu: Well, the woman turned out to be—(*glancing over his shoulder, then dropping his voice to a whisper*) the mistress herself!

Feng: The mistress?

Lu: And the man—was Master Ping.

Feng: No!

Lu: Yes, it was him all right. He and his stepmother were the ghosts who'd been haunting the place nights.

FENG (*with affected unconcern*): I don't believe it. You must have made a mistake.

LU: Not me. Don't you kid yourself. You see now, Ssu-feng, why I say you should come down to earth and stop being so silly. That's the Chous for you!

FENG: No, it's impossible.

LU: You're forgetting that Master Ping is only six or seven years younger than the mistress.

(*Still refusing to believe it, Ssu-feng shakes her head.*)

LU: All right. Please yourself whether you believe it or not, but don't say I didn't warn you. The reason the mistress hasn't been in a very good mood about you lately is because you—er—because you and—

FENG (*hurriedly changing the subject*): If the mistress knew it was you, she'd never forgive you.

LU: You're telling me. Though I was in a cold sweat at the time, and I didn't wait to be caught. I got out, quick.

FENG: But I can't imagine the mistress letting it go at that.

LU: She was very worried about it, of course not. She kept on sounding me and trying to trap me into saying something, but I didn't breathe a word. Still, that was over two years ago, and I expect by now they've decided it must have been a ghost they heard coughing that night.

FENG (*to herself*): No, no. I can't believe it.

LU: You can't? You and your day-dreams! Don't you realize who you are, and who he is? Do you imagine for one moment that a young gentleman in his position could ever be serious about you? Why, the mere fact that your father's no good is enough to—

FENG (*suddenly*): Stop it! I suppose you're talking all this silly nonsense to upset me just because I'm so happy about Mother coming home today! Lot of twaddle!

LU: There you go again! I tell you the truth, and you go off the deep end! Ah, I don't know. (*With a brief, supercilious glance at Ssu-feng he walks across to the low table and, with a practiced hand, conveys some of the cigarettes on it to his own battered old cigarette-case.*)

FENG (*coldly, as she watches him*): If that's all, I'll be going. (*She picks up the bowl of medicine and turns to go.*)

LU: Wait a minute. I haven't finished yet. (*Casually.*) Your mother will be coming here to see you.

FENG (*turning pale*): What?

LU: She's coming straight here from the station.

FENG: What did you have to tell her to come here for? You know she never wanted me to go into service: Anyway, I always go home in the evening, so what's the point of bringing her here?

Lu: It's none of my doing, Ssu-feng. The mistress wanted me to fetch her here.

FENG: The mistress, did you say?

Lu: That's right. (*Mysteriously.*) Queer, isn't it? She's no relation of your mother's, or friend either, and yet she goes out of her way to invite her here for a little chat.

FENG: Would you mind not being so mysterious about it and tell me what it's all about?

Lu: Do you know why the mistress is hiding herself upstairs on her own and pretending to be ill?

FENG: Well, she always does that whenever the master comes home.

Lu: Wouldn't you say it was different this time?

FENG: In what way?

Lu: Don't you feel there's something wrong?—Hasn't Master Ping mentioned anything?

FENG: No. All I know is, for the last six months or so he hasn't had much to say to the mistress.

Lu: I see—and how's she been treating you?

FENG: Better than ever these last few days.

Lu: Just as I thought! Now listen. She knows I don't want you to leave this job, so this time she's going to speak to your mother direct and get her to take you away, bag and baggage!

FENG (*in a low voice*): So she wants to get rid of me—but—but why?

Lu: You know very well without me telling you.

FENG (*still in a low voice*): But what can she want Mother here for?

Lu: She must have something to tell her.

FENG (*the truth suddenly dawning on her*): Oh, Dad! Whatever happens, Mother mustn't find out what I've been up to here. (*Overcome by remorse and apprehension, she bursts into tears.*) Just think, Dad. When Mother went away two years ago, she told you to look after me and not bring me to this place to work. You didn't take any notice of what she said and you insisted on me coming here. Mother still doesn't know about it. I just couldn't bear her to find out just what I've been doing here. (*Flinging herself down on the table.*) Oh, Mother! Mother!

Lu: There, there! (*Stroking her tenderly.*) Now, your dad's on your side, see? Your dad loves you, and you've got nothing to worry about. There's nothing she can do about it, and you won't get the sack. You see, there's one person in this house that she's afraid of.

178

FENG: Who's that?

LU: She's afraid of me. Remember the two ghosts I told you about? When I asked her to give you a day off last night, she said I could bring your mother here when she comes. Well, seeing what sort of a mood she'd been in these last few days, I put two and two together. Then, casual-like, I dropped a word or two about what happened that night. She's all there, you know, and she must have realized what I was getting at.—Humph! If she tries to come the old acid with me, she'll find herself in an awkward situation, especially with the master at home now! I know she can be a nasty piece of work, but anybody who tries to push my daughter around will have me to deal with first!

FENG (*looking up*): Don't go doing anything rash, though!

LU: I don't think much of anybody in this house, except the old man. Don't worry, your dad'll look after you. Anyway, I may be wrong about her. Perhaps she isn't thinking of doing anything of the sort. In fact, she did say she only wanted to meet your mother because she'd heard your mother could read and write.

FENG (*suddenly straining her ears to listen*): Sh-h! I think I can hear someone coughing in the dining-room.

LU (*listening*): It's not the mistress, is it? (*He goes across to the door leading to the dining-room, peeps through the keyhole, and hurries back to her.*) It is, too. Funny, her coming downstairs like that. Now, don't panic and don't breathe a word to her about anything. I'd better make myself scarce now.

FENG (*drying her tears*): All right, but be sure to let me know the minute Mother arrives.

LU: Yes, and when she does come, pretend you haven't heard a thing. Got it? (*He goes across to the center door, then speaks over his shoulder.*) And don't forget to tell the mistress that Lu Kuei is anxious to know how she is. (*He hurries out through the center door.*) (*Ssu-feng picks up the bowl of medicine once again and goes towards the dining-room, but just as she reaches the door, it opens and Chou Fan-yi appears. She is obviously a woman of ruthless determination. The faint red of her lips is the only touch of color in her otherwise pale face. Her large, dark eyes and straight nose give her face a certain beauty, though a beauty with a sinister cast to it. The eyes beneath her long, steady lashes betray her unhappiness. Sometimes, when the smoldering fires of misery in her heart blaze into life, these eyes will fill with all the anguish and resentment of a frustrated woman. The corners of her mouth are slightly drawn back, revealing her to be a repressed woman controlling herself with difficulty. Whenever she*)

179

coughs in her quiet way, her slender, delicate white hands press against her flat, emaciated chest, and when the coughing is over, leaving her panting for breath, they will go up to feel her face, now flushed with coughing. With her delicate health, her secret sorrows, her intelligence and her love of poetry and literature, she is a woman of old China; yet there is a primitive wildness in her which shows in her courage, in her almost fanatical reasoning, and in her sudden, unaccountable strength in moments of crisis. The sum impression which one gains of her is of a crystalline transparency, as if she is the sort of woman who can offer a man no companionship but the platonic kind, and her broad, unclouded forehead is expressive of a subtle intelligence; but when, lost in sentimental reverie, she breaks into a sudden smile of happiness, or when, at the sight of someone dear to her, a flush of pleasure suffuses her face and dimples appear on her cheeks, one feels for the first time that it would be possible to love her and that she does indeed deserve to be loved—one realizes, in fact, that she is a woman after all, a woman no different from all the others. When she loves, she loves with a fiery passion, and when she hates, she hates as fiercely, with a hatred which can destroy; yet on the surface she appears quiet and wistful, and when she stops beside one, it is like a leaf falling by one's side on a late autumn afternoon. She seems to feel that the summer of her life is now over, and that the shades of evening are falling around her.

She is dressed all in black, and her dress is trimmed with silver-grey pipings. A round fan hangs from her fingers. As she comes in she looks casually at Ssu-feng.)

FENG: Why, madam! I didn't know you'd come downstairs! I was just coming up with the medicine.

FAN-YI: Is the master in the study?

FENG: Yes, he's got a visitor.

FAN: Who is it?

FENG: Well, it was the police superintendent in there a minute ago, but I don't know who it is now. Did you want to see him?

FAN: No. *(She pauses and looks all round.)* After two weeks upstairs, this room looks quite different.

FENG: I know. The master didn't like the way it was arranged before, so he had some of your new furniture moved out again. He's got the room arranged just the way he wants it.

FAN *(noticing the bureau on the right)*: I see he's had that old bureau put back where it used to be. *(She coughs and sits down.)*

FENG: Your face looks feverish, madam. Wouldn't it be better if you
went back upstairs and lay down?

FAN: No, it's too hot up there. *(She coughs again.)*

FENG: The master says that as you're not very well, madam, you'd best
stay quietly upstairs in bed.

FAN: I don't want to stay in bed.—Oh, I forgot to ask you. When did the
master get back from the mine?

FENG: Three days ago, late at night. When he saw how feverish you
were, he told us not to disturb you. He's been sleeping downstairs on
his own.

FAN: But I don't seem to have seen him in the daytime, either.

FENG: Well, since he's back he's been out every day to meetings at the
provincial government offices, and each time he's got home and gone
up to see you in the evening your door's been locked.

FAN *(unconcernedly)*: I see.—Why, it's just as stifling downstairs.

FENG: Yes, it's very close. But it's been very cloudy, dark and overcast
since first thing this morning. I expect we're in for a storm.

FAN: Give me a larger fan. I'm practically suffocating. *(Ssu-feng hands
her a large palm-leaf fan. Fan-yi looks at her for a moment, then
deliberately turns her face away.)*

FAN: How is it I haven't seen anything of Master Ping just lately?

FENG: He's probably very busy.

FAN: I hear he's off to the mine. Is that true?

FENG: I don't know.

FAN: Haven't you heard about it, then?

FENG: No. Though I do know his maid's been busy packing his things.

FAN: What's your father doing?

FENG: I don't know.—Oh, he said he was anxious to know how you're
getting on.

FAN: Humph, he would be. *(After a pause, suddenly.)* Isn't he up yet?

FENG: Who?

FAN *(rather taken aback by the unexpected question, but hastily recov-
ering herself)*: Why—er—Master Ping.

FENG: I don't know.

FAN *(casting a swift glance at her)*: You don't?

FENG: I haven't seen him.

FAN: What time did he get home last night?

FENG *(blushing)*: I don't know. I sleep at home every night.

FAN *(forgetting herself)*: Sleep at home every night, indeed! *(Realizing
that she has made a faux pas.)* But why should you go home every

181

night now that the master's at home with no one to wait on him?

FENG: But, madam, didn't you tell me to yourself?

FAN: Yes, but the master wasn't at home then.

FENG: I thought a religious man like the master wouldn't like having a girl staying on to wait on him.

FAN: I see. (*Suddenly looking up.*) Though if he is leaving in a day or two, where else can he be going?

FENG (*timidly*): Master Ping, you mean?

FAN (*staring hard at her*): Of course.

FENG: I haven't heard a thing. (*Hesitantly.*) He—he never gets in till two or three in the morning. This morning my father was muttering something about having to open the gate for him in the early hours of the morning.

FAN: Was he drunk again?

FENG: I'm not sure. (*Changing the subject.*)—Madam, what about having your medicine now?

FAN: Medicine? Whose idea's this?

FENG: The master had it made up for you.

FAN: But how can there be any medicine when I haven't even seen a doctor?

FENG: The master said it must be your liver again, and this morning he happened to remember about the prescription you had last time, so he sent out for the ingredients and had it made up for you.

FAN: Is it ready?

FENG: Yes. It's been here getting cool for some time now. (*Handing her the bowl.*) Here you are, madam.

FAN (*taking a sip at it*): It's terribly bitter. Who made it up?

FENG: I did.

FAN: It tastes abominable. Pour it away.

FENG: Pour it away?

FAN (*deterred by the thought of her husband's stern face*): Oh, well, perhaps you'd better leave it on the table for the time being.—No. (*With loathing.*) You'd best pour it away.

FENG (*hesitantly*): All right, then.

FAN: For years I've been taking this revolting stuff. I've had more than enough of it already.

FENG (*holding out the bowl*): Now be brave, madam. Do try to take it. The worse it tastes, the more good it'll do you.

FAN (*flaring up*): Who asked you for advice? Pour it away, I say! (*Realizing that this outburst is rather undignified.*) My maid tells me the master looks much thinner this time.

FENG: Yes, he is thinner, and darker in the face, too. I hear the miners are out on strike just now, and that the master's very worried about it.

FAN: Is he very cross?

FENG: He's the same as usual. Except for seeing visitors and going out, he hasn't said a word to anybody in the house.

FAN: Not even to Master Ping and Master Chung?

FENG: He just nodded when he saw Master Ping. He didn't say a word to him. Only when he saw Master Chung, he asked him about school. —Oh yes, that reminds me: Master Chung was asking after you only this morning.

FAN: You can tell him I'm quite well.—And tell them in the office to give him forty dollars. Say it's for him to buy books with.

FENG: Master Chung was hoping to have a word with you.

FAN: Tell him to come and see me upstairs, then. (*She stands up and walks a few steps.*) What a horribly stuffy room this is! The whole place smells so musty.

FENG (*after a moment's hesitation*): I wonder if I might have the afternoon off, madam?

FAN: Because your mother's coming back from Tsinan, do you mean? Your father was saying something about it.

CHUNG'S VOICE (*from the garden*): Ssu-feng! Ssu-feng!

FAN: That's Master Chung calling you. Go and see what he wants.

CHUNG'S VOICE: Ssu-feng!

FENG: Here I am.

(*Chou Chung comes in through the center door.*) ·

CHUNG (*seeing only Ssu-feng*): Ah, here you are, Ssu-feng. I've been looking for you all the morning. (*Noticing Fan-yi.*) Mother! What are you doing downstairs?

FAN: Why, Chung, what have you been doing? Your face is streaming.

CHUNG: Oh, I've just been playing tennis with a school-friend. (*Affectionately.*) I've been wanting to see you. I've got so many things to tell you about. Are you feeling any better now? (*He sits down beside her.*) I've been up to see you several times in the past few days, but your door's always locked.

FAN: I wanted to be left alone. How do you think I look?—Ssu-feng, you might fetch Master Chung a bottle of mineral water. Why, you're blushing! (*Ssu-feng goes into the dining-room.*)

CHUNG (*delighted*): Let me have a look at you. Well, so far as I can see, you're perfectly all right—nothing wrong with you at all. I don't see why they should always be saying you're ill. While you've been shut

away in your room, Father's been home three days and you haven't
even seen him yet.

FAN (*looking at him sadly*): I don't feel myself, somehow. (*Suddenly.*)
Chung, you're seventeen, aren't you?

CHUNG: Now, Mother, if you forget my age again, I'll be really angry
with you.

FAN (*smiling*): Yes, I know it's silly of me, but sometimes I even forget
where I am. (*Lost in thought.*) Yes, it's now eighteen years since I
came to live in this house.—But tell me: don't you think I'm getting
old?

CHUNG: No. Why, what's worrying you?

FAN: Nothing.

(*Ssu-feng comes in with the mineral water.*)

FENG: Here you are, Master Chung.

CHUNG: Thank you.

(*Blushing, Ssu-feng pours it out for him.*)

CHUNG: Do you mind fetching another glass for the mistress?

(*Ssu-feng goes out.*)

FAN (*who has been watching them closely all this time*): Chung, why are
you two being so polite to one another?

CHUNG (*drinking*): Well, Mother, that's just what I wanted to tell you
about. It's because—

(*Ssu-feng comes in again.*)

CHUNG: —I'll tell you about it some other time. Why is it so stuffy in
this room?

FAN: Probably because the windows are closed.

CHUNG: I'll open them then.

FENG: The master said they weren't to be opened. He says it's hotter
outdoors than in.

FAN: Nonsense. Let's have them open. He's usually away two years at a
time, and doesn't realize how stale and airless this room can be.

(*Ssu-feng draws aside the curtains.*)

CHUNG (*seeing that Ssu-feng is having some difficulty moving the
flower-pots on the window-sill*): Don't bother, Ssu-feng. I'll do it. (*He
goes across to the window.*)

FAN (*turning to Ssu-feng*): Go down to the kitchen, will you, and see
what they're getting for the master in the way of vegetarian food.

(*Ssu-feng goes out through the center door.*)

FAN: Chung!

(*Chou Chung comes back across the room to her.*)

FAN: Now, sit down and tell me all about it.

CHUNG (*looking at her with eyes bright with hope and happiness*):
Mother, I've been very happy these last few days.

FAN: If you can be happy in this house, so much the better.

CHUNG: I've never had any secrets from you, Mother. You're not just an
ordinary mother. You're the most courageous, the most imaginative,
the most sympathetic of mothers—sympathetic to my ideas.

FAN: Go on, then.

CHUNG: I want to tell you something—or rather, I want to talk
something over with you.

FAN: Well, let's hear what it is.

CHUNG: Mother—(*Guardedly.*) You won't be cross with me?

FAN: No. Go on.

CHUNG (*elated*): Oh, Mother—(*He hesitates.*) No, I don't think I will
tell you.

FAN (*breaking into a smile*): Why not?

CHUNG: Well, I—I'm afraid you'll be angry. Will you still love me just
the same after I've told you?

FAN: Of course I will, you silly boy. Always.

CHUNG (*smiling*): Dear Mother! You mean that? You'll still love me?
And not be angry?

FAN: Of course. Now tell me all about it.

CHUNG: But you mustn't laugh at me when you hear what it is.

FAN: I won't.

CHUNG: Promise.

FAN: Yes, I promise.

CHUNG: Well, Mother, I'm in love.

FAN (*her suspicions and fears confirmed*): Indeed!

CHUNG (*meeting her stare*): Now, Mother! You're looking disapproving
already.

FAN (*shaking her head*): Not at all. I want to hear more. (*More cheerfully.*) Who's the girl?

CHUNG (*his enthusiasm undaunted*): Oh, she's the most—the most—
(*casting a glance at his mother*) well, anyway, I think she's the most
wonderful girl in the world. She has a heart of gold; she knows how to
enjoy life; she's understanding and kind; and she realizes the importance of hard work. What's most important, she isn't one of these
aristocratic young ladies who've been pampered and spoiled all their
lives.

FAN (*casually*): I should have thought you'd prefer an educated girl. Has
she been to school?

CHUNG: Oh, no. Though that's her only—I mean it seems to be her

185

only shortcoming.—Though you can't very well hold that against her.

FAN: I see. (*The sparkle has now faded from her eyes, but she cannot very well abandon her questioning now.*) Chung, I suppose you wouldn't be referring to—er—Ssu-feng?

CHUNG: Yes, Mother, I am.—Oh, I know people will laugh at me, Mother, but I'm sure *you'll* understand.

FAN (*to herself, in a stunned voice*): But my own son—it's fantastic!

CHUNG (*becoming anxious*): Why, don't you approve? You don't think I've done wrong, do you?

FAN: No, no, it's not that. It's just that I doubt whether a girl like her could make you happy.

CHUNG: But she will! She's intelligent and warmhearted—and she understands me.

FAN: You're reckoning without your father—he may not approve.

CHUNG: This is my own affair.

FAN: And if people talk when they hear about it?

CHUNG: That would worry me even less.

FAN: Like mother, like son. Though I'm afraid you're going the wrong way. In the first place, when all's said and done, she's still an uneducated girl from the lower classes. For a girl in her position it must seem a marvellous stroke of luck to have a young man like you fall in love with her.

CHUNG: Now, Mother! Don't you think she has a mind of her own?

FAN: You're always setting people up on pedestals, Chung.

CHUNG: I think you're doing her a great injustice, Mother. She's the purest, most independent, nicest girl alive. When I proposed to her yesterday—

FAN (*with growing astonishment*): What! Proposed to her? (*Laughing.*) You mean to say you proposed to her?

CHUNG (*annoyed by his mother's attitude*): There's no need to laugh about it! She turned me down.—But I'm glad, in a way, because it strengthens my conviction, that she's a girl in a million. She said she didn't want to marry me.

FAN: Humph!

CHUNG: Now, don't imagine she's just putting on an act by refusing, because it just isn't true. She said her heart belonged to another.

FAN: Who? Did she say?

CHUNG: I didn't ask. Most probably some neighbor of hers, someone she sees every day.—Still, the course of true love never runs smooth. I love her, and gradually she'll come to understand me and love me in return.

FAN (*unable to control herself any longer*): No son of mine shall ever marry a girl like her!

CHUNG (*taken aback*): Don't be like that about it, Mother! Ssu-feng's a decent girl. Whenever she mentions you behind your back, it's always with the greatest deference and respect.

FAN: What are you going to do now?

CHUNG: I intend to tell Father all about it.

FAN: You forget what sort of man your father is.

CHUNG: I must tell him. Of course, it's not absolutely certain that I'll ever marry her, but even if she doesn't want me for a husband, I'll still have great respect for her and try to help her. In the meantime, I'd like to see her getting an education. I'm hoping that Father will let me give her half the money set aside for my education, so that she can go to school.

FAN: What a child you are!

CHUNG (*crossly*): No, Mother, I'm not a child any longer.

FAN: One word from your father, and all your castles in the air will collapse.

CHUNG: I don't think so. (*A shade despondently.*) All right, don't let's talk about it any more. I saw Ping yesterday, Mother. He said he really is going to the mine to work this time and that he's leaving tomorrow. He said would I tell you he's terribly busy and probably won't have time to go upstairs and say good-bye to you himself. You won't mind, I hope?

FAN: Why should I?

CHUNG: Somehow I can't help feeling you don't get on with him as well as you used to. You know, Mother, when you consider that he lost his own mother when he was still a child, it's not really surprising that he should have such an odd disposition. His mother must have been a very emotional sort of woman, judging from what he's like.

FAN: Now that your father's at home, it would be better if you didn't mention Ping's mother; otherwise your father will be going around looking as black as thunder again and making everybody feel miserable.

CHUNG: But there's no getting away from it that Ping has been acting rather oddly just lately. He's taken to drinking heavily, and he'll snap your head off as soon as he looks at you. The other day, when he was drunk, he took me by the hand and told me he hated himself, and

187

then reeled off a whole long rigmarole that I couldn't make head or tail of.

FAN: Oh!

CHUNG: In the end he suddenly told me that he'd once loved a woman that he never should have loved!

FAN (*to herself*): Once?

CHUNG: After that he burst into tears, and the next moment he bundled me out of his room.

FAN: Did he say anything more after that?

CHUNG: No, nothing. He looked so forlorn that I felt really sorry for him. Why hasn't he ever got married?

FAN (*in a murmur*): Who knows? Who knows?

CHUNG (*looking round at the sound of footsteps outside the door*): Why, if it isn't Ping himself!

(*The center door is pushed open and Chou Ping comes in. He is about twenty-eight, very pale, and slightly taller than his half-brother. His features are well formed—one might even say handsome, though he is not exactly the sort of young man who makes women swoon at a glance. His bushy black eyebrows, his thick-lobed ears, and his large, powerful hands may give one the impression, at first sight, of simple honesty; but if you remain in his company a little longer you will realize that his appearance of rough, likable simplicity is deceptive. In his dull, troubled eyes you will discover uncertainty, hesitation, timidity, and conflict. The corners of his mouth droop slackly, and at the slightest fatigue his eyes will become set in a lifeless stare, so that you feel he is unable to exert any control over himself or settle down permanently to any regular occupation. He is conscious of his weakness and tries to remedy it—no, perhaps it would be more accurate to say that he suffers perpetual remorse for something wrong which he once did. Nevertheless, when some fresh impulse seizes him, all his passion and desire come flooding back in an overwhelming torrent, and what little is left of his reason becomes nothing more than a dead twig caught up in a whirlpool. Under these circumstances it is quite natural that one act of folly should be succeeded by an even greater one. And so, being in his own estimation a man with a moral outlook and a sensitive nature, he suffers agonies; he hates himself; and he envies all those who, untroubled by scruples, dare abandon themselves to any wickedness. At the same time, he also envies those who can firmly embrace a career and forge steadily ahead with it, keep to the beaten track of what is generally accepted as morality, and finally emerge as model citizens and model family*) men. It is this that lies behind his admiration for his father, who, so far as he can judge from his own limited experience, is a man of flawless character—except for a certain amount of obstinacy and coldness, and he admires him even for this, for these are traits which he is conscious of lacking himself. He feels he has done wrong in deceiving his father, and wants to rid himself of this feeling, but for this he needs new strength—anything so long as it will help him extricate himself from the morass of tormenting indecision which is dragging him down. His search has brought him to Ssu-feng, and he has discovered in her the things which he most desperately needs: for she has youth, beauty, and passion in overflowing abundance. It is true that he finds her rather unrefined, but he has now realized that this lack of refinement is just what he needs, and he has now come to loathe over-wistful women and the subtler emotions.

Yet his mind is still troubled by a hidden, fitful undercurrent of dissatisfaction. Whenever he becomes obsessed by the idea that Ssu-feng is incapable of understanding and comforting him, he plunges headlong into heavy drinking and all the usual round of riotous pleasure and debauchery. This leaves him more listless and depressed than ever, a prey to perpetual restlessness.

At the moment he is wearing a dark blue silk gown, European-style trousers, and patent leather shoes. He is unshaven and generally untidy. He is yawning.)

CHUNG: Hullo, Ping.

PING: So here you are.

FAN (feeling slighted): Ping!

PING: Oh. (Lowers his eyes, then looks up again.) I—er—I didn't know you were here, too.

FAN: I've just come downstairs.

PING (turning to Chou Chung): I suppose Father's still here?

CHUNG: Yes, he is. Did you want to see him?

PING: I was thinking of having a chat with him before I go. (Walks straight towards the door of the study.)

CHUNG: You can't go in now.

PING: Why, what's Father doing, then?

CHUNG: Probably having a business discussion with a visitor. When I saw him a moment ago, he said he'd be out soon and told us to wait for him here.

PING: I'd better get back to my room and write a letter first, then. (Turns to go.)

CHUNG: Oh no, you don't. Mother says she hasn't seen you for a long time. Why not sit down with us and have a chat?

FAN: Don't stop him, Chung. Let him go and have a rest if he wants to. I expect he wants to be left alone.

PING (*somewhat nettled*): Not at all. It's just that I thought you'd be very busy now that Father's at home, and I—

CHUNG: But don't you realize Mother's been ill?

FAN: Why should *he* worry his head about my being ill?

CHUNG: Mother!

PING: Are you better now?

FAN: Yes, thank you. I've just this moment come downstairs.

PING: Good. I'm leaving for the mine tomorrow.

FAN: Oh. (*After a pause.*) That'll be nice for you.—When do you expect to be back?

PING: Job to say, really. I may be gone two years, perhaps three. Whew, it's suffocating in here!

CHUNG: Well, we've opened all the windows.—Seems to me we're in for a heavy storm.

FAN (*after a pause*): What will you be doing at the mine?

CHUNG: Don't forget, Mother, that Ping specialized in mining when he was at the university.

FAN: Is that the reason why you're going, Ping?

PING (*picking up a newspaper*): I don't quite know how to put it. I feel I've been at home too long and I'm getting fed up.

FAN (*with a smile*): I rather think it's because you're afraid.

PING: How do you mean?

FAN: You've forgotten that this room was haunted once.

PING: No, I haven't forgotten. I've lived here long enough, that's all.

FAN (*smiling*): If I were in your place, I'd be absolutely sick and tired of everybody here, and I'd get out of this ghastly place, too.

CHUNG: You mustn't say such things, Mother.

PING (*gloomily*): Ah, I can't hate myself enough: Who am I to be sick and tired of other people? (*Heaving a sigh.*)—Well, Chung, I'm off to my room. (*He stands up.*)
(*The door of the study opens.*)

CHUNG: Don't go: I think Father's coming out now.

CHOU PU-YAN'S VOICE: Well, I think if we do it like that it'll be plain sailing. Right, well, goodbye. . . . Find your own way out?
(*The door opens wide and Chou Pu-yuan appears. He could be anywhere between fifty and sixty. His hair is already greying at the*

190

temples. He wears oval, gold-rimmed spectacles, and his deep-set eyes flash with a hawk-like intensity. Like all founders of family fortunes, his forbidding presence overawes his children. He is dressed in the latest fashion of twenty years ago—a patterned satin gown with a white silk shirt underneath and the collar unbuttoned to reveal a fleshy neck. His clothes, neat and spotlessly clean, look roomy and comfortable. He is rather fat, and has a slight stoop and a loose, flabby jowl. His eyes are sunken, yet they glitter hard and keen. The lines on his face tell a tale of long years of toiling and scheming, and his cold, insolent stare and the sardonic smile which occasionally twists the corners of his mouth proclaim his tyrannical temper, self-righteousness and obstinacy. All signs of the wild abandon of his youth are now buried deep beneath his wrinkles, except that his hair, though greying, still retains its youthful lustre. It is neatly parted and combed back from the forehead, sleek and glossy. In the sunlight his face will take on that silvery sheen which is popularly supposed to be the distinguishing mark of a man of wealth and position. This is the secret of his success as a mine-owner, no doubt.)

PING ⎱
CHUNG ⎰: Hullo, Father.

CHUNG: Your visitor gone?

CHOU (*nodding, then turning to Fan-yi*): I'm surprised to see you up. Better?

FAN: Oh, I wasn't so very ill in any case. How are you this time?

CHOU: Well enough.—I think you ought to go back upstairs and rest, though. Well, Chung, how do you think your mother looks compared with her usual self?

CHUNG: There's never been anything wrong with her at all.

CHOU (*who does not like having his sons answer him back like this*): Where did you get that idea from? I hope you made it your business to inquire after your mother's health all the time I was away? (*He sits down on a sofa.*)

FAN (*sensing that one of his usual lectures is imminent*): Pu-yuan, you seem to have got thinner since last time.—What's happened about the strike at the mine?

CHOU: Oh, they've been back at work since yesterday morning. It's all blown over now.

CHUNG: Then why is Lu Ta-hai still here waiting to see you, Father?

CHOU: Who's Lu Ta-hai?

CHUNG: Lu Kuei's son. You know: Lu Kuei got you to give him a job the

191

year before last. He's just turned up as the miners' representative.

CHOU: Oh, him! Put up to it by somebody outside, unless I'm much mistaken. Anyway, he's already been sacked.

CHUNG: Sacked! But Father, the man knows what he's talking about. I've just this moment had a chat with him. You can hardly sack a man just because he's a strikers' representative.

CHOU: H'm! It seems to be quite the fashion nowadays for young men to hobnob with the workers and go around mouthing meaningless words of sympathy with them!

CHUNG: I think we ought to sympathize with them. After all, they're only doing their best to help their own people. Besides, it's not right that people who are as well off as we are should grudge them enough to keep body and soul together. And it's not a matter of fashion, either.

CHOU (*turning up his eyes*): What do you know about society? How many books on sociology and economics have you read? I remember how I used to have the same sort of ideas when I was a student in Germany—except that my ideas were much more thorough than your half-baked notions!

CHUNG (*thoroughly browbeaten, yet firing a parting shot*): Father, I hear the miners who were injured this time didn't get a penny in the way of compensation.

CHOU (*looking swiftly up*): I think you've said more than enough for the time being. (*Turning to Fan-yi.*) He's been getting just like you these past two years. (*Looking at the clock.*) I've got another appointment in ten minutes' time. Now, have any of you got anything to see me about?

PING: Yes, I wanted to see you, Father.

CHOU: Oh, yes? What about?

PING: I want to leave for the mine tomorrow.

CHOU: Have you finished handing over at Head Office?

PING: Just about. I hope you'll give me some real work to do this time. I don't want to just stand by and watch.

CHOU (*pausing a moment, then looking him full in the face*): You think you're up to a really tough job? There'd be no backing out once you'd taken it on, you know. I won't have a son of mine make a fool of himself.

PING: I've been having much too easy a time here these last two years, and I'm really keen on getting away from the city and having a spell in the interior.

192

CHOU: Now let me think. (*A pause.*) Yes, you may as well leave tomorrow if you want to. I'll send you a wire when you get there and let you know exactly what your job will be.

(*Ssu-feng comes in from the dining-room with a bowl of Yunnan tea.*)

CHUNG (*hesitantly*): Er, Father.

CHOU (*sensing fresh trouble from this quarter*): What is it now?

CHUNG: There's something rather important I'd like to discuss with you.

CHOU: Well?

CHUNG (*hanging his head*): I'd like to share my allowance with someone.

CHOU: Eh?

CHUNG (*screwing up his courage*): My school allowance. I'd like to share it with—

(*Ssu-feng places the tea in front of Chou Pu-yuan.*)

CHOU: Ssu-feng—(*to Chou Chung*) just a minute—(*to Ssu-feng again*) what about the medicine I told you to get ready for the mistress?

FENG: I've done it.

CHOU: Then why isn't it here?

(*Ssu-feng says nothing, but looks at Fan-yi.*)

FAN (*sensing a certain tension in the air*): She got it for me just a short while ago, but I didn't take it.

CHOU: Why not? (*Pauses, then turns to Ssu-feng.*) Where is it now?

FAN (*quickly*): Down the sink. I told her to pour it away.

CHOU (*slowly*): Pour it away? I—see! (*To Ssu-feng.*) Is there any of it left?

FENG: There's still a little drop left in the jar.

CHOU: Go and get it.

FAN (*protesting*): I won't touch it—it's too bitter.

CHOU (*to Ssu-feng*): Go on.

(*Ssu-feng walks across to the left and pours the medicine into a small bowl.*)

CHUNG: But, Father! If Mother doesn't want it, there's no need to force her to take it.

CHOU: Neither you nor your mother knows what's wrong with either of you. (*To his wife, in a low voice.*) Come now, it'll make you quite well again if you'll only take it. (*Seeing that Ssu-feng seems still undecided, he points to the medicine bowl.*) Hand it to the mistress.

FAN (*forcing herself to agree to it*): All right. Put it down here for the moment.

(*Ssu-feng puts down the bowl.*)

CHOU (*with annoyance*): I think you'd better take it at once.

193

FAN (*bursting out*): Ssu-feng, take it away!

CHOU (*with a sudden harshness*): Take it, I say! Don't be so headstrong. And in front of the children, too!

FAN (*her voice trembling*): But I don't want it.

CHOU: Chung, hand your mother the medicine.

CHUNG (*protesting*): Now, Father!

CHOU (*glaring*): Go on!

(*Chou Chung reluctantly takes the medicine across to Fan-yi.*)

CHOU: Now ask her to take it.

CHUNG (*holding the medicine bowl with trembling hands*): Father, you're taking it too far!

CHOU: What's that?

PING (*going across with bent head to Chou Chung and speaking in an undertone*): You'd better do as Father says. You know what he's like.

CHUNG (*to his mother, with tears in his eyes*): Please take it, Mother, if only for my sake. Father won't let up until you do.

FAN (*pleading*): Can't I leave it now and take it in the evening?

CHOU (*with icy severity*): Fan-yi, as a mother, you've got to be constantly thinking of the children. Even if you don't particularly care about your own health, you should at least set the children an example by being obedient.

FAN (*looking from Chou Pu-yuan to Chou Ping, then picking up the bowl and putting it down again*): No! I can't!

CHOU: Ping, persuade your mother to take it.

PING: But Father, I—

CHOU: Go on! Down on your knees and persuade her!

PING (*going across to Fan-yi, then looking appealingly towards Chou Pu-yuan*): Father!

CHOU (*shouting*): Down on your knees!

(*Chou Ping looks dumbly at Fan-yi, who is in tears, while Chou Chung trembles with rage.*)

CHOU: Down on your knees, I said!

(*Chou Ping is about to kneel down, when—*)

FAN (*hurriedly, her eyes on Chou Ping*): All right! I'll take it now. (*She takes a couple of sips, but immediately the tears stream down her cheeks again. Then, with a glance at her harsh-eyed husband and the distressed Chou Ping, she swallows her resentment and finishes the medicine at a single gulp.*) Oh—oh—oh— (*She runs out weeping through the dining-room door.*)

(*A long silence.*)

CHOU (*looking at his watch*): There's still three minutes to spare. (*To Chou Chung.*) You were saying?

CHUNG (*looking up, slowly*): Eh?

CHOU: You were saying something about wanting to share your allowance with someone.—Well, what's it all about?

CHUNG (*in a low voice*): I've changed my mind about it now.

CHOU: You're quite sure there's nothing worrying you?

CHUNG (*with a sob in his voice*): No, nothing, nothing.—Mother was right. (*He hurries towards the dining-room.*)

CHOU: Chung! Where are you going?

CHUNG: Upstairs to see Mother.

CHOU: Just like that? Where are your manners?

CHUNG (*controlling himself and turning back*): Sorry, Father. May I be excused?

CHOU: All right. You may go now.

(*Chou Chung turns and makes for the dining-room again.*)

CHOU: Come back.

CHUNG: Yes, Father?

CHOU: Tell your mother I've asked Dr. Kramer to come and have a look at her.

CHUNG: But she's already taken the medicine you got for her.

CHOU: I think your mother's becoming mentally unbalanced. It looks serious to me. (*Over his shoulder to Chou Ping.*) And the same goes for you, too.

PING: Well, Father, I think I'll go back to my room for a rest.

CHOU: No, don't go yet. I want to have a talk with you. (*To Chou Chung.*) Tell her Dr. Kramer is a famous German psychiatrist—a specialist. I knew him when I was in Germany. When he calls, she must see him without fail. Got it?

CHUNG: Yes, all right. (*Turning back after a few steps.*) Anything else, Father?

CHOU: No. Off you go.

(*Chou Chung goes out into the dining-room.*)

CHOU (*turning and finding Ssu-feng still there*): Ssu-feng, I seem to remember telling you once that the servants are not to hang around in this room when they're not wanted.

FENG: Very well, sir. (*She also goes out through the dining-room door.*)
(*Lu Kuei enters from the study.*)

LU (*becoming incoherent upon suddenly finding himself confronted by his master*): Oh, er, a—a gentleman to see you, sir.

CHOU: Oh, show him into the big drawing-room.

LU: Very good, sir. *(He goes out.)*

CHOU: Hullo! Who's been opening the windows?

PING: Chung and I opened them.

CHOU: Shut 'em. *(Taking off his spectacles and wiping them.)* I don't want the servants running in and out of this room all the times. I shall be resting in here presently, and I don't want to be disturbed.

PING: I'll see to it.

CHOU *(still wiping his spectacles, and looking all round at the furniture)*: Most of the things in this room were your own mother's favorites. That's why, when we moved up here from the south, and all the times we've moved house since then, I've never been able to bring myself to part with any of it. *(He puts on his spectacles and coughs.)* I want the furniture in this room kept just the way it was arranged thirty years ago. It makes me feel better to see it like that. *(He strolls across to the bureau and looks at the photograph on it.)* Your own mother always liked the windows closed in summer.

PING *(with a forced smile)*: Though even if you do want to keep up Mother's memory, I still don't see why you've got to—

CHOU *(suddenly looking up)*: I hear you've been behaving rather discreditably.

PING *(alarmed)*: Wh—What!

CHOU *(walking up to him)*: Do you realize that what you're doing is a disgrace to your father? And also *(pauses)*—to your mother?

PING *(beginning to panic)*: Father!

CHOU *(kindly)*: You're my eldest son, and I don't think this need go any farther than the two of us. *(He pauses a moment, then his voice becomes stern.)* I hear your private life's been highly irregular while I've been away these last two years.

PING *(with growing alarm)*: Oh, no, Father, it just isn't true!

CHOU: If a man takes a risk, he must be prepared to accept the consequences.

PING *(the color draining from his cheeks)*: Father!

CHOU: They told me at Head Office that you spend all your time hanging around the dance-halls, and that the last two or three months you've got worse: out all night drinking and gambling.

PING: Oh, that. *(With obvious relief.)* You mean—

CHOU: Is all this true? *(After a long pause.)* Come on, I want the truth!

PING: It's quite true, Father. *(He blushes.)*

CHOU: A man approaching thirty should have learned a certain amount of self-respect!—Do you remember why you were named Ping?

PING: Yes.

CHOU: Tell me why, then.

PING: It's because Mother's name was Shih-ping. She gave me the name "Ping" herself, on her deathbed.

CHOU: Then perhaps you'll mend your ways out of respect for your own mother.

PING: I will, Father. It was only a momentary lapse.

(Lu Kuei enters from the study.)

LU: Excuse me, sir, but the visitor's—er—he's been here some time now.

CHOU: All right.

(Lu Kuei withdraws.)

CHOU: I pride myself on having one of the most satisfactory and well-behaved families possible, and I think my sons are both good, healthy lads. I've brought the two of you up, and I won't have you giving anybody an excuse to gossip about you.

PING: No, Father.

CHOU: Hullo, there, a servant! *(To himself.)* Why, I feel suddenly tired. *(Chou Ping takes his father's arm and steers him to a sofa, where he sits down.)*

(Lu Kuei comes in.)

LU: Yes, sir?

CHOU: Show the visitor in here.

LU: Very good, sir.

PING: Won't you have a rest first, Father?

CHOU: No. Don't worry about me. *(To Lu Kuei.)* Show him in, then.

LU: Yes, sir. *(He goes out.)*

(Chou Pu-yuan produces a cigar, and Chou Ping gives him a light. He sits sedately, puffing slowly at the cigar.)

—CURTAIN—

ACT TWO

After lunch. Beneath a dark, overcast sky, the afternoon is even more sultry and oppressive than the morning has been. The close, damp air is of the kind that makes one lose one's temper on the slightest provocation. Chou Ping appears from the dining-room. He is alone. He peers out at the garden: it is silent and deserted. He tiptoes across to the door of the study: the study is empty. He suddenly remembers that his father is seeing visitors in another part of the house. Reassured by this thought, he goes over to the window again, opens it, and looks out at the green, tree-canopied garden. He gives a peculiar whistle and calls "Ssu-feng!" several times in a low voice.

Ssu-feng slips stealthily into the room.

PING (*turning and speaking softly and with warmth*): Ssu-feng! (*He takes her hands in his.*)

FENG: No. (*Pushing him away.*) Don't. (*Listening tensely and glancing all round.*) There may be someone about.

PING: Not a soul, Feng. Come and sit down. (*He steers her to a sofa.*)

FENG (*uneasily*): Where's the master, then?

PING: Oh, he's seeing visitors in the large drawing-room.

FENG (*sitting down, then looking up into his face with a long sigh*): It's always like this, always so underhand.

PING: Mm.

FENG: You don't even dare call out my name.

PING: That's why I'm leaving.

FENG (*after a moment's thought*): I'm really sorry for the mistress after the way the master lost his temper with her. It's the first time he's seen her since he's been back, too.

PING: That's Father all over. His word is law, and he'll never take anything back once he's said it.

FENG (*nervously*): I—I'm terribly afraid.

PING: What of?

FENG: In case the master should find out about us. I'm terrified. You said once you'd tell him about us.

PING (*shaking his head, darkly*): There are worse things than that to worry about.

FENG: Such as?

PING (*suddenly*): You haven't heard anything?

FENG: Eh? (*After a pause.*) Why, no.

PING: Nothing about me?

FENG: No.

PING: Have you never heard anything at all?

FENG (*finding the topic distasteful to her*): No, never.—What do you mean, anyway?

PING: Well, er—oh, nothing. Nothing at all.

FENG (*earnestly*): I trust you. I trust you to be true to me, always. That's all I want.—A little while ago you were saying you'd be leaving for the mine tomorrow.

198

PING: I told you all about it last night.

FENG (*coming straight to the point*): Why won't you take me with you?

PING: Because—(*he smiles*) because I don't choose to.

FENG: But you know I'll have to leave this job sooner or later. Any day now the mistress is likely to give me the sack—perhaps even today.

PING (*to whom such a possibility has never occurred*): Give you the sack!—But why should she want to do that?

FENG: Never you mind why.

PING: But I want to know.

FENG: Well, for not doing my job properly, of course. Though I may be wrong—making wild guesses.—I don't expect she will, though. (*After a pause.*) You will take me with you, won't you, Ping?

PING: No.

FENG (*tenderly*): I'll do everything I can to make you comfortable, Ping. You need someone like me to look after you. I'll cook for you and sew on your buttons and darn your socks for you—I'm very good at all that sort of thing—if only you'll let me go with you!

(*Chou Ping says nothing.*)

FENG: I know for certain that once you get away from home you'll be lost without someone to look after you.

PING: But don't you see, Feng? I just can't take you with me.—Now don't you think you're being rather childish about it?

FENG: Do take me with you, Ping! I promise I won't be any trouble to you. If people started gossiping about you because of me, I'd go away at once. You needn't be afraid of scandal.

PING (*irritably*): Now, Feng! You don't imagine I'm that selfish, do you? You mustn't think I'm that sort.—Humph. Afraid of scandal indeed! (*Unable to restrain himself.*) For years now my heart has been dead, and for years I've hated myself with all the hatred I could muster. Do you imagine that now, now that I've begun to revive and summoned up the courage to fall in love with a woman—do you imagine I'm going to start worrying about what people say? Huh! Let'em say! Let them say what they like about "young Mr. Chou falling for one of the servants"—what do I care? I love her.

FENG (*soothingly*): There, Ping. Don't let it upset you. Whatever you've done, I won't hold it against you. (*She becomes lost in thought.*)

PING (*calmer now*): Penny for your thoughts?

FENG: He's repeated what he said a month ago.

PING: You mean that he loves you?

FENG: No, he's proposed.

PING: And what did you say to that?

FENG: I said I was already engaged to somebody else.

PING: Didn't he want to know more?

FENG: No. Though he did say he'd like to pay for me to go to school.

PING: Go to school? (*He laughs.*) The young idiot!—Still, who knows? You may find you're better off with him after all. I'm almost thirty, and you're only eighteen. And my prospects are no better than his, either. Besides, I've done a lot of—of unspeakable things.

FENG: Oh, do be serious, Ping. I'm really worried about it all. You must help me find a way out. He's still only a boy, you see, and I just hate having to keep him on a piece of string like this all the time, and you not letting me tell him the truth.

PING: I never said you couldn't tell him.

FENG: But every time you see me with him, you *will* look so—so—

PING: Well, naturally I look unhappy. When I see the girl I love best of all always going about with someone else, even if he is my own brother, well, of course I don't like it.

FENG: There you go again, getting away from the subject. Let's get down to brass tacks. Tell me honestly how you really feel about me.

PING: How I feel about you? (*He smiles as he remembers another woman who once asked him the same question, and decides that all women have a touch of stupidity about them.*) You want me to tell you honestly? (*He laughs.*) Well, what do you want me to say?

FENG (*unhappily*): I wish you wouldn't treat me like this, Ping. You know very well that I'm yours now, all yours, and yet you—you keep on taking the rise out of me.

PING (*annoyed at this, and feeling at the same time that she still misunderstands him to a certain extent*): Eh? (*Heaving a sigh.*) Oh, God!

FENG: You know how it is, Ping: my father's only interested in cadging money off me; my brother looks down on me because he says I haven't got any character; and my mother, if she found out about us, she certainly wouldn't have anything more to do with me. You're all I have, Ping. They may throw me over one day, but you can't, you can't. (*She breaks down sobbing.*)

PING: Now, just a minute, Feng. Just give me time to think things out.

FENG: My mother really does love me. She was always against me going into service, and I'm afraid she might find out about us and—and that you may not be serious about me at all. If that happened it—it would break her heart. (*Sobbing.*) And besides—

PING (*rising*): Don't be so suspicious of me, Feng. Tell you what: I'll come round to your place tonight.

FENG: You can't: Mother's coming home today.

PING: What about meeting somewhere outside, then?

FENG: No go. Mother's bound to want to have a chat with me this evening.

PING: But I'm leaving on the first train tomorrow morning.

FENG: So you've made up your mind not to take me with you, then?

PING: But my dear girl! How can I take you?

FENG: In that case, you—let me think about it.

PING: Now, my idea is that I leave home first, and then, once I'm out of it, I can find some way of talking Father round and getting him to let you come out and join me.

FENG (*looking him in the eye*): Oh, all right, then, I suppose you'd better come round to my place tonight. I expect Dad and Mum will be sleeping in the front room, and Ta-hai never sleeps at home, so by midnight I should have the back room all to myself.

PING: Well, then, shall I whistle first, as usual? You'll be able to hear me all right, won't you?

FENG: No, don't. If the coast is clear, I'll have a lamp in the window. If there's no lamp there when you come, you mustn't come near the place.

PING: No?

FENG: No, because that'll mean that I've got company and I've changed my mind.

PING: All right, as you say. Eleven o'clock, then.

FENG: Yes, eleven.

(*Lu Kuei appears through the center door.*)

LU: Oh! (*To Ssu-feng.*) I was just looking for you. (*To Chou Ping.*) Good afternoon, Master Ping.

FENG: What did you want me for?

LU: Your mother's arrived.

FENG (*her face lighting up with delight*): She's here? Where is she?

LU: In the porter's lodge. Your brother's just gone down to see her, and they're having a chat.

(*Ssu-feng hurries towards the center door.*)

PING (*calling after her*): Give my regards to your mother, Ssu-feng.

FENG: Thank you. See you later. (*She goes out.*)

LU: Is it tomorrow you're leaving, sir?

PING: Um.

LU: May I see you off at the station?

PING: Don't bother. Thanks all the same.

LU: You've always been so kind to us. My daughter and I will miss you.

PING (*smiling*): You mean you're broke again, eh?

LU: You're pulling my leg, sir.—I really mean what I said. Ssu-feng can tell you how highly I always speak of you, sir.

PING: Mm, yes.—You're not—after anything, are you?

LU: Oh no, nothing like that. I just thought you might be able to spare a moment for a little chat. As you know, Ssu-feng's mother's here—the mistress wants to see her—(*He breaks off: out of the corner of his eye he has glimpsed Fan-yi coming in from the dining-room.*) Why, madam! you're downstairs! Are you quite well again, madam? (*Fan-yi nods briefly.*)

LU: I kept inquiring how you were.

FAN: All right, you may go now.

(*Lu Kuei bows and goes out through the center door.*)

FAN (*to Chou Ping*): Where's he gone?

PING (*blankly*): Who?

FAN: Your father.

PING: Oh, he's busy—got a visitor. Shouldn't be long. Where's Chung?

FAN: He's gone out, the cry-baby.

PING (*ill at ease now that he is left alone with her in the room*): Oh, I see. (*Pauses.*) I must be going now: I've got some packing to do. (*He goes towards the dining-room.*)

FAN: Just a moment.

(*Chou Ping stops.*)

FAN: I wish you'd stay with me a moment.

PING: What for?

FAN (*unhappily*): I want to talk to you.

(*Chou Ping walks back to her and stands there in silence.*)

FAN: I hope you fully realize what that scene this morning was all about. It's not just an isolated incident, you know.

PING (*evasively*): Oh, well, Father's always been like that. What he says goes.

FAN: It's not in my nature to do just as I'm told by anybody.

PING: Yes, I know what you're like. (*Forcing a smile.*) Just don't take any notice of him, then.

FAN: Oh, Ping, I wish you'd be as warm and human as you used to be. I don't like to see you adopting this attitude of blasé cynicism that's so fashionable these days. You must realize that it's bad enough for me as it is, not being able to have you near me.

PING: That's why I'm going away. So that we won't have to keep seeing one another and being reminded of what we most regret.

FAN: I don't regret it. I've never regretted anything.

PING (*somewhat reluctantly*): I think I've made my position quite clear now. I've been keeping out of your way all these days—I think you understand why.

FAN: Only too well.

PING: I've been stupid, an utter fool. Now I'm sorry, because I realize I've made such a mess of my life. I'm a disgrace to myself, to my brother, and what's worse, to my father.

FAN (*in an ominously low voice*): But you're forgetting the person you disgraced most of all. A little too readily, I think.

PING: Why, who do you mean?

FAN: Me, your stepmother, the woman you seduced!

PING (*uneasily*): You must be mad.

FAN: You're in my debt. You've incurred certain responsibilities. You can't just run off on your own the moment the chance of a new life offers itself.

PING: That's an outrageous thing to say! You can't talk like that in a—a respectable family like Father's.

FAN (*furious*): "Father"! "Father"! To hell with your father! "Respectable"! From you of all people! (*With a sneer.*) Eighteen years now I've been in this "respectable family" of yours. I've heard all about the sins of the Chous—and seen them—and committed them myself. Not that I've ever considered myself one of you: what I've done, I've done on my own responsibility. No, I'm not like your grandfather, or your great-uncle, or your dear father himself—doing the most atrocious things in private, and wearing a mask of morality in public. Philanthropists, respectable citizens, pillars of society!

PING: Well, of course, you have the occasional black sheep in any big family, but our branch—

FAN: You're all the same, and your father's the biggest hypocrite of the lot. Years ago now he seduced a girl from the lower classes.

PING: There's no need to go dragging up that sort of thing.

FAN: And you—you're the illegitimate child he gave her!

PING (*overwhelmed and helpless with astonishment*): You're lying! What proof have you got?

FAN: Go and ask your "respectable" father yourself. He told me all about it one night fifteen years ago, when he was drunk. (*Pointing to the photograph on the bureau.*) That girl was your mother. Your father turned her out, so she drowned herself.

PING: You're—you're—you're just—oh, all right, all right—(*he smiles wryly*) I'll take your word for it. Well, what are you going to do? What is it you want with me?

FAN: Your father let me down. He tricked me into coming here—the same old wiles. There was no escape for me, and so I had Chung. All these years he's been the hateful tyrant that you saw this morning. He gradually ground me down until I became as cold and dead as a stone. Then, suddenly, you appeared from our place in the country, where you'd been living. It was you who made me what I am, half step-mother, half mistress. It was you who seduced me!

PING: "Seduced" indeed! I'd rather you didn't use that word, if you don't mind. Do you remember what actually took place?

FAN: Have you forgotten what you told me here in this very room, in the middle of the night? You said you hated your father. You said you wished he were dead. You said that even the prospect of putting yourself beyond the pale wouldn't deter you from loving me.

PING: Ah, but don't forget I was much younger then. I came out with all this nonsense on the impulse of the moment.

FAN: Aren't you forgetting something? There may have been only a few years between us, but that doesn't alter the fact that I was still your stepmother. Don't you see you had no right to say such things to me?

PING: You mean you can't forgive a young man for doing wrong in a moment of folly? *(He frowns uncomfortably.)*

FAN: It's not a question of forgiving anything. I'd resigned myself to my fate, when along came someone who must need revive me—and then tire of me and cast me aside, and leave me to wither away and slowly die of thirst. Now you can tell me what I should do.

PING: Er, well—I've no idea. What do you think?

FAN *(hammering out her words one by one)*: I don't want you to go away.

PING: Eh? You mean you want me to stay here with you, in this god-forsaken place? So that every day we're reminded of our past sins, until they gradually suffocate us?

FAN: But if you realize what a soul-destroying place this is, how can you have the heart to go away on your own and leave me here?

PING: You've no right to say that. You're still Chung's mother.

FAN: No! I'm not! Ever since I placed my life and my reputation in your hands I've shut myself off from everything else. No, I'm not his mother, no more than I'm Chou Pu-yuan's wife!

PING *(icily)*: Even if you don't regard yourself as my father's wife, I still recognize myself as his son.

FAN *(rendered speechless for a moment by this unexpected remark)*: I see, so you're your father's son.—I suppose the reason you've made a

204

point of not coming to see me lately is that you're afraid of your father?

PING: I suppose you could put it like that.

FAN: And the reason why you're going away to the mine is that you're following your father's heroic example and throwing over the one person who really understands and loves you?

PING: I see no reason why you shouldn't interpret it like that, if you want to.

FAN *(coldly)*: Spoken like a true son of your father. *(She laughs.)* His father's son! *(Suddenly calm.)* Pah! You're both the same. Useless, cowardly creatures, not worth anyone's self-sacrifice! I'm only sorry I didn't find you out sooner!

PING: Well, you know now, don't you! As for wronging you, I've explained to you at great length that I find this relationship between us repugnant. Yes, repugnant. You say I did wrong, and I freely admit it; but you cannot disclaim all responsibility for what I did. I've always looked upon you as a very intelligent and understanding woman, and so I'm sure that one day you'll understand and forgive me. I expect you'll accuse me of being cynical or irresponsible, but I want to tell you this: I hope this meeting will be our last. *(He goes towards the dining-room door.)*

FAN *(in a heavy voice)*: Wait.

(Chou Ping stops.)

FAN: I hope you understand what I meant just now. I'm not asking you for anything. I just want you to think back, and go over in your mind all the *(she pauses, distressed)*—all the things we ever said to one another in this room. Remember, no woman can be expected to submit to humiliation at the hands of two generations. Just think it over.

PING: I've already thought it over—from top to bottom. I don't think you can be entirely unaware of the torment I've gone through these past few days. And now perhaps you'll excuse me. *(He disappears into the dining-room.)*

(As Fan-yi watches him go, tears start to her eyes. She buries her face in the sofa and sobs.)

(Lu Kuei comes in stealthily through the center door and sees that she is weeping.)

LU *(softly)*: Madam!

FAN *(starting up)*: What are you doing here?

LU: Lu Ma's here. She's been here some time.

205

FAN: Who? Who's been here some time?

LU: My wife. You asked me to bring her here, I believe, madam.

FAN: Why didn't you tell me earlier?

LU: I meant to, only I—*(lowering his voice)* I saw you were having a conversation with Master Ping, I didn't like to disturb you.

FAN: Oh, so you—you were—?

LU: Me? Ho, I've been waiting on the master and his visitor in the main drawing-room. *(Pretending not to understand her suggestion.)* Why, did you want me for something, madam?

FAN: No. Well, you'd better show Mrs. Lu in.

LU *(smiling obsequiously)*: You mustn't mind my wife, madam. She's no class, really, and she hasn't much idea of how to behave.

FAN: She's a human being the same as anyone else. I only want to make her acquaintance and have a little chat with her.

LU: It's very kind of you, madam.—Oh, and while I think of it, madam, the master told me to ask you to find that old raincoat of his, as he thinks we're in for a storm.

FAN: Ssu-feng looks after his clothes. Can't she get it for him?

LU: Well, that's what I said to the master, seeing that you're not feeling very well, but he insists that you should get it, madam.

FAN: Oh, well, I'll get it presently.

LU: The master says he wants it now. He may be going out any minute.

FAN: Oh, I see. Well, I'd better go and get it straight away.—Ask your wife to come in and wait in here.

LU: Very good, madam. *(He goes out.)*

(Fan-yi's face is paler than ever now; she is making a great effort to suppress her feelings of resentment.)

FAN *(drawing a deep breath and speaking to herself)*: God, this heat! It's absolutely stifling!—I can't go on much longer like this! *(She gazes listlessly out of the window.)*

(Lu Kuei re-enters.)

LU: The master's just sent somebody along about the raincoat: he insists on having it at once.

FAN *(lifting her head)*: All right. You needn't wait. I'll have it sent along by one of the maids. *(She goes out through the dining-room.)*

(Lu Kuei goes out through the center door.)

(After a while, Lu Ma—Lu Shih-ping—comes in with Ssu-feng. She is about forty-seven, and her hair is beginning to grey at the temples. Her complexion is fair and clear, and makes her look eight or nine years younger. Her eyes are dull and lifeless, and from time to time will become fixed in an unseeing stare; yet there is something about

the long, delicate lashes and the large, round pupils that tells us of the charm and sparkle that must have been hers in her younger days. Her clothes are plain but neat, and she wears them like a woman of good family who has fallen on evil days. Around her head is a white towel, apparently there to keep the dust off her hair during her train journey. Whenever she speaks, the faintest of smiles comes to her lips. Her voice is low and steady, and her accent is that of a southerner who has lived a long time in the north: only the occasional peculiarity and the generally lighter intonation betray her place of birth. She speaks clearly, never swallowing her syllables. Her teeth are good and evenly set, and when she smiles deep dimples appear at the corners of her mouth. She comes in hand-in-hand with her daughter Ssu-feng, who is nestling affectionately up against her. Lu Kuei comes in behind them carrying a bundle wrapped in an old piece of cloth.)

FENG: Where's the mistress?

LU: She'll be down in a minute.

FENG: Sit down, Mother.

(*Lu Ma sits down.*)

FENG: You're tired, I expect.

MA: Not a bit.

FENG (*in high spirits*): Well, just wait there a minute while I get you a glass of iced water.

MA: No, don't bother. I don't feel hot.

LU: Get your mother a bottle of mineral water, Ssu-feng. (*To his wife.*) In a big house like this they have everything! Now that it's summer, there's lemonade, fruit juice, water-melon, oranges, bananas, fresh litchis—have what you like.

MA: No, don't, Ssu-feng. Don't listen to your father. We've no right to help ourselves to other people's things. You just stay here with me a little longer and then, when Mrs. Chou comes, we can see her together. I'll enjoy that more than all your cold drinks.

LU: The mistress should be down any minute now. What about your headscarf? You don't seem in much of a hurry to take it off.

MA (*with a good-natured smile*): Well, well. That's what comes of talking so much. (*Beaming at Ssu-feng.*) Fancy me forgetting that. I only put it on for the train. (*She removes it.*) No smuts on my face, are there? It was so dusty on the train. Does my hair look all right? I don't want to look a sight.

FENG: No, you're perfectly all right. You know, you haven't changed a bit these two years you've been away.

MA: Oh, Feng, I almost forgot. You see what a bad memory I have? I've been so busy talking all this time that I've forgotten to show you the one thing I'm sure you'll like best of all.

FENG: What is it, Mother?

MA (*producing a small packet*): Have a look. You're sure to like it.

FENG: No, don't let me see it yet. Let me try and guess.

MA: All right, then; let's see if you can.

FENG: Little stone figures?

MA (*shaking her head*): No, you're too big for things like that.

FENG: A little powder-puff?

MA (*shaking her head again*): What use would that be to you?

FENG: It must be a little needle-case, then.

MA (*smiling*): You're getting warmer.

FENG: I give up. Let me see. (*She undoes the packet.*) Why, Mother! A thimble, a silver thimble! Look, Dad, look what I've got! (*She shows it to Lu Kuei.*)

LU (*without looking at it*): Yes, very nice, too.

FENG: But it's such a pretty thimble! And there's a precious stone set in it.

LU: What! (*Coming quickly across to inspect it closely.*) Let's see it.

MA: It's a present from the headmaster's wife. You see, the headmaster lost an important purse. I found it and returned it to him, and his wife insisted on giving me a present. She brought out a whole lot of little trinkets and told me to choose one—for my daughter, she said. Well, this is the one I chose for you. Do you like it?

FENG: You couldn't have chosen better, Mother. It's just what I've always wanted.

LU: Huh! Humph! (*Handing the thimble back to Ssu-feng.*) Here you are. (*To his wife.*) Trust you to choose paste!

FENG (*contemptuously, her tongue loosened by the excitement of seeing her mother again*): Humph! That's just like you! Even real stones would turn to paste in your hands!

MA: Ssu-feng, you're not to speak to your father like that.

FENG (*petulantly*): But Mother, you've no idea how Dad's been taking it out on me while you've been away. He's been bullying me all the time.

LU (*contemptuously*): Well, don't just sit there chattering away in a corner like a couple of poor relations when you should be making the most of being in a big house and admiring your splendid surroundings. Ssu-feng, show your mother all the clothes you've bought these last two years.

FENG: Mother's not interested in such things.

Lu: And haven't you got a bit of jewellery of your own, too? Bring it out and show her, and then see who she thinks was right: her, who wanted to keep you shut up at home, or me?

Ma (to Lu Kuei): I told you before I went that I wouldn't have my daughter go into service, and every time I've written to you over the past two years I've reminded you about it. Yet you still go and— (Suddenly breaking off as she remembers that this is no place to discuss family matters, and turning to her daughter instead.) Where's Ta-hai?

Feng: I thought he was waiting for us at the porter's lodge.

Lu: It's not you two he's waiting for, it's the master he wants to see. (To his wife.) I sent word to you last year about Ta-hai. He managed to get a job in the mine.—Only because I put in a word for him here, though.

Feng (finding her father's repeated boasting distasteful): You needn't keep harping on that, Dad. Hadn't you better go and look after Ta-hai?

Lu: Oh, well. I'd forgotten all about him. (Going towards the center door, then stopping and turning for a last few words.) You'd better stay here in this room for the time being and not go roaming around all over the place, because the mistress will be down any minute. (He goes out.)

(Once he is out of the room, Lu Ma and her daughter relax. They look at each other with a wry smile.)

Ma (holding out her hand to Ssu-feng): Let me have a good look at you, child.

(Ssu-feng goes across to her mother.)

Feng: You're not cross with me, are you, Mother?

Ma: No. What's done is done.—But why have you kept quiet about it all this time?

Feng: I didn't dare tell you, because I was afraid you'd be angry with me.—Though I don't see that it matters all that much really that I should be in service like this.

Ma: You don't imagine it's because I don't like being poor, do you? Or that I'm afraid of having people laugh at us because we're poor? No, child, it's not that at all, I've learned to accept all that. The thing that really worries me is that you're still very young, and you might easily go and do something foolish. (Heaving a sigh.) Well, there's no need to talk about it now. (She gets up.) I wonder what your mistress wants to see me about. Strange, isn't it?

Feng: I suppose it is. (Becoming apprehensive, but still trying to be *optimistic.)* Though, you know, Mother, the mistress here hasn't got many friends. She's heard that you can read and write, so perhaps she feels you've got something in common and wants to have a little chat with you about that.

MA: D'you think so? *(She looks slowly round the room at the furniture, then points to the old bureau with the mirror on it.)* This room's very elegantly furnished—though the furniture looks rather too old.

FENG: It is, too. It's all thirty years old. They say his first wife was very fond of all these things—the young master's mother, that is. They did have some clumsy furniture in those days, didn't they?

MA *(dabbing her face with a handkerchief)*: That's funny—why should all the windows be kept closed in this weather?

FENG: Yes, it is queer, isn't it? One of the master's queer notions. He will have the windows closed in the summer.

MA *(trying to remember something)*: You know, Feng, I seem to have seen this room somewhere before.

FENG *(laughing)*: Have you? You must have been thinking about me too much, and come here in a dream.

MA: Yes, it does seem like a dream.—I can't get over it, it all looks so familiar. *(She hangs her head.)*

FENG *(alarmed)*: Ma, Mother, are you feeling all right? It must be the heat. Shall I go and get you a glass of water?

MA: No, I'm all right. Don't go.

FENG: What's the matter with you, Mother?

MA *(scrutinizing everything in the room and lost in thought)*: Strange —*(reaching out and grasping Ssu-feng by the hand)* Ssu-feng!

FENG *(feeling her mother's hands)*: Why, your hands are like ice, Mother.

MA: Don't worry. I'm all right. It really does seem as if I've been here before, though—if not in body, then in spirit.

FENG: Oh, don't be so silly, Mother. How can you have been here before? It's twenty years since they moved up north here, and you were still living down south then, weren't you?

MA: I can't help that. I still say I've been here before. These pieces of furniture—I've seen them before somewhere—though where, I just can't think.

FENG: What are you looking at, Mother?

MA: The bureau, that bureau there. *(Her voice dwindles to a whisper as she racks her brains to remember.)*

FENG: Oh, that used to belong to the first mistress, the one who died.

MA *(to herself)*: No, it can't be, it can't be.

FENG (*feeling sorry for her mother*): Don't talk any more, Mother. Just relax for a while.

MA: It's all right.—I gathered when I was down at the porter's lodge just now that there are two sons.

FENG: Yes, there are. Very nice, both of them. In fact, all the Chous are very nice people.

MA: The Chous? Is that their name?

FENG: Now Mother. Didn't you have to ask the way to the Chous' when you came. You can't have forgotten already. You must have got a touch of the sun on your way here. I'll get you a drink of water. (*As she goes past the bureau.*) Look Mother, here's a photo of the master's first wife. (*She brings the photograph across and holds it over her mother's shoulder from behind for her to look at.*)

MA (*taking the photograph and looking at it*): Oh! (*She is too astonished to say another word.*)

FENG (*still standing behind her*): You can see how good-looking she was. She was the eldest son's mother. They say I look like her. It's a pity about her dying.

(*Lu Ma's hand trembles as it holds the photograph.*)

FENG: Mother!

MA: Get me a drink of water.

FENG: You'd better come over here. (*She takes her mother's arm and leads her across to the large sofa.*)

(*Lu Ma still has the photograph clutched tightly in her hand.*)

FENG: Just lie down here for a minute. I'll go and get you some water. (*She hurries out into the dining-room.*)

MA: Oh, my God! . . . So I'm dead.—But this photo, and this furniture. . . . Can it be true? Oh, isn't the world big enough to—? To think that after all these years of misery my own poor child should have to go and find herself in his—his house of all places. Oh, God!

(*Ssu-feng comes in with the water.*)

FENG: Here you are, Mother.

(*Lu Ma drinks.*)

FENG: Feel a bit better now?

MA: Mm, yes, I'm all right now. You're coming straight home with me, Ssu-feng.

FENG (*surprised*): Why, what's the matter now?

(*Fan-yi's voice calls "Ssu-feng!" from the dining-room.*)

FENG (*stopping to listen*): It's the mistress.

FAN-YI'S VOICE: Ssu-feng!

FENG: Yes, madam?

FAN-YI'S VOICE: Come here, Ssu-feng, where have you put the master's raincoat?

FENG (*loudly*): I'm just coming. (*To her mother.*) I won't be a minute, Mother.

MA: Go on, then.

(*Ssu-feng goes out. Lu Ma looks all round the room, then goes across to the bureau and puts the photograph back. Suddenly hearing footsteps from the garden, she turns round, waiting.*)

(*Lu Kuei comes in through the center door.*)

LU: Where's Ssu-feng?

MA: Her mistress shouted for her.

LU: Well, when you see the mistress presently, tell her she needn't send the raincoat along when she's found it, because the master will be coming along here himself as he wants to see her about something.

MA: You say the master's coming along to this room here?

LU: Yes, and make sure you tell her properly, because if you don't, and she's not here when he comes, the old man will go right up in the air.

MA: You'd better tell her yourself.

LU: I'm up to my eyes in work with all these servants to look after. I haven't got time to stand about here.

MA: Well, I'm going home. I won't be seeing your mistress after all.

LU: But why not? She's sent for you, and you never know: She might have something important to see you about.

MA: I'm taking Ssu-feng home with me. She won't be working here any longer.

LU: What! Who d'you think you—

(*Fan-yi enters from the dining-room.*)

LU: Madam!

FAN (*speaking back into the dining-room*): Bring the other two as well, Ssu-feng, and let the master choose. (*Turning to Lu Ma.*) Ah, you'll be Ssu-feng's mother, I think? I'm sorry I've kept you waiting all this time.

LU: You shouldn't apologize to her, madam. You've done her a great honor by allowing her to come and pay her respects to you.

(*Ssu-feng enters from the dining-room with the raincoats.*)

FAN: Won't you sit down? You must have been waiting a long time.

MA (*looking Fan-yi up and down, but not sitting down*): Only a few moments, madam.

FENG: Shall I take all three raincoats along to the master, madam?

LU: The master wants them left here as he's coming along for them himself. Oh, and madam: he said would you please wait for him here, as he'd like to have a word with you.

FAN: Very well. *(To Ssu-feng.)* Go to the kitchen and see how they're getting on with dinner. Make sure they know what's wanted.

FENG: Very good, madam. *(Shooting a glance first at Lu Kuei and then, apprehensively, at Fan-yi, she goes out through the center door.)*

FAN: Lu Kuei, tell the master I'm engaged here with Ssu-feng's mother and that I'll let him know when I'm ready to see him.

LU: Very good, madam. *(He does not move.)*

FAN *(seeing that he is still there)*: Was there something else you wanted to see me about?

LU: Yes, madam: this morning the master had me make an appointment for you with the German doctor.

FAN: I know. Master Chung's already told me about it.

LU: The master was just saying that he'd like you to see the doctor as soon as he arrives, madam.

FAN: All right. You can go now.

(Lu Kuei goes out through the center door.)

FAN *(to Lu Ma)*: Let's sit down, then. Make yourself at home. *(She sits down on a sofa.)*

MA *(sitting down on a nearby chair)*: The moment I got off the train, I was told you wanted to see me.

FAN: Yes, I'd heard so much about you from Ssu-feng: she tells me you've had an education and that you come from a very good family.

MA *(not wishing to bring up the past)*: Ssu-feng's a silly child. Not much sense. She must have been a great trial to you.

FAN: On the contrary, she's very intelligent and I'm very fond of her. I don't think a girl like her should be in service at all. She should be given a better start in life.

MA: I realize that. I've been against her going into service all along.

FAN: I know just what you mean. Now, I know you're an educated, sensible person, and one can tell at a glance that you're not one for beating about the bush, so I may as well tell you straight out why I asked you to come.

MA *(having misgivings)*: Why, has this girl of mine been behaving in a way that causes gossip?

FAN *(smiling and assuming an air of complete assurance)*: Oh no, nothing like that.

(Lu Kuei comes in through the center door.)

LU: Madam.

213

FAN: What is it?

LU: Dr. Kramer's here. He's waiting in the small drawing-room.

FAN: I have a visitor.

LU: A visitor?—But the master would like you to see the doctor now, madam.

FAN: All right. You needn't wait.

(*Lu Kuei goes out.*)

FAN (*to Lu Ma*): Well, I'd better tell you something about the family first. You see, there are hardly any women in the house.

MA: I suppose not.

FAN: In fact, there's only myself and one or two maids. Then there's my husband, and my two sons. That leaves the rest of the servants—all men.

MA: I see.

FAN: Ssu-feng's very young; only nineteen, isn't she?

MA: Eighteen.

FAN (*with artful guile*): Oh yes, that's right. I remember now, she does look about a year older than my son. Yes, so young, so attractive—and working away from home.

MA (*anxiously*): Look, if Ssu-feng's done anything that she shouldn't have, you must tell me. Please don't keep anything from me.

FAN: No, it's nothing like that. (*She smiles again.*) She's a very nice girl. I'm only telling you how things are here. I've got a son, just seventeen—you may have seen him in the garden when you came in—not particularly bright.

(*Lu Kuei comes in from the study.*)

LU: The master's becoming insistent about you seeing the doctor, madam.

FAN: Is there no one to keep the doctor company?

LU: Yes, the master's with him himself. The superintendent's just left.

FAN: You can tell the master that I'm not ill, nor have I asked for a doctor.

LU: Very good, madam. (*He remains where he is.*)

FAN (*looking round at him*): What are you waiting for?

LU: I thought there might be something further, madam.

FAN (*struck by a sudden thought*): Yes, there is something. After you've told the master what I said, go and find an electrician. I've just heard that an old electric cable on the wistaria-trellis has snapped. It's trailing loose and it's live. Tell him to get it mended as soon as possible. We don't want any accidents.

214

(Lu Kuei goes out through the center door.)

FAN *(seeing that Lu Ma is on her feet)*: There's no need to get up, Mrs. Lu. Phew, this room's getting more stifling than ever. *(She goes across to a window, opens it, then returns to her seat.)* Just lately I've noticed that my son isn't quite his usual self. Well, to my great surprise, he suddenly tells me that he's very fond of Ssu-feng.

MA *(startled)*: What!

FAN: He wants to share his school allowance with her to pay for her education. He even says— *(with a smile) silly boy!*—that he wants to marry her.

MA: You needn't go on. I quite understand.

FAN: Ssu-feng is older than my son, and she's a very intelligent girl. In a situation like this—

MA *(resenting Fan-yi's mysterious tone of voice)*: I think I can trust my daughter. I'm satisfied that she's a sensible girl and knows the difference between right and wrong. I've always been against her going into service in a big house, but I've got confidence in her and I don't think she could have done anything foolish in the two years that she's been with you.

FAN: Yes, Mrs. Lu, I agree that Ssu-feng's a sensible girl; but now that this unfortunate situation has arisen, well, I'm afraid it rather lends itself to misunderstanding.

MA *(with a sigh)*: I never expected to find myself here today. I'm thinking of taking her with me when I go back, so if you'd be kind enough to let her leave you at once. . . .

FAN: Well—if you think it would be for the best, I've got nothing against it. Though there is one thing: my son's rather wild, and I'm afraid he may try to see Ssu-feng at your home.

MA: You needn't worry about that. I can see now how stupid I was. I should never have left her for her father to look after. I'm leaving here in three days' time, so I don't think she'll ever see anything more of the Chous. Madam, I'd like to take her away from here at once.

FAN: Well, if you insist. I'll get the office to make up her wages, and her personal belongings can be taken round to your house by a servant —And I'll send a suitcase of some of my old clothes which she may have some use for at home.

MA *(to herself)*: My poor child!

FAN *(going up to her)*: Don't take it so much to heart, Mrs. Lu. If you have any difficulty with money because of this, please don't hesitate to come and see me. You can rely on me to help you. Now, take her

215

home where you can look after her. With a good mother like you to guide her, she'll be much better off than working here.

(Chou Pu-yuan enters from the study.)

CHOU: Fan-yi!

(Fan-yi turns, while Lu Ma slips away into a corner.)

CHOU: Why haven't you gone yet?

FAN *(all innocence)*: Gone where?

CHOU: Aren't you aware you're keeping Dr. Kramer waiting?

FAN: Dr. Kramer? Who's he?

CHOU: Why, the Dr. Kramer that you saw before.

FAN: But there's nothing wrong with me now.

CHOU *(patiently)*: Dr. Kramer's been a good friend of mine since we first met in Germany. Specializes in nervous troubles. Your nerves are a little upset, but I'm sure he'll soon put you right.

FAN *(exploding)*: What do you mean, my nerves are upset? Why must you all keep saying such wicked things about me? There's nothing the matter with me, I tell you, nothing at all!

CHOU *(coldly)*: Well, you've got all the symptoms of being neurotic—raving and screaming in front of other people, and refusing to have a doctor when you're ill, or even admit that you're ill.

FAN: Humph! If there *were* anything the matter with me, it wouldn't be anything a doctor could cure. *(She goes towards the dining-room door.)*

CHOU *(at the top of his voice)*: Stop! Where do you think you're going?

FAN *(nonchalantly)*: I'm going upstairs.

CHOU *(imperiously)*: Do as you're told!

FAN: Take orders from you? *(She looks him disdainfully up and down.)* And who, pray, do you think you are? *(Without more ado she goes out through the dining-room.)*

CHOU: Here, somebody!

(A servant appears.)

SERVANT: Yes, sir?

CHOU: The mistress is upstairs. Tell Master Ping to take Dr. Kramer up to her room.

SERVANT: Very good, sir.

CHOU: And tell Master Ping to ask the doctor to excuse me. I'm tired and I'll have to leave him on his own.

SERVANT: Very good, sir. *(He goes out.)*

CHOU *(lights a cigar, then, noticing the raincoats on the table, addresses Lu Ma)*: Are these the raincoats the mistress hunted out?

MA *(looking at him)*: I think so.

216

CHOU: Well, they're the wrong ones. They're all new ones. It's my old one that I want, tell her.

MA: Um.

CHOU (*seeing that she does not stir*): Don't you know that servants aren't allowed to be in this room unless they're sent for?

MA: No, I didn't know that, sir.

CHOU: Are you a new servant here?

MA: No, I came to see my daughter.

CHOU: Your daughter?

MA: My daughter Ssu-feng.

CHOU: Then you've got into the wrong room.

MA: Oh.—Will that be all, sir.

CHOU (*indicating the open window*): Who's opened that window?

MA: Oh, yes. (*She strolls across to the window as if quite at home here, closes it, then goes slowly towards the center door.*)

CHOU (*suddenly struck by something odd about the way she closes the window*): Wait a minute.

(*Lu Ma stops.*)

CHOU: Who—what's your name?

MA: Lu.

CHOU: I see; Lu. You don't sound like a northerner from your accent.

MA: You're quite right: I'm not. I'm from Kiangsu.

CHOU: It sounds rather like a Wusih accent.

MA: Well, I was born and bred in Wusih.

CHOU (*in deep thought*): Wusih, eh? Wusih. . . . (*Suddenly.*) When were you there, in Wusih?

MA: About thirty years ago.

CHOU: So you were in Wusih thirty years ago, eh?

MA: Yes. Thirty years ago. I remember we still didn't use matches in those days.

CHOU (*deep in thought again*): Thirty years ago. . . . Yes, it's a long time. Let's see, I must have been in my twenties then. Yes, I was still in Wusih then.

MA: So you're from Wusih too, are you, sir?

CHOU: Yes. (*Meditatively.*) Nice place, Wusih.

MA: Yes, very nice.

CHOU: And you say you were there thirty years ago?

MA: That's right, sir.

CHOU: Something happened in Wusih thirty years ago, quite a to-do—

MA: Oh.

CHOU: You know the incident I mean?

217

MA: Well, I might still remember if I knew what you were referring to, sir.

CHOU: Oh, it happened so long ago that I expect everyone's forgotten all about it.

MA: You never know. There may be someone who still remembers it.

CHOU: I've asked dozens of people who were in Wusih at that time, and I've sent people down to make inquiries on the spot; but the people who were there at the time are either getting on in years or else they're dead, and the few who are still alive either knew nothing about it or else they've forgotten all about it. Though you might know. Well, there was a family in Wusih thirty years ago called the Meis.

MA: The Meis?

CHOU: There was a young lady in the family, a clever girl, and very decently behaved, too. One night, she suddenly went and drowned herself. Then, afterwards—you heard about it?

MA: I don't think so.

CHOU: Oh.

MA: Though I did know a girl by the name of Mei, but that was twenty-seven years ago.

CHOU: Oh? Tell me about her.

MA: But she wasn't a lady, and not particularly clever—and not very well behaved either, by all accounts.

CHOU: Perhaps—perhaps you're talking about the wrong girl.—Though I'd like you to go on, all the same.

MA: Well, this girl Mei threw herself in the river one night, though she wasn't alone: she was holding in her arms a three-day-old baby boy. She'd been leading a rather irregular life, so they said.

CHOU (wincing): Oh?

MA: She was a low-class girl who'd been getting above herself. It seems she'd been having an affair with a gentleman's son by the name of Chou, and that she'd had two sons by him. Well, a matter of three days after the second one was born, this young Mr. Chou suddenly turned her out. The elder child was left with the family, but the new-born baby was in her arms when she threw herself in the river. That was on a New Year's Eve.

CHOU (with beads of perspiration on his forehead): Oh!

MA: But she was no lady, only the daughter of a maid at the Chous' in Wusih. Her name was Shih-ping.

CHOU (looking up): What's your name?

MA: My name's Lu, sir.

CHOU (heaving a sigh and becoming lost in thought): Yes, Shih-ping,

Shih-ping, that was the name. They say some poor man found her body and had it buried. Could you make inquiries and find out where her grave is?

MA: But I don't see why you take such an interest in all this business, sir.

CHOU: She was a sort of relative of ours.

MA: A relative?

CHOU: Yes, er—we'd like to look after her grave.

MA: Oh, but there's no need to do that.

CHOU: How do you mean?

MA: She's still alive.

CHOU (*shaken*): What!

MA: She never died.

CHOU: Still alive, you say? But I don't see how she can be. I saw her clothes on the bank of the river, and inside them was a note she'd left.

MA: She was rescued, though.

CHOU: She was?

MA: But as she was never seen in Wusih again after that, everybody there thought she was dead.

CHOU: Where is she now, then?

MA: She's living alone, miles away from Wusih.

CHOU: What about the baby?

MA: He's alive, too.

CHOU (*suddenly standing up*): Who are you, anyway?

MA: I am Ssu-feng's mother, sir.

CHOU: H'm.

MA: She's getting on now. She's married to a poor man and they've got a daughter. She doesn't have an easy time of it.

CHOU: Have you any idea where she is at the moment?

MA: I saw her only the other day.

CHOU: What! You mean she's here of all places? In the city?

MA: Yes, not far from here.

CHOU: Well. I'm damned!

MA: Would you like to see her, sir?

CHOU (*hurriedly*): No, no, not particularly.

MA: Times are hard for her now. After she left the Chous, the young Mr. Chou married a rich, well-connected young lady. But this girl Mei was on her own, far from home, without a single relative or friend to help her. And she had this child to support. She did everything—from begging to sewing, from working as a maid to being a servant in a school.

CHOU: But why didn't she go back to the Chous?

219

MA: I don't expect the idea appealed to her. For the child's sake she got married twice.

CHOU: She did, eh?

MA: Yes, and both times to very low-class people. She's been unlucky in her husbands. Perhaps you'd like to help her in some way, sir?

CHOU: Well, I think you'd better go now.

MA: Will that be all, sir? *(She gazes at him, her eyes filling with tears.)*

CHOU: Er—oh, you can tell Ssu-feng to get my old raincoat out of the camphor-wood chest—and she can fish out those old shirts while she's about it.

MA: Old shirts, did you say?

CHOU: Yes, tell her they're in the very old chest—silk ones, with no collars.

MA: But aren't there five of those silk shirts, sir? Which one did you want?

CHOU: What do you mean, "which one"?

MA: Well, hasn't one of them got a hole burnt in the right sleeve, and wasn't it mended by having a plum-blossom embroidered over the hole? And then there's the one—

CHOU *(startled)*: A plum-blossom, you say?

MA: Yes, and the name "Ping" was embroidered beside it, too.

CHOU *(rising slowly to his feet)*: Then you—then you—you're—

MA: I used to be one of your servants.

CHOU: Shih-ping! *(In a low voice.)* So it is you, then?

MA: Of course you never expected to see Shih-ping looking so old that even you wouldn't recognize her. *(Chou Pu-yuan glances automatically at the photograph on the bureau, then looks back at Lu Ma.)* *(There is a long pause.)*

CHOU *(suddenly stern)*: What did you come here for?

MA: I didn't ask to come.

CHOU: Who sent you here, then?

MA *(bitterly)*: Fate! Unjust fate brought me here!

CHOU *(coldly)*: So you've found me, after more than twenty years.

MA *(indignantly)*: But I haven't; I haven't been looking for you. I thought you were dead long ago. I never expected to find myself here today. It's fate that meant us to meet again.

CHOU: Well, you might be a bit calmer about it. We've both got families of our own now. If you think you've got a grievance, let's at least begin by dispensing with all these tears. We're a bit too old for that sort of thing.

MA: Tears? I've cried my eyes dry long ago. No, I've got no grievance: all

I've got left is hatred, and regret, and the memory of the misery I've gone through, day in day out, for the past twenty years and more. Though I expect you've forgotten what you did: twenty-seven years ago, on New Year's Eve, just three days after I'd given birth to your second child, you turned me out of your house in a snowstorm, because you were in a hurry to get rid of me so that you could marry a young lady with money and position.

CHOU: What's the point of raking up old scores after all these years?

MA: The point? Because our young Mr. Chou has been a success in life and is now a respectable member of society! I didn't succeed in killing myself after I was turned out by your family, but the shock killed my mother. And your family forced me to leave my two babies behind at your house.

CHOU: But you took the younger one with you, didn't you?

MA: Yes, your mother eventually let me take him—but only because she thought he wouldn't survive long. (*To herself.*) My God! It all seems like a bad dream!

CHOU: I don't see the need to go on raking up the past like this.

MA: But I do! I do! I've kept it pent up inside me more than twenty years, and now it's got to come out! After you married and moved out of the district, I thought I'd never see you again for the rest of my life. The last thing I expected was that my own daughter would come to work in your house of all places and follow in her mother's footsteps.

CHOU: No wonder Ssu-feng's the image of you.

MA: I waited on you, and now my child is waiting on your sons. It's a punishment. That's what it is: a punishment.

CHOU: Now, steady on. Let's be sensible about it. I'm not as cold-blooded as you think. You don't imagine anyone can stifle his conscience as easily as that? You've only got to look at this room: all your favorite furniture of the old days is here. I've kept it all these years to remember you by.

MA (*with bent head*): Um.

CHOU: I always remember your birthday, April the eighteenth. So far as everyone here is concerned you were my lawful wedded wife. Remember how you insisted on keeping the windows closed because of your delicate health after you had Ping? Well, I still keep them closed in memory of you to help make up for the wrong I did you.

MA (*with a sigh*): Please don't go on. We're both too old for that sort of thing.

CHOU: I couldn't agree more. Now we can have a straight talk.

MA: I don't think there's anything to talk about.

221

CHOU: On the contrary. You don't seem to have altered much in temperament—Lu Kuei strikes me as being rather a shifty character.

MA: You've got nothing to worry about on that score. He'll never know anything about it.

CHOU: Which is a good thing for both of us. There is one other thing I'd like to know: what's become of the boy you took with you?

MA: He's working at your mine.

CHOU: I mean, where is he at this moment?

MA: In the porter's lodge, waiting to see you.

CHOU: What! Lu Ta-hai? You mean—he's my son?

MA: He certainly is! Only he and you are poles apart.

CHOU (*wryly*): And so my own flesh and blood turns against me and foments a strike in my mine!

MA: Don't think he'll own you as his father, though.

CHOU (*suddenly*): All right! Let's have it! How much do you want?

MA: What do you mean?

CHOU: To keep you in your old age.

MA (*with a twisted smile*): Ha! So you still think I came here purposely to blackmail you, do you?

CHOU: All right, let's say no more about that for the moment. I'll tell you first of all what I propose to do. Well now, Lu Kuei will have to go, and Ssu-feng can't very well stay here, either. However—

MA: You needn't be afraid. You think I'd blackmail you with our relationship? Don't worry, I won't. In three days' time I'll be going back to where I came from, and I'll be taking Ssu-feng with me. This is all a bad dream. I just couldn't bear to stay in the place any longer.

CHOU: Good idea. I'll pay all your fares and expenses.

MA: You'll do what?

CHOU: It'll make me feel a bit better.

MA: Oh no, you don't! (*She laughs derisively.*) Do you imagine I'd fall back on your charity now, after managing single-handed for twenty-seven years?

CHOU: All right, all right. What is it you want, anyway?

MA (*after a pause*): Well, there is—there is one thing I'd like.

CHOU: And what's that?—Mm?

MA (*blinded by tears*): I—I just want to have a last look at my son Ping.

CHOU: You want to see him?

MA: Yes. Where is he?

CHOU: He's upstairs with his stepmother and her doctor. I can send for him now if you like. Though—(*he hesitates*) he's grown up now, and he—(*hesitating*) he thinks his mother's been dead for years now.

MA: Now you don't imagine I'm going to fall on his neck in a flood of tears and tell him I'm his long-lost mother, do you? I'm not as silly as that. I quite realize that I'm not the sort of mother that any son could feel proud of. I appreciate that his position in life and his education wouldn't allow him to own such a woman as me as his mother. I have learned a thing or two all these years, you know. No, all I want is just to see him. After all, he is my own child. You've got nothing to worry about, though: even if I did spoil everything for him by telling him, he'd still never own me.

CHOU: So that's settled, then. I'll have him down here and let you have a look at him, and after that, no Lu will ever set foot inside this house again.

MA: All right, then. And I hope I'll never set eyes on you again as long as I live.

CHOU (*taking a check-book from an inside pocket and making out a check*): Fair enough. Here's a check of five thousand dollars, which I hope you'll accept. I hope it'll help to make up for the wrong I've done you.

(*Lu Ma takes the check and tears it up.*)

CHOU: Shih-ping!

MA: No amount of your money can cancel out all these years of heart-break.

CHOU: But you—

(*He is cut short by angry voices outside. Lu Ta-hai's voice is heard shouting "Get out of my way. I'm going in." Then come the voices of several footmen: "Stop. You can't go in. The master's resting." The noise of a struggle follows.*)

CHOU (*going to the center door*): Come here, somebody!

(*A servant appears in the doorway.*)

CHOU: Who's that making all that noise?

SERVANT: It's that miner, Lu Ta-hai. He won't be reasonable about it, but insists on seeing you now, sir.

CHOU: I see. (*He hesitates a moment.*) You'd better let him come in, then. Wait a minute: send someone upstairs for Master Ping. I want to see him.

SERVANT: Very good, sir. (*He goes out through the center door.*)

CHOU (*to Lu Ma*): Don't be so pig-headed, Shih-ping. If you don't take the money, you'll regret it one day.

(*Lu Ma looks at him without so much as a word.*)

(*Three or four servants bring in Lu Ta-hai. He stands on the left with the servants clustering round him.*)

HAI (*noticing his mother*): Mother, I didn't know you were still here.

CHOU (*sizing him up*): What's your name?

HAI: Don't you put on airs with me. Are you trying to tell me you don't know who I am?

CHOU: All I know is that you were the biggest trouble-maker during the strike.

HAI: Precisely. That's why I've come to pay you a visit.

CHOU: What is it you want?

HAI: As chairman of the board of directors you know very well what I want.

CHOU (*shaking his head*): I'm afraid I don't.

HAI: We've come all this way from the mine, and since six o'clock this morning I've been cooling my heels in your porter's lodge, just so that I can ask you, Mr. Chairman, what exactly you're going to do about our demands. Do you accept them or not?

CHOU: H'm.—What's become of the other three representatives, then?

HAI: I'll tell you: they're busy enlisting the support of other trade unions.

CHOU: I see. But didn't they tell you anything else?

HAI: It's none of your business what they told me.—And now I want to know what exactly you think you're playing at, blowing hot and cold all the time.

(*Chou Ping comes in from the dining-room. Seeing that his father has company, he turns to go.*)

CHOU (*catching sight of Chou Ping*): Don't go, Ping.

(*He glances at Lu Ma.*)

PING: Very well, Father.

CHOU (*gesturing to one side*): Come and stand here by me. (*To Ta-hai.*) You'll find you need something more than mere emotion if you're going to be a negotiator.

HAI: Humph! Don't think I don't know your tricks! I know them all. All this hanging about and putting off is to give you time to buy over a few miserable blacklegs. You're just keeping us here out of the way until you've done it.

CHOU: I must admit that that supposition is not entirely inaccurate.

HAI: But you're wasting your time. The miners are solid behind the strike this time, and they're properly organized. This time we representatives are not coming to you on our bended knees. Get that straight: we're not on our bended knees. If you accept our demands, well and good; if not, then the strike goes on until you do. We know just how long you can last out: two months, and you'll have to close down.

CHOU: So you think all these representatives and leaders of yours are reliable, eh?

HAI: At least they're much more reliable than anybody in your money-grabbing concerns.

CHOU: Then let me show you something.

(*He looks for a telegram on the table. A servant hands it to him. Just at this moment Chou Chung slips unobtrusively in from the study and stands there listening.*)

CHOU (*handing the telegram to Lu Ta-hai*): This telegram came from the mine yesterday.

HAI (*reading it*): What! They've gone back! (*Putting the telegram down.*) They can't have done.

CHOU: The miners went back yesterday morning. You mean to say you didn't know, and you one of their representatives?

HAI (*angrily*): So the mine police can get away with opening fire on the miners and killing thirty of them, eh? (*He bursts out laughing.*) Huh, it's a fake. You faked this telegram yourselves to split us. What a dirty, low trick!

PING (*unable to contain himself any longer*): Who do you think you are? How dare you speak like that!

CHOU: You keep out of this! (*To Lu Ta-hai.*) So you have complete confidence in the other representatives who came with you, eh?

HAI: All right, don't waste your breath: I know what you're getting at.

CHOU: Very well, then, what if I show you the written agreement to call off the strike?

HAI (*laughing*): You needn't try and bluff me: I wasn't born yesterday. An agreement doesn't mean a thing without the representatives' signatures on it.

CHOU: Get the agreement.

(*A servant goes into the study and returns with a document, which he hands to Chou Pu-yuan.*)

CHOU: There you are: the agreement, complete with the signatures of the other three.

HAI (*looking at it*): What! (*Slowly.*) They've signed it. All three of them. (*Reaching out for the document to examine it more closely.*) How could they just sign like that, without consulting me? They can't just ignore me like this!

CHOU (*whipping the document away and handing it to a servant*): So

225

there you are, you young fool. Shouting and blustering won't get you anywhere: experience is what you want.

HAI: Where are the other three?

CHOU: They caught a train back last night.

HAI (*as the scales finally fall from his eyes*): So the three of them have double-crossed me, the spineless rats! And sold their mates, too! So your money's done the trick again, your nasty pieces of work! You're all the same, you bosses!

PING (*angered*): Why, you insolent scoundrel!

CHOU: Hold your tongue. (*Turning back to Lu Ta-hai.*) You're no longer in a position to speak to me, Lu Ta-hai—the firm's already sacked you.

HAI: Sacked me!

CHUNG: That's not playing the game, Father.

CHOU (*turning to Chou Chung*): You shut up and get out!

(*Chou Chung departs in high dudgeon through the center door.*)

HAI: All right, then. (*Grinding his teeth.*) Your dirty tricks are nothing new to me. You'd stoop to anything so long as there was money in it. You get the police to mow down your men, and then you—

CHOU: How dare you!

MA (*going to Lu Ta-hai*): Come on, let's go. That's enough.

HAI: Yes, and I know all about your record, too! When you contracted to repair that bridge over the river at Harbin, you deliberately breached the dyke—

CHOU (*harshly*): Get out of here!

SERVANTS (*tugging at Lu Ta-hai*): Come on! Outside! Out!

HAI: You drowned two thousand two hundred coolies in cold blood, and for each life lost you raked in three hundred dollars! I tell you, creature, you've made your money by killing people, and you and your sons stand accursed for ever! And now on top of that you—

PING (*hurling himself on Lu Ta-hai and striking him twice in the face*): Take that, you lying swine!

(*Lu Ta-hai returns a blow, but is seized and held by the servants.*)

PING: Give him what for!

HAI (*to Chou Ping*): You—!

(*The servants set upon him. Blood appears on his face.*)

CHOU (*harshly*): Stop! Leave him alone!

(*The servants stop but still keep hold of Lu Ta-hai.*)

HAI (*struggling*): Let go of me, you hooligans!

PING (*to the servants*): Hustle him outside!

MA (*breaking down*): You *are* hooligans, too! (*Going across to Chou*

Ping.) You're my—mighty free with your fists! What right have you to hit my son?

PING: Who are you?

MA: I'm your—your victim's mother.

HAI: Take no notice of the rat, Mother. You don't want him setting on to you, as well.

MA *(staring dazedly at Chou Ping's face, then bursting into tears again):* Oh, Ta-hai, let's go! Let's get out of here!

(Lu Ta-hai is shepherded out by the servants, followed by Lu Ma. Only Chou Pu-yuan and Chou Ping remain on the stage.)

PING *(apologetically):* Father.

CHOU: You might have been less impetuous.

PING: But the fellow had no right to throw mud at you like that.

(A pause.)

CHOU: Did your mother see the doctor?

PING: Yes, but he couldn't find anything wrong with her.

CHOU: H'm. *(Lost in thought for a while, then, abruptly.)* Here, somebody!

(A servant comes in through the center door.)

CHOU: Tell the mistress I've dismissed Lu Kuei and Ssu-feng, so she can make up their wages.

SERVANT: Very good, sir.

PING: But I say! What have they done wrong?

CHOU: Aren't you aware that this fellow we had here just now is also a Lu Ssu-feng's brother, in fact?

PING *(taken aback):* That fellow Ssu-feng's brother? Why, Father—

CHOU *(to the servant):* Tell the mistress that the office is to give Lu Kuei and Ssu-feng two months' extra pay, but they must leave the house today. That's all.

(The servant goes out through the dining-room.)

PING: But, Father, Ssu-feng and Lu Kuei have both been excellent servants, and very loyal.

CHOU: H'm. *(Yawning.)* I'm tired. Think I'll go and have a rest in the study. Tell them to bring me a cup of Yunnan tea—strong.

PING: Very well, Father.

(Chou Pu-yuan goes into the study.)

PING *(heaving a sigh):* Phew! *(He hurries towards the center door.)*

(Just at that moment Chou Chung comes in through the same door.)

CHUNG *(anxiously):* Ping, where's Ssu-feng?

PING: I've no idea.

CHUNG: Is it true that Father's dismissed her?

PING: Yes, and Lu Kuei, too.

CHUNG: Even if her brother did upset Father, he got a good hiding for it, didn't he? No point in taking it out on the girl, is there?

PING: Go and ask Father.

CHUNG: But it's quite preposterous.

PING: Yes, isn't it?

CHUNG: Where is Father?

PING: In the study.

(Chou Chung goes into the study, leaving Chou Ping pacing up and down. Ssu-feng comes in through the center door, drying her eyes.)

PING *(hurrying across to her)*: I'm sorry, Ssu-feng. I really had no idea who he was.

(Ssu-feng gestures helplessly. Her heart is too full for words.)

PING: Your brother shouldn't have said such wild things, though.

FENG: No use bringing it up again. *(She makes straight for the dining-room.)*

PING: Where are you off to now?

FENG: I'm going to pack my things. It's good-bye now. Since you'll be leaving tomorrow, I may never see you again.

PING: No, don't go. *(He stands in her way.)*

FENG: No, let me go. Don't you realize we've already got the sack from this place?

PING *(hurt)*: Feng, you—you don't blame me, do you?

FENG: I knew it would end up like this sooner or later. Don't come to see me tonight whatever you do.

PING: But—what about the future?

FENG: Well—we'll just have to wait and see.

PING: Yes, Ssu-feng, I will see you this evening—I must. I've got so many things to talk over with you. Ssu-feng, you—

FENG: No. Whatever happens, you mustn't come.

PING: Then you'll have to find some other way of seeing me.

FENG: There isn't any other way. Can't you see how things are?

PING: Whatever you say, I'm coming round.

FENG: No, you mustn't. Don't be a fool. I absolutely forbid you—

(Chou Fan-yi enters from the dining-room.)

FENG: Oh, madam.

FAN: Oh, I didn't know you two were here. *(To Ssu-feng.)* I'll have your things sent round in a short while. Either your father can take them, or else one of the servants can come.—Where do you live?

FENG: No. 10, Almond Blossom Lane.

FAN: Don't let it upset you. You can come and see me whenever you're

228

free, as often as you like. Yes, I'll have one of the servants take your things along. No. 10, Almond Blossom Lane, you said?

FENG: Yes. Thank you, madam.

LU MA'S VOICE: Ssu-feng! Ssu-feng!

FENG: Yes, Mother? I'm in here.

(Lu Ma comes in through the center door.)

MA: Come on, Ssu-feng, pack up your odds and ends and let's go before it comes on to pour.

(Noise of wind, and distant thunder approaching.)

FENG: All right, Mother.

MA *(to Fan-yi)*: I'll say good-bye to you now, madam. *(To her daughter.)* Thank your mistress for everything, Ssu-feng.

FENG *(dropping a curtsey to Fan-yi)*: Thank you, madam! *(She gazes tearfully at Chou Ping, who slowly turns his head away.)*

(Lu Ma and Ssu-feng go out through the center door.)

FAN: Now, Ping, what were you and Ssu-feng talking about just now?

PING: You've no right to ask me that.

FAN: Don't imagine she could ever understand you.

PING: What do you mean?

FAN: Don't try and put me off with lies again. I want to know where you said you were going.

PING: It's none of your business. I should have thought you had more self-respect than ask a thing like that.

FAN: You must tell me: where is it you're proposing to go tonight?

PING: I—*(abruptly)* I'm going to see her. Now, what are you going to do about it?

FAN *(menacingly)*: Do you realize who she is and who you are?

PING: No. All I know is that I'm really in love with her now, and that she loves me in return. I'm well aware that you've known all about it all the time. Since you now want to have it out in the open, there's no reason why I should conceal it from you any longer.

FAN: To think of a well-educated young man like you carrying on with such a low-class girl, a mere servant's daughter—

PING *(exploding)*: How dare you! Who are you to call her low class, you of all people!

FAN *(with a sneer)*: Take care. Take care. Don't drive a disappointed woman too hard. She's capable of anything.

PING: I'm prepared for the worst.

FAN: All right. Go, then! But be careful—*(looking out of the window, half to herself)* there's a storm coming!

PING *(understanding her)*: I know.

229

(Chou Pu-yuan comes in from the study.)

CHOU: Hullo, what are you all talking about?

PING: I was just telling Mother what had happened.

CHOU: Have they gone?

FAN: Yes.

CHOU: Fan-yi, I've gone and made Chung burst into tears again. Call him out and calm him down, would you?

FAN *(going across to the door of the study)*: Chung! Chung! *(Receiving no answer, she goes into the study.)*

(Outside, wind and thunder howl and roar together.)

(Chou goes over to the window. A shrieking gust of wind sends flower-pots on the window-sill outside crashing to the ground.)

CHOU: Ping, the flower-pots are being blown down by the wind. Tell the servants to hurry up and close the shutters. I expect there's a storm coming.

PING: Very well, Father. *(He goes out through the center door.)*

(Chou Pu-yuan stands in front of the window, watching the lightning outside.)

—CURTAIN—

ACT THREE

Inside Lu Kuei's house—at No. 10, Almond Blossom Lane.

First, let us look at the scene outside the house:

The station clock has struck ten, and the people of Almond Blossom Lane, old and young, are taking the air along the banks of a pond which, although it is the source of evil exhalations drawn up by the summer sun in the daytime, provides late at night an open space where one may catch the fresh, cool breezes that blow in from the less crowded area of the foreign concessions. Despite a sharp downpour a moment ago, it is still unbearably hot and close, and the sky is dark with thunderclouds, black and ominous. It is the sort of weather that makes people feel like sun-scorched blades of grass, which, although they have been moistened by a light dew during the night, are still parched inside and thirsting for another thunderstorm. Yet the frogs that crouch among the reeds by the pond are as untiringly strident as ever. The sound of the strollers' voices comes in desultory snatches. From time to time a silent flash of lightning splashes the starless sky with a harsh blue glare and for one startled moment shows us the weeping willows by the pond, drooping and trembling over the water. Then, just as suddenly, it is dark again.

Then, one by one, the strollers drift away and silence closes in on all sides. A rumble of distant thunder seems to cow even the frogs into silence; a breeze springs up again and sifts through the rustling leaves of the willows. From some echoing alleyway comes the lonely, frantic barking of stray dogs.

Presently the lightning blazes again, stark and terrifying, then a jarring burst of thunder goes shuddering across the sky. In its wake comes a close, oppressive silence, broken only by the occasional croaking of a frog and, what is louder, the sharp clack of a night-watchman's bamboo "gong." A storm is about to break.

When the storm does come, it will last right through to the final curtain.

All the audience can see, however, is the interior of Ssu-feng's room. (It is, in fact, the back room of Lu Kuei's two-roomed hut.) Of the scene just described, apart from the sounds, the audience can see only what is visible through the window in the middle of the back wall.

Now let us examine Ssu-feng's room:

The Lus have just finished their evening meal. All four of them are in an unpleasant mood, and each of them is occupied with his or her own thoughts. Ta-hai is sitting in a corner cleaning something. Lu Ma and Ssu-feng keep an uncomfortable silence. The former, her head bent, is clearing away the bowls and chopsticks from the round table in the center of the room. A drink-fuddled Lu Kuei sits slumped back in a rickety easy-chair on the left. Monkey-like, he stares at his wife from bloodshot eyes and hiccups. He puts his bare feet now on the staves of the chair, now on the floor with his legs sprawled wide apart. He wears a white singlet, sweat-soaked and clinging. He fans himself incessantly with a palm-leaf fan.

Ssu-feng is standing in front of the window. Her back is towards the audience as she stares anxiously out. From outside the window comes the croaking of the frogs and the light-hearted voices of passers-by. She seems to be listening uneasily for something, and from time to time she looks round at her father and then looks swiftly away again in disgust. Beside her, standing against the left wall, is a plank-bed covered with a mat and a spotless double quilt. A mat pillow and a palm-leaf fan are neatly arranged on it.

The room is very small and, as is always the case in the houses of the poor, the ceiling comes oppressively low over one's head. On the wall over the head of the bed hangs an illustrated poster advertising a brand of cigarettes, while on the left-hand wall is pasted an old reproduction originally put up as a New Year decoration and now very tattered and torn. A small table stands by the only chair in the room—now occupied by Lu Kuei—with a mirror, a comb and various cheap cosmetics on it: apparently Ssu-feng's dressing-table. Along the left-hand wall stands a bench, and by the table in the middle of the room there is a solitary stool. Under Ssu-feng's bed, there is a trunk draped with a white cloth and with several pairs of fashionable shoes, a teapot and several cheap bowls on it. An oil lamp with a bright red-paper lampshade stands on the round table. The light is not very strong, yet one sees enough of the articles on the table to know that it is a woman's bedroom.

The room has two doors, of which the one on the left—the side where the bed is—is no more than a gaudily patterned red curtain hanging over a recess which, besides providing storage-space for a heap of coal and bits of old furniture, also serves as Ssu-feng's dressing-room. The door on the right is of cracked and battered planks and leads to the front room. This is Lu Kuei's room, and it is in this front room that he and his wife will sleep tonight. From the front room a door opens on the muddy path leading to the edge of the pond. Just inside the door between the two rooms, leaning against the wall, are several long planks for making a bed with.

When the curtain rises, Lu Kuei has just delivered a voluble and highly-colored lecture to his family. In the tense silence which follows this spirited outburst one can hear the strains of some indelicate love-song coming from the direction of the pond, mingled with the murmur of conversation from the people outside relaxing in the cool of the evening. Inside the room, the four heads are bent in silent preoccupation. Hard drinking and the effort involved in the delivery of such a forceful lecture have bathed Lu Kuei in perspiration from head to foot and now he sits with slobbering lips and his face an ugly red. He is apparently revelling in his position of authority as head of the family, judging by the gusto with which he brandishes his tattered palm-leaf fan and the way he points and gestures with it. His sweat-soaked, flesh-draped head is thrust forward and his glazed eyes swing from one member of his family to another.

Ta-hai is still busy cleaning the object in his hand, which the audience now sees to be a pistol. The two women wait in silence for Lu Kuei to launch another shrill tirade against them. The croaking of the frogs and the voices of street-singers now drift in through the window.

Still standing in front of the window, Ssu-feng now and then heaves a deep sigh.

232

Lu (*coughing*): God almighty! (*Heatedly.*) Just look at you. There's not one of you can look me in the face! (*Turning to Ta-hai and Ssu-feng.*) It's no good you pretending not to hear, either. I've worked my fingers to the bone to bring you two up, both of you, but what have either of you ever done to show your gratitude? (*To Ta-hai.*) Eh? (*To Ssu-feng.*) Answer me that! (*To Lu Ma, who is standing by the round table in the center.*) Or perhaps *you* can tell me, seeing that they're your precious children?

(*Silence. From outside comes the sound of someone singing to the accompaniment of a Chinese fiddle.*)

HAI (*to Ssu-feng*): Who's that still singing at this time of night? It's almost half past ten.

FENG (*listlessly*): Oh, some blind man and his wife. They're round here every day. Street-singers. (*She heaves a faint sigh as she fans herself.*)

Lu: All my life I've just had one patch of bad luck after another, and every time it's been because some miserable nobody has put a spoke in my wheel. Just when I've been with the Chous two years and got my children fixed up with good jobs, you (*pointing at his wife*) have to come along and undo all that I've done. Every time you come home there's trouble. Look at what happened today: I go out to fetch an electrician and when I get back what do I find? Ssu-feng's lost her job and I'm out on my neck in the bargain. If you hadn't come home, damn you, (*pointing at her again*) all this would never have happened!

HAI (*putting down the revolver*): If you want to swear at me, just get on with it. There's no need to take it out on Mother instead.

Lu: Me swear at you? As if I'd dare swear at a young gentleman like you! You, who even swear at rich people to their face!

HAI (*losing patience with him*): You get two or three drinks inside you and you're off. You've been gabbing on and on for half an hour now. Can't you give it a rest?

Lu: Give it a rest? Not on your life! I've just about had a bellyful of her, and I'm going to have my say. Oh no, I haven't finished yet! It's not as if your old dad had always been a servant: there was a time when I had people waiting on me. I lived like a lord and had a good time—only the best was good enough. But from the day I married your mother, I started going to rack and ruin. Things have been going from bad to worse. Yes, from bad to worse. . . .

FENG: You know very well it's gambling that's ruined you!

HAI: Take no notice of him. Let him ramble on.

Lu (*carried away by his own eloquence, as if he has been the only one to*

233

suffer): I tell you, I've been going to rack and ruin, from bad to worse. I've had to swallow insults from the people I've worked for, as well as insults from you. But now I haven't even got any employers to be insulted by! I've just got to stay here and starve to death with you! Now just ask yourselves: What have you ever done for me that you can be proud of? *(He suddenly finds that he has nothing to rest his legs on.)* Shih-ping, bring that stool over here for me to put my legs on.

HAI *(frowning discouragement at his mother):* No, Mother! *(Nevertheless, Lu Ma brings the only stool in the room and places it at Lu Kuei's feet. He puts his legs on it.)*

LU *(looking across at Ta-hai):* And who's to blame for it all? If you have to go and call people names and upset them, it's only natural that they're going to give us the sack. I can't help it if I'm your father, can I? Now just think, Ta-hai. Think of me, an old man, having to starve to death because of what you've done. If I did die, you'd have it on your conscience, now, wouldn't you? Eh? If I did die like this?

HAI *(rising, unable to contain himself any longer):* Get on with it and die, then! Who do you think you are, anyway?

LU *(brought back to earth with a jolt):* Well, I'm damned!

MA ⎱ *(together):* Ta-hai!
FENG ⎰

LU *(awed by Ta-hai's tall, muscular body and the gun in his hand, he smiles nervously):* Well, well! Proper temper the lad's got, hasn't he! *(After a pause.)* Though you know, on second thoughts, I don't think it's all Ta-hai's fault. There isn't a single decent Chou in the whole of their family. I've been with them two years, and what I haven't found out about their little antics isn't worth knowing. Still, it's always the same for people with plenty of money—they can get away with anything. The worse they behave the more respectable they pretend to be. The more they give themselves airs, the nastier their minds, the dirty beasts! Look at the way they carried on when I left this afternoon. There they were, both of them, trying to smooth me down with their soft-soap. Well, just you wait and see, my hearties! They think I don't know about the little capers they cut!

FENG: That's enough. No scandal, now.

LU *(with unconscious complacency):* Ha! Wait until I start putting it all round—about the goings-on between the lady of the house and the eldest son: that ought to bring her old man himself round to see me on his bended knees, the old swine! Ungrateful lot they are! *(He*

234

coughs with satisfaction.) I'll show 'em! (*To his daughter.*) Where's my tea?

FENG: I think you must be drunk, Dad. Didn't you see me put it on the table for you a minute ago?

LU (*picking up the cup, inspecting it and turning back to Ssu-feng*): What's this, my lady? Plain water? (*He empties the cup on the floor.*)

FENG (*coldly*): Of course it is. There isn't any tea.

LU: What the devil do you mean? You know very well I always have a nice cup of tea after my dinner!

HAI: Well, well, so Father would like tea after his dinner. (*To Ssu-feng.*) What do you mean by it, Ssu-feng? Upsetting Father like that! You should have made him a pot of best-quality Lungching—it's only four dollars eighty an ounce.

FENG: Lungching! Why, there isn't even a pinch of dust in the tea-caddy.

HAI (*to Lu Kuei*): Hear that? You'll have to make do with boiled water and lump it, and stop being so damned fussy. (*He pours out a cup of boiled water, puts it on the table beside Lu Kuei, then walks away.*)

LU: This is my house, and if you don't like it you can clear out.

HAI (*advancing on him*): Now, you—

MA (*holding him back*): No, don't do anything, there's a good lad. Don't quarrel with him, for my sake.

LU: You really think you're somebody, don't you! You haven't been here two days before you manage to cause all this upset, and then before I've even breathed a word about it you're threatening to attack me! Go on, get out of my sight!

HAI (*keeping his temper*): I'm not staying here any longer if he's going to be like this, Mother. I'm going.

MA: Don't be silly. It'll come on to rain any minute. Where would you go, anyway?

HAI: I've got some business to attend to. If I don't pull it off, I'll probably go rickshaw-pulling.

MA: Now look here, Ta-hai—

LU: Out he goes. Don't stop him. Cocky young whippersnapper! He can get out. Right out. Go on!

HAI: You'd better watch it. Don't get me too riled.

LU (*brazening it out*): Don't forget your mother's here. You wouldn't dare do a thing to me with her here, you bastard!

HAI: What was that? Who do you think you're swearing at?

LU: At you, you bloody—

235

MA (*to Lu Kuei*): Now shut up and stop making such an exhibition of yourself.

LU: Me make an exhibition of myself? Look who's talking! At least I didn't produce bastards—and take one of them—(*pointing at Ta-hai*) along with me when I got married.

MA (*hurt and incensed*): Why, you—!

HAI (*drawing his pistol*): I'll—I'll kill you for that, you old swine!

LU (*leaping to his feet and shouting*): Help! Help! He'll shoot me! (*He stands petrified with fear.*)

FENG (*rushing across to Ta-hai and seizing his wrist*): Ta-hai!

MA: Put it away, Ta-hai.

HAI (*to Lu Kuei*): Now, tell Mother you're in the wrong, and promise that you'll never say such vile things to her again.

LU: Er—

HAI (*taking a step forward*): Say it!

LU (*intimidated*): If—if—if you put that gun down first.

HAI (*angrily*): No. You say it first.

LU: All right. (*To Lu Ma.*) It was wrong of me, and I'll never say such vile things to you again.

HAI (*pointing to the only chair in the room*): And sit over there again!

LU (*completely deflated, he sits down on the chair. He hangs his head and mutters to himself*): Bastard!

HAI: Humph! You're not worth me wasting my energy on!

MA: Put that gun down, Ta-hai.

HAI (*putting it down and smiling*): Don't worry, Mother. I only wanted to put the wind up him.

MA: Give it to me. Where did you get it from?

HAI: I brought it from the mine. Police dropped it in the scuffle when they fired on us.

MA: What have you got it on you now for?

HAI: No particular reason.

MA: Oh yes, you have. Now tell me.

HAI (*smiling grimly*): It's nothing, really. If the Chous drive me to the wall, this will be one way out.

MA: Nonsense. Give it to me.

HAI (*protesting*): Oh, Mother!

MA: I told you all about it at dinner. Our family's finished with the Chous, and we'll never mention them again.

HAI (*quietly and slowly*): And what about the blood they spilt at the mine? What about the slap in the face I got from that young

236

Mr. Chou? You expect me to forget these things just like that?

MA: Yes, I do. These scores can never be properly settled. Once you start retaliating there'll be no end to it. What is to be will be. I only hope you don't have to suffer too much.

HAI: It's all right for you, Mother, but I—

MA (*raising her voice*): Now, listen to me, Ta-hai. You're my favorite child, and I've never talked to you like this before; but let me tell you this: if you hurt any of the Chous—I don't care whether it's the master or the young gentlemen—if you so much as lay a hand on any of them, I'll have nothing more to do with you so long as I live.

HAI (*pleading*): But surely, Mother—

MA (*categorically*): You ought to know what I'm like by now. If you go and do the one thing I just couldn't bear you to do, I'll kill myself before your eyes. Give me that gun.

(*Ta-hai refuses.*)

MA: Give it to me! (*She goes up to him and seizes hold of the pistol.*)

HAI (*hurt*): But Mother, you—

FENG: Let Mother have it, Ta-hai.

HAI: All right. You'd better have it, then. But you must tell me where you put it.

MA: Very well, I'll put it in this chest here. (*She puts it in the chest by the bed.*) But—(*looking at Ta-hai*) I'll take it round to the police and hand it in first thing tomorrow morning.

LU: Quite right. That's the most sensible thing you can do.

HAI: You shut up!

MA: Ta-hai, you mustn't speak to your father like that.

HAI (*looking at Lu Kuei, then turning back to Lu Ma*): Well, Mother, I'm off now. I'll go down the rickshaw rank and see if I can find any of my old mates.

MA: Go on, then. But you must be sure to come back. We can't have all the family falling out with each other like this.

HAI: All right. I'll come straight back. (*He goes out through the outer room on the left.*)

(*The sound of Ta-hai closing the outer door is heard.*)

LU (*muttering to himself*): The bastard! (*Turning to Lu Ma.*) Why didn't you buy some tea? I told you to, didn't I?

MA: We can't afford it.

LU: But, Ssu-feng, where's my money?—The wages you brought from the Chous' this afternoon?

FENG: You mean the two months' extra pay?

237

Lu: Yes. There should be sixty dollars altogether.

Feng (*realizing that he will have to be told the truth sooner or later*): It's all gone. To pay off your debts.

Lu: What do you mean, "all gone"?

Feng: That fellow Chao was here again not long ago. Wouldn't go away till we'd paid off your gambling debts. So Mother gave him the money.

Lu (*turning to Lu Ma for corroboration*): The whole sixty dollars? You gave him the lot?

Ma: Yes. Which means that your latest gambling debts are as good as settled up.

Lu (*really anxious now*): My God! No wonder you've ruined me, if that's the way you carry on. What's this—quarter-day or something?

Ma (*unemotionally*): It's better to have all your debts paid. I've decided to give up this house.

Lu: You've what?

Ma: I'm thinking of going back to Tsinan in three days' time.

Lu: But when you've gone, there'll still be Ssu-feng and myself here. We'll still need the place even if you don't.

Ma: I'm taking Ssu-feng with me this time. I'm not going to leave her here on her own any more.

Lu (*smiling at Ssu-feng*): Hear that, Ssu-feng? Your mother wants to take you away with her.

Ma: When I went away last time, I didn't know how this job of mine would turn out. I was going to a strange place and I hadn't got any friends there, and all the while she stayed here she'd at least have Mrs. Chang next door to look after her, so naturally I didn't take her with me. I know now that the job's a steady one, and she's lost her job here, so why shouldn't I take her with me?

Feng (*alarmed*): So you—you really want to take me with you?

Ma (*in a pained voice*): Yes. Nothing will ever induce me to leave you on your own any more.

Lu: Here, hold on. We'll have to talk all this over properly first.

Ma: What is there to talk about? If you feel so inclined, you can come with us, and we can all go together. Though it'll mean leaving all your cronies that you gamble with if you do.

Lu: Tsinan's the last place I want to go. Though I still don't see why you should want to take Ssu-feng with you.

Ma: It's only natural that a girl should be with her mother. It's just that I had no choice but to leave her here last time.

Lu (*glibly*): If Ssu-feng stays with me she won't have to worry about a thing. She'll live in comfort and she'll only mix with the best people. If she goes with you, her life won't be worth living. So what's the point?

MA (*giving him up as hopeless*): Oh, it's no good talking to you. You just *won't* understand. You'd better ask her if she wants to come with me or to stay with you.

LU: She wants to stay with me, of course.

MA: Ask her!

LU (*confident of winning*): Come here, Ssu-feng. Now, you've heard what it's all about. Well, which do you want to do? Up to you entirely. Will you go with your mother, or stay here with me?

(*Ssu-feng turns round, her face streaming with tears.*)

LU: Well, I'll be—what are you crying for?

MA: Oh, Feng!

LU: Well, come on. It's not as if you were swearing your life away! Who's it to be?

MA (*comforting her*): That's all right, Feng, you can tell me. You promised to come with me a little while ago, but perhaps you've changed your mind now? Tell me, my dear, tell me truly. I'll still love you whichever way you choose.

LU: You see, you've upset her with all your talk about taking her with you. I happen to know that she can't tear herself away from this place. (*He smiles.*)

FENG (*to Lu Kuei*): Oh, go away! (*To her mother.*) Don't ask me, Mother. I can't bear it. Oh, Mother, my dear, dear mother! I will go with you. Oh, Mother! (*She flings herself sobbing into her mother's arms.*)

MA: There, there, my dear. I know you've had a bad time of it today.

LU: See what I mean? She's too much of a lady with her little scenes. She'll find it tough going if she goes with you.

MA (*to her husband*): Be quiet, you. (*To Ssu-feng.*) I'm sorry I didn't look after you properly. But from now on you'll be with me, and no one will take advantage of you. My own dear child.

(*Lu Ta-hai enters from the right.*)

HAI: Mrs. Chang's back now, Mother. I ran into her on my way home.

MA: Did you say anything to her about selling our furniture?

HAI: Yes, I did mention it. She said she can help.

MA: Did you find anybody you knew down at the rickshaw rank?

HAI: Yes, but I'll have to go out again to find a guarantor.

MA: We can go together, then. I won't be a minute, Ssu-feng, I'll be straight back.

HAI (*to Lu Kuei*): Are you sobering up yet? (*To Ssu-feng.*) I won't be home tonight.

(*He and his mother go out together.*)

LU (*following them out with his eyes*): Blast him! (*Noticing that Ssu-feng has gone back to her place at the window, he turns to her.*) Well, that's your mother out of the way, Ssu-feng. Now, tell me, what are you going to do?

(*Ssu-feng sighs, but pays him no attention. She stands listening to the croaking of the frogs outside and the rumble of distant thunder.*)

LU (*scornfully*): All this business is a bigger headache for you than you thought it would be, isn't it?

FENG (*with assumed indifference*): A headache for me? Nothing of the sort. It's just that I feel uncomfortable when the weather's as close as this.

LU: You can't fool me. Ever since supper-time you've been miles away, just staring into space. What's worrying you?

FENG: Nothing.

LU: Now be sensible about it, my dear. You're my only daughter—all I have got. If you go away with your mother, I'll be left here all on my own.

FENG: Please don't go on. I feel all mixed up inside as it is. (*There is a flicker of lightning outside.*) Listen, it's thundering now.

LU: Don't change the subject. Have you really made up your mind to go to Tsinan with your mother?

FENG: Yes. (*She heaves a short sigh.*)

LU (*singing dispiritedly*):

Every springtime brings the flowers
Which died in last year's autumn rain;
The springtime of this life of ours,
Once past, can ne'er come back again. . . .

(*Suddenly.*) You know, Ssu-feng, we're only young once, and we have to make the most of it. And opportunity only knocks once.

FENG: Oh, please go. I'm ready for bed.

LU: You haven't got to worry about your job at the Chous'. Once I get going I'll have us back there overnight. Do you really believe you could tear yourself away from a nice place like this, though? Could you really bear to leave the Chous'—?

FENG: Oh, I wish you'd stop talking and go to bed! Look, everybody's gone home outside.

LU: Don't you be a little idiot. All these fancy notions about things. You can't rely on anybody in this life. Money's the only real thing.

240

Though of course you and your mother haven't the sense to appreciate it.

FENG: Listen. I thought I heard a knock.

(A knock is heard at the front door.)

LU: Who can it be at this time of night? It's nearly eleven.

FENG: Let me go and see, Dad.

LU: No, I'll go. *(Opening the door leading to the outer room.)* Who is it?

CHUNG'S VOICE: Hullo! Is this where the Lus live?

LU: Yes. What do you want?

CHUNG'S VOICE: I've come to see someone.

LU: Who are you?

CHUNG'S VOICE: My name's Chou.

LU *(his face lighting up)*: There you are! What did I say? Somebody from the Chous.

FENG *(alarmed)*: No, Dad. Tell him there's nobody at home.

LU: Eh? *(Throwing her a shrewd glance.)* What's the idea? *(He goes out.)*

(Ssu-feng hurriedly straightens up the room as best she can. She tidies some of the things away into the curtained recess, then stands waiting for the visitor.)

(In the meantime, Chou Chung can be heard in conversation with Lu Kuei. After a moment they both come in.)

CHUNG *(delighted to find Ssu-feng here)*: Why, Ssu-feng!

FENG: Master Chung!

LU *(smiling obsequiously)*: I hope you don't mind, sir. This isn't much of a place to welcome you to.

CHUNG: It was the devil's own job to get to. You've got quite a stretch of water outside—*(smiling)* most attractive.

LU: You must take a seat, Master Chung. Ssu-feng, bring the good chair over here.

CHUNG *(struck by Ssu-feng's silence)*: What's the matter, Ssu-feng? Aren't you feeling well or something?

FENG: I'm all right.—Master Chung, why did you have to come here? If the mistress finds out, you'll—

CHUNG: But it was Mother who sent me.

LU *(beginning to understand)*: The mistress herself sent you?

CHUNG: Yes, but I wanted to see you all in any case. *(To Ssu-feng.)* Where are your brother and your mother?

LU: They've gone out.

FENG: How did you find out where we live?

241

CHUNG (*naively*): Mother told me. I didn't expect to find such a lot of water outside. And it's so slippery after the rain. You have to be careful in the dark; otherwise, you'd soon come a cropper.

LU: I hope you didn't do anything like that, Master Chung?

CHUNG: Oh no. I came in our own rickshaw. Great fun. (*His eyes stray round the room and finally come to rest on Ssu-feng. He beams at her.*) So this is where you live!

FENG: I think you'd better hurry up and get back.

LU: What!

CHUNG (*struck by a sudden thought*): Oh yes, I was almost forgetting what I came for. Mother says she's rather concerned about you all now that you've left. She was afraid you might not be able to find a job straight away, so she's sent a hundred dollars for your mother. (*He produces the money.*)

FENG: What!

LU (*taking this to be an act of appeasement on the part of the Chou family, he smiles smugly at Ssu-feng*): You see how kind and considerate they are? After all, you know, they are rich people.

FENG: No, Master Chung. Please thank madam for us, but we can manage all right on our own. Please take it back.

LU (*turning to Ssu-feng*): Here, what do you think you're saying? It would be rude of us to refuse it after madam's been so kind as to send Master Chung along with it in person! (*He takes the money.*) Give madam our best regards and tell her we're quite all right, all of us. Tell her not to worry about us, and thank her for everything.

FENG (*obstinately*): You can't do this, Father.

LU: You're too young to understand.

FENG: Mother and Ta-hai would never let you keep the money if you did take it.

LU (*ignoring her and turning to Chou Chung*): Thank you for coming all this way. I'll just dash out and buy you some fruit now, if you'll excuse me a moment. Ssu-feng will keep you company.

FENG: You mustn't go, Father! You can't do this!

LU: Stop arguing and pour Master Chung a cup of tea. I won't be long. (*He hurries out.*)

CHUNG: There's no harm in letting him go.

FENG (*with loathing*): Ugh! It's sickening!—(*Displeased.*) What business is it of yours to come here with money?

CHUNG: You—er—you don't seem particularly pleased to see me. What's the matter?

FENG (*making conversation*): Has the master had his dinner yet?

242

CHUNG: Yes, he's just finished. He lost his temper again, and Mother rushed upstairs before she'd finished eating. She was in a tearing rage. I went up to her and spent a long time trying to cheer her up; otherwise, I'd have got here a bit earlier.

FENG (*casually*): How's Master Ping?

CHUNG: I haven't seen him, but I know he's pretty upset. He's been drinking in his room again, so he's probably drunk by now.

FENG: Oh! (*She heaves a sigh.*)—Why couldn't you send one of the servants round with the money? There was no need for you to come to this slum of ours yourself.

CHUNG (*earnestly*): You've got a grudge against us now, isn't that it?—(*Shamefaced.*) That was a bad business today. It made me feel ashamed to see you treated like that. You mustn't think Ping really meant any harm. He's terribly sorry now for what he did. He's still very fond of you, you know.

FENG: Master Chung. Please remember that I'm not one of your family's servants now.

CHUNG: But can't we always remain good friends?

FENG: I'm going back with my mother. To Tsinan.

CHUNG: No, don't go yet. We can get you and your father back with us sooner or later. By the time we've moved into our new house, Father will probably have gone back to the mine. Then you can come back to us, and I'll be jolly glad to have you back, I can tell you!

FENG: You're very kind-hearted, really.

CHUNG: Ssu-feng, you mustn't let a little thing like this upset you. The world is such a big place. You ought to go to school, and then you'd learn that there have been lots of people like us in the world—putting up with suffering, working hard and biding their time, and in the end enjoying the happiness they've won.

FENG: Ah, but a woman's only a woman after all! (*Suddenly.*) Listen! (*The croaking of frogs is heard.*)

CHUNG: No, you're no ordinary woman. You've got strength, and you can put up with hardship. We're both young yet and we've got all our lives ahead of us to work for the welfare of mankind. I hate this present society of ours—it's so unfair. I hate people whose only language is brute force. I loathe my father. You and I are in the same boat together—we're both victims of oppression.

FENG: You must be thirsty, Master Chung. I'll get you some water. (*She stands up and pours him a cup of water.*)

CHUNG: No, it's all right.

FENG: Yes, let me wait on you once again.

CHUNG: You mustn't say things like that. The world as it is now should never have come into existence. I've never thought of you as a servant: you've always been my elder sister, my guide. Our world, the real world, is not this one.

FENG: You certainly know how to talk!

CHUNG: Sometimes I forget the present—(*with a rapt expression on his face*) I forget my home, I forget you, I forget my mother—I even forget myself. It seems like a winter morning, with a brilliant sky overhead . . . on a boundless sea . . . there's a little sailing-boat, light as a gull. When the sea-breeze gets stronger, and there's a salty tang in the air, the white sails billow out like the wings of a hawk and the boat skims over the sea, just kissing the waves, racing towards the horizon. The sky is empty except for a few patches of white cloud floating lazily on the horizon. We sit in the bows, gazing ahead, for ahead of us is our world.

FENG: Ours?

CHUNG: Yes, yours and mine. We can fly—fly to a place that is truly clean and happy, a place, where there is no conflict, no hypocrisy, no inequality, no—(*Lifting his head as though such a world were there before his eyes, then, abruptly.*) Do you like it?

FENG: You've got a wonderful imagination.

CHUNG (*warmly*): Will you go there with me? You could even bring him too, if you wanted to.

FENG: Who?

CHUNG: The one you told me about yesterday, when you said your heart already belonged to another. I'm sure he must be just like you—someone nice and friendly.

(*Ta-hai comes in.*)

FENG: Hullo, Ta-hai.

HAI (*coldly*): What's all this?

CHUNG: Ah, Mr. Lu!

FENG: Master Chung from the Chous has come round to see us.

HAI: Oh. I didn't expect to come in and find you two here. Where's Father?

FENG: He's gone out shopping.

HAI (*to Chou Chung*): I can't for the life of me imagine why you should want to come down to this wretched slum at this time of night—to see us!

CHUNG: It was you that I really came to see. I feel I owe you an apology.

HAI: What for?

CHUNG (*blushing*): What happened at our place this afternoon, when you—

244

HAI (*flaring up*): Cut it out!

FENG: Don't be like that, Ta-hai. He's come with the best of intentions—to offer us his sympathy.

HAI: We've no use for your sympathy, Master Chung. We were born and bred in poverty and we're used to being treated like that. We don't need to have anybody coming here in the middle of the night to give us their sympathy.

CHUNG: Oh, I think you've got me all wrong.

HAI (*distinctly*): I haven't, you know. (*Turning to Ssu-feng.*) Go on out.

FENG: But, Ta-hai!

HAI: Go and leave us on our own. I want to have a word with him. (*Ssu-feng makes no move.*) Go on! (*Ssu-feng goes out slowly through the door on the right.*)

HAI: I've already had a chat with you, and I realize you're a little more enlightened than the rest of your family. But remember this: if you ever come here again to—to be kind to us, (*with a sudden ferocity*) I'll lose my temper with you.

CHUNG (*with a smile*): But I don't see how anybody can be offended by an offer of sympathy.

HAI: There could never be any sympathy between you and me. Our stations in life are too far apart.

CHUNG: I think your prejudices get the better of you sometimes, Ta-hai. It's no crime to be wealthy, so why should wealth stand in the way of our being friends?

HAI: You're too young to understand. I'd be wasting my breath if I tried to explain it any further. I'll just say this much: you should never have come here. This is no place for you.

CHUNG: But why?—Only this morning you said you'd like to be friends with me, and I think Ssu-feng would like to be friends with me, too; so why won't you even let me come and offer my help?

HAI: Don't imagine you're doing us a good turn, Master Chung. They tell me you wanted to send Ssu-feng to school; that right? Well, she's my sister, the daughter of a poor man, and her lot in life will be to marry somebody from her own class—a life of washing, cooking and scrabbling among the cinders for scraps of coal. Schooling? Education? Humph! That's something for young *ladies* to dream about!

CHUNG: There's something in what you say, of course, but—

HAI: So if you're really concerned about Ssu-feng, Sir Mine-owner's-son, you'll oblige by not having anything more to do with her.

CHUNG: I think you're too prejudiced. Just because my father's a mine-owner, that's no reason why you should say that you—

HAI (*glaring at him*): Now I'm warning you—

CHUNG: Warning me?

HAI: If I ever catch you here with my sister again, I'll—(*some of the tension suddenly goes out of him*) oh, well, it's getting late. Time for bed.

CHUNG: I—I never expected that you'd be like that about it. I never expected that what Father said would turn out to be right after all.

HAI (*exploding*): Your father's an old swine!

CHUNG:.What!

HAI: And your brother's a—

(*Ssu-feng comes running back into the room.*)

FENG: Stop! Stop saying such things! (*Pointing at Ta-hai.*) I think you're—you're being utterly beastly!

HAI: Idiot!

FENG: I've nothing more to say to you! (*To Chou Chung.*) Now go. Don't say another word to him.

CHUNG (*looking helplessly at Ta-hai*): All right, then, I'll go. (*To Ssu-feng.*) I'm really terribly sorry. I didn't realize I'd only make things more unpleasant for you by coming here.

FENG: Forget it, and please go.

CHUNG: All right, I'm going. (*To Ta-hai, goodnaturedly.*) I'd still like to be friends with you. (*Holding out his hand.*) Won't you shake hands with me? (*Ta-hai ignores him and turns away.*)

FENG: Humph!

(*Having nothing more to say, Chou Chung makes for the door. Just then, Lu Kuei comes in with fruit, wine and various kinds of food.*)

LU (*seeing that Chou Chung is leaving*): What's this?

HAI: Get out of the way. He's going.

LU: No, wait, wait. Why are you rushing off like this, Master Chung? You've only just got here.

FENG (*angrily*): Ask Ta-hai!

LU (*with a smile, to Chou Chung*): Don't mind him. Stay a little longer, won't you?

CHUNG: No, I really am going.

LU: But you'll have something to eat first, won't you, sir? I've been a long way to get these things for you. You will have a bite and a glass of wine before you go, won't you?

CHUNG: No, it's getting late now. I'll have to be getting along.

HAI (*to Ssu-feng*): Where did he get the money to buy all this stuff?

LU (*turning round*): It was my own money, that I'd earned myself.

FENG: No, it wasn't, Father: it was money from the Chous. And you're squandering it. (*Turning to Ta-hai.*) Mrs. Chou sent Mother a

246

hundred dollars. Mother was out, and Dad would insist on taking it. He wouldn't listen to me.

Lu (*looking daggers at Ssu-feng, then turning to Ta-hai*): Master Chung brought it in person; so I couldn't very well refuse it, now, could I?

Hai (*going up to Chou Chung*): So! You came to bring us money, did you?

Feng (*to Ta-hai*): Now perhaps you'll understand!

Lu: You see what kind-hearted people the Chous are?

Hai (*turning to Lu Kuei*): Give me the money!

Lu (*apprehensively*): What for?

Hai: Are you going to give it to me or aren't you? (*With menacing voice and eyes.*) If you don't, well, just remember what's in the chest there.

Lu (*terrified*): All right, you can have it! (*He fishes the notes out of his pocket and hands them over to Ta-hai.*) Here you are. A hundred dollars.

Hai (*after counting the notes*): Two dollars short. Well?

Lu (*forcing a smile*): Well—er—I—I've spent it.

Chung (*not wishing to see any more*): Well, cheerio. I'm off now.

Hai (*grasping his arm*): Oh no, you don't. Don't imagine we can be caught as easily as that.

Chung: What do you mean?

Hai: Now I've got some money somewhere. Ah, yes. Just two dollars left in my pocket. (*He produces some silver and small notes, then counts them.*) Two dollars exactly. Here's your money back. We've no use for it.

Lu: This is outrageous!

Chung: You don't seem to be able to appreciate kindness.

Hai: You're quite right. I don't. And the same goes for your family's hypocrisy and crocodile tears, and for their—

Feng: Ta-hai!

Hai: Take it away. Now get out. Go on, out!

Chung (*his illusions shattered, he stands there for a moment, then suddenly picks up the money*): All right. I'm going. I'm sorry.

Hai: Now I'm telling you: if any of you Chous come here after this, I'll kill you, whoever you are!

Chung: Well, thank you! Though I don't suppose for one moment that anyone else in the family would be so foolish as to do what I've done. Good-bye! (*He goes towards the door on the right.*)

Lu: Ta-hai!

Hai (*shouting*): Get him out of here!

Lu: All right, all right. I'll show you a light. It's dark in the front room.

CHUNG: Thank you.

(Lu Kuei and Chou Chung go out through the door on the right.)

FENG: Master Chung! *(She runs out after them.)*

(Lu Ma comes in through the door on the right.)

HAI: Did you know that Master Chung from the Chous was here?

MA: Well, I saw a rickshaw outside the door, but I didn't dare come in as I didn't know who it was that had come to see us.

HAI: You realize I've just thrown him out?

MA *(nodding)*: Yes, I know. I've been listening at the door for a while.

HAI: Mrs. Chou sent you round a hundred dollars.

MA *(indignantly)*: I don't want any money from her. I'm leaving to-morrow and taking Ssu-feng with me.

HAI: Tomorrow?

MA: Yes, tomorrow, I've changed my mind.

HAI: Glad to hear it! Then there's no need for me to tell you the rest of it.

MA: What's that?

HAI: Nothing, really. Just that when I got back I found Ssu-feng here passing the time of day with this Master Chung.

MA *(anxiously, in spite of herself)*: What were they talking about?

HAI: I don't know.

MA *(to herself)*: Silly girl!

HAI: Well, I'll be off now, Mother.

MA: Where to?

HAI: The last of my money's gone, so I'm thinking of doing a night's rickshaw-pulling.

MA: What for? There's no need to do that. I've got some money here. You can stay here the night.

HAI: Keep it. You may need it yourself. I'm away, then. *(He goes out through the door on the right.)*

MA *(calling after him)*: Ta-hai! Ta-hai!

(Ssu-feng comes in.)

FENG: Hullo, Mother. *(Uneasily.)* You're back, then.

MA: You were too busy seeing your young Mr. Chou off to notice me.

FENG *(making an effort to explain)*: It was his mother who told him to come.

MA: Ta-hai tells me you had a long chat together.

FENG: You mean me and Master Chung?

MA: Yes. What did he say to you?

FENG: Nothing much. Just the usual sort of thing.

MA: You're sure?

FENG: What's Ta-hai been telling you now?

MA (*sternly*): Feng! (*She looks her daughter full in the face.*)

FENG: What's the matter, Mother?

MA: Don't you know that I love you more than anyone else?

FENG: Why do you ask that?

MA: I want to ask a favor of you.

FENG: Of course. What is it?

MA: You've got to tell me what there is between you and that Chou boy.

FENG: That's Ta-hai's silly nonsense again. What's he been telling you?

MA: No, it's not Ta-hai. He hasn't told me anything. It's just that I want to know.

(*The rumble of distant thunder is heard.*)

FENG: But what makes you ask these things, Mother? Haven't I told you there's nothing at all between us? There isn't, Mother.

(*The sound of thunder again.*)

MA: Listen. There's thunder. Now be fair with your poor mother. I can't have my own daughter continually deceiving me about such things!

FENG (*after a pause*): I'm not deceiving you, Mother! Haven't I told you that all the time you've been away—

LU'S VOICE (*from the front room*): Shih-ping. Come on in to bed. It's late.

MA: Don't worry about me. Get to bed yourself. (*To Ssu-feng.*) What were you saying?

FENG: Haven't I told you that all the time you've been away I've come home—every night?

MA: Now you must tell me the truth, child. I couldn't bear to have anything really serious happen to you.

FENG: Mother, (*sobbing*) why can't you trust your own daughter? (*She flings herself into her mother's arms.*)

MA (*shedding tears*): My poor child, it's not that I don't trust you— (*with anguish in her voice*) but that I don't trust the world. You've no idea, you silly girl, all that I've been through all these years. I could never begin to describe it. I never had anyone to warn me when I was young. And that's the pity of it. One false step, and I lost my way completely. You're the only daughter I ever had, Feng, and I can't bear to see you go the way I did. You do love me, don't you, Feng? I just couldn't bear you to deceive me ever. Oh, my poor child!

FENG: No, Mother, I'll never deceive you. From now on I'll be yours —always.

MA (*abruptly changing the subject*): I shan't be able to set my mind at rest all the time I stay here, Feng. We must go tomorrow—get away from this place.

FENG (*rising*): Tomorrow? As soon as that?

MA (*with finality*): Yes. I've changed my mind. We'll go tomorrow and we'll never come back here again.

FENG: What, never? But Mother, why have we got to go rushing off like this?

MA: You've got nothing else to do here before you go, have you?

FENG (*hesitantly*): I—er—

MA: Don't you *want* to leave here with me as soon as we can?

FENG (*with a sigh and a wry smile*): All right, then. Let's go tomorrow.

MA (*suddenly suspicious again*): Ssu-feng, I think there's still something you're keeping from me.

FENG (*wiping her eyes*): No, there isn't, Mother.

MA (*tenderly*): You'll remember what I was telling you just now, my dear?

FENG: Yes, Mother, I will!

MA: Feng, I want you never to see any of the Chous again so long as you live!

FENG: All right, I won't.

MA (*gravely*): No, you must swear that you won't. (*Ssu-feng looks fearfully at her mother's stern face.*)

FENG: Oh, must I?

MA (*as gravely as before*): Yes, you must.

FENG (*falling to her knees*): Mother—(*throwing herself against Lu Ma's knees*) I—I can't.

MA (*with tears streaming down her cheeks*): Do you want to break your mother's heart? You forget that for your sake—all my life I've—(*She turns her head aside and sobs.*)

FENG: All right, Mother. I'll swear.

MA (*rising*): Then do it on your knees, as you are now.

FENG: I promise, Mother, that I'll never see any of the Chous again. (*A peal of thunder rolls across the sky.*)

MA: Hear the thunder? Now, what if you should forget what I've told you and see any of the Chous again?

FENG (*apprehensively*): But I won't, Mother, I won't.

MA: No, my child, you must swear that you won't. If you should ever forget what I've told you— (*A peal of thunder.*)

FENG (*in desperation*): —Then may I be struck dead by lightning.

(Flinging herself into her mother's arms.) Oh, Mother, Mother! *(She bursts into tears.)*

(Crashes of thunder.)

MA *(her arms around Ssu-feng)*: Feng, my child!

(Lu Kuei comes in, shirtless and wearing only a singlet.)

LU *(to his wife)*: Aren't you ever coming to bed tonight? What's all the jaw about?

MA: None of your business.

LU: What!

FENG: Now go on, Mother. Please go to bed now and leave me to myself.

LU: The poor kid's had enough to put up with for one day. What have you got to keep on at her for?

MA: You sure you don't want me to keep you company?

FENG: No, Mother. I only want to be left on my own.

(Lu Kuei goes out.)

MA: All right, go to bed like a good girl, then.

FENG: Yes, Mother.

(Lu Ma goes out.)

(Ssu-feng closes the door behind her. In the next room Lu Kuei is singing his song again: "Every springtime brings the flowers. . . ." She goes over to the round table and turns the lamp down to a glimmer. From outside come the croaking of the frogs and the barking of dogs. She undoes two or three buttons as she paces restlessly up and down, then goes and sits on the edge of the bed. Finally, she heaves a deep sigh and throws herself down on the bed. The regular, hollow clop-clop-clop of a night-watchman's bamboo "gong" breaks the silence. Ssu-feng sits up again and fans herself vigorously with her palm-leaf fan. Finding the air too close and stifling, she opens the window and stands in front of it.)

(Lu Kuei comes in, his bare feet in heelless slippers.)

LU: What, still up?

FENG *(throwing him a brief glance)*: Mm.

LU *(picking up the bottle of wine and the food he bought for Chou Chung)*: Come on, now, get some sleep.

FENG *(absent-mindedly)*: Mm.

LU *(at the door)*: It's getting late. *(He goes out.)*

(Ssu-feng goes across to the door on the right and closes it. She stands by the door for a few moments, listening to her parents talking in the next room, then goes back to the round table with a long sigh and throws herself down across it, sobbing and quietly pounding the

251

table-top. Suddenly, someone whistles outside. Ssu-feng starts up, turns up the lamp and runs across to the window. She puts her head out for a quick look round, then closes the window and stands leaning against the window-sill in a state of great agitation. The whistles become more distinct. She puts the lamp with the red-paper lamp-shade in the window. The whistles come nearer and nearer. There is a distant rumble of thunder, then the sound of footsteps outside the window.)

(There is a tap on the window.)

FENG *(gasping)*: Oh!

PING'S VOICE *(in an undertone)*: Hey! Open up!

FENG: Who is it?

PING'S VOICE *(disguised)*: Guess!

FENG *(her voice trembling)*: What—what are you doing here?

PING'S VOICE: Guess!

FENG: I can't see you now *(Desperately.)* Mother's at home.

PING'S VOICE: You can't put me off with that: she's gone to bed.

FENG *(with a note of concern in her voice)*: You'd better be careful. My brother hates you like poison.

PING'S VOICE *(indifferently)*: I happen to know he's not at home.

FENG: You must go away!

PING'S VOICE: Not likely!

(He tries to force the window open by pushing it inwards, but Ssu-feng holds it shut by pressing as hard as she can against it.)

FENG *(anxiously)*: No, don't. You can't come in.

PING'S VOICE *(in an undertone)*: Now, come on, Ssu-feng. Open up. Please!

FENG: No, I can't! It's the middle of the night, and I've already got undressed.

PING'S VOICE *(urgently)*: What?

FENG: I've already gone to bed!

PING'S VOICE: In that case. . . . I'd—I'd better—*(He heaves a long sigh.)*

FENG *(pleading)*: Then you will go away, won't you?

PING'S VOICE *(submissively)*: All right, then. If I must. I'll be off, then. *(Suddenly becoming urgent once more.)* But first open the window a minute, so that I can—

FENG: No. You must go away at once!

PING'S VOICE *(urgently)*: Now listen! All I want is—is to give you a kiss.

FENG *(as if it hurts her to say it)*: Oh, Master Ping, you're not at home now. You must forgive me this time.

PING'S VOICE *(bitterly)*: So you've forgotten me. You no longer want to—

FENG (*resolutely*): Yes, I've forgotten you. Now go away.

PING'S VOICE (*suddenly*): Wasn't my brother here a short while ago?

FENG: Yes. (*Hesitantly.*) He was.

PING'S VOICE (*acidly*): Oh! (*Heaving a deep sigh.*) That explains it. (*Viciously.*) If you *have* thrown me over, you heartless little—

FENG: What do you mean, "thrown you over"?

PING'S VOICE (*impatiently*): Then why won't you open the window and let me in? Don't you realize that I—love you?

FENG: Please don't pester me any more. All day you've been making trouble for us. Don't you think you've done enough?

PING'S VOICE: I know I did wrong. But now I want to see you—I must.

FENG (*with a sigh*): All right, we'll see about it tomorrow. I'll do what you like tomorrow.

PING'S VOICE (*suspiciously*): Tomorrow? You really mean that?

FENG: Yes, I do. I really mean it.

PING'S VOICE: All right, then, we'll leave it like that. You'd better not be leading me on, though.
(*The sound of footsteps.*)

FENG: You going now?

PING'S VOICE: Yes, I'm off.
(*The footsteps fade into the distance.*)

FENG (*to herself, as if a weight has been lifted from her mind*): He's gone! (*She opens the window to let in the breeze.*) Oh!
(*Chou Ping suddenly appears at the window.*)

FENG: Help! Mother! (*She quickly pushes the window to.*)

PING (*forcing the window ajar and continuing to press against it*): You won't get rid of me so easily this time!

FENG (*straining to hold the window shut*): No—no—go away!
(*Chou Ping finally succeeds in forcing his way into the room. He is smothered in mud and his face is bloody.*)

PING: You see? I've got in after all.

FENG (*recoiling from him*): You're drunk again!

PING: Why did you want to get rid of me? Why were you afraid to see me? (*He turns towards her.*)

FENG (*frightened*): What's happened to your face?

PING (*feeling his face with his hand, which comes away covered in blood*): That's where I fell over on my way here—just to see you. (*He closes the window.*)

FENG: You must go! Please, *please*—

PING (*with a strange laugh*): No. I want to have a good look at you first. (*A peal of thunder.*)

FENG (*shrinking away from him*): No, I'm afraid.

PING (*closing in on her*): What are you afraid of?

FENG (*her voice trembling*): Because—(*still retreating*) there's blood all over your face . . . I just don't recognize you—you—

PING (*again with a strange laugh*): Who do you think I am? You silly girl! (*He takes her hand.*)

(*Against the background of a crescendo of thunder there is a deafening crash overhead.*)

FENG: Oh, Mother! (*Taking refuge in Chou Ping's arms.*) I'm frightened!

(*As the thunder roars and the rain pours down in torrents, the lights are gradually dimmed. The window opens, pushed from outside. It is pitch-dark outside the window. A sudden blue flash of lightning lights up an eerie white face at the window. It is Fan-yi. She looks like a corpse as she stands there, heedless of the rain that pelts down on her dishevelled hair. She reaches out and pulls the window to again, then fastens it on the outside. As the thunder crashes and roars louder than ever, the stage is plunged into complete darkness.*)

FENG (*at the sound of the thunder*): Hold me tight. I'm afraid.

(*The lights gradually come on again.*)

(*Lu Ta-hai's voice is heard outside shouting to be let in. Chou Ping is sitting on the chair, while Ssu-feng stands by the door, her face tense.*)

PING (*listening*): Who's that?

FENG: Sh! Don't make a sound!

MA'S VOICE: What, back again, Ta-hai?

HAI'S VOICE: It's been raining so hard that the sheds at the rickshaw rank have collapsed.

FENG (*in a low, urgent voice*): It's my brother. You'll have to get out. Fast.

(*Chou Ping dashes to the window and tugs at it.*)

PING (*unable to make it budge*): That's funny!

FENG: What is?

PING (*anxiously*): Someone's fastened the window from the outside.

FENG (*frightened*): No! Who could have done that?

PING (*tugging at the window again*): It's no good; it won't budge.

FENG: Quiet! They're just outside the door.

HAI'S VOICE: Where are the bed-planks?

MA'S VOICE: In Ssu-feng's room.

FENG: They're coming in. Hide yourself in here, quick.

(*Just as she is bundling Chou Ping into the curtained recess, Ta-hai comes in with a lamp.*)

254

HAI: What's this? (*He sees the pair of them standing petrified.*) Mother! Come in here, quick! I'm seeing things!
(*Lu Ma runs in.*)

MA (*gasping*): God!

FENG (*bursting out of the room*): Oh!
(*Lu Ma, clinging to the door, almost faints.*)

HAI: So it's you, is it! (*He snatches the kitchen knife from the table and rushes at Chou Ping with it.*)

MA (*catching him by the sleeve and holding him back with all her strength*): Stop, Ta-hai, stop! Over my dead body!

HAI: Let me go! Leave go of me! (*He stamps his foot.*)

MA (*realizing that Chou Ping is still standing there rooted to the spot*): Run, you fool! Don't just stand there!
(*Chou Ping runs out through the door on the right.*)

HAI (*shouting*): Grab him, Dad! Grab him!

MA (*waits until she is satisfied that Chou Ping has made good his escape before releasing Ta-hai, then sits down on the floor in a stupor*): My God!

HAI (*stamping his foot*): Mother, Mother! What an idiotic thing to do!
(*Lu Kuei comes in.*)

LU: Has he gone? Whew!—Where's Ssu-feng?

HAI: She's bolted, the little bitch.

MA: Oh, my child! The river's in flood out there! You mustn't do it! Ssu-feng! (*She goes to run out.*)

HAI (*holding her back*): Where are you going?

MA: No, no! I've got to find her! I've got to find her!

HAI: All right. I'm coming with you.

MA: Quick, then! (*Shouting.*) Ssu-feng! (*She runs out.*)
(*Suddenly, Lu Kuei puts on his hat and follows them out. Ta-hai goes across to the chest and takes out the pistol. Thrusting it inside his coat, he hurries out.*)
(*Noise of raging storm outside.*)

—QUICK CURTAIN—

ACT FOUR

In the Chous' drawing-room. About two o'clock in the morning.

When the curtain rises, Chou Pu-yuan is sitting on a sofa, reading a newspaper by the light of a floor-lamp beside him. The rest of the room is in darkness.

The hiss of the rain is loud even in the room, though the curtains are drawn and the center door closed. Beyond the glass-panelled door the garden is shrouded in utter darkness.

CHOU (*putting down his paper and stretching wearily*): Hullo, there! Here, somebody! (*He walks across to the dining-room door, polishing his spectacles as he goes.*) Anybody there?
  (*Flashes of lightning outside. He goes over to the bureau and rings.*)
  (*A servant appears.*)
SERVANT: You rang, sir?
CHOU: I've been calling you long enough.
SERVANT: Job to hear anything with this rain, sir.
CHOU (*indicating the clock*): What's happened to the clock? It's stopped.
SERVANT: Well, you see, sir, it was always Ssu-feng's job to wind it, but as she's gone today, it's been overlooked.
CHOU: What's the time now?
SERVANT: Er—must be about two.
CHOU: I told the office to have some money sent to Tsinan. Are they clear what they've got to do?
SERVANT: The money that was to go to somebody in Tsinan by the name of—er—Lu, you mean, sir?
CHOU: Yes.
SERVANT: It's been attended to.
  (*Flashes of lightning outside. Chou Pu-yuan turns and looks out at the garden.*)
CHOU: The electric cable down by the wistaria-trellis—did your mistress send for someone to mend it?
SERVANT: Yes, but the electrician said he couldn't work in this heavy rain and that he'd have to come back tomorrow.
CHOU: I see.—Er, what did you say the time was?
SERVANT: Nearly two o'clock. Will you be retiring now, sir?

CHOU: You can ask your mistress to come down here.

SERVANT: She's retired for the night.

CHOU (*casually*): What about Master Chung?

SERVANT: He went up some time ago.

CHOU: Well, see if Master Ping's still up, then.

SERVANT: Master Ping went out after dinner and isn't back yet. (*A pause.*)

CHOU (*going back to his seat on the sofa and speaking in a mournful voice*): So there's no one else in the house still up, then?

SERVANT: No, sir. They've all gone to bed.

CHOU: All right. That'll be all.

SERVANT: Nothing more you require, sir?

CHOU: No.

(*The servant goes through the center door. Chou Pu-yuan gets up again and paces moodily up and down. Presently he stops in front of the bureau, switches on the main light, and gazes abstractedly at Shih-ping's photograph.*)

(*Chou Chung comes in from the dining-room.*)

CHUNG (*not expecting to find his father here*): Father!

CHOU (*obviously glad of the interruption*): Haven't—haven't you gone to bed yet?

CHUNG: No.

CHOU: Did you want to see me?

CHUNG: No, I thought I'd find Mother here.

CHOU (*disappointed*): Oh—er—your mother's upstairs.

CHUNG: I don't think she is, though. I knocked at her door a long time, until I found it was locked.—Though of course she may have been there all the time.—Well, I'll be going now, Father.

CHOU: Chung.

(*Chou Chung stops.*)

CHOU: Don't go yet.

CHUNG: Is there anything I can do for you?

CHOU: No. (*Affectionately.*) How is it you're still up?

CHUNG (*submissively*): Sorry, Father. I am up rather late. I'll turn in straight away.

CHOU: Did you take the medicine Dr. Kramer gave you?

CHUNG: Yes, I did.

CHOU: Have a game of tennis today?

CHUNG: Yes.

CHOU: Happy?

CHUNG: Mm.

CHOU (*getting up and taking Chou Chung by the hand*): What's the matter? Afraid of me?

CHUNG: Yes, I am, Father.

CHOU (*drily*): You seem to be dissatisfied about something. Is that it?

CHUNG (*ill at ease*): I—I hardly know how to put it, Father.

(*A pause. Chou Pu-yuan goes back to the sofa and sits down with a sigh. He beckons Chou Chung across to him.*)

CHOU (*mournfully*): Today I—er, well, I somehow feel I'm getting old. (*Pauses.*) Know what I mean?

CHUNG (*indifferently*): No, I don't.

CHOU (*abruptly*): If I should die one of these days and leave you alone, with no one to look after you, wouldn't you be worried?

CHUNG (*without any trace of emotion*): I expect I would.

CHOU (*affectionately, in an attempt to put his son at his ease*): You said this morning you'd like to share your school allowance with someone —Well, let's hear all about it. I'm open to any suggestions within reason.

CHUNG: I was just being silly. I promise I won't say anything like that again.

(*A long pause.*)

CHOU (*gazing reproachfully into Chou Chung's face*): You don't seem to have much to say to me.

CHUNG: I—I don't know what to say. As a rule, you don't seem particularly willing to see us. (*Falteringly.*) But—but today you seem rather different, somehow. You—

CHOU (*who has heard enough*): All right. You may go now.

CHUNG: Very well, Father. (*He goes out through the dining-room.*)

(*Chou Pu-yuan looks disappointed as he watches his son out of the room. When he is alone, he picks up Shih-ping's photograph again.*)

(*Chou Fan-yi comes in quietly through the center door. Her raincoat is still dripping wet. Her face is pale and haggard, and her hair drenched.*)

FAN (*assuming an air of unconcern when she sees the startled look that her husband gives her*): Still up? (*She remains standing by the door.*)

CHOU: Well I'm damned! (*Going across to her.*) Where have you been? Chung's been looking for you all the evening.

FAN (*simply*): I've been for a walk.

CHOU: What, when it's pouring like this?

FAN: Mm.—(*Suddenly vindictive.*) I'm neurotic, remember?

CHOU: And now perhaps you'll tell me where you've been?

FAN (*crossly*): None of your business.

CHOU (*looking her up and down*): You're wet through. You'd best hurry up and get those wet things off.

FAN: I felt feverish in my mind, so I went out to cool off in the rain.

CHOU (*impatiently*): Don't talk such utter nonsense. Where exactly have you been?

FAN (*looking him full in the face, a syllable at a time*): I've been at your place!

CHOU (*annoyed*): At my place?

FAN (*with a faint smile*): Mm. Enjoying the rain in the garden!

CHOU: What, all this time?

FAN (*cheerfully*): Yes, I've had a nice long soak.

(*A pause. Pu-yuan stares at her in startled bewilderment. She just stands where she is by the door, impassive as a statue.*)

CHOU: Fan-yi, I think you'd best go upstairs and get some rest.

FAN (*stubbornly*): No. (*Suddenly.*) What's that you've got in your hand? (*Scornfully.*) Humph! That woman's photograph again! (*She reaches out for it.*)

CHOU: You needn't look at it. It's Ping's mother, you know.

FAN (*snatching it from him and looking at it under the light*): Ping's mother was very good-looking.

(*Pu-yuan ignores her, and goes and sits down on the sofa.*)

FAN: Mm? Don't you think so?

CHOU: I suppose so.

FAN: She looks very good-natured.

(*Pu-yuan ignores her.*)

FAN: Intelligent, too.

CHOU (*absorbed in his own thoughts*): Mm.

FAN (*appreciatively*): And so young!

CHOU (*unconsciously echoing her*): Yes, so young.

FAN (*putting the photograph down*): It's funny, I seem to have seen her somewhere.

CHOU (*looking up suspiciously*): Impossible! Where could you have seen her? Now, come on, time for bed. (*He gets up and takes the photograph from her.*)

FAN: Well, don't just stand there holding it.

(*Pu-yuan gazes through her but makes no reply.*)

FAN (*taking the photograph from him*): Put it over here! (*With an unnatural laugh.*) You won't lose it. I'll look after it for you. (*She puts it on the table.*)

CHOU: Don't pretend you're mad! You're playing the fool with me!

FAN: But I *am* mad. And I'd rather you left me alone.

CHOU (*annoyed*): All right. Now go on up to bed. I want to be left on my own here to have a rest.

FAN: Oh no. *I* want to be left here on my own to have a rest. You'll have to get out.

CHOU (*glowering at her*): Fan-yi, I'm telling you to go upstairs!

FAN (*contemptuously*): I don't wish to. You hear? I don't wish to.
    (*A pause.*)

CHOU (*in a low voice*): What you've got to be careful of—(*tapping his own head*) is this. Remember what Dr. Kramer said. He wants you to be quiet and not talk so much. He'll be here again tomorrow. I've made an appointment for you.

FAN (*looking straight in front of her*): Here again tomorrow? Humph!
    (*A chap-fallen Chou Ping comes in from the dining-room and walks with bent head towards the study.*)

CHOU: Ping.

PING (*looking up with a start*): Why, Father! You're still up.

CHOU (*censoriously*): Only just got back home, I suppose?

PING: Oh no, Father. I've been back some time now. I only went out to do some shopping.

CHOU: What do you want here?

PING: I was going to the study to see if your letter of introduction was ready.

CHOU: But you're not leaving until tomorrow morning, are you?

PING: I suddenly remembered there was a train leaving at half-past two tonight, so I've decided to go straight away.

FAN (*suddenly*): Straight away?

PING: Mm.

FAN: You're in a tearing hurry, aren't you?

PING: Yes, Mother.

CHOU (*pleasantly*): But it's raining hard just now. Not much of weather to go out in at this time of night.

PING: If I go on this train, I'll get there first thing in the morning, which will give me more time to look up all the people I've got to see.

CHOU: The letter's on the desk in the study. I suppose you'd better go now, if you think you must. (*Chou Ping nods and turns to go into the study.*)

CHOU: Wait. You needn't fetch it yourself. (*To Fan-yi.*) Go and get the letter for him, will you?

FAN (*looking distrustfully at her husband*): All right. (*She goes into the study.*)

CHOU (*waiting until she has gone out and then, cautiously*): She refuses to go upstairs. I want you to take her up to her room and tell one of the maids to see her into bed all right.

PING: Very well, Father.

CHOU (*even more cautiously*): Come here!

(*Chou Ping comes closer.*)

CHOU (*in an undertone*): And tell the servants to keep their wits about them. (*With annoyance.*) I think her nerves are getting worse than ever. A short while ago she suddenly went off on her own.

PING: Went off?

CHOU: Yes. (*Gravely.*) She'd been standing out in the rain all the evening. And she says such funny things! I don't like the look of it at all.—I'm getting on in years, and I want everything to go smoothly in the family—

PING (*uneasily*): I think, Father, if only you don't attach too much importance to these things, you'll find they'll straighten themselves out.

CHOU (*as though overawed by something*): No, no. Sometimes things turn out in a way you'd never have imagined. The world's a—a funny place. What's happened today has made me suddenly realize just how difficult, how terribly difficult life can be. (*Wearily.*) I'm glad you want to go to the mine for a bit of real hard work. I've got something here for you to take with you. (*He takes Chou Ping over to a square table and opens a drawer for him to look into.*) But it's strictly for self-defence. Don't go getting into mischief with it. (*He locks the drawer.*) Here's the key. Don't forget to take it with you when you go. (*He gives Chou Ping the key.*)

(*Fan-yi comes back in with the letter.*)

FAN (*resentfully*): Here's your letter!

CHOU (*coming back to earth with a start and turning again to Chou Ping*): All right, off you go, then. I'm going to bed. You'd better get some rest, too, Fan-yi.

FAN (*eager to get rid of him*): Yes, all right.

(*Chou Pu-yuan goes out through the study.*)

FAN (*as soon as Chou Pu-yuan is gone, despondently*): So you've really made up your mind to go, then.

PING: Yes.

FAN (*suddenly*): What was your father saying to you just now?

PING (*evasively*): He said I was to see you up to your room and ask you to go to bed.

FAN (*with a sardonic smile*): I should have thought he'd have had me dragged upstairs by the servants and locked in!

PING (*pretending not to understand*): What on earth do you mean?

FAN (*letting fly*): Don't think you can pull the wool over my eyes! I know all about it. (*Bitterly.*) He's been telling you I'm neurotic—mad. I know quite well he's trying to convince you that I am. He's trying to convince everybody that I am.

PING (*nervously*): Oh no, you mustn't go getting ideas like that.

FAN (*making a wry face*): You, too? Even you trying to deceive me? (*Morosely.*) I can see it in your eyes, both of you. You and your father are both the same—you want me to go mad! You and your father, you sneer about me behind my back, and laugh at me, and plot against me!

PING (*calmly*): You're imagining things. I'll see you up to your room.

FAN (*sharply*): I don't want your help! Get away from me! (*Faintly.*) I haven't got to the stage yet where your father needs to go behind my back and tell you to be careful and see the lunatic up to her room!

PING (*suppressing his distaste and annoyance*): If that's the case, perhaps you'll give me the letter, so that I can get out of your way.

FAN (*puzzled*): Where are you going, then?

PING (*helplessly*): I'm going away. I've got some packing to do.

FAN (*suddenly cold and calm*): Might I inquire where you went tonight?

PING (*with animosity*): You don't need to ask. You know very well.

FAN (*menacingly*): So you went to see her after all. (*A pause. Fan-yi stares at Chou Ping until he drops his eyes to the floor.*)

PING (*with an air of finality*): Yes. I did. (*Challenging her.*) What are you going to do about it?

FAN (*crumpling*): Nothing. (*Forcing a smile.*) It was wrong of me to say what I did this afternoon. You mustn't think too badly of me because of that. There's just one thing I want to know: what are you going to do about her after you've gone?

PING: After I've gone?—(*Impulsively.*) I'll marry her!

FAN: Marry her?

PING: Yes.

FAN: What about your father?

PING (*nonchalantly*): Plenty of time to think about that.

FAN (*mysteriously*): Ping, I'll give you a chance.

PING (*blankly*): Eh?

FAN (*persuasively*): If you don't leave today, I think I can get round your father for you.

PING: Thanks, but there's no need to. This business is quite square and above board so far as I'm concerned. I don't care who knows.

FAN (*miserably*): Oh, Ping!

PING: Well?

FAN (*moodily*): You realize what will become of me after you've gone?

PING: I've no idea.

FAN (*trembling at the prospect*): Can't you imagine what it will be like? You've only got to look at the way your father goes on.

PING: I don't understand what you mean.

FAN (*tapping her head*): This. Know what I mean?

PING (*not sure whether he understands or not*): What exactly *do* you mean?

FAN (*with an air of detachment, as though she were speaking about someone else*): Well, first of all, this specialist, Dr. Kramer, is bound to come here every day, giving me medicine and forcing me to take it. And so it'll go on: medicine, medicine, medicine, day in and day out! Gradually there'll be more and more people to wait on me, to look after me, to keep watch over me, as if I were something peculiar—a freak. They'll—

PING (*become impatient with her*): Now listen to me: you're just imagining things.

FAN: They'll gradually start talking the way your father does: Be careful, watch your step, she's got a touch of insanity. Wherever I go, I'll hear people whispering behind my back, gossiping about me. Gradually everyone will become wary of me, and no one will dare come and see me. Finally, I'll be put in chains, and by that time I really shall have gone mad.

PING (*at a complete loss*): Well! (*Glancing at his watch.*) It's getting late. Give me the letter, then: I've still got some packing to do.

FAN (*pleading*): Ping, don't think that that can't happen. Think it over, Ping. Haven't you even a—even a spark of feeling?

PING: If you—(*with deliberate venom*) if you're so set on taking that road, what can I do about it?

FAN (*indignantly*): What! Have you forgotten that your own mother was also hounded to her death by this father of yours?

PING (*abandoning all reserve*): My mother wasn't like you. She knew what love meant. She loved her son, and she was at least faithful to my father.

FAN (*her eyes ablaze with the light of madness*): What right have you to say a thing like that? Have you forgotten what you did three years ago, in this very room? You forget that it's you yourself that's the guilty one. You forget we—(*checking herself abruptly*) but what's the use of bringing all that up again? It's over and done with.

(*Chou Ping, his head bowed, drops into a sofa.*)

FAN (*turning to Chou Ping*): All right, Ping. This time I'm begging

263

you—begging you for the last time. I've never gone down on my hands and knees like this to anyone else, and now I'm begging you to have pity on me. I can't stand this house any longer. (*Plaintively.*) You saw with your own eyes what I went through today, and it isn't only going to be today: it'll go on for days, months, years at a time, and it won't stop until I'm dead. He hates the sight of me, your father. And he's afraid of me, because I can see through him, and know all about him. He wants everybody to think I'm a freak, a lunatic! Oh, Ping!—

PING (*profoundly disturbed*): Don't—don't talk like that.

FAN (*insistently*): I've got no relatives, Ping, no friends, nobody I can trust. I beg you, Ping, stay a little longer—

PING (*trying to put her off*): Oh, no, I couldn't do that.

FAN (*imploring him*): Well, if you must go, take me with you. Anything to get away from this—

PING (*horrified*): What! You're off your head!

FAN (*still imploring him*): I'm not, I'm not. Take me with you, away from this place! (*Becoming desperate.*) And afterwards, if you wanted to have Ssu-feng come and—and live with you, I'd agree to that, even, if only—if only—(*frantically*) if only you don't leave me!

PING (*looking at her in horror and astonishment*): I'm—I'm beginning to think you really are mad!

FAN: No, you mustn't say things like that. I'm the only person that really understands you. I know your failings—and you know mine. I know you inside out. (*Suddenly putting on a seductive smile.*) Come here. What—what are you afraid of?

PING (*gazing at her and shouting in spite of himself*): Stop smiling like that! (*More emphatically still.*) Don't smile at me like that! (*Beating his head in distress.*) Oh, I hate myself. I wish I were dead!

FAN (*bitterly*): Am I such a burden to you? But you know I haven't got many more years to live.

PING (*in an anguished voice*): But surely you realize that such a relationship must seem revolting to anyone else?

FAN (*coldly*): How many times have I told you that I don't look at it like that? My conscience isn't made that way. (*Solemnly.*) Ping, I was wrong in what I did this afternoon. If you'll follow my advice now and not go away, I can get Ssu-feng to come back here.

PING: What!

FAN (*distinctly*): It's still not too late to get her back.

PING (*going up to her and speaking in a low, level voice*): Get out of my sight!

FAN: What!

PING: You sound as if you'd taken leave of your senses. Get upstairs to bed.

FAN (*resigning herself to the inevitable*): That's that, then.

PING (*seizing this opportunity to snatch the letter from her*): Yes. Now off you go.

FAN (*despairingly*): I saw you with Ssu-feng at the Lus' tonight.

PING (*astounded*): Eh? Is that where you went, then?

FAN (*sitting down*): Yes. I spent quite a long time standing about near their place.

PING (*disturbed*): What time were you there?

FAN (*hanging her head*): I watched you get in through the window.

PING (*anxiously*): Then what?

FAN (*looking straight ahead with lifeless eyes*): Then I went over to the window and stood there.

PING: How long were you there?

FAN (*distinctly*): Right up until the time you left.

PING (*going across to her*): So it was you that closed the window!

FAN (*gloomily*): Yes, it was me.

PING (*revolted*): Why, you're more of a monster than I ever imagined!

FAN (*looking up*): What?

PING: You *are* a lunatic after all!

FAN (*looking at him without any expression on her face*): Well, what are you going to do about it?

PING (*ferociously*): Oh, go to hell! (*He goes out through the dining-room, slamming the door behind him.*)

(*Fan sits there in a daze, staring at the dining-room door. Catching sight of the photograph, she picks it up and puts it down again after a glance at it. Then, calm and poised, she stands up and begins pacing up and down.*)

FAN: What *is* it that I want to do? I wonder.

(*The center door opens quietly. Fan-yi turns to find Lu Kuei stealing in.*)

LU (*with a slight bow*): Good evening, madam.

FAN (*somewhat taken aback*): What are you doing here?

LU (*with an oily smile*): I've come to see how you're getting on, madam. I've been waiting outside the door for some time.

FAN (*calmly*): I see, outside the door, were you?

LU: That's right. (*Mysteriously.*) When I saw that Master Ping was quarrelling with you, I—(*with a mirthless smile*) I didn't like to come in.

FAN (*still poised and unruffled*): What do you want?

265

LU (*with complete assurance*): Well, I really came to tell you that Master Ping got drunk again tonight and came round to our place. But now, seeing that you were there yourself, madam, there's nothing more for me to say.

FAN (*with disgust*): What are you after now?

LU (*haughtily*): I'd like to see the master.

FAN: The master's gone to bed. What do you want to see him about?

LU: Oh, nothing important. If you'd like to see to it yourself, madam, then we needn't trouble the master.—(*With a meaningful look.*) It all depends on you, madam.

FAN (*deciding, after a pause, to put up with him*): Very well, then: tell me what it is. Perhaps I can help you.

LU (*craftily*): If you would like to handle the matter and save me seeing the master, everybody will be spared a lot of unnecessary trouble. All we want is to ask you to give us our jobs back, madam.

FAN (*crossly*): Do you suppose I—(*suddenly unbending*) very well, I think we can manage that.

LU (*pleased with himself*): Thank you, madam. (*Shrewdly.*) Then perhaps you'd fix a definite date for us to come back, madam?

FAN (*simply*): Make it the day after tomorrow, then.

LU (*bowing*): Thank you for your kindness, madam. (*Suddenly.*) Oh, I almost forgot. Have you seen Master Chung, madam?

FAN: No.

LU: Didn't you send him round to our place with a present of a hundred dollars?

FAN (*irritated*): Well?

LU: Well, you see, the money was sent back by our own young gentleman.

FAN: Your young gentleman?

LU (*explaining*): That's to say Ta-hai—that wretched son of mine.

FAN: Well, what about it?

LU (*smoothly*): Well, Shih-ping—our Shih-ping, still knows nothing about it.

FAN: Shih-ping? (*With a look of alarm.*) Who's Shih-ping?
(*The center door opens.*)

LU (*looking round*): Who is it?
(*Lu Ta-hai comes in, his clothes drenched and his face glum. Fan-yi looks at him in astonishment.*)

HAI (*to Lu Kuei*): So here you are!

LU: How did you get in?

266

HAI (*coldly*): The gates were shut and I couldn't make anybody hear, so I climbed over the wall.

LU: What are you doing here? What's happened to Ssu-feng?

HAI (*wiping the rain off his face with a wet handkerchief*): Can't find her. Mother's waiting outside.

LU (*frowning with annoyance at what he regards as a lot of fuss about nothing*): Oh, give it up. Ssu-feng will be back home any minute. Now you come home with me. I've fixed everything up with the Chous here. Everything's all right now. Let's be off, then.

HAI: Not yet—not until you've got me the young gentleman here. I can't find him.

LU (*apprehensively*): What are you up to now?

HAI (*calmly*): Nothing. I just want to have a little chat with him.

LU (*disbelieving him*): Oh no, you don't. I know what your little game is—

HAI (*glowering at him*): Will you find him for me or won't you?

LU (*cowed*): Only if you don't do more than talk.

HAI: You can take it from me that I haven't come here to quarrel with him.

FAN (*calmly*): Go and fetch him, Lu Kuei. It'll be all right with me here.

HAI: Go on, then, but if you sneak away without fetching him, you'd better look out!—And tell them to open the gate and let Mother in.

LU: All right, all right. But as soon as I've finished I'm off—(*In an undertone, to himself.*) The young bastard! (*He goes out through the dining-room.*)

FAN (*getting up*): Who are you?

HAI: Ssu-feng's brother.

FAN: You want to see Master Ping, you say?

HAI: Yes.

FAN (*easily*): I think he's just off to the station to catch a train.

HAI (*looking round*): Eh?

FAN: In fact, he's leaving immediately.

HAI: Running away, eh?

FAN: He certainly is!

(*Chou Ping comes in from the dining-room. He catches sight of Ta-hai at once.*)

PING (*steadying himself with an effort*): Oh!

HAI: Ah, good, you're still here. (*Looking round.*) Ask the lady to leave us. I want to have a word with you alone.

267

PING (*looks at Fan-yi, and when she does not move he goes across to her*): Please go upstairs.

FAN: All right. (*She goes out through the dining-room.*)
(*A pause. Ta-hai glares angrily at Chou Ping.*)

PING (*unable to bear the suspense any longer*): I didn't expect to see you again so soon.

HAI (*ominously*): I hear you're going away.

PING (*forcing a smile*): It's still not too late, though. You got here in plenty of time. What is it you want? I'm ready.

HAI (*ferociously*): Ready, you say?

PING (*looking him full in the face*): Yes.

HAI (*going up to him*): Take that! (*He strikes Chou Ping hard in the face.*)

PING (*his face bleeding, his fists clenched in an effort to control himself*): Why, you—(*He takes a handkerchief out of his pocket and wipes the blood off his face with it.*)

HAI (*grinding his teeth*): Humph! So you were going to run away!
(*A pause.*)

PING (*suppressing his anger and explaining*): I'd arranged to go away some time ago.

HAI (*with a malignant laugh*): You had, eh?

PING (*becoming calmer*): I think there are too many misunderstandings between us.

HAI: Misunderstandings! (*Notices the blood on his hand and wipes it off on his clothes.*) There isn't much I misunderstand about you! All you care about is yourself, you spineless thing!

PING (*in a soft, even voice*): We've met twice, but on both occasions I've been in a filthy temper. I'm afraid you must have got a rather bad impression of me.

HAI (*contemptuously*): Keep your excuses. You may be a young gentleman, but you act like a rat. Life's too easy for people like you. You've got plenty of surplus energy and nothing to do with it; so you pick up a poor man's daughter to amuse yourself with; then, when you've finished with her, off you go and responsibility be damned.

PING: I can see it's no use explaining anything to you now. I know you're here for something. (*Calmly.*) Well, out with your gun or your knife or whatever it is. Dispose of me as you think fit.

HAI: Very generous of you!—And in your own house, too! You're very clever. But you're not worth it. You won't catch me risking my own useful life for the sake of putting a dead-and-alive thing like you out of its misery.

PING (*looking him full in the face*): I suppose you think I'm afraid of you. Well, you're wrong. I'm more afraid of myself than I am of you. I've made one mistake, and I don't want to make another.

HAI (*scornfully*): So far as I can see, your biggest mistake was to be born. If it hadn't been for my mother, I'd have slaughtered you there and then! I hold your life in my hand even now.

PING: Death would be a welcome release for me. You imagine I'm afraid of death? Well, I'm not. Far from it—I'm glad to see you. I've had enough of life; I'm fed up with it.

HAI (*disgustedly*): Oh, so you're fed up with life, are you?—But not too much to make my sister share it with you, eh?

PING (*with a wry smile*): You mean I'm selfish? You really think I'm a heartless creature who only wants her for the amusement he can get out of her? Just ask your sister, will you? She knows I'm really in love with her. She's all I live for now.

HAI: You've got a smooth tongue, haven't you! (*Suddenly.*) Then why don't you—why don't you come out into the open with it all?

PING (*after a slight pause*): That's just what I hate myself most for. My position is an extremely difficult one. Can you imagine a family like mine approving of a thing like that?

HAI (*with pungent scorn*): So you think you can say you really do love her, and make that an excuse for doing whatever you like with her, while at the same time you say you've got to consider your family and your father's position as chairman of the board, eh? Then in the end they'll let you throw her over as and when you like so that you can marry some rich young lady who'll be a social asset to your family—is that it?

PING: I wish you'd go and ask Ssu-feng. She can tell you why I'm going away: it's to get away from my family and try to shake myself free of my father, so that I'll have a chance to marry her.

HAI (*mocking him*): You talked your way out of that pretty well! But how do you account for this business of coming round to our place in the middle of the night?

PING (*roused*): I'm not talking my way out of anything, and I don't need to make excuses to you. I'm only telling you all this because you're Ssu-feng's brother. I love her. And she loves me. We're both young, and we're both human. When two young people are in each other's company day after day, something's bound to happen. But I'm sure I'll be able to do the right thing by her one day and marry her. My conscience is perfectly clear.

HAI: You'd have us believe your intentions were strictly honorable,

269

then? And who do you imagine's going to believe that you, the boss's son and heir, had fallen in love with a poor girl whose brother's a miner and whose mother's a servant?

PING (*after some deliberation*): Well, I—er—I may as well tell you: my hand was forced by a woman who left me no alternative.

HAI: What? You mean there's another woman involved?

PING: Yes. The lady that was here just now.

HAI: Her?

PING (*distraught*): Yes, my stepmother!—All these years I've kept this secret bottled up inside me. I've never dared tell anyone.—She's had a good education and all that, but—the moment she set eyes on me she developed a passion for me and wanted me to—(*breaking off abruptly*) though of course I can't disclaim all responsibility for what happened.

HAI: Does Ssu-feng know about this?

PING: Yes, I'm sure of it. (*With tears in his eyes.*) I was a fool ever to have started. As time went on I became more and more afraid, and the whole business became more distasteful and hateful to me. I hated this unnatural relationship. Can you understand? I wanted to leave her, but she tightened her grip on me. She wouldn't let me go. She's a monster, capable of anything. My life was a burden to me. In the end I got so mad that I was prepared to do anything—anything to be free of her. Even death seemed preferable. And then Ssu-feng came along. She gave me hope—and another year of life.

HAI: I see.

PING: All this—I've never been able to bring myself to tell anybody about it, and yet—(*slowly*) the funny thing is, I've suddenly told it all to you!

HAI (*grimly*): This is a judgment on your father.

PING (*rather put out by Ta-hai's unexpected remark*): Why, you—! The reason I'm telling you all this is because you're Ssu-feng's brother. I want you to believe that I'm sincere. I've never had the slightest intention of deceiving her.

HAI (*unbending a little*): Then you really intend to marry Ssu-feng? You know she's a silly girl. She'd never marry anybody else after this.

PING (*quickly*): I realize that. I'm leaving today, but in a month or two I'll be back to fetch her.

HAI: Now look here, you son-of-the-boss you, you don't expect me to swallow that, do you?

PING (*taking a letter out of his pocket*): You can read this letter that I've just written to her. It's all explained here.

HAI: I don't want to see it. I—I haven't got time now.

270

PING (*looking up after a moment's silence*): Then I'm afraid there's no other way of proving my good faith. Though that lethal weapon you've got there in your pocket should be guarantee enough. If you still don't believe me, I'm still at your mercy, you know.

HAI (*acidly*): You think I'm going to let you get away with it as easily as that? (*With a sudden ferocity.*) You really think I am? (*He suddenly whips out his pistol.*)

PING (*panic-stricken*): What are you going to do?

HAI (*fiercely*): I'm going to kill you! (*Taking aim at Chou Ping.*) You spineless thing!

PING: All right, go on, then! (*He shuts his eyes in terror.*)

(*A pause.*)

HAI (*he exhales sharply, lowers the gun and speaks with distaste*): Open your eyes!

PING (*puzzled*): What's the matter?

HAI (*miserably*): Nothing. Only my mother. My sister is all she lives for. If you can give Ssu-feng a decent life, I'll let you go this once.

(*Chou Ping opens his mouth to speak, but Ta-hai stops him with a wave of the hand.*)

HAI (*peremptorily*): And now fetch my sister in.

PING (*bewildered*): What?

HAI: Ssu-feng. I take it she's here.

PING: No, no, she's not here. I thought she was at home.

HAI (*uncertainly*): Well, that's queer. Mother and I spent two hours looking for her in the rain, but there wasn't a sign of her. I naturally assumed she must be here.

PING (*anxiously*): You mean she's been out wandering around in the rain for two hours? Isn't there—anywhere else she could have gone to?

HAI (*positively*): No! Where could she have gone in the middle of the night?

PING (*as a terrible suspicion crosses his mind*): No! Don't say she's gone and—

HAI: You think she's—no, she wouldn't do that. (*Contemptuously.*) No, I don't think she'd have the guts.

PING (*his voice trembling*): Yes, she would. You don't know her. She's proud, and strong-willed, and she—but she should have seen me first. She shouldn't have been so rash.

(*A pause.*)

HAI (*suddenly*): Humph! A fine bit of play-acting that was! Think you can put me off with tricks like that? Don't kid yourself.—She's here! She must be here!

(*A whistle is heard outside the window.*)

PING (*raising his hand for silence*): Sh! Stop shouting. (*The whistling comes nearer and nearer.*) That's her! Here she is! I can hear her!

HAI: Eh?

PING: That's her. When we meet, we always whistle first.

HAI: Where is she, then?

PING: Probably out in the garden. (*He opens the window and whistles back.*)

(*A pause.*)

PING (*over his shoulder*): Here she comes!

(*There is a knock on the center door.*)

PING (*to Ta-hai*): I think you'd better keep out of sight in the next room for the time being. She wouldn't be expecting to find you here. I don't think she could stand many more shocks. (*He shows Ta-hai into the dining-room.*)

SSU-FENG'S VOICE: Ping!

PING (*hurrying across to the center door*): Feng! (*Opening the door.*) Come in!

(*Ssu-feng comes in, her face wet with tears and rain, and her tangled, dripping hair hanging in her eyes. She stares at Chou Ping as if in a trance.*)

FENG: Ping!—(*Timidly.*) Anyone about?

PING (*perturbed*): No, it's all right. (*He grasps her hands.*)

FENG: Oh, Ping! (*She flings her arms round him and sobs convulsively.*)

PING: How—how did you get into such a state? How did you know I was here? (*Babbling with relief.*) How did you get in?

FENG: I slipped in through the back way.

PING: Your hands are like ice. You'd better hurry up and get those wet things off.

FENG: No—(*with a sob*) let me have a look at you first.

PING (*taking her over to a sofa and sitting her down beside him*): But—but where have you been?

FENG (*looking at Chou Ping with her eyes full of tears*): Here you are at last, Ping. It seems ages since I last saw you.

PING: My poor darling, how can you be so silly? But where have you been, my silly girl?

FENG: I just ran on and on in the rain until I didn't know where I was. The noise of the thunder seemed to drive everything out of my mind. I thought I heard Mother calling after me, but I was afraid, and I ran as fast as I could. I was looking for the river out in front of our place. I was going to throw myself in.

PING (*aghast*): Feng!

272

FENG: —But somehow I couldn't find it, though I went round and round in circles looking for it.

PING: Oh, Feng, it's all my fault. Please forgive me. Don't hold it against me.

FENG: Somehow I stumbled here in a daze. Suddenly I saw there was a light in your window and I realized you were in. All of a sudden I felt that I couldn't just die: I couldn't bear to be parted from you. I think we can still go away—only we must go away together.

PING (*solemnly*): Yes, we must go away together.

FENG (*earnestly*): It's the only way out, Ping. I've got no home to go to now. (*With feeling.*) Ta-hai hates me, and I just couldn't face Mother now. I've got nothing now—no family, no friends. I've got only you, Ping. Take me away with you tomorrow.

(*A pause.*)

PING (*after a pause*): No, no.

FENG (*in despair*): Ping!

PING (*gravely*): We must go right now.

FENG (*incredulous*): What, this minute?

PING (*tenderly*): Yes. I was intending to go alone and then come back for you later, but there's no need to wait now.

FENG (*still incredulous*): You really mean it? We'll go together?

PING: Yes, I really do mean it.

FENG (*delirious with joy, she seizes Chou Ping's hands and kisses them wildly, while the tears stream down her cheeks*): So it's true! It's true, then! Oh, Ping! You darling, you! You're the dearest darling in the whole world. You—you've saved my life!

PING (*fervently*): From now on we'll always be together.

FENG: Yes, once we get away from this place, we'll never be parted from each other.

PING (*getting up*): All right, Feng, but before we go there's someone you must see. As soon as we've done that, we'll be away.

FENG: Who do you mean?

PING: Your brother.

FENG: Ta-hai?

PING: He's been looking for you. He's in the dining-room there.

FENG (*frightened*): No, no, don't see him. He hates you. He'll hurt you. Let's go—let's get out—quick.

PING: I've already seen him.—And now we must see him once more—- (*with an air of finality*) otherwise we just won't be able to go.

FENG (*timorously*): But, Ping, you—

(*Chou Ping goes across to the dining-room door and opens it.*)

PING *(calling)*: Lu Ta-hai! Lu Ta-hai!—I say! He's gone! That's funny. He must have gone out through the other door. *(He looks at Ssu-feng.)*

FENG *(going up to Chou Ping and pleading with him)*: Come on, Ping, let's go. *(Dragging him towards the center door.)* Let's go just as we are. *(As Ssu-feng gets Chou Ping to the door, it opens. Lu Ma and Lu Ta-hai come in.)*

(Lu Ma looks a changed woman. She has cried and shouted herself hoarse in the rain. She seems to have aged considerably.)

FENG *(in alarm)*: Mother!

(A slight pause.)

MA *(in an agonized voice, her arms held out towards Ssu-feng)*: Feng.

(Ssu-feng rushes towards her mother.)

FENG: Oh, Mother!

MA *(stroking Ssu-feng's head)*: My child, my poor, poor child.

FENG *(sobbing quietly)*: Oh, Mother, forgive me, forgive me.

MA: Why didn't you tell me earlier?

FENG *(hanging her head)*: I was afraid. I was afraid you might be angry with me, and despise me, and turn me out. I just didn't dare tell you.

MA *(sorrowfully)*: It's my own fault for being so stupid. I should have thought of it before. *(Bitterly.)* But who could have expected anything like this? And to think that it should have happened to my own child of all people! My own fate's been hard enough, but you—

HAI *(unemotionally)*: Let's get going, then. Ssu-feng will be going home with you for the time being.—I've arranged everything with him— *(pointing to Chou Ping)* he can go on in advance and come back for Ssu-feng later.

MA *(bewildered)*: What are you saying? What are you saying?

HAI *(looking at his mother, unperturbed)*: I know what's worrying you, Mother, but there's no other way out. So—*(after a pause)* we may as well let them go.

MA: What! Let them go?

PING *(hesitantly)*: You can trust me, Mrs. Lu. I'll be good to her. I'm taking her with me and leaving at once.

MA *(her voice trembling)*: Do you want to go with him, Feng?

FENG *(tightly gripping her mother's hands)*: Mother, I'm afraid I'll have to leave you for a while.

MA: You can't live together!

HAI *(surprised)*: What's the matter, Mother?

MA *(firmly)*: No! It wouldn't do!

FENG: Mother!

MA: Ssu-feng, we're going home. *(To Ta-hai.)* Go and call a rickshaw. I don't suppose Ssu-feng can do any more walking. We must go—as fast as we can!

FENG *(recoiling from her in desperation)*: You can't do this to me, Mother!

MA: It wouldn't do, I say. *(Woodenly.)* Come on, we must go.

FENG *(imploring her)*: Do you want to drive your daughter to distraction and see her die of worry before your very eyes?

PING *(going up to Lu Ma)*: Mrs. Lu, I know I've done you wrong, but I'll do my best to make up for it. Now that things have come to such a pass, you—

HAI *(at a loss to understand his mother's behavior)*: What's the matter with you, Mother?

MA *(sternly)*: You go and get a rickshaw! *(To Ssu-feng.)* Now listen to me, Feng: I'd rather lose you than see you living with him!—Come on, then.

(Just as Ta-hai gets to the door, Ssu-feng screams.)

FENG: A—a—ah! Mother! *(She faints into her mother's arms.)*

MA *(holding her in her arms)*: My child! You—

PING *(agitated)*: She's fainted.

MA *(feeling Ssu-feng's forehead and softly calling her name)*: Ssu-feng. *(Chou Ping runs towards the dining-room.)*

HAI: Don't panic: a drop of cold water and she'll be all right. She was like that when she was little.

(Chou Ping gets some cold water and sprinkles it on Ssu-feng's face. She gradually comes to.)

MA *(splashing more cold water on her face)*: Wake up, wake up, Ssu-feng.

FENG *(drawing a deep breath)*: Ah, Mother.

MA *(trying to comfort her)*: Don't be hard on me, child. I'm not being hard-hearted. I just can't tell you what I'm going through.

FENG *(sighing deeply)*: Mother.

MA: What is it?

FENG *(to Chou Ping)*: I—there's something I've got to tell you.

PING: Feel better now, Feng?

FENG: I—I've been keeping it from you all the time. *(Looking piteously at her mother.)* I couldn't even bring myself to tell you, Mother.

MA: What is it, child?

FENG *(sobbing)*: I—we're going to have a—*(She breaks down in a flood of tears.)*

MA: What? You mean you— *(Words fail her.)*

275

PING (*seizing Ssu-feng's hand*): Ssu-feng! You mean it? You—

FENG (*weeping*): Yes.

PING: But when? How long?

FENG (*hanging her head*): About three months now.

PING: But, Ssu-feng, why didn't you tell me? I—oh, my—

MA (*hoarsely*): My God!

PING (*going over to Lu Ma*): You just can't stand in our way now, Mrs. Lu. It's all my fault. Now, please, *please* let her go. I give you my word I'll be worthy of her, and a credit to you.

FENG (*going down on her knees at her mother's feet*): Have pity on us, Mother. Say "yes" and let us go.

MA (*sitting there in a daze, unable to speak for a moment*): I must be dreaming. My children, my own children, after thirty years—oh, my God! (*She buries her face in her hands and bursts into tears, then waves them away.*) Go away! I don't know you! (*She turns her face away.*)

PING: In that case—(*rising*) we'd better go.

(*Ssu-feng gets to her feet again.*)

MA (*unable to control herself*): No, you can't do it!

FENG (*falling on her knees again and pleading with her*): What's the matter with you, Mother? My mind's made up. Whoever he is, I belong to him now. My heart was promised to him from the very first, and there can never be anybody else for me but him. I've got now so that wherever he goes I'll go with him and whatever he does I'll do too. Can't you understand, Mother, that I—

MA (*stopping her with a gesture, distressed*): Child!

HAI: Well, things being as they are, I don't see why we shouldn't let her go.

PING: Mrs. Lu, if you refuse to let her go, we'll have no alternative but to disobey you and just go.—Feng!

FENG (*shaking her head*): No—(*still looking up at Lu Ma*) Mother!

MA (*in a low voice*): Oh, God knows what this is a punishment for— what have I ever done to bring such a calamity down on our heads?—My poor children, they didn't know what they were doing. Oh, God, if anyone has to be punished, why can't it just be me? It's my fault and no one else's: it all began when I took the first false step. (*Heart-broken.*) They're my innocent children; they deserve a chance in life. The guilt is here in my heart, and I should be the one to suffer for it. (*She rises to her feet and looks heavenwards.*) And tonight, here I am letting them go away together. I know I'm doing wrong, but this way the responsibility will all be mine; all this trouble was caused by me in the first place. My children haven't done anything wrong: they're too good and innocent to do anything wrong. If there must be a punishment, let me bear it—alone. *(Looking away.)* Feng—

FENG *(uneasily)*: What's the matter with you, Mother? What are you talking about?

MA *(turning her face away)*: It doesn't matter. *(Gently.)* Now get up. And go. Both of you.

FENG *(getting up and embracing her mother)*: Oh, Mother!

PING: Come on, then. *(Looking at his watch.)* We haven't got much time. Only twenty-five minutes before the train goes. Tell them to get the car out. Come on.

MA *(calmly)*: No, don't do that, Feng. If you're going away secretly like this in the middle of the night, it would be best not to attract too much attention. *(To Ta-hai.)* Ta-hai, you can go and get a rickshaw. I'm going home now. You can see them off at the station.

HAI: All right. *(He goes out through the center door.)*

MA *(to Ssu-feng, with a sad tenderness)*: Come here, my child. Let me kiss you good-bye.

(Ssu-feng goes up to her mother and embraces her.)

MA *(to Chou Ping)*: You come here, too. Let me have a look at you.

(Chou Ping goes and stands in front of Lu Ma, his head bent.)

MA *(looking at him and wiping her eyes)*: Go on, then. Off you go.—I want you both to promise me one thing before you go, though.

PING: What is it?

MA: If you don't promise, then I won't let Ssu-feng go after all.

FENG: Tell us what it is, Mother. I'll promise.

MA *(looking from one to the other)*: When you go, you'd best go as far as you can and never come back. Once you've left tonight, you must never see me again as long as you live.

FENG *(in distress)*: Oh, Mother, don't—

PING *(tipping her a wink and whispering)*: She's overwrought just now—will be all right later on.

FENG: Yes, all right, then.—We'll be off now, then, Mother. *(Her eyes fill with tears as she kneels for a farewell kowtow to her mother.)*

(Lu Ma is controlling her own emotions with an effort.)

MA *(waving them away)*: Off you go, then.

PING: Let's go out through the dining-room. I've still got some of my things in there.

(Just as the three of them get to the dining-room door, it opens and Fan-yi comes in.)

FENG *(involuntarily)*: Madam!

FAN (*with composure*): Why, where are you all going? There's still a thunderstorm on outside, you know!

PING (*to Fan-yi*): So you've been eavesdropping at the door, have you?

FAN: Yes, and I'm not the only one. There's someone else here. (*Turning back to the dining-room.*) Come out, you!

(*A sheepish Chou Chung emerges from the dining-room.*)

FENG (*startled*): Master Chung!

CHUNG (*disconcerted*): Hullo, Ssu-feng!

PING (*annoyed*): I didn't expect such behavior from you, Chung.

CHUNG (*still at sea*): It was Mother who told me to come here. I'd no idea what was going on.

FAN (*coldly*): You'll know soon enough.

PING (*to Fan-yi, fuming*): Now what's the meaning of all this?

FAN (*mockingly*): I just wanted your brother to come and give you a send-off.

PING (*furiously*): What a dirty, mean trick!—

CHUNG: Now, Ping!

PING (*to Chou Chung*): I'm sorry! (*Rounding abruptly on Fan-yi again.*) But there isn't another mother like you on earth!

CHUNG (*bewildered*): What's going on, then, Mother?

FAN: See for yourself! (*To Ssu-feng.*) Where are you going, Ssu-feng?

FENG (*falteringly*): I—er—I—

PING: Nothing silly, now. Tell them we're going away together.

CHUNG (*now that the light has dawned*): What's this, Ssu-feng? You're going away with him?

FENG: Yes, Master Chung. I—I'm—

CHUNG (*somewhat reproachfully*): Then why didn't you tell me so before?

FENG: But I did. I told you to leave me alone because I—I was no longer a—

PING (*to Ssu-feng*): Go on, tell them all about it! (*Pointing to Fan-yi.*) Tell her that you're going to marry me!

CHUNG (*rather taken aback*): Ssu-feng, you—

FAN (*to Chou Chung*): Now you know what it's all about.

(*Chou Chung hangs his head.*)

PING (*rounding on Fan-yi with a sudden viciousness*): You spiteful creature! You think he'll spoil everything to help you? Well, Chung? What ideas have you got on the subject? Eh? What are you going to do about it? Eh?

(*Chou Chung looks from his mother to Ssu-feng, then hangs his head in silence.*)

FAN: Come on, Chung! (*After a pause, more insistently.*) Why don't you say something, Chung? Why don't you ask him? Why don't you ask your brother something?

(Another pause. Everybody looks at Chou Chung, who stands mute.)

FAN: Say something, Chung! You're not dead, are you? Or dumb? Or are you just a stupid child? Surely you're not just going to stand there with all this going on and not make a murmur?

CHUNG *(lifting his head and replying with a lamb-like bleat)*: No, Mother. *(He looks at Ssu-feng again, then hangs his head.)* So long as Ssu-feng is willing, I've no objection.

PING *(going up to Chou Chung)*: Spoken like a sensible fellow, Chung!

CHUNG *(with a puzzled frown)*: No. I've suddenly realized—it's just come to me—that I wasn't really in love with Ssu-feng after all. *(Staring abstractedly into space.)* What I felt about her was—probably only a silly infatuation. *(Shrinking back from the triumphant Chou Ping.)* Yes, take her away with you—only be good to her.

FAN *(all her hopes dashed)*: Ugh, you! *(With a sudden fury.)* You're no son of mine! *(Incoherently.)* You're no man at all! If I were you—- *(turning on Ssu-feng)* I'd smash her, burn her, kill her! You're just a poor, feeble idiot—not a spark of life in you! I should have known better—you're none of mine—no son of mine!

CHUNG *(pained)*: What's the matter with you, Mother?

FAN *(to Chou Chung, hysterically)*: Don't think I'm your mother. *(Raising her voice.)* Your mother died long ago. She was crushed and smothered by your father. *(Wiping her eyes, in an anguished voice.)* After all these eighteen years of misery in this soul-destroying place, this "residence of the Chou family" that's more like a prison, married to a hateful tyrant—after all these years my spirit is still not dead. Your father may have made me have you, Chung, but my heart—my soul is still my own. *(Pointing to Chou Ping.)* He's the only one that's ever possessed me body and soul. But now he doesn't want me; he doesn't want me any more.

CHUNG *(considerably distressed)*: Mother, my dearest mother, what *is* all this about?

PING: Take no notice of her. She's going off her head!

FAN *(heatedly)*: Copying your father now, are you? You hypocrite, you! No, I'm not mad—not in the least! And now it's your turn to speak, and tell them all about it—it's my last chance to get even with you!

PING *(embarrassed)*: What is there for me to tell? I think you'd better go up to bed.

FAN *(sneering)*: Stop pretending! Tell them that I'm not your step-mother at all.

(General astonishment. A short pause.)

279

CHUNG (*at his wit's end*): Mother!

FAN (*recklessly*): Go on, tell them. Tell Ssu-feng. Go on, tell her!

FENG (*overcome*): Oh, Mother! (*She throws herself into her mother's arms.*)

FAN: Remember: it was you, and you alone, that deceived your brother, and deceived me, and deceived your father! (*She looks at him with a contemptuous sneer.*)

PING (*to Ssu-feng*): Take no notice of her. Let's get out of here.

FAN: You wouldn't get far. The gate's locked. Your father will be down any minute. I've sent for him.

MA: God!

PING: What are you trying to do?

FAN (*with icy calm*): I want your father to meet his dear future daughter-in-law before you leave. (*Calling her husband.*) Pu-yuan! Pu-yuan!—

CHUNG: Mother, please!

PING (*advancing on Fan-yi*): Don't you dare shout again, you lunatic! (*Fan-yi runs to the door of the study and shouts again.*)

MA (*in great agitation*): Let's get out of here, Ssu-feng.

FAN: No. He's coming!
    (*Chou Pu-yuan comes in from the study. There is a deathly hush, and no one moves an inch.*)

CHOU (*in the doorway*): What's all the shouting for? You ought to be in bed by now.

FAN (*haughtily*): I want you to meet some relatives of yours.

CHOU (*amazed to find Lu Ma and Ssu-feng here*): Why, what the—what are you two doing here?

FAN (*taking Ssu-feng's hand and turning to Pu-yuan*): Let me introduce your daughter-in-law. (*To Ssu-feng, indicating Pu-yuan.*) Say hullo to your father! (*Then to Pu-yuan, indicating Lu Ma.*) And I'd like you to meet this lady here, too!

MA: Oh, madam!

FAN: Come here, Ping! You can pay your respects to your new mother now that your father's here.

PING (*embarrassed*): Father, I—I—

CHOU (*taking in the situation*): Why—(*To Lu Ma.*) So you've come back again after all, Shih-ping.

FAN (*startled*): What?

MA (*desperately*): No, no, you're mistaken.

CHOU (*remorsefully*): Yes, Shih-ping. I thought you'd be back.

MA: No! No! (*Hanging her head.*) Oh, God!

FAN (*stupefied*): Shih-ping? You mean she's Shih-ping?

CHOU (*irritated*): Don't start pretending you didn't know, and asking silly questions. She's Ping's mother, the one that died thirty years ago.

FAN: In Heaven's name!

(*A long silence, broken only by a cry of anguish from Ssu-feng as she stares at her mother, who sits there with her head bent, as if in pain. Dazedly, Chou Ping's eyes travel from his father to Lu Ma, while Fan-yi steals round to Chou Chung. She is gradually becoming aware that a far greater tragedy than her own is unfolding before her eyes.*)

CHOU (*with a heavy heart*): Ping, come here. Your own mother never died at all. She's here, alive.

PING (*beside himself*): No, it can't be her! Father, say it's not her!

CHOU (*severely*): Idiot! Don't talk such utter nonsense! She may not be from a good family, but she's your mother just the same.

PING (*in utter despair*): Oh, Father!

CHOU (*seriously*): Don't forget that you owe her something for bringing you into the world, even if it is a bit of a blow to find that Ssu-feng's your half-sister.

FENG (*overcome with grief*): Oh, Mother!

CHOU (*despondently*): Forgive me, Ping. This was the only real mistake I ever made. I never imagined for one moment that she was still alive and that one day she'd find us here. I can only put it down to divine justice. (*Turning to Lu Ma with a sigh.*) I'm getting old now. I felt very sorry after I told you to go this afternoon, and I've arranged to have twenty thousand dollars sent to you. Now that you've come back again, I think Ping will be a good son to you and look after you. He'll help to make amends for the wrong I did you.

PING (*to Lu Ma*): So you—you're my—

MA (*unable to control herself any longer*): Oh, Ping!—(*She turns her head away and sobs.*)

CHOU: Down on your knees to her, Ping! You're not dreaming. She's your mother.

FENG (*in utter bewilderment*): This can't be true, Mother.

(*Lu Ma makes no reply.*)

FAN (*to Chou Ping, repentantly*): I never expected it to—to turn out like this, Ping!—

PING (*to Pu-yuan*): Father! (*To Lu Ma.*) Mother!

FENG (*she and Chou Ping stare at one another until, suddenly, she can bear it no longer*): Oh, my God! (*She rushes out through the center door.*)

(Chou Ping throws himself down on the sofa and buries his head in his arms. Lu Ma stands motionless, lifeless.)

FAN *(calling anxiously)*: Ssu-feng! Ssu-feng! *(Turning to Chou Chung.)* I don't like the look of this, Chung. You'd better hurry out and find her.

(Chou Chung runs out through the center door, calling after Ssu-feng.)

CHOU *(going up to Chou Ping)*: Now, Ping, what's all this about?

PING *(bursting out)*: You should never have fathered me! *(He runs out through the dining-room.)*

(Suddenly, a scream is heard from Ssu-feng in the distance, followed by Chou Chung's frantic shouting of "Ssu-feng! Ssu-feng!" Then comes a scream from Chou Chung.)

MA *(shouting)*: Ssu-feng, what's happened?

FAN *(simultaneously)*: Chung! My boy!

(They both run out through the center door.)

CHOU *(hurries to the window, pulls aside the curtain, and quavers)*: What's happened? What's happened?

(A servant comes running in through the center door.)

SERVANT *(gasping)*: Sir!

CHOU: Quick! What's happened?

SERVANT *(in a panic-stricken gabble)*: Ssu-feng—she's—she's dead!

CHOU *(aghast)*: What about Chung?

SERVANT: He's—he's dead, too.

CHOU *(in a trembling voice)*: No! . . . No! What—what happened?

SERVANT: Ssu-feng ran into the electric cable. It's live. Master Chung didn't know about it, and he caught hold of her. They were both electrocuted.

CHOU: No, it can't be true! It's—it's impossible! Just impossible! *(He hurries out with the servant.)*

(Chou Ping comes in from the dining-room. He is deathly pale, yet his manner is perfectly calm. He goes over to the square table, opens the drawer and takes out a pistol. Then he goes into the study.)

(There is a hubbub of voices outside—a babel of weeping, shouting, and altercation. Lu Ma comes in through the center door, followed by an old servant with a torch.)

(Lu Ma stands silent in the center of the stage.)

OLD SERVANT *(trying to comfort her)*: Now come on, my dear, don't stand there dumb. What you want is a good cry. You'll feel better when you've had a good cry.

MA *(expressionless)*: I can't cry!

OLD SERVANT: Well, there's nothing else you can do now—now come on, you must have a cry.

MA: No, I—I—*(She stands there in a daze.)*

(The center door is flung wide open and Fan-yi appears in the doorway, supported by a number of servants. It is difficult to decide whether she is laughing or crying.)

SERVANTS *(behind her in the doorway)*: You'd best go in, madam, and not look.

(The servants shepherd her into the room, but she stops just inside the door. She leans against the door-post in a fit of hysterical laughter.)

FAN: Why are you gaping at me like that, Chung? Why are you smiling at me like that?—Oh, Chung, my silly boy!

(Chou Pu-yuan comes in through the center door.)

CHOU: Come on in, Fan-yi! My hands feel numb. You mustn't look at them any more.

OLD SERVANT: Come on in, madam. They're burned to a cinder, and there's nothing anybody can do about it now.

FAN *(coming forward into the room, convulsed with sobs)*: Chung, my boy, my boy! You were alive and well a moment ago. How can you be dead—so horribly dead?

CHOU: Steady, now. Steady. *(He wipes his eyes.)*

FAN *(laughing hysterically)*: You deserve to die, Chung, you deserve to die! With a mother like me you deserve to die!

(From outside comes the noise of a scuffle between Lu Ta-hai and the servants.)

CHOU: Who's that? Who's that making a disturbance at a time like this?

(The old servant goes out to find out. Another servant comes in immediately.)

CHOU: What's going on out there?

SERVANT: It's that Lu Ta-hai again, the one who was here this morning. He's back again now, and starting a fight with us.

CHOU: Tell him to come in.

SERVANT: He's gone now, sir. Got out the back way.—After he'd done quite a bit of damage to some of us with his fists and his feet.

CHOU: Got away, you say?

SERVANT: Yes, sir.

CHOU *(suddenly)*: Go after him, then, and bring him back here.

SERVANT: Very good, sir.

(All the servants go out, leaving only Pu-yuan, his wife and Lu Ma in the room.)

283

CHOU (*broken-hearted*): I've lost one son. I can't afford to lose another. (*They all sit down.*)

MA: Let them all go! Perhaps it's best that he has gone. I know what the boy's like. He's bursting with hatred. He won't come back.

CHOU (*as if bewildered by the sudden quiet*): It doesn't seem true that the youngsters have gone first and left us old—(*Suddenly.*) Ping! Where's Ping? Ping! Ping! (*No reply.*) Come here, somebody! Where are you all? (*Still no reply.*) Go and find him for me! Where's my eldest son?

(*The sound of a pistol shot from the study is followed by a deathly silence in the room.*)

FAN (*suddenly*): Oh! (*She runs into the study. Pu-yuan stands motionless, like a man in a trance. Fan-yi returns at once, wailing dementedly.*) He—he—

CHOU: He—he—

(*They both run into the study.*)

—CURTAIN—

ESSAYS AND SPEECHES

The importance of Mao Tse-tung's *Talks at the Yenan Forum* cannot be overstressed. Anyone who wishes to understand the development of all literature in China from the period of its war with Japan to the present and to be able to judge that work properly must study this essay with care.

Kuo Mo-jo (1892-   ) has enjoyed a most successful career in the good graces of the Communist Party. Poet, dramatist, historian, editor, and essayist, he has managed to be both an effective writer and a significant political figure since the early 1920's. And this is particularly remarkable when it is revealed that innumerable colleagues in both politics and the arts have felt the unrelenting and sometimes unpredictable hand of Party control. Tremendously inspired in his youth by Western writers—Goethe, Nietzsche, Turgenev, Shelley, Upton Sinclair, and Galsworthy, among others—he first printed his views on "Revolution and Literature" in 1926. Few would call him a writer of enduring merit, but he has contributed a noteworthy body of poetry and plays in addition to his translations of Western literary works and his histories which suggest his social idealism. His post-Cultural Revolution position as Minister of Culture attests to his political astuteness while his essays remain a good measure of Party line and personal convictions at the time of their composition.

Talks at the Yenan Forum
on Literature and Art*

by Mao Tse-tung

INTRODUCTION

MAY 2, 1942

Comrades! You have been invited to this forum today to exchange ideas and examine the relationship between work in the literary and artistic fields and revolutionary work in general. Our aim is to ensure that revolutionary literature and art follow the correct path of development and provide better help to other revolutionary work in facilitating the overthrow of our national enemy and the accomplishment of the task of national liberation.

In our struggle for the liberation of the Chinese people there are various fronts, among which there are the fronts of the pen and of the gun, the cultural and the military fronts. To defeat the enemy we must rely primarily on the army with guns. But this army alone is not enough; we must also have a cultural army, which is absolutely indispensable for uniting our own ranks and defeating the enemy. Since the May 4th Movement[1] such a cultural army has taken shape in China, and it has helped the Chinese revolution, gradually reduced the domain of China's feudal culture and of the comprador culture which serves imperialist aggression, and weakened their influence. To oppose the new culture the Chinese reactionaries can now only "pit quantity against quality." In other words, reactionaries have money, and though they can produce

* Reprinted from *Mao Tse-tung on Literature and Art* (Peking: Foreign Languages Press, 1967), pp. 1-43.

286

nothing good, they can go all out and produce in quantity. Literature and art have been an important and successful part of the cultural front since the May 4th Movement. During the ten years' civil war, the revolutionary literature and art movement grew greatly. That movement and the revolutionary war both headed in the same general direction, but these two fraternal armies were not linked together in their practical work because the reactionaries had cut them off from each other. It is very good that since the outbreak of the War of Resistance Against Japan, more and more revolutionary writers and artists have been coming to Yenan and our other anti-Japanese base areas. But it does not necessarily follow that, having come to the base areas, they have already integrated themselves completely with the masses of the people here. The two must be completely integrated if we are to push ahead with our revolutionary work. The purpose of our meeting today is precisely to ensure that literature and art fit well into the whole revolutionary machine as a component part, that they operate as powerful weapons for uniting and educating the people and for attacking and destroying the enemy, and that they help the people fight the enemy with one heart and one mind. What are the problems that must be solved to achieve this objective? I think they are the problems of the class stand of the writers and artists, their attitude, their audience, their work and their study.

The problem of class stand. Our stand is that of the proletariat and of the masses. For members of the Communist Party, this means keeping to the stand of the Party, keeping to Party spirit and Party policy. Are there any of our literary and art workers who are still mistaken or not clear in their understanding of this problem? I think there are. Many of our comrades have frequently departed from the correct stand.

The problem of attitude. From one's stand there follow specific attitudes towards specific matters. For instance, is one to extol or to expose? This is a question of attitude. Which attitude is wanted? I would say both. The question is, whom are you dealing with? There are three kinds of persons, the enemy, our allies in the united front and our own people; the last are the masses and their vanguard. We need to adopt a different attitude towards each of the three. With regard to the enemy, that is, Japanese imperialism and all the other enemies of the people, the task of revolutionary writers and artists is to expose their duplicity and cruelty and at the same time to point out the inevitability of their defeat, so as to encourage the anti-Japanese army and people to fight staunchly with one heart and one mind for their overthrow. With regard to our different allies in the united front, our attitude should be one of both alliance and criticism, and there should be different kinds of alliance and different kinds of criticism. We support them in their resistance to Japan and praise them for any achievement. But if they are not active in the War of Resistance, we should criticize them. If anyone opposes the Communist Party and the people and keeps moving down the path of reaction, we will firmly oppose him. As for the masses of the people, their toil and their struggle, their army and their Party, we should certainly praise them. The people, too, have their shortcomings. Among the proletariat many retain petty-bourgeois ideas, while both the peasants and the urban petty bourgeoisie have backward ideas; these are burdens hampering them in their struggle. We should be patient and spend a long time in educating them and helping them to get these loads off their backs and combat their own shortcomings and errors, so that they can advance with great strides. They have remolded themselves in struggle or are doing so, and our literature and art should depict this process. As long as they do not persist in their errors, we should not dwell on their negative side and consequently make the mistake of ridiculing them or, worse still, of being hostile to them. Our writings should help them to unite, to make progress, to press ahead with one heart and one mind, to discard what is backward and develop what is revolutionary, and should certainly not do the opposite.

The problem of audience, *i.e.*, the people for whom our works of literature and art are produced. In the Shensi-Kansu-Ningsia Border Region[2] and the anti-Japanese base areas of northern and central China, this problem differs from that in the Kuomintang areas, and differs still more from that in Shanghai before the War of Resistance. In the Shanghai period, the audience for works of revolutionary literature and art consisted mainly of a section of the students, office workers and shop assistants. After the outbreak of the War of Resistance the audience in the Kuomintang areas became somewhat wider, but it still consisted mainly of the same kind of people because the government there prevented the workers, peasants and soldiers from having access to revolutionary literature and art. In our base areas the situation is entirely different. Here the audience for works of literature and art consists of workers, peasants, soldiers and revolutionary cadres. There are students in the base areas, too, but they are different from students of the old type; they are either former or future cadres. The cadres of all types, fighters in the army, workers in the factories and peasants in the villages all want to read books and newspapers once they become literate, and those who are illiterate want to see plays and operas, look at drawings and paintings, sing songs and hear music; they are the audience for our works of literature and art. Take the cadres alone. Do not think they are few; they far outnumber the readers of any book published in the Kuomintang areas. There, an edition usually runs to only 2,000 copies, and even three editions add up to only 6,000; but as for the cadres in the base areas, in Yenan alone there are more than 10,000 who read books. Many of them, moreover, are tempered revolutionaries of long standing, who have come from all parts of the country and will go out to work in different places, so it is very important to do educational work among them. Our literary and art workers must do a good job in this respect.

Since the audience for our literature and art consists of workers, peasants and soldiers and of their cadres, the problem arises of understanding them and knowing them well. A great deal of work has to be done in order to understand them and know them well, to understand and know well all the different kinds of people and phenomena in the Party and government organizations, in the villages and factories and in the Eighth Route and New Fourth Armies. Our writers and artists have their literary and art work to do, but their primary task is to understand people and know them well. In this regard, how have matters stood with our writers and artists? I would say they have been lacking in knowledge and understanding; they have been like "a hero with no place to display his prowess." What does lacking in knowledge mean? Not knowing people well. The writers and artists do not have a good knowledge either of those whom they describe or of their audience; indeed, they may hardly know them at all. They do not know the workers or peasants or soldiers well, and do not know the cadres well either. What does lacking in understanding mean? Not understanding the language, that is, not being familiar with the rich, lively language of the masses. Since many writers and artists stand aloof from the masses and lead empty lives, naturally they are unfamiliar with the language of the people. Accordingly, their works are not only insipid in language but often contain nondescript expressions of their own coining which run counter to popular usage. Many comrades like to talk about "a mass style." But what does it really mean? It means that the thoughts and feelings of our writers and artists should be fused with those of the masses of workers, peasants and soldiers. To achieve this fusion, they should conscientiously learn the language of the masses. How can you talk of literary and artistic creation if you find the very language of the masses largely incomprehensible? By "a hero with no place to display his prowess," we mean that your collection of great truths is not appreciated by the masses. The more you put on the airs of a veteran before the masses and play the "hero," the more you try to peddle such stuff to the masses, the less likely they are to accept it. If you want the masses to understand you, if you want to be one with the masses, you must make up your mind to undergo a long and even painful process of tempering. Here I might mention the experience of how my own feelings changed. I began life as a student and at school acquired the ways of a student; I then used to feel it undignified to do even a little manual labor, such as carrying my own luggage in the presence of my fellow students, who were incapable of carrying anything, either on their shoulders or in their hands. At that time I felt that intellectuals were the only clean people in the world, while in comparison workers and peasants were dirty. I did not mind wearing the clothes of other intellectuals, believing them clean, but I would not put on clothes belonging to a worker or peasant, believing them dirty. But after I became a revolutionary and lived with workers and peasants and with soldiers of the revolutionary army, I gradually came to know them well, and they gradually came to know me well too. It was then, and only then, that I fundamentally changed the bourgeois and petty-bourgeois feelings implanted in me in the bourgeois schools. I came to feel that compared with the workers and peasants the unremolded intellectuals were not clean and that, in the last analysis, the workers and peasants were the cleanest people and, even though their hands were soiled and their feet smeared with cow-dung, they were really cleaner than the bourgeois and petty-bourgeois intellectuals. That is what is meant by a change in feelings, a change from one class to another. If our writers and artists who come from the intelligentsia want their works to be well received by the masses, they must change and remold their thinking and their feelings. Without such a change, without such remolding, they can do nothing well and will be misfits.

The last problem is study, by which I mean the study of Marxism-Leninism and of society. Anyone who considers himself a revolutionary Marxist writer, and especially any writer who is a member of the Communist Party, must have a knowledge of Marxism-Leninism. At present, however, some comrades are lacking in the basic concepts of Marxism. For instance, it is a basic Marxist concept that being determines consciousness, that the objective realities of class struggle and national struggle determine our thoughts and feelings. But some of our comrades turn this upside down and maintain that everything ought to start from "love." Now as for love, in a class society there can be only class love; but these comrades are seeking a love transcending classes, love in the abstract and also freedom in the abstract, truth in the abstract, human nature in the abstract, etc. This shows that they have been very deeply influenced by the bourgeoisie. They should thoroughly rid themselves of this influence and modestly study Marxism-Leninism. It is right for writers and artists to study literary and artistic creation, but the science of Marxism-Leninism must be studied by all revolutionaries, writers and artists not excepted. Writers and artists should study society, that is to say, should study the various classes in society, their mutual relations and respective conditions, their physiognomy and their psychology. Only when we grasp all this clearly can we have a literature and art that is rich in content and correct in orientation.

I am merely raising these problems today by way of introduction; I hope all of you will express your views on these and other relevant problems.

CONCLUSION

MAY 23, 1942

Comrades! Our forum has had three meetings this month. In the pursuit of truth we have carried on spirited debates in which scores of Party and non-Party comrades have spoken, laying bare the issues and making them more concrete. This, I believe, will very much benefit the whole literary and artistic movement.

In discussing a problem, we should start from reality and not from definitions. We would be following a wrong method if we first looked up definitions of literature and art in textbooks and then used them to determine the guiding principles for the present-day literary and artistic movement and to judge the different opinions and controversies that arise today. We are Marxists, and Marxism teaches that in our approach to a problem we should start from objective facts, not from abstract definitions, and that we should derive our guiding principles, policies and measures from an analysis of these facts. We should do the same in our present discussion of literary and artistic work.

What are the facts at present? The facts are: the War of Resistance Against Japan which China has been fighting for five years; the world-wide anti-fascist war; the vacillations of China's big landlord class and big bourgeoisie in the War of Resistance and their policy of high-handed oppression of the people; the revolutionary movement in literature and art since the May 4th Movement—its great contributions to the revolution during the last twenty-three years and its many shortcomings; the anti-Japanese democratic base areas of the Eighth Route and New Fourth Armies and the integration of large numbers of writers and artists with these armies and with the workers and peasants

291

in these areas; the difference in both environment and tasks between the writers and artists in the base areas and those in the Kuomintang areas; and the controversial issues concerning literature and art which have arisen in Yenan and the other anti-Japanese base areas. These are the actual, undeniable facts in the light of which we have to consider our problems.

What then is the crux of the matter? In my opinion, it consists fundamentally of the problems of working for the masses and how to work for the masses. Unless these two problems are solved, or solved properly, our writers and artists will be ill-adapted to their environment and their tasks and will come up against a series of difficulties from without and within. My concluding remarks will center on these two problems and also touch upon some related ones.

I

The first problem is: literature and art for whom?

This problem was solved long ago by Marxists, especially by Lenin. As far back as 1905 Lenin pointed out emphatically that our literature and art should "serve ... the millions and tens of millions of working people." [3] For comrades engaged in literary and artistic work in the anti-Japanese base areas it might seem that this problem is already solved and needs no further discussion. Actually, that is not the case. Many comrades have not found a clear solution. Consequently their sentiments, their works, their actions and their views on the guiding principles for literature and art have inevitably been more or less at variance with the needs of the masses and of the practical struggle. Of course, among the numerous men of culture, writers, artists and other literary and artistic workers engaged in the great struggle for liberation together with the Communist Party and the Eighth Route and New Fourth Armies, a few may be careerists who are with us only temporarily, but the overwhelming majority are working energetically for the common cause. By relying on these comrades, we have achieved a great deal in our literature, drama, music and fine arts. Many of these writers and artists have begun their work since the outbreak of the War of Resistance; many others did much revolutionary work before the war, endured many hardships and influenced broad masses of the people by their activities and works. Why do we say, then, that even among these comrades there are some who have not reached a clear solution of the problem of whom literature and art are for? Is it conceivable that there are still some who maintain that revolutionary literature and art are not for the masses of the people but for the exploiters and oppressors?

Indeed, literature and art exist which are for the exploiters and oppressors. Literature and art for the landlord class are feudal literature and art. Such were the literature and art of the ruling class in China's feudal era. To this day such literature and art still have considerable influence in China. Literature and art for the bourgeoisie are bourgeois literature and art. People like Liang Shih-chiu,[4] whom Lu Hsun criticized, talk about literature and art as transcending classes, but in fact they uphold bourgeois literature and art and oppose proletarian literature and art. Then literature and art exist which serve the imperialists— for example, the works of Chou Tso-jen, Chang Tzu-ping[5] and their like—which we call traitor literature and art. With us, literature and art are for the people, not for any of the above groups. We have said that China's new culture at the present stage is an anti-imperialist, anti-feudal culture of the masses of the people under the leadership of the proletariat. Today, anything that is truly of the masses must necessarily be led by the proletariat. Whatever is under the leadership of the bourgeoisie cannot possibly be of the masses. Naturally, the same applies to the new literature and art which are part of the new culture. We should take over the rich legacy and the good traditions in literature and art that have been handed down from past ages in China and foreign countries, but the aim must still be to serve the masses of the people. Nor do we refuse to utilize the literary and artistic forms of the past, but in our hands these old forms, remolded and infused with new content, also become something revolutionary in the service of the people.

Who, then, are the masses of the people? The broadest sections of the people, constituting more than 90 per cent of our total population, are the workers, peasants, soldiers and urban petty bourgeoisie. Therefore, our literature and art are first for the workers, the class that leads the revolution. Secondly, they are for the peasants, the most numerous and most steadfast of our allies in the revolution. Thirdly, they are for the armed workers and peasants, namely, the Eighth Route and New Fourth Armies and the other armed units of the people, which are the main forces of the revolutionary war. Fourthly, they are for the laboring masses of the urban petty bourgeoisie and for the petty-bourgeois intellectuals, both of whom are also our allies in the revolution and capable of long-term co-operation with us. These four kinds of people constitute the overwhelming majority of the Chinese nation, the broadest masses of the people.

Our literature and art should be for the four kinds of people we have

enumerated. To serve them, we must take the class stand of the proletariat and not that of the petty bourgeoisie. Today, writers who cling to
an individualist, petty-bourgeois stand cannot truly serve the masses of
revolutionary workers, peasants and soldiers. Their interest is mainly
focused on the small number of petty-bourgeois intellectuals. This is the
crucial reason why some of our comrades cannot correctly solve the
problem of "for whom?" In saying this I am not referring to theory. In
theory, or in words, no one in our ranks regards the masses of workers,
peasants and soldiers as less important than the petty-bourgeois intellectuals. I am referring to practice, to action. In practice, in action, do they
regard petty-bourgeois intellectuals as more important than workers,
peasants and soldiers? I think they do. Many comrades concern themselves with studying the petty-bourgeois intellectuals and analyzing their
psychology, and they concentrate on portraying these intellectuals and
excusing or defending their shortcomings, instead of guiding the intellectuals to join with them in getting closer to the masses of workers,
peasants and soldiers, taking part in the practical struggles of the masses,
portraying and educating the masses. Coming from the petty bourgeoisie
and being themselves intellectuals, many comrades seek friends only
among intellectuals and concentrate on studying and describing them.
Such study and description are proper if done from a proletarian position. But that is not what they do, or not what they do fully. They take
the petty-bourgeois stand and produce works that are the self-expression
of the petty bourgeoisie, as can be seen in quite a number of literary and
artistic products. Often they show heartfelt sympathy for intellectuals of
petty-bourgeois origin, to the extent of sympathizing with or even
praising their shortcomings. On the other hand, these comrades seldom
come into contact with the masses of workers, peasants and soldiers, do
not understand or study them, do not have intimate friends among them
and are not good at portraying them; when they do depict them, the
clothes are the clothes of working people but the faces are those of
petty-bourgeois intellectuals. In certain respects they are fond of the
workers, peasants and soldiers and the cadres stemming from them; but
there are times when they do not like them and there are some respects in
which they do not like them: they do not like their feelings or their
manner or their nascent literature and art (the wall newspapers, murals,
folk songs, folk tales, etc.). At times they are fond of these things too, but
that is when they are hunting for novelty, for something with which to
embellish their own works, or even for certain backward features. At
other times they openly despise these things and are partial to what
belongs to the petty-bourgeois intellectuals or even to the bourgeoisie.

294

These comrades have their feet planted on the side of the petty-bourgeois intellectuals; or, to put it more elegantly, their innermost soul is still
a kingdom of the petty-bourgeois intelligentsia. Thus they have not yet
solved, or not yet clearly solved, the problem of "for whom?" This applies
not only to newcomers to Yenan; even among comrades who have been
to the front and worked for a number of years in our base areas and in the
Eighth Route and New Fourth Armies, many have not completely
solved this problem. It requires a long period of time, at least eight or ten
years, to solve it thoroughly. But however long it takes, solve it we must
and solve it unequivocally and thoroughly. Our literary and art workers
must accomplish this task and shift their stand; they must gradually move
their feet over to the side of the workers, peasants and soldiers, to the side
of the proletariat, through the process of going into their very midst and
into the thick of practical struggles and through the process of studying
Marxism and society. Only in this way can we have a literature and art
that are truly for the workers, peasants and soldiers, a truly proletarian
literature and art.

This question of "for whom?" is fundamental; it is a question of
principle. The controversies and divergences, the opposition and disunity
arising among some comrades in the past were not on this fundamental
question of principle but on secondary questions, or even on issues
involving no principle. On this question of principle, however, there has
been hardly any divergence between the two contending sides and they
have shown almost complete agreement; to some extent, both tend to
look down upon the workers, peasants and soldiers and divorce themselves from the masses. I say "to some extent" because, generally speaking, these comrades do not look down upon the workers, peasants and
soldiers or divorce themselves from the masses in the same way as the
Kuomintang does. Nevertheless, the tendency is there. Unless this
fundamental problem is solved, many other problems will not be easy to
solve. Take, for instance, the sectarianism in literary and art circles. This
too is a question of principle, but sectarianism can only be eradicated by
putting forward and faithfully applying the slogans, "For the workers and
peasants!", "For the Eighth Route and New Fourth Armies!" and "Go
among the masses!" Otherwise the problem of sectarianism can never be
solved. Lu Hsun once said:

> A common aim is the prerequisite for a united front. . . . The
> fact that our front is not united shows that we have not been
> able to unify our aims, and that some people are working only
> for small groups or indeed only for themselves. If we all aim at

serving the masses of workers and peasants, our front will of course be united.[6]

The problem existed then in Shanghai; now it exists in Chungking, too. In such places the problem can hardly be solved thoroughly, because the rulers oppress the revolutionary writers and artists and deny them the freedom to go out among the masses of workers, peasants and soldiers. Here with us the situation is entirely different. We encourage revolutionary writers and artists to be active in forming intimate contacts with the workers, peasants and soldiers, giving them complete freedom to go among the masses and to create a genuinely revolutionary literature and art. Therefore, here among us the problem is nearing solution. But nearing solution is not the same as a complete and thorough solution. We must study Marxism and study society, as we have been saying, precisely in order to achieve a complete and thorough solution. By Marxism we mean living Marxism which plays an effective role in the life and struggle of the masses, not Marxism in words. With Marxism in words transformed into Marxism in real life, there will be no more sectarianism. Not only will the problem of sectarianism be solved, but many other problems as well.

II

Having settled the problem of whom to serve, we come to the next problem, how to serve. To put it in the words of some of our comrades: should we devote ourselves to raising standards, or should we devote ourselves to popularization?

In the past, some comrades, to a certain or even a serious extent, belittled and neglected popularization and laid undue stress on raising standards. Stress should be laid on raising standards, but to do so one-sidedly and exclusively, to do so excessively, is a mistake. The lack of a clear solution to the problem of "for whom?", which I referred to earlier, also manifests itself in this connection. As these comrades are not clear on the problem of "for whom?", they have no correct criteria for the "raising of standards" and the "popularization" they speak of, and are naturally still less able to find the correct relationship between the two. Since our literature and art are basically for the workers, peasants and soldiers, "popularization" means to popularize among the workers, peasants and soldiers, and "raising standards" means to advance from their present level. What should we popularize among them? Popularize what is needed and can be readily accepted by the feudal landlord class? Popularize what is needed and can be readily accepted by the bourgeoisie? Popularize what is needed and can be readily accepted by the petty-bourgeois intellectuals? No, none of these will do. We must popularize only what is needed and can be readily accepted by the workers, peasants and soldiers themselves. Consequently, prior to the task of educating the workers, peasants and soldiers, there is the task of learning from them. This is even more true of raising standards. There must be a basis from which to raise. Take a bucket of water, for instance; where is it to be raised from if not from the ground? From mid-air? From what basis, then, are literature and art to be raised? From the basis of the feudal classes? From the basis of the bourgeoisie? From the basis of the petty-bourgeois intellectuals? No, not from any of these; only from the basis of the masses of workers, peasants and soldiers. Nor does this mean raising the workers, peasants and soldiers to the "heights" of the feudal classes, the bourgeoisie or the petty-bourgeois intellectuals; it means raising the level of literature and art in the direction in which the workers, peasants and soldiers are themselves advancing, in the direction in which the proletariat is advancing. Here again the task of learning from the workers, peasants and soldiers comes in. Only by starting from the workers, peasants and soldiers can we have a correct understanding of popularization and of the raising of standards and find the proper relationship between the two.

In the last analysis, what is the source of all literature and art? Works of literature and art, as ideological forms, are products of the reflection in the human brain of the life of a given society. Revolutionary literature and art are the products of the reflection of the life of the people in the brains of revolutionary writers and artists. The life of the people is always a mine of the raw materials for literature and art, materials in their natural form, materials that are crude, but most vital, rich and fundamental; they make all literature and art seem pallid by comparison; they provide literature and art with an inexhaustible source, their only source. They are the only source, for there can be no other. Some may ask, is there not another source in books, in the literature and art of ancient times and of foreign countries? In fact, the literary and artistic works of the past are not a source but a stream; they were created by our predecessors and the foreigners out of the literary and artistic raw materials they found in the life of the people of their time and place. We must take over all the fine things in our literary and artistic heritage, critically assimilate whatever is beneficial, and use them as examples

297

when we create works out of the literary and artistic raw materials in the life of the people of our own time and place. It makes a difference whether or not we have such examples, the difference between crudeness and refinement, between roughness and polish, between a low and a high level, and between slower and faster work. Therefore, we must on no account reject the legacies of the ancients and the foreigners or refuse to learn from them, even though they are the works of the feudal or bourgeois classes. But taking over legacies and using them as examples must never replace our own creative work; nothing can do that. Uncritical transplantation or copying from the ancients and the foreigners is the most sterile and harmful dogmatism in literature and art. China's revolutionary writers and artists, writers and artists of promise, must go among the masses; they must for a long period of time unreservedly and wholeheartedly go among the masses of workers, peasants and soldiers, go into the heat of the struggle, go to the only source, the broadest and richest source, in order to observe, experience, study and analyze all the different kinds of people, all the classes, all the masses, all the vivid patterns of life and struggle, all the raw materials of literature and art. Only then can they proceed to creative work. Otherwise, you will have nothing to work with and you will be nothing but a phoney writer or artist, the kind that Lu Hsun in his will so earnestly cautioned his son never to become.[7]

Although man's social life is the only source of literature and art and is incomparably livelier and richer in content, the people are not satisfied with life alone and demand literature and art as well. Why? Because, while both are beautiful, life as reflected in works of literature and art can and ought to be on a higher plane, more intense, more concentrated, more typical, nearer the ideal, and therefore more universal than actual everyday life. Revolutionary literature and art should create a variety of characters out of real life and help the masses to propel history forward. For example, there is suffering from hunger, cold and oppression on the one hand, and exploitation and oppression of man by man on the other. These facts exist everywhere and people look upon them as commonplace. Writers and artists concentrate such everyday phenomena, typify the contradictions and struggles within them and produce works which awaken the masses, fire them with enthusiasm and impel them to unite and struggle to transform their environment. Without such literature and art, this task could not be fulfilled, or at least not so effectively and speedily.

What is meant by popularizing and by raising standards in works of literature and art? What is the relationship between these two tasks?

Popular works are simpler and plainer, and therefore more readily accepted by the broad masses of the people today. Works of a higher quality, being more polished, are more difficult to produce and in general do not circulate so easily and quickly among the masses at present. The problem facing the workers, peasants and soldiers is this: they are now engaged in a bitter and bloody struggle with the enemy but are illiterate and uneducated as a result of long years of rule by the feudal and bourgeois classes, and therefore they are eagerly demanding enlightenment, education and works of literature and art which meet their urgent needs and which are easy to absorb, in order to heighten their enthusiasm in struggle and confidence in victory, strengthen their unity and fight the enemy with one heart and one mind. For them the prime need is not "more flowers on the brocade" but "fuel in snowy weather." In present conditions, therefore, popularization is the more pressing task. It is wrong to belittle or neglect popularization.

Nevertheless, no hard and fast line can be drawn between popularization and the raising of standards. Not only is it possible to popularize some works of higher quality even now, but the cultural level of the broad masses is steadily rising. If popularization remains at the same level for ever, with the same stuff being supplied month after month and year after year, always the same "Little Cowherd" [8] and the same "man, hand, mouth, knife, cow, goat," [9] will not the educators and those being educated be six of one and half a dozen of the other? What would be the sense of such popularization? The people demand popularization and, following that, higher standards; they demand higher standards month by month and year by year. Here popularization means popularizing for the people and raising of standards means raising the level for the people. And such raising is not from mid-air, or behind closed doors, but is actually based on popularization. It is determined by and at the same time guides popularization. In China as a whole the development of the revolution and of revolutionary culture is uneven and their spread is gradual. While in one place there is popularization and then raising of standards on the basis of popularization, in other places popularization has not even begun. Hence good experience in popularization leading to higher standards in one locality can be applied in other localities and serve to guide popularization and the raising of standards there, saving many twists and turns along the road. Internationally, the good experience of foreign countries, and especially Soviet experience, can also serve to guide us. With us, therefore, the raising of standards is based on popularization, while popularization is guided by the raising of standards. Precisely for this reason, so far from being an obstacle to the raising

299

of standards, the work of popularization we are speaking of supplies the basis for the work of raising standards which we are now doing on a limited scale, and prepares the necessary conditions for us to raise standards in the future on a much broader scale.

Besides such raising of standards as meets the needs of the masses directly, there is the kind which meets their needs indirectly, that is, the kind which is needed by the cadres. The cadres are the advanced elements of the masses and generally have received more education; literature and art of a higher level are entirely necessary for them. To ignore this would be a mistake. Whatever is done for the cadres is also entirely for the masses, because it is only through the cadres that we can educate and guide the masses. If we go against this aim, if what we give the cadres cannot help them educate and guide the masses, our work of raising standards will be like shooting at random and will depart from the fundamental principle of serving the masses of the people.

To sum up: through the creative labor of revolutionary writers and artists, the raw materials found in the life of the people are shaped into the ideological form of literature and art serving the masses of the people. Included here are the more advanced literature and art as developed on the basis of elementary literature and art and as required by those sections of the masses whose level has been raised, or, more immediately, by the cadres among the masses. Also included here are elementary literature and art which, conversely, are guided by more advanced literature and art and are needed primarily by the overwhelming majority of the masses at present. Whether more advanced or elementary, all our literature and art are for the masses of the people, and in the first place for the workers, peasants and soldiers; they are created for the workers, peasants and soldiers and are for their use.

Now that we have settled the problem of the relationship between the raising of standards and popularization, that of the relationship between the specialists and the popularizers can also be settled. Our specialists are not only for the cadres, but also, and indeed chiefly, for the masses. Our specialists in literature should pay attention to the wall newspapers of the masses and to the reportage written in the army and the villages. Our specialists in drama should pay attention to the small troupes in the army and the villages. Our specialists in music should pay attention to the songs of the masses. Our specialists in the fine arts should pay attention to the fine arts of the masses. All these comrades should make close contact with comrades engaged in the work of popularizing literature and art among the masses. On the one hand, they should help and guide the popularizers, and on the other, they should learn from these comrades and, through them, draw nourishment from the masses to replenish and enrich themselves so that their specialities do not become "ivory towers," detached from the masses and from reality and devoid of content or life. We should esteem the specialists, for they are very valuable to our cause. But we should tell them that no revolutionary writer or artist can do any meaningful work unless he is closely linked with the masses, gives expression to their thoughts and feelings and serves them as a loyal spokesman. Only by speaking for the masses can he educate them and only by being their pupil can he be their teacher. If he regards himself as their master, as an aristocrat who lords it over the "lower orders," then, no matter how talented he may be, he will not be needed by the masses and his work will have no future.

Is this attitude of ours utilitarian? Materialists do not oppose utilitarianism in general but the utilitarianism of the feudal, bourgeois and petty-bourgeois classes; they oppose those hypocrites who attack utilitarianism in words but in deeds embrace the most selfish and short-sighted utilitarianism. There is no "ism" in the world that transcends utilitarian considerations; in class society there can be only the utilitarianism of this or that class. We are proletarian revolutionary utilitarians and take as our point of departure the unity of the present and future interests of the broadest masses, who constitute over 90 per cent of the population; hence we are revolutionary utilitarians aiming for the broadest and most long-range objectives, not narrow utilitarians concerned only with the partial and the immediate. If, for instance, you reproach the masses for their utilitarianism and yet for your own utility, or that of a narrow clique, force on the market and propagandize among the masses a work which pleases only the few but is useless or even harmful to the majority, then you are not only insulting the masses but also revealing your own lack of self-knowledge. A thing is good only when it brings real benefit to the masses of the people. Your work may be as good as "The Spring Snow," but if for the time being it caters only to the few and the masses are still singing the "Song of the Rustic Poor," [10] you will get nowhere by simply scolding them instead of trying to raise their level. The question now is to bring about a unity between "The Spring Snow" and the "Song of the Rustic Poor," between higher standards and popularization. Without such a unity, the highest art of any expert cannot help being utilitarian in the narrowest sense; you may call this art "pure and lofty" but that is merely your own name for it which the masses will not endorse.

Once we have solved the problems of fundamental policy, of serving the workers, peasants and soldiers and of how to serve them, such other problems as whether to write about the bright or the dark side of life and the problem of unity will also be solved. If everyone agrees on the fundamental policy, it should be adhered to by all our workers, all our schools, publications and organizations in the field of literature and art and in all our literary and artistic activities. It is wrong to depart from this policy and anything at variance with it must be duly corrected.

III

Since our literature and art are for the masses of the people, we can proceed to discuss a problem of inner-Party relations, *i.e.*, the relation between the Party's work in literature and art and the Party's work as a whole, and in addition a problem of the Party's external relations, *i.e.*, the relation between the Party's work in literature and art and the work of non-Party people in this field, a problem of the united front in literary and art circles.

Let us consider the first problem. In the world today all culture, all literature and art belong to definite classes and are geared to definite political lines. There is in fact no such thing as art for art's sake, art that stands above classes or art that is detached from or independent of politics. Proletarian literature and art are part of the whole proletarian revolutionary cause; they are, as Lenin said, cogs and wheels[11] in the whole revolutionary machine. Therefore, Party work in literature and art occupies a definite and assigned position in Party revolutionary work as a whole and is subordinated to the revolutionary tasks set by the Party in a given revolutionary period. Opposition to this arrangement is certain to lead to dualism or pluralism, and in essence amounts to "politics—Marxist, art—bourgeois," as with Trotsky. We do not favor overstressing the importance of literature and art, but neither do we favor underestimating their importance. Literature and art are subordinate to politics, but in their turn exert a great influence on politics. Revolutionary literature and art are part of the whole revolutionary cause, they are cogs and wheels in it, and though in comparison with certain other and more important parts they may be less significant and less urgent and may occupy a secondary position, nevertheless, they are indispensable cogs and wheels in the whole machine, an indispensable part of the entire revolutionary cause. If we had no literature and art even in the broadest and most ordinary sense, we could not carry on the revolutionary movement and win victory. Failure to recognize this is wrong. Furthermore, when we say that literature and art are subordinate to politics, we mean class politics, the politics of the masses, not the politics of a few so-called statesmen. Politics, whether revolutionary or counter-revolutionary, is the struggle of class against class, not the activity of a few individuals. The revolutionary struggle on the ideological and artistic fronts must be subordinate to the political struggle because only through politics can the needs of the class and the masses find expression in concentrated form. Revolutionary statesmen, the political specialists who know the science or art of revolutionary politics, are simply the leaders of millions upon millions of statesmen—the masses. Their task is to collect the opinions of these mass statesmen, sift and refine them, and return them to the masses, who then take them and put them into practice. They are therefore not the kind of aristocratic "statesmen" who work behind closed doors and fancy they have a monopoly of wisdom. Herein lies the difference in principle between proletarian statesmen and decadent bourgeois statesmen. This is precisely why there can be complete unity between the political character of our literary and artistic works and their truthfulness. It would be wrong to fail to realize this and to debase the politics and the statesmen of the proletariat.

Let us consider next the question of the united front in the world of literature and art. Since literature and art are subordinate to politics and since the fundamental problem in China's politics today is resistance to Japan, our Party writers and artists must in the first place unite on this issue of resistance to Japan with all non-Party writers and artists (ranging from Party sympathizers and petty-bourgeois writers and artists to all those writers and artists of the bourgeois and landlord classes who are in favor of resistance to Japan). Secondly, we should unite with them on the issue of democracy. On this issue there is a section of anti-Japanese writers and artists who do not agree with us, so the range of unity will unavoidably be somewhat more limited. Thirdly, we should unite with them on issues peculiar to the literary and artistic world, questions of method and style in literature and art; here again, as we are for socialist realism and some people do not agree, the range of unity will be narrower still. While on one issue there is unity, on another there is struggle, there is criticism. The issues are at once separate and interrelated, so that even on the very ones which give rise to unity, such as resistance to Japan, there are at the same time struggle and criticism. In a united front, "all unity and no struggle" and "all struggle and no unity" are both wrong policies —as with the Right capitulationism and tailism, or the "Left" exclusivism and sectarianism, practiced by some comrades in the past. This is as true in literature and art as in politics.

The petty-bourgeois writers and artists constitute an important force

303

among the forces of the united front in literary and art circles in China. There are many shortcomings in both their thinking and their works, but, comparatively speaking, they are inclined towards the revolution and are close to the working people. Therefore, it is an especially important task to help them overcome their shortcomings and to win them over to the front which serves the working people.

IV

Literary and art criticism is one of the principal methods of struggle in the world of literature and art. It should be developed and, as comrades have rightly pointed out, our past work in this respect has been quite inadequate. Literary and art criticism is a complex question which requires a great deal of special study. Here I shall concentrate only on the basic problem of criteria in criticism. I shall also comment briefly on a few specific problems raised by some comrades and on certain incorrect views.

In literary and art criticism there are two criteria, the political and the artistic. According to the political criterion, everything is good that is helpful to unity and resistance to Japan, that encourages the masses to be of one heart and one mind, that opposes retrogression and promotes progress; on the other hand, everything is bad that is detrimental to unity and resistance to Japan, foments dissension and discord among the masses and opposes progress and drags people back. How can we tell the good from the bad—by the motive (the subjective intention) or by the effect (social practice)? Idealists stress motive and ignore effect, while mechanical materialists stress effect and ignore motive. In contradistinction to both, we dialectical materialists insist on the unity of motive and effect. The motive of serving the masses is inseparably linked with the effect of winning their approval; the two must be united. The motive of serving the individual or a small clique is not good, nor is it good to have the motive of serving the masses without the effect of winning their approval and benefiting them. In examining the subjective intention of a writer or artists, that is, whether his motive is correct and good, we do not judge by his declarations but by the effect of his actions (mainly his works) on the masses in society. The criterion for judging subjective intention or motive is social practice and its effect. We want no sectarianism in our literary and art criticism and, subject to the general principle of unity for resistance to Japan, we should tolerate literary and art works with a variety of political attitudes. But at the same time, in our criticism we must adhere firmly to principle and severely criticize and repudiate all works of literature and art expressing views in opposition to the nation, to science, to the masses and to the Communist Party, because these so-called works of literature and art proceed from the motive and produce the effect of undermining unity for resistance to Japan. According to the artistic criterion, all works of a higher artistic quality are good or comparatively good, while those of a lower artistic quality are bad or comparatively bad. Here, too, of course, social effect must be taken into account. There is hardly a writer or artist who does not consider his own work beautiful, and our criticism ought to permit the free competition of all varieties of works of art; but it is also entirely necessary to subject these works to correct criticism according to the criteria of the science of aesthetics, so that art of a lower level can be gradually raised to a higher and art which does not meet the demands of the struggle of the broad masses can be transformed into art that does.

There is the political criterion and there is the artistic criterion; what is the relationship between the two? Politics cannot be equated with art, nor can a general world outlook be equated with a method of artistic creation and criticism. We deny not only that there is an abstract and absolutely unchangeable political criterion, but also that there is an abstract and absolutely unchangeable artistic criterion; each class in every class society has its own political and artistic criteria. But all classes in all class societies invariably put the political criterion first and the artistic criterion second. The bourgeoisie always shuts out proletarian literature and art, however great their artistic merit. The proletariat must similarly distinguish among the literary and art works of past ages and determine its attitude towards them only after examining their attitude to the people and whether or not they had any progressive significance historically. Some works which politically are downright reactionary may have a certain artistic quality. The more reactionary their content and the higher their artistic quality, the more poisonous they are to the people, and the more necessary it is to reject them. A common characteristic of the literature and art of all exploiting classes in their period of decline is the contradiction between their reactionary political content and their artistic form. What we demand is the unity of politics and art, the unity of content and form, the unity of revolutionary political content and the highest possible perfection of artistic form. Works of art which lack artistic quality have no force, however progressive they are politically. Therefore, we oppose both the tendency to produce works of art with a wrong political viewpoint and

305

the tendency towards the "poster and slogan style" which is correct in political viewpoint but lacking in artistic power. On questions of literature and art we must carry on a struggle on two fronts.

Both these tendencies can be found in the thinking of many comrades. A good number of comrades tend to neglect artistic technique; it is therefore necessary to give attention to the raising of artistic standards. But as I see it, the political side is more of a problem at present. Some comrades lack elementary political knowledge and consequently have all sorts of muddled ideas. Let me cite a few examples from Yenan.

"The theory of human nature." Is there such a thing as human nature? Of course there is. But there is only human nature in the concrete, no human nature in the abstract. In class society there is only human nature of a class character; there is no human nature above classes. We uphold the human nature of the proletariat and of the masses of the people, while the landlord and bourgeois classes uphold the human nature of their own classes, only they do not say so but make it out to be the only human nature in existence. The human nature boosted by certain petty-bourgeois intellectuals is also divorced from or opposed to the masses; what they call human nature is in essence nothing but bourgeois individualism, and so, in their eyes, proletarian human nature is contrary to human nature. "The theory of human nature" which some people in Yenan advocate as the basis of their so-called theory of literature and art puts the matter in just this way and is wholly wrong.

"The fundamental point of departure for literature and art is love, love of humanity." Now love may serve as a point of departure, but there is a more basic one. Love as an idea is a product of objective practice. Fundamentally, we do not start from ideas but from objective practice. Our writers and artists who come from the ranks of the intellectuals love the proletariat because society has made them feel that they and the proletariat share a common fate. We hate Japanese imperialism because Japanese imperialism oppresses us. There is absolutely no such thing in the world as love or hatred without reason or cause. As for the so-called love of humanity, there has been no such all-inclusive love since humanity was divided into classes. All the ruling classes of the past were fond of advocating it, and so were many so-called sages and wise men, but nobody has ever really practiced it, because it is impossible in class society. There will be genuine love of humanity —after classes are eliminated all over the world. Classes have split society into many antagonistic groupings; there will be love of all humanity when classes are eliminated, but not now. We cannot love enemies, we cannot love social evils, our aim is to destroy them. This is common sense; can it be that some of our writers and artists still do not understand this?

"Literary and artistic works have always laid equal stress on the bright and the dark, half and half." This statement contains many muddled ideas. It is not true that literature and art have always done this. Many petty-bourgeois writers have never discovered the bright side. Their works only expose the dark and are known as the "literature of exposure." Some of their works simply specialize in preaching pessimism and world-weariness. On the other hand, Soviet literature in the period of socialist construction portrays mainly the bright. It, too, describes shortcomings in work and portrays negative characters, but this only serves as a contrast to bring out the brightness of the whole picture and is not a so-called half-and-half basis. The writers and artists of the bourgeoisie in its period of reaction depict the revolutionary masses as mobs and themselves as saints, thus reversing the bright and the dark. Only truly revolutionary writers and artists can correctly solve the problem of whether to extol or to expose. All the dark forces harming the masses of the people must be exposed and all the revolutionary struggles of the masses of the people must be extolled; this is the fundamental task of revolutionary writers and artists.

"The task of literature and art has always been to expose." This assertion, like the previous one, arises from ignorance of the science of history. Literature and art, as we have shown, have never been devoted solely to exposure. For revolutionary writers and artists the targets for exposure can never be the masses, but only the aggressors, exploiters and oppressors and the evil influence they have on the people. The masses too have shortcomings, which should be overcome by criticism and self-criticism within the people's own ranks, and such criticism and self-criticism is also one of the most important tasks of literature and art. But this should not be regarded as any sort of "exposure of the people." As for the people, the question is basically one of education and of raising their level. Only counter-revolutionary writers and artists describe the people as "born fools" and the revolutionary masses as "tyrannical mobs."

"This is still the period of the satirical essay, and Lu Hsun's style of writing is still needed." Living under the rule of the dark forces and deprived of freedom of speech, Lu Hsun used burning satire and freezing irony, cast in the form of essays, to do battle; and he was entirely right. We, too, must hold up to sharp ridicule the fascists, the Chinese reactionaries and everything that harms the people; but in the Shensi-

Kansu-Ningsia Border Region and the anti-Japanese base areas behind the enemy lines, where democracy and freedom are granted in full to the revolutionary writers and artists and withheld only from the counter-revolutionaries, the style of the essay should not simply be like Lu Hsun's. Here we can shout at the top of our voices and have no need for veiled and roundabout expressions, which are hard for the people to understand. When dealing with the people and not with their enemies, Lu Hsun never ridiculed or attacked the revolutionary people and the revolutionary Party in his "satirical essay period," and these essays were entirely different in manner from those directed against the enemy. To criticize the people's shortcomings is necessary, as we have already said, but in doing so we must truly take the stand of the people and speak out of whole-hearted eagerness to protect and educate them. To treat comrades like enemies is to go over to the stand of the enemy. Are we then to abolish satire? No. Satire is always necessary. But there are several kinds of satire, each with a different attitude, satire to deal with our enemies, satire to deal with our allies and satire to deal with our own ranks. We are not opposed to satire in general; what we must abolish is the abuse of satire.

"I am not given to praise and eulogy. The works of people who eulogize what is bright are not necessarily great and the works of those who depict the dark are not necessarily paltry." If you are a bourgeois writer or artist, you will eulogize not the proletariat but the bourgeoisie, and if you are a proletarian writer or artist, you will eulogize not the bourgeoisie but the proletariat and working people: it must be one or the other. The works of the eulogists of the bourgeoisie are not necessarily great, nor are the works of those who show that the bourgeoisie is dark necessarily paltry; the works of the eulogists of the proletariat are not necessarily not great, but the works of those who depict the so-called "darkness" of the proletariat are bound to be paltry—are these not facts of history as regards literature and art? Why should we not eulogize the people, the creators of the history of mankind? Why should we not eulogize the proletariat, the Communist Party, New Democracy and socialism? There is a type of person who has no enthusiasm for the people's cause and looks coldly from the side-lines at the struggles and victories of the proletariat and its vanguard; what he is interested in, and will never weary of eulogizing, is himself, plus perhaps a few figures in his small coterie. Of course, such petty-bourgeois individualists are unwilling to eulogize the deeds and virtues of the revolutionary people or heighten their courage in struggle and their confidence in victory. Persons of this type are merely termites in the revolutionary ranks; of course, the revolutionary people have no need for these "singers."

"It is not a question of stand; my class stand is correct, my intentions are good and I understand all right, but I am not good at expressing myself and so the effect turns out bad." I have already spoken about the dialectical materialist view of motive and effect. Now I want to ask, is not the question of effect one of stand? A person who acts solely by motive and does not inquire what effect his action will have is like a doctor who merely writes prescriptions but does not care how many patients die of them. Or take a political party which merely makes declarations but does not care whether they are carried out. It may well be asked, is this a correct stand? And is the intention here good? Of course, mistakes may occur even though the effect has been taken into account beforehand, but is the intention good when one continues in the same old rut after facts have proved that the effect is bad? In judging a party or a doctor, we must look at practice, at the effect. The same applies in judging a writer. A person with truly good intentions must take the effect into account, sum up experience and study the methods or, in creative work, study the technique of expression. A person with truly good intentions must criticize the shortcomings and mistakes in his own work with the utmost candor and resolve to correct them. This is precisely why Communists employ the method of self-criticism. This alone is the correct stand. Only in this process of serious and responsible practice is it possible gradually to understand what the correct stand is and gradually obtain a good grasp of it. If one does not move in this direction in practice, if there is simply the complacent assertion that one "understands all right," then in fact one has not understood at all.

"To call on us to study Marxism is to repeat the mistake of the dialectical materialist creative method, which will harm the creative mood." To study Marxism means to apply the dialectical materialist and historical materialist viewpoint in our observation of the world, of society and of literature and art; it does not mean writing philosophical lectures into our works of literature and art. Marxism embraces but cannot replace realism in literary and artistic creation, just as it embraces but cannot replace the atomic and electronic theories in physics. Empty, dry dogmatic formulas do indeed destroy the creative mood; not only that, they first destroy Marxism. Dogmatic "Marxism" is not Marxism, it is anti-Marxism. Then does not Marxism destroy the creative mood? Yes, it does. It definitely destroys creative moods that are

309

feudal, bourgeois, petty-bourgeois, liberalistic, individualist, nihilist, art-for-art's sake, aristocratic, decadent or pessimistic, and every other creative mood that is alien to the masses of the people and to the proletariat. So far as proletarian writers and artists are concerned, should not these kinds of creative moods be destroyed? I think they should; they should be utterly destroyed. And while they are being destroyed, something new can be constructed.

V

The problems discussed here exist in our literary and art circles in Yenan. What does that show? It shows that wrong styles of work still exist to a serious extent in our literary and art circles and that there are still many defects among our comrades, such as idealism, dogmatism, empty illusions, empty talk, contempt for practice and aloofness from the masses, all of which call for an effective and serious campaign of rectification.

We have many comrades who are still not very clear on the difference between the proletariat and the petty bourgeoisie. There are many Party members who have joined the Communist Party organizationally but have not yet joined the Party wholly or at all ideologically. Those who have not joined the Party ideologically still carry a great deal of the muck of the exploiting classes in their heads, and have no idea at all of what proletarian ideology, or communism, or the Party is. "Proletarian ideology?" they think. "The same old stuff!" Little do they know that it is no easy matter to acquire this stuff. Some will never have the slightest Communist flavor about them as long as they live and can only end up by leaving the Party. Therefore, though the majority in our Party and in our ranks are clean and honest, we must in all seriousness put things in order both ideologically and organizationally if we are to develop the revolutionary movement more effectively and bring it to speedier success. To put things in order organizationally requires our first doing so ideologically, our launching a struggle of proletarian ideology against non-proletarian ideology. An ideological struggle is already under way in literary and art circles in Yenan, and it is most necessary. Intellectuals of petty-bourgeois origin always stubbornly try in all sorts of ways, including literary and artistic ways, to project themselves and spread their views, and they want the Party and the world to be remolded in their own image. In the circumstances it is our duty to jolt these "comrades" and tell them sharply, "That won't work! The proletariat cannot accommodate itself to you; to yield to you would actually be to yield to the big landlord class and the big bourgeoisie and to run the risk of undermining our Party and our country." Whom then must we yield to? We can mold the Party and the world only in the image of the proletarian vanguard. We hope our comrades in literary and art circles will realize the seriousness of this great debate and join actively in this struggle, so that every comrade may become sound and our entire ranks may become truly united and consolidated ideologically and organizationally.

Because of confusion in their thinking, many of our comrades are not quite able to draw a real distinction between our revolutionary base areas and the Kuomintang areas and they make many mistakes as a consequence. A good number of comrades have come here from the garrets of Shanghai, and in coming from those garrets to the revolutionary base areas, they have passed not only from one kind of place to another but from one historical epoch to another. One society is semifeudal, semi-colonial, under the rule of the big landlords and big bourgeoisie, the other is a revolutionary new-democratic society under the leadership of the proletariat. To come to the revolutionary bases means to enter an epoch unprecedented in the thousands of years of Chinese history, an epoch in which the masses of the people wield state power. Here the people around us and the audience for our propaganda are totally different. The past epoch is gone, never to return. Therefore, we must integrate ourselves with the new masses without any hesitation. If, living among the new masses, some comrades, as I said before, are still "lacking in knowledge and understanding" and remain "heroes with no place to display their prowess," then difficulties will arise for them, and not only when they go out to the villages; right here in Yenan difficulties will arise for them. Some comrades may think, "Well, I had better continue writing for the readers in the Great Rear Area;[12] it is a job I know well and has 'national significance.' " This idea is entirely wrong. The Great Rear Area is also changing. Readers there expect authors in the revolutionary base areas to tell about the new people and the new world and not to bore them with the same old tales. Therefore, the more a work is written for the masses in the revolutionary base areas, the more national significance will it have. Fadeyev in The Debacle[13] only told the story of a small guerrilla unit and had no intention of pandering to the palate of readers in the old world; yet the book has exerted world-wide influence. At any rate in China its influence is very great, as you know. China is moving forward, not back, and it is the revolutionary base areas, not any of the backward, retrogressive areas, that are leading China forward. This is a fundamental issue that, above all, comrades must come to understand in the rectification movement.

Since integration into the new epoch of the masses is essential, it is necessary thoroughly to solve the problem of the relationship between the individual and the masses. This couplet from a poem by Lu Hsun should be our motto:

Fierce-browed, I coolly defy a thousand pointing fingers,
Head-bowed, like a willing ox I serve the children.[14]

The "thousand pointing fingers" are our enemies, and we will never yield to them, no matter how ferocious. The "children" here symbolize the proletariat and the masses. All Communists, all revolutionaries, all revolutionary literary and art workers should learn from the example of Lu Hsun and be "oxen" for the proletariat and the masses, bending their backs to the task until their dying day. Intellectuals who want to integrate themselves with the masses, who want to serve the masses, must go through a process in which they and the masses come to know each other well. This process may, and certainly will, involve much pain and friction, but if you have the determination, you will be able to fulfill these requirements.

Today I have discussed only some of the problems of fundamental orientation for our literature and art movement; many specific problems remain which will require further study. I am confident that comrades here are determined to move in the direction indicated. I believe that in the course of the rectification movement and in the long period of study and work to come, you will surely be able to bring about a transformation in yourselves and in your works, to create many fine works which will be warmly welcomed by the masses of the people, and to advance the literature and art movement in the revolutionary base areas and throughout China to a glorious new stage.

NOTES

1. The May 4th Movement was an anti-imperialist and anti-feudal revolutionary movement which began on May 4, 1919. In the first half of that year, the victors of World War I, *i.e.*, Britain, France, the United States, Japan, Italy and other imperialist countries, met in Paris to divide the spoils and decided that Japan should take over all the privileges previously enjoyed by Germany in Shantung Province, China. The students of Peking were the first to show determined opposition to this scheme, holding rallies and demonstrations on

May 4. The Northern warlord government arrested more than thirty students in an effort to suppress this opposition. In protest, the students of Peking went on strike and large numbers of students in other parts of the country responded. On June 3 the Northern warlord government started arresting students in Peking en masse, and within two days about a thousand were taken into custody. This aroused still greater indignation throughout the country. From June 5 onwards, the workers of Shanghai and many other cities went on strike and the merchants in these places shut their shops. Thus, what was at first a patriotic movement consisting mainly of intellectuals rapidly developed into a national patriotic movement embracing the proletariat, the urban petty bourgeoisie and the bourgeoisie. And along with the growth of this patriotic movement, the new cultural movement which had begun before May 4 as a movement against feudalism and for the promotion of science and democracy, grew into a vigorous and powerful revolutionary cultural movement whose main current was the propagation of Marxism-Leninism.

2. The Shensi-Kansu-Ningsia Border Region was the revolutionary base area which was gradually built up after 1931 through revolutionary guerrilla warfare in northern Shensi. When the Central Red Army arrived in northern Shensi after the Long March, it became the seat of the Central Committee of the Chinese Communist Party and the central base area of the revolution. The Shensi-Kansu-Ningsia Red Area was changed into the Shensi-Kansu-Ningsia Border Region after the formation of the Anti-Japanese National United Front in 1937. Nearly thirty counties, *i.e.*, Yenan, Fuhsien, Kanchuan, Yenchuan, Yenchang, Anting (now Tzechang), Ansai, Chihtan, Chingpien, Shenmu, Fuku, Tingpien, Hsunyi, Chunhua, Huanhsien, Chingyang, Hoshui, Chenyuan, Ninghsien, Chengning, Yenchih, Suitch, Chingchien, Wupao, Michih, Chia Hsien, etc., were under its jurisdiction.

3. See V. I. Lenin, "Party Organization and Party Literature," in which he described the characteristics of proletarian literature as follows:

> It will be a free literature, because the idea of socialism and sympathy with the working people, and not greed or careerism, will bring ever new forces to its ranks. It will be a free literature, because it will serve, not some satiated heroine, not the bored "upper ten thousand" suffering from fatty degeneration, but the millions and tens of millions of working people—the flower of the country, its strength and its future. It will be a free literature, enriching the last word in the revolutionary thought of mankind with the experience and living work of the socialist proletariat, bringing about permanent interaction between the experience of the past (scientific socialism, the completion of the development of socialism from its primitive, utopian forms) and the experience of the present (the present struggle of the worker comrades). (*Collected Works*, Eng. ed., FLPH, Moscow, 1962, Vol. X, pp. 48-49.)

4. Liang Shih-chiu, a member of the counter-revolutionary National Socialist Party, for a long time propagated reactionary American bourgeois ideas on literature and art. He stubbornly opposed the revolution and reviled revolutionary literature and art.

313

5. Chou Tso-jen and Chang Tzu-ping capitulated to the Japanese aggressors after the Japanese occupied Peking and Shanghai in 1937.

6. Lu Hsun, "My View on the League of Left-Wing Writers" in the collection *Two Hearts, Complete Works*, Chin. ed., 1957, Vol. IV.

7. See Lu Hsun's essay, "Death," in the "Addenda," *The Last Collection of Essays Written in a Garret in the Quasi-Concession, Complete Works*, Chin. ed., 1958, Vol. VI.

8. The "Little Cowherd" is a popular Chinese folk operetta with only two people acting in it, a cowherd and a village girl, who sing a question and answer duet. In the early days of the War of Resistance Against Japan, this form was used, with new words, for anti-Japanese propaganda and for a time found great favor with the public.

9. The Chinese characters for these six words are written simply, with only a few strokes, and were usually included in the first lessons in old primers.

10. "The Spring Snow" and the "Song of the Rustic Poor" were songs of the Kingdom of Chu in the 3rd century B.C. The music of the first was on a higher level than that of the second. As the story is told in "Sung Yu's Reply to the King of Chu" in Prince Chao Ming's *Anthology of Prose and Poetry*, when someone sang "The Spring Snow" in the Chu capital, only a few dozen people joined in, but when the "Song of the Rustic Poor" was sung, thousands did so.

11. See V. I. Lenin, "Party Organization and Party Literature": "Literature must become *part* of the common cause of the proletariat, 'a cog and a screw' of one single great Social-Democratic mechanism set in motion by the entire politically-conscious vanguard of the entire working class." (*Collected Works*, Eng. ed., FLPH, Moscow, 1962, Vol. X, p. 45.)

12. The Great Rear Area was the name given during the War of Resistance to the vast areas under Kuomintang control in southwestern and northwestern China which were not occupied by the Japanese invaders, as distinguished from the "small rear area," the anti-Japanese base areas behind the enemy lines under the leadership of the Communist Party.

13. *The Debacle* by the famous Soviet writer Alexander Fadeyev was published in 1927 and translated into Chinese by Lu Hsun. The novel describes the struggle of a partisan detachment of workers, peasants and revolutionary intellectuals in Siberia against the counter-revolutionary brigands during the Soviet civil war.

14. This couplet is from Lu Hsun's "In Mockery of Myself" in *The Collection Outside the Collection, Complete Works*, Chin. ed., 1958, Vol. VII.

Romanticism and Realism*

by Kuo Mo-Jo

In an essay in the July 1 issue of "Hongqi" (Red Flag), Kuo Mo-jo, poet and historian, expresses his views on revolutionary romanticism and revolutionary realism, a question which is now being discussed in China's literary circles. We present an abridged translation of the article.
—Ed.

Since the victory of the October Socialist Revolution forty years ago, more than a third of the entire human race, guided by Marxism-Leninism, has taken its destiny into its own hands and is daily working miracles never known before in history. In the sphere of literature, Marxism-Leninism has supplied romanticism with an ideal and realism with a soul, thus providing the revolutionary romanticism and revolutionary realism which we need today, or the appropriate synthesis of both—socialist realism:

For the last hundred years and more China has been continuously influenced by Western ideas; but owing to the semi-colonial status into which the country gradually lapsed, the Chinese bourgeoisie was never able to lead the bourgeois democratic revolution to victory. When the May the Fourth Movement was launched in 1919, the Chinese literary movement came into direct contact with Western ideas. Such terms as romanticism and realism were then introduced to China, and were used by some as labels for the literary groups which appeared after that time. Thus the Creation Society was called "romantic" and the Literary Research Association "realist," when in fact they merely bore certain resemblances to these schools. This method of distinction is not with-

* Reprinted from *Peking Review*, July 15, 1958, pp. 7-11. (All notes are those of the *Peking Review* editor.)

out merit, however. It shows that romanticism and realism arose at the same time in modern China. Both were anti-imperialist and anti-feudal, and in less than a decade, developing simultaneously, they covered the ground traversed in the last century or two of modern European history. Under the leadership of the Chinese Communist Party, the "Romantic School" and "Realist School" were, in the main, long ago merged to form a cultural army for the revolution. This army, as Mao Tse-tung said, "has helped the Chinese revolution in gradually reducing the domain and weakening the influence of China's feudal culture and her comprador culture which is adapted to imperialist aggression." China's historical conditions made this inevitable. Chinese romanticism never lost its revolutionary character, but early accepted a distinct idea; while Chinese realism remained uncontaminated by the decadent influence of the West, and early acquired a revolutionary soul. This was particularly true after the publication in 1942 of Mao Tse-tung's *Talks at the Yenan Forum on Art and Literature* which, we have no hesitation in saying, gave a clearer orientation to the revolutionary literature of the Chinese proletariat.

IMAGINATION AND FANTASY

Strictly speaking, there are occasions when it is quite difficult to distinguish between the romantic and realist spirit and essence in literature. In general, romanticism lays stress on the emotions, realism on the intellect. But as each individual's spiritual life is a compound of emotions and intellect, no one can have one alone without the other. It is probably safe to say that most men have more of romanticism and less of realism in their young days, while when they grow older the situation may be reversed altogether. Thus it is impossible to analyze a writer or a work of literature by chemical methods of qualitative or quantitative analysis to determine the percentage of romanticism and the percentage of realism. Literature is a reflection and criticism of actual life, and in this sense its nature should be realistic. But creative writing means thinking in images, and allows for the exercise of imagination and indeed of exaggeration. The truly great writers invariably make a synthesis based on life itself, to create typical characters in typical circumstances; and since this creative process involves fantasy, we should also be justified in calling it romantic. If we compare writing with scientific research, it is obvious that science is relatively realistic and literature relatively romantic. But even in science you require imagination and the ability to synthetize. Sometimes a scientist has to deduce ten possible facts from one known premise by the exercise of scientific prevision. In such cases he must rely upon a well-regulated imagination. A synthesis of the results of different research projects may produce something quite new in the world of nature, such as the incomparable sputnik—which required a high degree of creative correlation. Hence even scientific research has a rich share of romanticism. Karl Marx's *Capital* has been called a supreme drama, and this description brings out the essential identity or dialectic unity of art and science, romanticism and realism. It is frequently very hard to say whether the greatest writers of ancient or modern times are romantics or realists. Let me give a few examples of this.

Our great ancient poet, Chu Yuan, looks like a romantic. His *Li Sao*, *Nine Odes* and *Nine Elegies* draw heavily on the supernatural. He speaks of riding on the clouds, the rainbow, the dragon and the phoenix, of urging on the sun and moon, the wind and thunder, and wandering ceaselessly through the sky. He ascends to Paradise, returns to remote antiquity, soars to the roof of the world, or descends to the bottom of Tungting Lake. He caresses the comet in outer space, and talks of love to goddesses in the clouds. . . . Surely here we have an out-and-out romantic. But Chu Yuan makes no attempt to escape from reality in order to satisfy his personal desires, or to create art for art's sake. He seeks an ideal and an ideal ruler in order to save his country and its people and help to unify the China of his day. He sets out from completely realistic premises and finally returns to reality. Moreover he sets no store by his own life and death. He takes an interest in everything under the sun. Some of the questions about the universe he poses in the *Riddles* have not been answered to this day. We cannot, therefore, but admit that at the same time he is a great realist.

Another example is Lu Hsun, a great writer of our modern times. Most readers would acknowledge that he is beyond any doubt a realist. His stories in the *Call to Arms* and *Wandering* brim over with the spirit of modern realism. Some characterize Lu Hsun as: "Cold, cold, and cold again." On a superficial reading this view seems warranted, for Lu Hsun's razor-sharp scalpel can indeed "make you shiver though not with cold." But is Lu Hsun really cold? Far from it! His works are filled with passion, as everyone knows. His *Old Tales Retold* are based on material from fairy tales and legends, some of them dealing with the time before the creation of heaven and earth; and relying on his superb imagination he creates brilliant, kaleidoscopic pictures. Of course, he used these themes to satirize reality; but can anyone deny that those stories brim

317

over with a romantic spirit. This is why I affirm that Lu Hsun is not cold. His apparent coldness should be interpreted as white heat—a heat so intense that it throws off no sparks. He suppresses instead of showing his intense passion. His coldness is capable of burning your hand. "He stares icily at all who point the finger of scorn." Resolute fighters like Lu Hsun are bound to be intensely passionate. It follows that, while Lu Hsun is undeniably a great realist, he also evinces a high degree of romanticism. In fact, I should say he has these qualities in almost equal proportions.

A GOOD EXAMPLE

The clearest example of all is Comrade Mao Tse-tung, our great leader, who has developed Marxism-Leninism in the actual practice of the Chinese revolution. One of the greatest realists, he is also—I say this with full confidence—one of the greatest romantics. A great revolutionary, he is at the same time an outstanding writer and poet. His theoretical writing has tremendous appeal and, like the works of Marx and Lenin, is of a high literary order. But Comrade Mao Tse-tung does not merely write theoretical works. Over the past few years he has published nineteen poems in the classical style which, it is now generally agreed, are our finest example of a synthesis of revolutionary realism and revolutionary romanticism. To illustrate this, I will simply quote *The Immortals:* [1]

I lost my proud poplar, and you your willow; [2]
Poplar and willow spiralled to the heaven of heavens;
Wu Kang, [3] *when asked what he had to offer,*
Presented them with cassia wine.

The lonely goddess in the moon [4] *spreads her ample sleeves*
To dance for these good souls in the endless sky;
Of a sudden comes word of the Tiger's [5] *defeat on earth,*
And they break into tears of torrential rain.

The central theme of this poem is no mere remembrance of the past, but a proud approbation of the revolution. From it we can see: 1) The spirit of revolutionary martyrs is immortal. 2) Revolutionaries have revolutionary optimism, and are dedicated to the cause of the revolution beyond their lives. 3) All those with a sense of justice (represented here by Wu Kang and the goddess of the moon) have deep sympathy and respect for the revolution and the revolutionary martyrs. 4) The relationship between the revolutionary cadres and the people should be close and comradely. In sixty Chinese characters, this poem evokes a clear image of these ideas. Here we have the brave spirits of the revolutionary martyrs Yang Kai-hui and Liu Chih-hsun, as well as mythological figures; we have the palace of the moon, the cassia tree there and the wine made from the cassia; tears of joy can turn into torrential rain, and earth and heaven are one, for now we are with the immortals, now in the world of men. It is hardly necessary to say that here is none of the extravagant sentiment of certain classical poets, for even the heroic spirit of Su Tung-po (1036-1101) and Hsin Chi-chi (1140-1207), famous poets of the Sung dynasty, pales by comparison with this poem. Romantic exaggeration here throws the realist theme into relief in a completely natural and moving manner. We may truly say that this poetic way has never been surpassed. If we want to learn how to combine revolutionary realism with revolutionary romanticism in our writing, the poems of Comrade Mao Tse-tung are our best models.

Of course, as I pointed out earlier, Comrade Mao Tse-tung is skilled at using the methods of romanticism in his theoretical writing also to make his language sharper, more vivid and moving. I need not give any more examples here, for his works abound in them, and readers can read them for themselves. I will just quote one simple case to illustrate my meaning. That is a sentence from "Introducing a Co-operative" in the first issue of *Hongqi* (Red Flag): "There are undoubtedly some who will never change till their dying day, preferring to meet their maker with heads as hard as granite; but this does not affect the general situation." The phrase "preferring to meet their maker with heads as hard as granite" symbolizes "who will never change till their dying day," and this exaggerated image makes the statement clearer and more striking. I think even the rightist gentlemen, those with "heads as hard as granite," will think twice when they read this. Should they be stubborn to the end and "meet their maker with heads as hard as granite"? Or should they thoroughly change themselves to meet the makers of this world—the people? This is a very simple illustration of a concrete example. Lengthy abstract arguments are often less effective than one specific example like this. Herein lies the vitality of thinking in images.

EPITOME OF COLLECTIVISM

We should learn from Comrade Mao Tse-tung: learn from his skillful use of Marxism-Leninism applied to conditions in China, which has enabled the revolution to achieve victory and Marxism-Leninism to attain further development, and learn from his skillful integration of romanticism with realism which has enabled him to write immortal theoretical and literary works. I must say frankly that I have a tremendous admiration for Comrade Mao Tse-tung. This is not blind worship of the individual. I, for one, am opposed to the blind worship of individuals. By blind worship we mean the veneration of some individual who does not really represent the truth. If the individual is a leader who really represents the truth, such as Marx, Lenin and Mao Tse-tung, why shouldn't we respect him as our teacher? Of course, these outstanding teachers of ours have their own teachers—the people. Comrade Mao Tse-tung has said: "Only by becoming the pupil of the masses can he become their teacher." Marx, Lenin and Mao Tse-tung have pooled the wisdom of the masses. Mao Tse-tung has constantly urged us to adhere to the principle of "from the masses, to the masses."* He has absorbed the wisdom of the broad masses of the people and, as far as possible, all useful knowledge ancient and modern, Chinese and foreign. And precisely because he is a good student, he is a good thinker, speaker, man of action and teacher. He is a most democratic leader, and a teacher most skilled in guiding the people. Such outstanding individuals are the epitome of collectivism, and show the pre-eminence not of the individual but of the collective whole. We must not ignore the leading role in the revolution of individuals who stand for the pre-eminence of the collective merely because we oppose the "cult of the individual." Of course, we not merely respect but learn from them. If we learn well, we may excel our teachers. And I believe this is what Comrade Mao Tse-tung expects of us.

* This is a quotation from Mao Tse-tung's *On Methods of Leadership* meaning, as he himself puts it, "summing up (i.e. co-ordinating and systematizing after careful study) the views of the masses (i.e. views scattered and unsystematic), then taking the resulting ideas back to the masses, explaining and popularizing them until the masses embrace the ideas as their own, stand up for them and translate them into action by way of testing their correctness."—Ed.

To learn well is not easy, but neither is it impossible. To learn from Comrade Mao Tse-tung we must, of course, study his works; and writers should also make a careful study of the style of his poems. Naturally the study of poetry requires training in the use of the language. As the ancients said: "To find one word, the poet plucks several hairs from his beard." It looks as if anyone who wishes to become an eminent poet, will have to sacrifice his whole beard! I am sure Comrade Mao Tse-tung is too busy to pore over his poems like that, yet they have attained heights unrivalled by his predecessors. The secret here is that in order to be a poet one has first to be a real man. Poetry and literature are verbal arts, and writers must of course have some technical training. But it is not merely a question of technique. There have been a great many poets in ancient and modern times, in China and elsewhere, but how many of them can be said to be outstanding? We can say with certainty that all the outstanding poets not only write good poetry but are good men—in fact their lives may be even better than their poetry. If we want to learn from Comrade Mao Tse-tung, we must follow the example of his life.

Comrade Mao Tse-tung has told us to change our class standpoint, and set the example himself. Let me quote what he says about this in his *Talks at the Yenan Forum on Art and Literature*:

> If you want the masses to understand you and want to become one with them, you must be determined to undergo a long and even painful process of remolding. In this connection I might mention the transformation of my own feelings. I began as a student and acquired at school the habits of a student; in the presence of a crowd of students who could neither fetch nor carry for themselves, I used to feel it undignified to do any manual labor, such as shouldering my own luggage. At that time it seemed to me that the intellectuals were the only clean persons in the world, and the workers and peasants seemed rather dirty beside them. I could put on the clothes of other intellectuals because I thought they were clean, but I would not put on clothes belonging to a worker or peasant because I felt they were dirty. Having become a revolutionary I found myself in the same ranks as the workers, peasants and soldiers of the revolutionary army, and gradually I became familiar with them and they with me too. It was then and only then that a fundamental change occurred in the bourgeois and petty-bourgeois feelings implanted in me by the bourgeois schools. I came to feel that it was those unremolded intellectuals who were unclean as compared with the workers

321

and peasants, while the workers and peasants are after all the cleanest persons, cleaner than both the bourgeois and the petty-bourgeois intellectuals, even though their hands are soiled and their feet smeared with cow dung. This is what is meant by having one's feelings transformed changed from those of one class into those of another.

What a penetrating and inspiring description this is of Comrade Mao Tse-tung's personal experience! It is a pity that many of us have not learnt to do likewise although sixteen years have passed since these words were spoken. Of course, it is still not too late to learn. Here I feel very deeply the supreme correctness and importance of the policy now being carried out of sending government workers to the countryside or to factories. As Mao Tse-tung has so often advised us to go the villages or factories to "ride past and see the flowers" or "dismount and look at the flowers," I also went recently to the special administrative region of Changchiakou and spent two weeks there. That was a very good education for me. Today the great leap forward in industry and agriculture means that the enthusiasm of our people everywhere for construction is like a flame licking sky-high. New sights are to be seen on all sides, as well as poems and drawings so vivid and so lofty in thought that they take one's breath away. This is one vast melting-pot. Everyone who goes there will inevitably be carried away by it. The air is charged with energy and enthusiasm—not a trace of coldness or gloom. Yet there is no sign of fluster, nor are the people "so busy as to be completely tied down."

A FLOOD OF POEMS AND SONGS

If we want to find recent works of socialist realism we must surely look for them in the countryside, in the factories and the construction sites. The working people's enthusiasm for socialist construction has over-flowed into a flood of poems and songs. It is here that writers must look if they want to learn and are searching for a classroom. We can call the present period of the great leap forward the era of revolutionary romanticism and of revolutionary realism. Real life has raced ahead, and it is up to the writers to reflect this in their work. When I was at Changchiakou, I wrote dozens of poems on the spur of the moment, and the last of them ends: "How can I write down the poems which are all around?" That was how I felt then. These poems were not mine: they were composed by the working people—I simply jotted them down. How intimate human relations have become! Never before has such intimacy existed, no, not between brothers, not between fathers and sons, not even between man and wife. A new relationship has come into being, bringing genuine joy to each individual. It seems that flowers and trees, birds and beasts, mountains, rocks and minerals all feel the new wind which is blowing.

How can men remain unchanged in such a situation? Those who were trampled underfoot by landlords and rich peasants in the old days are now directors of co-operatives. Impulsive youngsters are now model workers who also play the fiddle well. Young girls have now mastered their job, are also teaching others to read and write and, taught by veteran actors after work, are able to perform Shansi opera. Now that rivers are climbing up hills and the earth is yielding its treasures, we can only say that the present age is the age of talents.

Moreover, this state of affairs is not transient but has come to stay. The sun above may set, but not the sun on earth. It seems that the sun in the sky is lagging behind. In a folk song about the great leap forward, men challenge the sun.

> *Hey, Sun!*
> *Will you take us on?*
>
> *We're out at work for hours*
> *While you're still snug abed;*
>
> *We grope our way home through the dark*
> *Long after you down tools and hide your head.*
>
> *Hey, Sun!*
> *Dare you take us on?*

I fancy Comrade Sun will have to raise his hands and say with a smile: I surrender! Allow me to answer the challenge for the sun with another poem.

> *Bravo! Well asked, my friend,*
> *I've to raise my hands and surrender.*
>
> *It's because I have to travel west*
> *That I desert your eastern sky so long.*

323

I tell you this: The West's a pretty mess,
With the privileged classes indulged in orgies.

You won't need fifteen years to catch up England—
That's absolutely certain!

All one can do after a short stay in the countryside is to absorb the atmosphere of revolutionary romanticism and write a few poems or short articles. Poetry has a lyric character, and it takes a special delight in romanticism. But a longer stay in the countryside enables you to observe things more closely, grasp them more deeply, conceive more perfect themes and so produce great works. In this way you are better able to express yourself in the style of revolutionary realism. The prospect before us is as clear as all that.

To me, romanticism and realism are both good so long as they are revolutionary. Revolutionary romanticism takes romanticism as its keynote, but blends it with realism. Perhaps this style is especially suited to poetry. Revolutionary realism takes realism as its keynote and blends it with romanticism. Perhaps novels are best able to develop this style. The forms of poetry and of the novel may change. I believe that those writers who have thrown themselves into the crucible of life and reality will one day melt down the old forms and forge new ones which accord with the spirit of the times and the needs of the people. This is to be expected.

1. This poem was written on May 11, 1957, for Li Shu-yi, a teacher in Changsha, Hunan Province. It refers to her husband Liu Chih-hsun, a Communist and a comrade-in-arms of the author, who fell in the Battle of Hunghu in Hupeh in 1933. Yang Kai-hui, the author's wife and a close friend of Li Shu-yi, was killed by the warlord Ho Chien when the Red Army withdrew from Changsha in 1930.

2. "Poplar" refers to Yang Kai-hui, for the character *yang* means "poplar." "Willow" refers to Liu Chih-hsun, for *liu* means "willow."

3. According to an ancient legend, Wu Kang committed some crimes during his search for immortality and was therefore condemned to cut down the cassia tree in the moon. Each time he raises his axe the tree becomes whole again. Thus he has to go on felling it for ever.

4. Tradition has it that Chang Ngo stole the elixir of immortality and fled to the moon, where she lives a lonely goddess.

5. In the Chinese original an allusion to the counter-revolution.

324

MISCELLANEOUS FORMS

Among the forms represented here are the folk tale, revolutionary aphorisms, reportage, and *tatzepao* or wall newspapers. These are popular and generally anonymously created art forms. By and for the great masses of Chinese people, they do not require the formality of authorship. Folk tales are part of any culture; so are aphorisms, although the "revolutionary" qualification suggests both the distinctiveness of these aphorisms as well as their use in China. Wall newspapers, also, are hardly a new form of expression. Anonymity fits them while their individual peculiarities reveal the people who create them.

Only reportage, a form of personal essay with an issue or message, suggests any need for an author's identification. Most are distinguished simply as from the many workers, peasants, and soldiers who, in their spare time, write of their experiences and thus become a major source of socialist literature. On the other hand, Chao Shu-li (1906-   ) was a writer well known in China for novels (*Sanliwan Village*), short stories ("Erh-hei's Marriage"), plays and reportage. A member of the Executive Committee of the Chinese Writers' Union before the Cultural Revolution when he was criticized as a "revisionist," his work is generally characterized by colloquial expressions and a strong folk flavor.

A Folk Tale—

Two Hired Hand Brothers*

There was once a family with two brothers.

One spring Big Brother went to work as a hired hand for a landlord.

"I'm a generous man," the landlord said. "I pay as high as anyone. Nine taels of silver a year. But we have a rule here for hired hands. If I tell you to do a job and you can't do it, I deduct three taels of silver from your wages."

Big Brother was an experienced hand. There was no work around a farm he couldn't do. He agreed without hesitation.

Until the tenth month he did his job smoothly and well—in the fields, on the threshing-ground. The landlord could find no fault. One day when the threshed grain was drying in the sun the landlord said:

"It's time to store this grain away. First, I want you to give the corners of the granary a good sunning."

Big Brother was astonished. "How can I do that?"

"You mean you can't do the job?"

"Of course not."

"Very well. That's three taels of silver off your wages."

Big Brother continued working to the eleventh month. The landlord told him to sweep the courtyard. In the yard were some vats, large and small, where the landlord raised lotus flowers in the summer.

"Put the big vats inside the little ones," the landlord directed. "Then the courtyard won't be so cluttered."

Big Brother was taken aback. "How can I do that?"

* An anonymous tale reprinted from *Chinese Literature*, No. 5 (1965), pp. 83-86.

326

"You mean you can't do the job?"

"Of course not."

"Very well. Another three taels off your wages."

Big Brother continued working till the last day of the twelfth month. Everyone was getting ready for the New Year holiday. Though the landlord's family was happy, Big Brother was sad. He consoled himself with the thought that tonight he would get three taels of silver for the year's hard work anyhow. He would go home and buy fuel and rice. He and his brother could at least have a decent meal on New Year's Eve.

After lunch the landlord ordered Big Brother to slaughter a pig. He did so. Just as he was starting to cut it up, the landlord strolled in, smoking his pipe.

"I want you to cut me a piece exactly the same weight as my head," the landlord directed. "Not a bit heavier and not a bit lighter."

Big Brother stared at him, stupified. "How can I do that?"

"You mean you can't do the job?"

Big Brother flung down the knife. "Of course not."

"That's another three taels of silver off your pay. Three times three is nine. I don't owe you a penny. You can't say I'm harsh. We agreed to this in advance."

Very angry, Big Brother returned home and told the whole story. Younger Brother comforted him as best he could. The two spent a poor New Year's Eve with neither rice nor fuel.

A few days later, Younger Brother went to the landlord and asked for a job as a hired hand. The landlord said:

"I'm a generous man. I pay as high as anyone. Nine taels of silver a year. But we have a rule here for hired hands. If I tell you to do a job and you can't do it, I deduct three taels of silver from your wages."

"Agreed," Younger Brother replied cheerfully. "But when I work as a hired hand, I have a rule of my own. If my master takes back any order he gives me, he has to pay me double wages."

The landlord thought a moment. "It's a deal."

Younger Brother worked until the tenth month. The threshed grain was drying on the threshing-ground. His old ailment acting up again, the landlord said:

"It's time to store this grain away. First, I want you to give the corners of the granary a good sunning."

"Right," said Younger Brother. He got a ladder, climbed up the side of the granary and started ripping the roof off. The landlord was incensed.

"What are you doing?"

327

"Didn't you tell me to give the corners of the granary a good sunning?"

"You—you—you. . . ." the landlord sputtered.

"You gave me the order yourself. Do you take it back?"

The landlord gnashed his teeth. "No!"

Younger Brother completely demolished the roof of the granary. It nearly broke the landlord's heart, but he couldn't say a word.

Younger Brother continued working. One day in the eleventh month, the landlord directed him to sweep the courtyard. The yard still had many vats in which the landlord raised lotus flowers in summer.

"Put the big vats inside the little ones. Then the courtyard won't be so cluttered," said the landlord.

"Right," replied Younger Brother. He got a hammer and smashed a large vat to bits. The landlord was enraged.

"What are you doing?"

"Didn't you tell me to put the big ones inside the little ones?"

"You—you—you. . . ." the landlord sputtered.

"You gave me the order yourself. Do you take it back?"

The landlord gnashed his teeth. "No!"

Younger Brother destroyed all the big vats in the yard, while the landlord watched with eyes popping out of his head.

Younger Brother continued working until the twelfth month. Everyone was getting ready for the New Year holiday. Though the landlord's family was bursting with rage, Younger Brother was serene. After lunch on the thirtieth, at the landlord's instructions, he slaughtered a pig. Just as he was starting to cut it up, the landlord approached him.

"I want you to cut me a piece exactly the same weight as my head. Not a bit heavier and not a bit lighter."

"Right," said Younger Brother. He hacked off the pig's head and handed it to the landlord. "Here you are."

The landlord clucked scornfully. "Whoever said a pig's head weighs the same as a man's? It looks like you can't do this job."

"Not so fast," replied Younger Brother. "I'm only half done. Now let me have your head and we'll weigh them both. I'll prove to you there's not an ounce of difference."

He grasped the landlord by the collar and raised his chopper. The landlord pulled in his neck like a turtle.

"No, no, you mustn't," he squawked.

"A piece the same weight as your head. You gave the order yourself." Younger Brother held him fast.

328

The landlord covered his head with his hands. He didn't dare speak. Younger Brother brandished the chopper.

"I'm going to cut," he warned.

"I take it back, I take it back," the landlord cried.

"Double wages, as agreed?"

"Yes, yes, double wages." The landlord was helpless.

He paid out eighteen taels of silver. Younger Brother released him and returned home with the money. To Big Brother he said:

"The landlord didn't get the better of us this time. We can have a happy New Year holiday at last."

Revolutionary Aphorisms*

Aphorisms form an integral part of Chinese folk literature. The people compose them whenever they want to state a general truth derived from their own experience of life. The following is a selection of new aphorisms widely circulated among the men of the Chinese People's Liberation Army.

> Chairman Mao's works shed a golden light,
> Like the red sun, for ever bright.

> Chairman Mao's works are the sun,
> It shines on the Four Seas and high they surge.

> All-powerful, the works of Mao Tse-tung;
> The Five Continents reel, racked with storm.

> Relying on mere physical strength is of little worth,
> But relying on Mao Tse-tung's thought we can make a new
>   heaven and earth.

* Reprinted from *Chinese Literature*, No. 9 (1966), pp. 142-146.

329

All rivers in the world flow to the sea,
All truths are found in the works of Mao Tse-tung.

Past counting, the stars in the sky;
Past measuring, the water in the sea;
Past telling, the might of Mao Tse-tung's thought.

Each word in Chairman Mao's works
Is a battle-drum,
Each sentence is the truth.

Bullets and shells
Are no match
For the spiritual atom-bomb of Mao Tse-tung's thought.

A revolutionary staunch and true
Reads Chairman Mao his whole life through.

Dearer than rain or dew to the parched crops
Are Chairman Mao's works to our troops.

Of all rules to remember, the first, best one
Is to practice the teachings of Mao Tse-tung.

However busy we may be,
We must never forget to study Chairman Mao's works
And apply them creatively.

Difficulties by thousands may hedge us around,
But with Chairman Mao's thought a solution is found.

Learn from Chairman Mao to keep a firm class stand,
Or you may betray the Party in the end.

If you don't study Chairman Mao
You will be blind;
If you do
A red sun will light up your mind.

Fish cannot live without water;
Without studying the works of Chairman Mao
Soldiers cannot be true revolutionaries.

Study Chairman Mao's writings well
And you will know right from wrong, you will see plain;
Take the road of communism
And you will stand firm, come tempest or pelting rain.

Study Mao Tse-tung's works well
And no trials will daunt you, however overwhelming;
His works will light up your mind
And speed communism's coming.

A soldier will fight like a hero
Only if on the thought of Mao Tse-tung he relies;
But armed with Mao Tse-tung's thought
He can cross seas of fire, climb hills of knives.

Without the sun, the moon can shed no light;
Without rain or dew, a crop dies;
Soldiers who don't study Chairman Mao's works and put
    them into practice
Will lose their way—even with open eyes.

Keep Chairman Mao's thought in mind
And no hardships can cause you dismay,
No setbacks can make you give way.

A man armed with the thought of Mao Tse-tung
Has a backbone stronger than iron,
A will firmer than steel.

Heads may fall,
Blood may flow;
But never let go
Of the thought of Mao Tse-tung.

A key in daily use
Sparkles with light,
Just as fresh-springing fountains
Are always clear and bright;
And men who study the works of Chairman Mao
Are full of drive and fight.

The eagle which soars through the sky must have strong wings;
The soldier who wants to take long views must rely on the
    thought of Mao Tse-tung.

Read Chairman Mao's works every day,
You'll not lose your way but see clear;
Read Chairman Mao's works every day,
And you'll have drive and to spare;
Read Chairman Mao's works every day
And you'll overcome hardships of every kind;
Read Chairman Mao's works every day
And nothing can poison your mind.

To solve a problem, read Chairman Mao's works;
When fresh problems crop up, read Chairman Mao's works.

You must hit the right spot when you're beating a drum,
You must pluck the right strings when you're playing a lute;
And to study Chairman Mao's works well
You must put what you've learned into practice.

Mao Tse-tung's thought is a telescope for a revolutionary
To see clearly what lies thousands of miles away.

Mao Tse-tung's thought is a microscope for a revolutionary,
All germs, all pests enabling him to see.

No matter how black a crow's wings,
They cannot shut out the bright sun;
No matter how vicious the lies of bourgeois "authorities,"
They cannot harm the great thought of Mao Tse-tung.

A fierce dog fears a stick,
A fierce wolf fears the hunter's gun,
The enemy fears most the thought of Mao Tse-tung.

Reportage—

A New Canteen and Old Memories*

by Chao Shu-li

My old home is on the west of the southern tip of the Taihang Mountains. I not only grew up and had my schooling there but worked in that mountainous region before liberation. So although I left home after liberation, I seize every chance that comes my way of going back there for a look.

As early as 1937 this district became a base in the War of Resistance to Japanese Aggression. Since liberation, naturally, like all the other old revolutionary bases, it has never lagged behind, even if we cannot boast of being in the vanguard all the time. Each visit home shows me something new. Most of my stories have been based on material collected there.

When I went home in the winter of 1958, because it was the year of the Big Leap in socialist construction there were more new things than usual. The first I noticed was the canteen built after the organization of the commune. This is a building facing south with the kitchen on the west side and the dining hall on the east. Inside the kitchen is a well. The well is an old one, but it has been incorporated in the kitchen so that when the cooks need water they do not have to fetch it from outside. The stove flues and chutes for adding coal and removing ashes lead directly out through the wall; hence when the fire is lit, there is no dust or smoke inside. The dining hall has two rows of square tables, each

* Reprinted from *Chinese Literature*, No. 12 (1959), pp. 107-111. (Translated by Yang Hsien-yi.)

with four benches around it, while two braziers stand in the broad space between the two rows of tables. The children who can't reach food on the tables like to have their meals around these braziers.

When I had my first meal in this canteen, I gave some comments to the leader of the work brigade. The canteen struck me as extremely well built, but since the commune had only just been set up, wasn't it rather extravagant to put up a building which had—so I heard—needed the combined efforts of about seventy families? Before the brigade-leader could answer my question, all those at the nearby tables laughed. One of them suggested that I should guess how much they had spent on this canteen. While I was hesitating over an estimate, someone else assured me I need not worry about the cost. They had not only hired no masons and bought no materials, but had not used much of their regular working hours. The canteen was built by the commune members in their spare time. They contributed the material and did all the work themselves, yet it took no more than a fortnight. Some of the achievements of our working people really seem like miracles!

I was most impressed by this inexpensive, excellent canteen. Its location reminded me of many folk I knew in the old days.

This place used to be called the South Compound. In the front court lived three brothers named Chao, distant relatives of ours. They were about my father's age but belonged to my generation. The eldest brother, Hsi-kuei, had no land of his own and went to another county to farm hilly country, but died without ever having married. The third brother, Ming-lun, was a good farmhand as a young man; but unable to wrest a living from the poor soil he rebelled against his hard lot and turned thief. In the end he was beaten to death by his own clan. He had many points in common with Ah Q, the hero in one of Lu Hsun's stories, and I wanted to write about him but never did. These two brothers, who died through poverty, left no descendants.

To the east of the canteen there had been a courtyard called The Store where lived two brothers also about my father's age. The elder, Lu Shuan-cheng, I called Elder Uncle; the younger, Lu Sui-cheng, I called Younger Uncle. Their sole property was this house they lived in. Lu Shuan-cheng died of typhoid leaving two sons, the elder of whom starved to death during a famine. The younger son lived with an uncle and did not come home till after the land reform. He is now a team-leader. Lu Sui-cheng died without having married, like Hsi-kuei. He was poisoned by some bad beef.

To the south of the canteen lived two generations of a family named Feng, who owned not an inch of land. The son, Fu-kuei, whom I called

Elder Brother, also starved to death after living as a beggar. Part of my short story *Fu-kuei* was based on his life.

Behind the house where Fu-kuei lived was the East Court, the home of the four Lu brothers, two of whom I addressed as Elder Uncle, two as Younger Uncle. They were carpenters with a few *mou* only of poor land. In our parts a man could not make a living as an artisan: a trade was no more than a side-line. Of these four brothers only the youngest married—and that not until his thirties. The three elder brothers could not afford to marry. They loved folk music and had several instruments; it was in their house that I learned to play the gong and drum. They are all dead now. The fourth brother, Liu-niu, died away from home during a famine and his son lives in another district.

Northeast of East Court there grew a great walnut tree with two windowless stone huts under it. There lived quite a number of people who had fled from Honan during the floods. Most refugees stayed there when they first came to our village; in fact some of them, unable to find other lodgings, remained there for several years. My *Rhymes of Li Yu-tsai* describes two categories of villagers: the "Old" and the "Little." Most of those called "Old" were based on these refugees.

I can recollect about a hundred of those "Old" people—if I included those in neighboring villages the number would come to several hundreds. Those familiar, kindly faces have long since disappeared: most of these old folk have died leaving no descendants. Had they not fallen victim to poverty and famine in the old society, many of them would now be leading officials or labor heroes, gathering cheerfully for their meal in this new canteen.

Busy recollecting these old friends, I dawdled over my meal till all the grown-ups had finished and gone back to work, leaving only a group of children under school age around the braziers. These children were not shy: when they saw the grown-ups had left they clustered around me and asked where I was from. One of them knew who I was—perhaps his father or mother had pointed me out. I stroked their heads and asked their names. They answered quickly, "Little" this and "Little" that. I did not catch any names, nothing but "Little." I suppose they may count as "Little" people too, but they are infinitely luckier than those of the "Little" category in the *Rhymes of Li Yu-tsai*. These children will never know what it is to fly from famine.

Tatzepao—Wall Newspaper

Rightful Owners*

Tools for production
return to their rightful
owners—those who use them;
the land comes back
to the people who till it;
the people turn to a new
way; hope of the ages becomes
reality.

* Reprinted from Rewi Alley, *The People Speak Out* (Peking: Foreign Languages Press, 1954), p. 78.

Tatzepao—Wall Newspaper

On Meals*

Two meals
in three days;
an empty belly
is not easy to take;
the cries of hungry children
bring to the old incessant pain,
to hell with the landlord!

* Reprinted from Rewi Alley, *The People Speak Out* (Peking: Foreign Languages Press, 1954), p. 76.